Leadership Communication

Leadership Communication

Third Edition

Deborah J. Barrett

Rice University

LEADERSHIP COMMUNICATION, THIRD EDITION
Published by McGraw-Hill/Irwin, a business unit of The McGraw-Hill Companies, Inc., 1221
Avenue of the Americas, New York, NY, 10020. Copyright © 2011 by The McGraw-Hill
Companies, Inc. All rights reserved. Previous editions © 2008 and 2006. No part of this
publication may be reproduced or distributed in any form or by any means, or stored in a
database or retrieval system, without the prior written consent of The McGraw-Hill Companies,
Inc., including, but not limited to, in any network or other electronic storage or transmission, or
broadcast for distance learning.

Some ancillaries, including electronic and print components, may not be available to customers
outside the United States.

This book is printed on acid-free paper.

2 3 4 5 6 7 8 9 0 DOC/DOC 1 0 9 8 7 6 5 4 3 2 1 0

ISBN: 978-0-07-337777-3
MHID: 0-07-337777-5

Vice President & Editor-in-Chief: *Brent Gordon*
Publisher: *Paul Ducham*
Managing Developmental Editor: *Laura Hurst Spell*
Marketing Manager: *Jaime Halteman*
Editorial Coordinator: *Jane Beck*
Project Manager: *Melissa M. Leick*
Design Coordinator: *Brenda Rolwes*
Production Supervisor: *Nicole Baumgartner*
Composition: *Glyph International*
Typeface: *10/12 New Aster*
Printer: *R. R. Donnelley Crawfordsville, IN*

All credits appearing on page or at the end of the book are considered to be an extension of the
copyright page.

Library of Congress Cataloging-in-Publication Data
Barrett, Deborah, 1949–
   Leadership communication / Deborah J. Barrett.—3rd ed.
      p. cm.
   ISBN-13: 978-0-07-337777-3 (alk. paper)
   ISBN-10: 0-07-337777-5
 1. Communication in management.   2. Communication in organizations.
3. Business communication.   4. Leadership.   I. Title.
   HD30.3.B387 2009
   658.4'5—dc22
                                                        2009036825

The Internet addresses listed in the text were accurate at the time of publication. The inclusion
of a Web site does not indicate an endorsement by the authors or McGraw-Hill, and McGraw-
Hill does not guarantee the accuracy of the information presented at these sites.

Dedicated in loving memory of my mother and father

Dedicated to Jim and to my children, Davy and Mary
—Deborah J. Barrett, PhD

Brief Contents

Table of Contents

About the Author

Deborah J. Barrett is professor of the Practice of Professional Communication and director of the Program for Communication Excellence at Rice University.

Deborah has taught communication for over 25 years, specializing in professional communication for the last 20 years. At Texas A&M University, she was a visiting assistant professor in technical writing; at Houston Baptist University, she was an associate professor in English and director of the writing specialization and English internship programs; and at Rice University, she was a lecturer of MBA communication at the Jones Graduate School of Management from 1988 to 1991 and from 1998 to 2006.

Deborah's leadership approach to communication has developed over many years of teaching but has also been influenced by her years as a consultant working independently and for McKinsey & Company and Hill & Knowlton. At McKinsey & Company, she was a communication consultant for over five years. She served as a leader in the change communication practice, developed and conducted firm training, and led and worked with McKinsey teams on communication and general management consulting projects throughout the world. She was one of the few communication consultants firmwide selected to attend McKinsey's Engagement Leadership Training, its advanced leadership training for senior associates. At Hill & Knowlton, Deborah was a senior managing director, brought in to build a change management practice.

In her consulting work, she has been able to put her academic experience and leadership communication concepts to the test. Her consulting work includes developing major change programs, designing and conducting vision/strategy development programs, writing strategic plans, creating communication strategy for mergers and acquisitions, and developing internal communication improvement programs. She has coached many senior-level executives, including CEOs of major corporations, in writing, speaking, and interpersonal skills and has conducted numerous workshops for leaders at all levels.

Deborah has published articles in professional journals and presented papers at professional conferences around the world on communication ethics, change communication, employee communication, cross-cultural communication, virtual teams, PowerPoint, effective MBA communication, emotional intelligence, and leadership communication. She serves on the editorial boards of the *Business Communication Quarterly, Education Review of Business Communication,*

Corporate Communication: An International Journal, and *International Journal of Knowledge, Culture, and Change Management.*

Her BA in English and speech and her MA in English are from the University of Houston, and her PhD in English is from Rice University.

Preface

Leadership Communication is a text to guide current and potential leaders in developing the communication capabilities needed to be transformational leaders. The content is based on research in communication and leadership and on the author's years of experience teaching professional communication and working as a consultant, independently as well as for one of the leading management-consulting firms and one of the leading public relations firms. This third edition of *Leadership Communication* maintains the instruction to help readers achieve the objectives of the previous editions by focusing on strategy and emotional intelligence, but it has been updated and changed specifically to emphasize transformational leadership, ethics, and integrity and to include guidance on the use of current social media.

Text Objectives

Leaders need core communication capabilities in strategy, speaking, and writing. They also need to be able to communicate effectively with diverse audiences, understand cultural differences, conduct productive meetings, manage global teams, create and communicate visions, lead change initiatives, and foster external relations. *Leadership Communication* includes all these subjects and covers important fundamental communication skills needed by all leaders.

Mastering leadership communication means learning to do the following:

1. Project a positive ethos.
2. Lead and communicate with integrity.
3. Analyze audiences and create targeted, meaningful messages.
4. Develop effective communication strategies for all situations.
5. Select and use the most effective media, including social media, to reach all audiences.
6. Use the language of leaders, communicating clearly, concisely, and correctly.
7. Create well-organized, coherent communication.
8. Deliver presentations and use presentation technology with confidence.
9. Display emotional intelligence and cross-cultural literacy.
10. Lead small groups, whether in teams or meetings.
11. Develop a vision and messages to guide and motivate others.
12. Design and deliver messages to reach all stakeholders with positive results.

These are the primary objectives of this text. Leaders use all possible communication tools within reach, and use them effectively. This text will help you know how to use those tools and show you how to improve your communication capabilities. As a result, you will learn to communicate more effectively and position yourself to be a transformational leader in your organization and beyond it.

Changes to This Edition

For those who have used previous editions of *Leadership Communication,* this edition has been revised with a specific emphasis on transformational leadership throughout and to appeal to and be useful to advanced undergraduates as well as graduate students and executive audiences. In addition, it includes the following changes:

1. Social media (blogging, Twitter, Facebook, LinkedIn, etc.) and other technology, such as electronic presentations, shared workspaces, research management (Zotero), are included throughout the text with applications calling on the use of these new media. Also, the written communication chapter includes several pages specifically on social media (blogging and microblogging), and the chapter on external relations includes recent media case situations as well as examples from *Groundswell* to illustrate the power and importance of Web presence and use for reputation management and client interactions.

2. All exercises have been updated and renamed "Applications" to emphasize the focus on applying the principles introduced in the chapters, whether using the text in a classroom setting or individually to improve communication abilities.

3. The Introduction is now Chapter 1, which has been expanded to include the following:

   a. More on leadership and on transformational leadership in particular.

   b. The placement of leadership communication in the field of professional communication overall.

   c. Several pages on ethics and an exercise on determining what is or is not a question of ethics.

   In addition, the self-assessment, formerly located at the end of the Introduction, has been moved to Appendix A, and overall applications on leadership communication have been added to this new Chapter 1.

4. Chapters 2 and 3, now Chapters 3 and 4, have been reversed, with the instruction on the language of leaders applying to all of leadership communication and including more on power, influence, and persuasion.

5. Chapters 4 and 5 (now Chapters 5 and 6), on presentations and graphics, include instruction on creating and delivering online and Web presentations.

6. The Managerial Leadership Communication level of the leadership communication framework and section of the text have been renamed "Organizational" to reflect the broader coverage of this section and the text overall.

7. Chapter 6, on emotional intelligence/interpersonal skills and cross-cultural communication, has been split into two chapters (now Chapters 7 and 8) with more content on both subjects. In addition, Chapter 7 includes new sections on motivation and on networking (including networking tools, such as Facebook and LinkedIn).

8. Chapters 9 and 10 include more on conducting virtual meetings and teams.

9. Chapter 11 includes more on change inspired by transformational leaders in particular.

10. Chapter 12 includes a discussion of using new media, such as blogs, Twitter, and Web monitoring and presence, to manage external reputations.

Instructor Supporting Materials

For instructors, this text is supported online at www.mhhe.com/barrett3e. Included on the site are PowerPoint lecture slides, suggested approaches to the chapters, discussions of all chapter applications with answers to exercises, a test bank, suggestions for using the book to prepare students for action or service learning or other similar consulting engagements, and sample syllabi.

Acknowledgments

Before recognizing each person to whom I am grateful, I want to thank three organizations for their direct and indirect contributions to the original creation and publication and the subsequent development of *Leadership Communication*:

McGraw-Hill/Irwin—The editors for their guidance and support and the talented production staff for making this edition a reality.

McKinsey & Company—The firm overall for the opportunity to work with some of the brightest thinkers and with executives and managers who exemplify leadership communication.

Rice University—The university for giving me the opportunity to work with excellent students, both the MBA students as I developed the concept of leadership communication and the outstanding undergraduates as I have expanded the leadership communication concepts to help students of all levels serve as leaders in the community and in whatever professional worlds they enter.

Thank you to the reviewers who were kind enough to review the book and offer their suggestions for improving this edition:

Judy Jones Tisdale, PhD, University of North Carolina at Chapel Hill; Carol White, Georgia State University; and Sandi L. Zeljko, PhD, Eastern University

I want to thank my communication colleagues who contributed their time, energy, expertise, and friendship when I first developed the book and over the years since the first edition was published in 2006: Chuck McCabe, Beth O'Sullivan, Beth Peters, and Larry Hampton.

For this edition, I want to thank another communication colleague, Sandra Elliott, who stepped in on very late notice to provide a fresh editorial eye and to add substantially to the social media instruction and exercises. Also, I want to thank Webtrends for allowing us to use Sandra's research on social media best practices and their examples and case studies.

Also, I owe a special thank you for this edition to Shar'-Lin Anderson, the program coordinator for our Program for Communication Excellence, for providing help with the manuscript at various stages, for managing the permission process, and for updating the URLs and other Web references.

I also owe a huge thank you to all my students over the years, who continue to be my inspiration for constantly looking for ways to improve the teaching of communication.

Finally, I want to thank Jim, my husband, friend, and partner, who put up with my many weekends of work and long days and frequent tests of new ideas on him, and for always being there to help keep some balance in my life. And as always, I have to thank Kramer, who slept in my lap, with his head resting on my arm, while I worked on this edition, just as on all of the others, no matter the clicking keyboard or late hour.

Core Leadership Communication

What Is Leadership Communication?

The art of communication is the language of leadership.

James C. Humes, speech writer for five U.S. presidents

Effective leadership is still largely a matter of communication.

Alan Axelrod, Elizabeth I, CEO: *Strategic Lessons from the Leader Who Built an Empire*

Aspiring individuals should seek to learn the skills necessary to become transformational leaders. Organizations throughout the world need transformational leaders who possess a high degree of integrity and are motivated to lead people to higher levels of performance. Transformational leaders provide new direction, new inspiration, and new behaviors for their organizations. Therefore, they are essential ingredients in organizational development and societal progress.

Bruce A. Tucker & Robert F. Russell, "The Influence of the Transformational Leader," *Journal of Leadership and Organizational Studies.*

Chapter Objectives

In this chapter, you will learn to do the following:

- Identify leadership with an emphasis on transformational leaders.
- Connect leadership to communication.
- Define leadership communication and the leadership communication framework.
- Appreciate the importance of projecting a positive ethos.
- Recognize and manage ethical issues and create an ethical organizational environment.

A leader must be able to communicate effectively. When asked to define leadership, theorists and practitioners alike frequently use the words "influence," "inspire," and "transform," all of which depend on communication, verbal and nonverbal. Leaders lead through their words and their actions. This text focuses on both, thus the emphasis throughout on emotional intelligence, the ability to understand the self and others. The leadership focus here is on inspirational and transformational leadership. The hope is that the present and future leaders using this text will learn to communicate to bring about positive results for themselves and for their organizations or communities.

In *Leading without Power: Finding Hope in Serving Community,* Max De Pree says, "Leaders are constantly communicating."[1] In a business setting, studies have shown that managers spend most of their day engaged in communication, with communication occupying 70 to 90 percent of their time every day.[2] The sheer amount of time we spend communicating underscores how important strong communication skills are in whatever leadership position we assume or in whatever career we pursue. Mastering leadership communication becomes a priority for all individuals who want to lead others and want their groups, their organizations, or the broader community to follow them, trust them, and consider them leaders.

This chapter begins by identifying leadership and exploring how leadership and communication are connected, then defines "leadership communication" and the framework that governs the organization of the text, and concludes by explaining the importance of projecting a positive ethos and of recognizing and managing questions of ethics.

Identifying Leadership

What exactly is leadership? Theorists and practitioners have devoted thousands of words and numerous articles and books to the subject. Google lists 154,000,000 entries under "leadership (definition)." Many universities offer leadership programs. Job descriptions frequently ask for candidates with leadership skills, and many corporations encourage and provide leadership development. In fact, "investment in leadership education and development by corporations has become increasingly popular, reaching nearly $50 billion in 2000."[3]

What, however, does leadership entail? Researchers seldom agree completely on how best to define it, some saying they know it when they see it. Pressed, most would agree that leaders are individuals who guide, direct, motivate, or inspire others. They are the men and women who influence others in an organization or in a community. They command others' attention. They persuade others to follow them or pursue goals they define. They control situations. They improve the performance of groups and organizations. They connect with others, and they get results.

These individuals may not be presidents of countries or CEOs of companies, but they could be. They could also be experienced employees who step forward to mentor those who are less experienced, researchers who discover a cure for some disease or invent something to make our lives easier, managers who direct successful project teams, vice presidents who lead divisions and motivate their staff to achieve company goals, educators who inspire their students to achieve their potential, or students who bring about positive change in their schools or in the broader community.

Leadership theorists define leadership by the traits leaders possess, by the tasks they perform, by the positions they hold, and by the accomplishments they achieve:

> Traditional theories of leadership focus on the traits of leaders (personality, charisma, referent power), the process by which individuals become leaders (the tasks, the people, and the situation), or the interactions individuals have with others that create their leadership status. In the last, the focus is either on the exchange or transaction between the leader and others, or on the impact the leader has on individuals or an organization which inspires change or a difference of some sort, a transformation.[4]

The leadership focus in this text is on the type of leadership called "transformational."[5] This type of leader possesses a positive ethos (authority and credibility), inspires trust and respect, connects with others individually and in groups, articulates a clear and motivating vision, and skillfully motivates and guides others to act. The transformational leader displays four primary behavioral characteristics: "idealized influence, inspirational motivation, intellectual stimulation, and individualized consideration."[6] In addition, he or she exhibits important communication abilities, such as listening, persuading, and articulating ideas effectively.[7]

Discussions on leadership often come back to one question: Is a leader born or developed? In other words, can individuals learn to be leaders? The short answer is yes they can: "Organizations and individuals can indeed directly influence the quality and the quantity of their leadership. . . . It is not a matter of whether leaders are born or made. They are born *and* made."[8] Avolio argues that, in particular, "transformational leadership skills can indeed be developed."[9] *Leadership Communication* is devoted to helping individuals develop as transformational leaders by mastering the most important capability they need, the ability to communicate effectively.

Connecting Leadership to Communication

The fundamental premise on which this book rests is that effective leadership depends on effective communication, that ability to connect to others and, through that connection, guide, direct, motivate, and inspire. Good communication skills enable, foster, and create the understanding and trust necessary to encourage others to follow a leader. Without effective communication, leaders accomplish little. Without effective communication, a leader is not a leader.

Being able to communicate effectively is what allows individuals to move into leadership positions. In business, for instance, an early Harvard Business School study on what it takes to achieve success and be promoted in an organization says that the individual who gets ahead in business is the person who "is able to communicate, to make sound decisions, and to get things done with and through people."[10] This text tackles the first of these capabilities directly, and by teaching individuals to communicate more effectively, it also helps them improve their ability to get things done with and through people. After all, communication is about people.

Defining Communication

Communication is the transmission of meaning from one person to another or to many people, whether verbally or nonverbally. Communication from one person to another is often called the "rhetorical situation," which is commonly depicted as a simple triangle consisting of the context, the sender, the message, and the receiver (Exhibit 1.1).

Exhibit 1.1 suggests very simple and ideal communication. There would be no miscommunication or misunderstandings. The sender would understand the context and the audience (receiver), select the right medium, and send a clear message. The receiver would receive and understand that message exactly as the sender intended.

In reality, communication is much more complex and interactive, with many opportunities for messages and meanings to go astray. Exhibit 1.2 shows some of the numerous interruptions or breakdowns when communicating even an apparently simple message.

EXHIBIT 1.1
The Traditional Diagram of the Rhetorical Situation

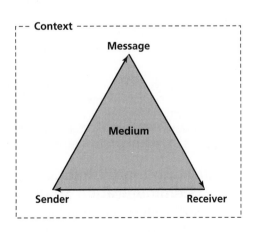

EXHIBIT 1.2
The Interruptions
to Communication

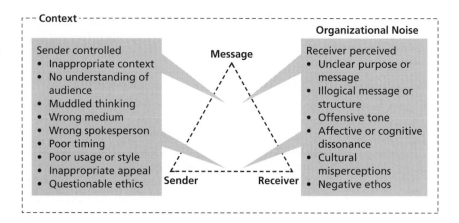

Complications in communication come from the interruptions or interferences in the transmission of a message, whether the context, sender, or receiver causes them. The context in which the information is sent, the noise that surrounds it, the selection of the medium, the words used in the message, the image of the speaker—all influence the meaning as it travels successfully, or as intended, from one person to another.

Defining Leadership Communication

Effective leadership communication requires the ability to anticipate the potential interruptions in the transmission of the message, appreciate the context, understand the audience, select the right medium, and craft clear messages that allow the meaning to reach the specific receiver as intended.

One goal of mastering all aspects of leadership communication is to move us as close as possible to the ideal of meaningful message transfer. Leadership communication necessitates minimizing or eliminating all interruptions and interferences by understanding the receivers (the audience) and developing a communication strategy (objective and plan) to facilitate the effective transmission of messages.

So what is leadership communication?

> Leadership communication is the controlled, purposeful transfer of meaning by which individuals influence a single person, a group, an organization, or a community by using the full range of their communication abilities and resources to connect positively with their audiences, overcome interferences, and create and deliver messages that guide, direct, motivate, or inspire others to action.

Relating Leadership Communication to Other Fields of Communication Studies

The discipline of communication consists of many fields of study that differ in their characteristics and the content they emphasize. For

EXHIBIT 1.3
The Positioning of Leadership Communication

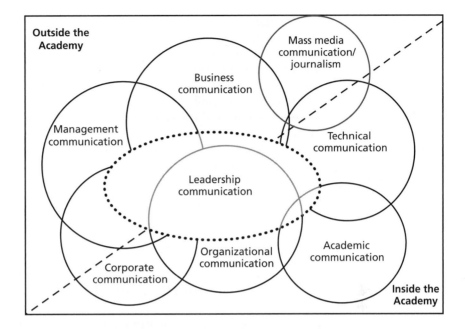

example, the field of business communication differs from technical communication, which differs from corporate communication, which differs from organizational communication. While little value here is gained by engaging in a scholarly debate on how one field of communication differs from another, it is useful to realize what differentiates leadership communication from the rest of the fields of communication studies in general. Exhibit 1.3 illustrates the number of fields within the discipline of communication and shows the placement of leadership communication in relation to them.[11]

Leadership communication rests on top and cuts across many of the others. Leadership communication includes some of the topics often included in the other fields because leaders emerge in all academic and professional arenas, and individuals wanting to develop the communication abilities for any leadership role in a professional setting need some of the abilities developed inside or outside of the academy. However, the emphasis in leadership communication is on leadership and on the most important communication subjects leaders need to master in professional settings.

Although all of us use some of the basics of business communication, such as how to deliver our messages effectively in memos and e-mails or how to create and deliver effective presentations, three of the fields emphasize subjects closer to those included in leadership communication: managerial communication, organizational communication, and corporate communication.

Managerial communication emphasizes the abilities managers need as they supervise and lead others in mostly business environments; organizational communication tends to focus on the behavioral and interactive and interpersonal skills individuals need to assume leadership roles inside an organization; and corporate communication emphasizes the abilities leaders need as they lead change efforts, develop visions and missions, and manage public relations and policy making.

These are the fields of communication most often associated with providing the instruction for business or similar professional settings, as opposed to academic and technical environments. Leadership communication's focus is also communication in professional and organizational settings, although effective communication abilities help leaders in academic and technical environments as well in leadership roles in the broader community.

Applying the Leadership Communication Framework

All professional communication, from business to corporate communication includes, to a lesser or greater extent, the following topics: developing communication strategy, understanding audiences, and writing and speaking effectively. The leadership communication framework used to organize this text begins with these core skills before focusing on the interpersonal, cross-cultural, and other leadership capabilities expected of individuals leading meetings and teams at the organizational level and then the visionary and broader community leadership abilities found at the corporate level of the framework.

Leadership communication as defined and used in this text consists of layered, expanding abilities from core strategy development and effective writing and speaking to the use of these skills in more complex situations. As leaders' perspectives and control expand, they will find that they need to improve their core skills with even greater analytical and synthesizing abilities.

Leadership Communication starts with the core communication topics represented in the center of the framework (Exhibit 1.4), then moves from the inside of the spiral to the outside, expanding outward to apply the core skills to a wider array of audiences and increasingly complex organizational situations.

The leadership communication framework is depicted as a spiral to avoid suggesting a hierarchy, since all effective communication depends on the core skills at the center. These are also our more individual skills. To be a leader, we need to master the skills at the core. We also need to expand our skills to include those needed to lead and supervise groups and, eventually, to incorporate those on the outer circle, the corporate

EXHIBIT 1.4
The Leadership
Communication
Framework

communication skills needed to interact successfully with all internal audiences and external stakeholders.

Core Communication

Communication strategy is included in the section on core skills (Section 1), but leaders will find they always need to take a strategic approach to be a master of leadership communication. Therefore, developing a communication strategy will be emphasized throughout all sections of the text as we move from inside to the outer rings of the spiral. Strategy is the foundation on which any effective communication depends. Leaders need to be able to analyze an audience in every situation and develop a communication strategy that facilitates accomplishing their communication objectives.

Leaders need to be able to structure and write effective simple and complex correspondence and documents, from text messages and e-mails to proposals and reports. They need to be able to write and speak in the language expected of leaders, language that is clear, correct, and concise. In addition, they need to be able to create and deliver oral presentations confidently and persuasively, using graphics that contribute to delivering the messages. These are the capabilities at the core of all professional communication.

Success in organizational and corporate communication depends on mastering these core capabilities. Although listening is a core skill in any rhetorical situation, it is included in the organizational section of the text (Section 2) instead of the core section because leading and interacting with others effectively requires even greater attention to hearing what others say, not simply what we think we hear them say.

Organizational Communication

Organizational communication builds on the core skills. These are the capabilities that individuals need when they interact with others, whether one-on-one, with groups, or in a broader organizational context. Organizational communication skills begin with emotional intelligence and interpersonal skills, the essential skills needed to interact effectively with others as individuals or groups. Next, the section covers cross-cultural literacy and communication, which involves having the ability to understand and appreciate cultural differences and communicate successfully across and work within different cultures. The organizational communication section also includes leading meetings and managing teams, both essential capabilities for today's leaders.

Corporate Communication

Corporate communication, the topic of Section 3, involves expanding from the organizational skills to those abilities needed to lead an organization and address a broader community. Communication becomes even more complex when we need to think about how best to communicate to all internal and external stakeholders. Again, any good communication depends on having a strategy, but as the audiences become more diverse and larger, the communication strategy becomes more complicated. Leaders find as they move into higher levels of an organization that they need to be able to direct change programs and lead vision development. In addition, they take on greater responsibility for the organization's reputation and become the company's face and voice for the public.

Projecting a Positive Leadership Ethos

Leadership communication at all levels and across the spiral depends on the ability to project a positive image, or more specifically, a positive ethos. The word "image" is often associated with illusion or superficiality. It embodies what an audience thinks of us initially based on mostly superficial perceptions. "Ethos" refers to qualities of greater depth and substance. It ties more directly to our character, which our audience judges according to the culture in which we are communicating.

"Charisma" is another term often used to describe someone who has the ability to persuade others and to connect with an audience. It resembles ethos in its effect on an audience, but it differs in that it suggests exuding a power over others based more on emotions than on reason. Public figures who were charismatic leaders and exemplified a positive ethos include John F. Kennedy, Mahatma Gandhi, and Martin Luther King, Jr.

Both image and charisma can be used to describe leaders, but since ethos ties more directly to the character of the speaker or writer, it serves as a better word to use in capturing the positive qualities leaders should possess. Projecting a positive ethos, then, better defines the goal leaders should seek in mastering leadership communication.

A positive ethos will take leaders a long way toward influencing their audiences with their intended message, whereas a negative ethos is one of the greatest barriers to effective communication. How leaders are perceived makes the difference in how well they are believed, how persuasive they are, and ultimately how effectively they communicate. Successful leadership communication depends on projecting a positive ethos.

Defining Ethos

To understand ethos, it helps to look back at the original definitions found in the writing of the Greek philosopher Aristotle, who identified three types of persuasive appeals:

- Logos
- Pathos
- Ethos

Logos is an appeal based on the logic of an argument, while *pathos* is an appeal based on the use of emotions. *Ethos* is an appeal based on the perceived character of the sender of the message: Is the person trustworthy, confident, believable, knowledgeable, and a man or woman of integrity? If the audience does not trust or believe the speaker or writer, logic or emotion will have little persuasive force.

According to Aristotle, ethos is the most important persuasive device and most critical ingredient in the rhetorical situation: The "character of the speaker may almost be called the most effective means of persuasion he possesses."[12] Therefore, "the orator must not only try to make the argument of his speech demonstrative and worthy of belief; he must also make his own character look right and put his hearers, who are to decide, into the right frame of mind."[13] An effective speaker can "inspire confidence in the orator's own character" and "induce" belief and acceptance in the audience.[14]

What is it that will help leaders inspire confidence and induce others to listen to them? One of the primary requirements is credibility. In their extensive research on leadership, James M. Kouzes and Barry Z. Posner found that credibility is the number one reason people follow someone.[15] To be an effective leader, we must be credible to our followers.

Credibility is essential to creating a positive ethos. Aristotle said, "Persuasion is achieved by the speaker's personal character when the speech is so spoken as to make us think him credible."[16]

For audiences to view leaders as credible, they must perceive them as knowledgeable, authoritative, confident, honest, and trustworthy. Leaders can achieve the first two through hard work and position. For instance, if we are giving a presentation on the future of energy production in the United States, we must know the industry and the market as well as something about politics and regulatory policy. We can learn the facts and appear knowledgeable. In addition, if we are a CEO of a major energy company, our audience will probably perceive us as someone with the authority to talk about energy.

We can exude confidence by being well prepared and feeling comfortable delivering presentations. We can even create an aura of honesty and trustworthiness through effective delivery techniques, such as maintaining steady eye contact, having an easy rapport with the audience, and being well prepared to answer questions. Thus, we can take specific actions to build greater credibility. By doing so, we can begin to establish a positive ethos.

Projecting a Positive Ethos

To build a positive ethos, leaders need to know how others perceive them; however, determining how all audiences perceive us is not easy. Research on managers' ability to judge how they are perceived found that "most managers overestimate their own credibility—considerably."[17] Discerning how others perceive us takes honest self-reflection and often the assessment of others. Few people really see themselves as others see them.

To see ourselves completely honestly would be a powerful advantage. To quote the Scottish poet Robert Burns from his poem "To a Louse": "O wad some Power the giftie gie us/To see oursels as ithers see us!" In this famous poem, Burns tells the story of a woman dressed immaculately who exudes an air of great superiority. On closer inspection, however, her observers see that she has lice and realize she is not as immaculate as she appears on the surface.

The idea that, when two people meet, six people are really in the room—the persons as they see themselves, the persons as the others see them, and the persons as they actually are—underscores the complexity of perception and self-perception.[18] Deciding which perception is the most accurate would lead to a philosophical tangle, although determining which one is most important would depend on the purpose of the encounter. If one of the individuals intends to influence the other, then the perception of the other takes on great importance and the need for that individual to know how he or she is perceived becomes critical.

What can leaders do to find out how they are perceived? They can develop greater emotional intelligence (see Appendix A for a self-assessment, which contains several questions related to emotional intelligence). In addition, leaders can obtain feedback from others; one popular performance tool is the 360-degree feedback, a multisource feedback process. It combines our self-evaluation with that of our superiors, our peers, and direct reports to create a well-rounded evaluation of us. It provides an excellent method for uncovering discrepancies between how we see ourselves and how others see us.

Self-exploration and some sought-after honest feedback from others will bring the greater self-awareness necessary to judge ourselves more accurately and to recognize the signals others send back to us, either in their words or, often more importantly, in their body language and their actions. This self-knowledge can help in building a positive ethos (for more information on self-assessments and ways to improve emotional intelligence, see Chapter 7).

In addition to critical self-reflection and the evaluation of others, we can improve our ability to suggest a positive ethos by building a positive reputation, improving our professional appearance, projecting greater confidence, and learning to communicate more effectively. Reputation could include title, organizational positions, past roles or accomplishments, and public opinion. We can achieve a positive appearance through appropriate and culturally expected dress and grooming. To suggest confidence to our audience, we can use eye contact, establish a rapport, and speak easily about a subject without notes when making a presentation. By using language effectively to capture the meaning and inspire trust, we can create believers in our message.

Connecting Ethos to Audience Motivation

The importance of understanding our audience cannot be overemphasized; therefore, several pages in Chapter 2 are devoted to analyzing audiences. An audience's receptivity to us, our ethos, or our message can assist or be a barrier to their receiving our message as we intend. Looking briefly at what makes an audience receptive to our message is helpful in expanding our understanding of ethos.

What is it that makes others attend to our message? What is it that persuades them to listen and to act? In a recent article in *Harvard Business Review*, Robert Cialdini argues that "no leader can succeed without mastering the art of persuasion."[19] Just as creating a positive ethos aids in the art of persuasion; understanding what motivates others to listen and to act helps as well.

People are obviously much more likely to listen to or care about what we say if our messages are meaningful to them or if they have an interest in them. Combine this interest with knowing how to encourage

EXHIBIT 1.5
Sources of Power

Source: French, J. R. P. and
Raven, B. (1958). The bases
of social power in D.
Cartwright, (Ed) *Studies in
Social Power*. Ann Arbor:
University of Michigan
Press. Used with permission;
Hocker, J. L., and Wilmont,
W.W. (1985). *Interpersonal
Conflict*, 2nd ed. Dubuque,
IA: Wm. C. Brown.

Power Type	Source of Persuasion
Coercive	The prospect of being punished
Reward	Prospective benefits or rewards
Legitimate	Recognized position or title
Referent	Personal attractiveness or charisma
Expert	Expertise of the speaker
Information	Possessor of needed information
Connection	Interpersonal relationships, linkages

the audience to trust us and believe our message, and we will have an attentive audience. When the audience has a stake in our subject and is inclined to believe us, they are prepared to be persuaded.

Power

The art (or, some might argue, science) of motivating people has been studied for years, by Freud, Jung, James, Maslow, Alderfer, and others. One useful approach is that of John French and Bertram Raven. They diagnosed five sources of power to persuade others to attend to a message (Exhibit 1.5). More recently, Hocker and Wilmot have added to these five sources of power the power of information and of connections through interpersonal relationships. They argue that power exists in all social interactions, with communication functioning to influence others, often through the power one person has over others.

The previous example of a CEO of a major energy company demonstrates creating an ethos based on the motivational power of expertise and legitimacy associated with title and position. When combined with the use of the "referent" appeal or the charisma of being a confident, effective presenter, the CEO establishes sources of persuasion. If we add to this scenario that the audience consists of energy analysts responsible for reporting on the industry's future, we have the appeal of "reward" and "information," a very receptive setting for persuasion to occur with five of the power influencers in place.

The CEO's persuasive ability depends on an emotional appeal and a positive ethos, a combination that may work as well as or better than facts and figures in many cases: "Arguments, per se, are only one part of the equation. Other factors matter just as much, such as the persuader's credibility and his or her ability to create a proper, mutually beneficial frame for a position, connect on the right emotional level with an audience, and communicate through vivid language that makes arguments come alive."[20]

Knowledge of what motivates others can help in creating a positive ethos, which will make us more persuasive. Words and how we use them reflect who we are. We can use the most effective words in any given situation, or put the right "spin" on a subject for a particular audience, but if we stray too far from what we believe, our audience will probably perceive us as untrustworthy. And trust is essential in persuading others.

Trust

Trust is complicated. What makes one person trust another? Two researchers looked specifically at trust and the relationship between superiors and subordinates in an organization and found five characteristics of the people others trust, four moral values and one behavioral:

1. **Integrity**—the reputation for honesty and truthfulness on the part of the trusted individual.
2. **Competence**—the technical knowledge and interpersonal skill needed to perform the job.
3. **Consistency**—reliability, predictability, and good judgment in handling situations.
4. **Loyalty**—benevolence, or the willingness to protect, support, and encourage others.
5. **Openness**—mental accessibility, or the willingness to share ideas and information freely with others.[21]

Being sensitive to the motivation of others is important to successful persuasion, but so are integrity and sincerity. Otherwise, we risk projecting a negative ethos.

Our ethos may be the most persuasive tool we possess. Although it may be difficult for a leader in business to be perceived as honest and trustworthy in today's scandal-laden business world, the success of individuals and companies often depends on it.

Two examples of the value of a positive ethos and business leaders with good reputations are Warren Buffet and Bill Gates and their two companies. Berkshire Hathaway and Microsoft are two of the highest performing and two of the highest ranked in any poll of positive reputations. Their leaders and their companies have a positive ethos.

The extensive research into emotional intelligence has shown that company leaders set the tone, create the mood, and determine the actions of the organization. They and their companies are trusted because of their reputation, because they are good at what they do, because of their knowledge, because they appear confident, and because they are believed to be ethical. All of these conditions lead to a positive ethos.

A positive ethos is essential to success as a leader and is critical in leadership communication. For some, achieving a positive ethos may mean making some changes in the outward manifestations on which we are often judged by others. This type of studied attempt to control perception is called image management, which can be seen as deception.

However, the type of leader being coached here is again the transformational leader, with all of the positives associated with this type of leader—as described by Bass, those "who are seeking the greatest good for the greatest number without violating individual rights, and are concerned about doing what is right and honest, [the leaders who] are likely to avoid stretching the truth or going beyond the evidence for they want to set an example to followers about the value of valid and accurate communication in maintaining the mutual trust of the leaders and their followers."[22]

The positive ethos for a transformational leader often comes down to trust. Trust creates credibility; credibility creates a positive ethos. Without question, trust is lost whenever leaders deceive others: "The credibility of the leaders suffers when the truth is stretched. Trust in the leaders is risked and . . . trust is the single most important variable moderating the effects of transformational *leadership* on the performance, attitudes, and satisfaction of the followers."[23] In other words, the transformational leader is expected to be honest. Therefore, behind that positive ethos should be positive ethics as well.

Connecting Ethos and Ethics

While we can control or develop some of the outward manifestations of a positive ethos, it is more difficult for an individual to change or for an audience to determine the true character of the communicator. For the transformational leader, a positive ethos exemplifies a strong inner character (Exhibit 1.6). We would hope all leaders are honest, honorable, truthful, fair, and ethical—in short, that they have integrity: "Integrity in all things precedes all else. The open demonstration of integrity is essential; followers must be wholeheartedly convinced of their leaders' integrity," writes Max De Pree in his book *Leadership Jazz*.[24]

We judge our leaders by the ethos they project: their outward manifestation in their dress, behavior, charismatic appeal, knowledge, and expertise; their inner character; and their communication actions. Do they speak and write clearly, confidently, and correctly? Are they good listeners, attending to their own nonverbal signals and those of others? Do they seem sincere in their connections to others? Do they show emotional intelligence and an understanding of and appreciation for cultural differences?

We can see leaders' outward projections of the self and the actions, but the inner character is below the surface, leaving us to judge based on what we see and on the behavior and actions. Our judgments, then, are filtered through our perceptions and influenced by our own view of the world and the clarity of our own cultural and experiential lens.

EXHIBIT 1.6 Ingredients for Creating a Positive Ethos

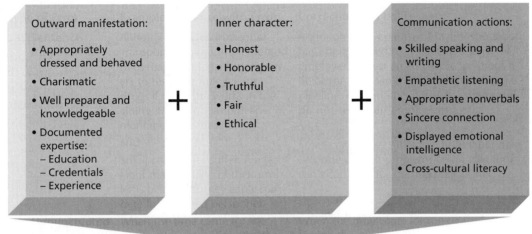

Outward manifestation:

- Appropriately dressed and behaved
- Charismatic
- Well prepared and knowledgeable
- Documented expertise:
  – Education
  – Credentials
  – Experience

+

Inner character:

- Honest
- Honorable
- Truthful
- Fair
- Ethical

+

Communication actions:

- Skilled speaking and writing
- Empathetic listening
- Appropriate nonverbals
- Sincere connection
- Displayed emotional intelligence
- Cross-cultural literacy

Positive Ethos

Therefore, unfortunately, we can be deceived. History shows that a person's projected image may not reflect reality. Ethos and ethics are not always aligned; someone can project a positive ethos and appear honest and trustworthy yet have little or no ethical foundation behind that projection. Someone skilled in deception can fool others; the absence of honesty and integrity is not always apparent to an audience.

When we judge the ethos of another, we have four possibilities:

1. The person is ethical and projects a positive ethos.
2. The person is ethical but projects a negative ethos.
3. The person is unethical and projects a negative ethos.
4. The person is unethical but projects a positive ethos.

Since effective leadership communication depends heavily on the ethos projected, we need to be sensitive to the ethical foundation below the surface. As James Kouzes and Barry Posner found in their research on leadership, "If people are going to follow someone willingly, whether it be into battle or into the boardroom, they first want to assure themselves that the person is worthy of their trust. They want to know that the would-be leader is truthful and ethical."[24]

Being an Ethical Leader

It is important for any leader to look critically at the motivation and meaning behind his or her words and actions. Today, in particular, organizations are looking for ethical leaders; therefore, our reflection on our ethos as part of the self-assessment should include some analysis of the ethical foundation it reflects. For instance, does our ethos suggest the characteristics of an "ethical leader": "fairness, mutual well-being, and harmony"?[25] A positive ethos suggests a "good" character, and a suggestion of a good character makes leaders more persuasive. As Aristotle said, "We believe good men [and women] more fully and more readily than others."[26] A good character suggests an ethical foundation that makes our audience trust us and be more receptive to what we say.

An ethical foundation and ethical behavior are expected of transformational leaders: "The effectiveness of genuine transformational leadership [is grounded] in three essential pillars: 1) moral character, 2) ethical values, and 3) the morality of the processes of ethical choices."[27] Transformational leaders are judged by how they treat others, and ethics become most obvious when interacting and making decisions about those working with and for them.

Exhibit 1.7 lists the typical kinds of ethical issues a leader confronts in a professional environment. According to Trevino and Nelson, 60 percent of the ethical issues that managers face are in the human resources (HR) area—for example, offering one job candidate more money than another for the same position in the same location, rewarding one employee with a larger bonus than another, not using the same evaluation criteria for all members of the same team, and providing privileges for one person over another. All of these violate fairness and can lead to lawsuits, which is one reason most organizations have HR professionals involved in hiring, firing, and performance situations.

EXHIBIT 1.7
Types of Ethical
Issues Common in
Organizations

Source: Trevino, L. K., and
Nelson, K. A. (2007).
Managing Business Ethics,
4th ed. Hoboken, NJ: John
Wiley.

Types	Definitions and Examples
Human resources issues	• Question of fairness • Privacy, performance evaluations, hiring, firing, discrimination, harassment
Conflicts of interest	• Compromised judgment or objectivity • Overt or covert bribes, trading influence or privileged information or appearance of doing so
Customer confidence	• Providing quality product or service at a fair price, representing both honestly, and protecting customer confidentiality • Product safety and effectiveness, truth in advertising, privacy, confidentiality, fiduciary responsibilities
Use of corporate resources	• Fulfilling your responsibility to your employer/organization • Truthful, honest, responsible use of corporate resources, care with corporate reputation and financial resources

Source: Barach, J. A.
(1985). The Ethics of Hard-
ball. *California Management
Review* 27, p. 2.

EXHIBIT 1.8
The Golden Rule
across Cultures

Religion	Variation on the Golden Rule
Buddhism	"Hurt not others in ways that you yourself would find hurtful."
Christianity	"Whatsoever you wish that men would do to you, do so to them, for this is the law and the prophets."
Confucianism	"Tsze-Kung asked, saying 'Is there one word which may serve as a rule of practice for all one's life? The Master said: 'Is not reciprocity such a word? What you do not want done to yourself, do not do to others.'"
Hinduism	"This is the sum of duty: do naught to others which would cause pain if done to you."
Islam	"No one of you is a believer until he desires for his brother that which he desires for himself."
Judaism	"What is hateful to you, do not to your fellow man. This is the entire Law: all the rest is commentary."

In many cases, though, leaders do not have someone to look over their shoulder and help them answer questions of ethics. Instead, they need to address them on their own. Having a defined and organized approach to making ethical decisions can prove very useful for all leaders. The next section provides a few approaches that can be used in any of the situations encountered in Exhibit 1.7.

Making Ethical Decisions

Throughout history, the golden rule—the principle of reciprocity, or doing unto others as we expect them to do unto us—has been one approach to determining ethical behavior. Interestingly, it crosses cultural boundaries and appears in some form in the teachings of the world's major religions, as illustrated in Exhibit 1.8.

Although what is considered ethical in one culture may differ from another, the golden rule and research indicate "that people around the world tend to identify a similar set of values, suggesting that people from different cultures generally agree that honesty, fairness, and respect for human life, for example, are important."[28] In most professional settings, tradition, professional codes of conduct, company codes of ethics or value statements, laws and regulations, international trade agreements, and contracts help individuals determine what is ethical for them or their organization. When faced with an ethical question not answered in one of these, a leader usually follows one of the traditional approaches:

1. **End results (consequentialist)**—focuses on harms and benefits to stakeholders to arrive at a decision that produces the greatest good for the greatest number.

2. **Duty (deontological)**—emphasizes duties, rights, and justice, based on moral standards, principles, and rules.
3. **Social contract (group virtue)**—bases ethical decisions on the customs and norms, the character and integrity of the moral community.
4. **Personal (individual virtue)**—bases ethical decisions on the conscience, what feels right to the individual.

Frequently, ethical questions call on a combination of these. For example, consider the following scenario:

> You have a friend who has sent you a sexist joke through e-mail at work. You are considering forwarding it to some of your closest friends.

Using the end result approach to ethics, you decide those receiving it will not be harmed and might actually benefit in having a laugh. In fact, knowing your friends well, you think, they will all find it funny, so you think it passes the "greatest good for the greatest number test." In terms of duty, the question becomes a little more complicated. A sexist joke violates today's moral standards. It also could violate most social or group virtues, particularly those of the organization in which you work, although you think the customs and norms of your group would allow such a joke. Finally, it comes down to your conscience. Does it feel right to you personally? That you are stopping to think about it suggests it does not, so you make the wise decision, not to send it.

For more complicated ethical decisions, we can apply a more analytical decision-making process, such as that developed by Hosmer (Exhibit 1.9).

Using the same scenario, our analysis would take us through each of the steps in the process as follows:

1. **Moral standards and impacts:** The joke could benefit some of your friends because they would get a laugh out of it, but it could harm others, particularly if your friends sent the e-mail to others, which

EXHIBIT 1.9 Hosmer's Analytical Process to Resolve Ethical Questions

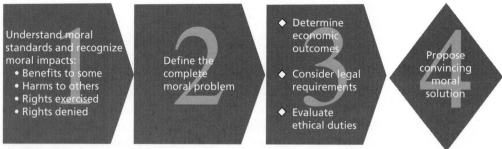

Understand moral standards and recognize moral impacts:
- Benefits to some
- Harms to others
- Rights exercised
- Rights denied

Define the complete moral problem

- Determine economic outcomes
- Consider legal requirements
- Evaluate ethical duties

Propose convincing moral solution

Content source: Hosmer, L.T. (2003). *The Ethics of Management.* New York: McGraw-Hill. Graphic original.

they could easily do. In that case, your company could find out about it, which would hurt you and it could go to people it would offend. You could argue that you are exercising your rights, that of the freedom of speech, but by doing so, you are potentially denying the rights of others, the group of people against whom the joke is aimed and any others who might be offended by it.

Given the leaning in this first step, you would not even need to go to the next step, but for the sake of illustration, let's do.

2. **The moral problem:** The moral problem is one of individual rights versus society's norms. Jokes at the expense of others are at the base of much humor. We can look at popular situation comedies so much a part of U.S. culture for numerous examples, such as *The Office, Two and a Half Men, Scrubs,* and, going back a few years, *Seinfeld.* Many of these shows contain sexist jokes. Some shows make political statements in their humor, which could offend large groups of people, such as *Boston Legal* and *Saturday Night Live,* so in completely analyzing the moral problem, we soon realize the issue can become complicated placed in the context of contemporary society's idea of what is right and what is wrong.

3. **This step has three parts: economical, legal, and ethical duty.** Economically, you could suffer, of course, if your company has a policy against using e-mail for personal use or for purposes that could be considered to violate the rights of others, which it probably does; if so, you could be fired. Also, if you own the company or are in a leadership role where your actions are noticed by stakeholders, your company could suffer financial loss if your e-mail hit the Internet or ended up in the hands of clients or customers. Legally, the e-mail potentially violates the law, particularly if it damages another's reputation, creates a hostile work environment, or otherwise causes duress for anyone else. Under the ethical duty portion of your analysis, you would look at the four traditional approaches to ethics presented above, particularly the ones on duty and social contract.

4. Finally, you come to your moral solution, which, given the balance between the pros and the cons in steps 1–3, would be the decision not to send the e-mail.

Whether a simple moral question or a more complicated ethical dilemma, leaders have to be prepared to make decisions, realizing that those decisions affect their ethos and that of their company. Having an analytical approach is not always warranted; however, often the decisions are complex, and such an approach is necessary. When possible, the leader can fall back on the "front-page" test, or perhaps today we ought to call this the "Internet test." Would he or she want to see his or her decision or action on the front page of the newspaper or on the Internet for all to see?

Establishing an Ethical Environment for Others

In addition to having to make ethical decisions, leaders are responsible for establishing the ethical culture for their organization. Leaders will want to create a climate of integrity to motivate ethical behavior across their organization. They will want to avoid any of the following negative organizational cultures, which the Ethics Resource Center found to result in unethical behavior:

- Lack of any of the following:
  - Satisfaction with information from top management
  - Trust that top management will keep promises and commitments
  - Satisfaction with information from supervisors
  - Trust that supervisors will keep promises and commitments
  - Trust that coworkers will keep promises and commitments
- Rewards for employees who are successful, even if it is through questionable means.[29]

Again, we can see how important trust is for the individual and the organization. Leaders need to create an open environment in which followers and employees feel free to speak up and come forward when and if they witness any unethical or questionable behavior. They need to exemplify in their own behavior the behavior they expect of others and display honesty and integrity in all they say and all they do. They need to make sure the members of their organization know the laws, rules, and norms that apply in their country, industry, and company.

Finally, to create an ethical organizational culture, leaders should take the following steps:

1. Set high standards and communicate them loudly and repeatedly in public and private.
2. Establish an environment of open communication within and outside of the immediate unit or division.
3. Be consistent and transparent.
4. Act swiftly when standards are violated.
5. Encourage complete candor with direct reports.
6. Don't shoot the messenger.
7. Get out and interact with employees at all levels.
8. In a crisis, be open, honest, and accessible.

This chapter has established the foundation for the rest of the text. It explores the transformational leader, which is the type of leader that mastering leadership communication will help individuals become. The text is designed to help current leaders and prospective leaders become effective communicators in all situations as it teaches them to be better leaders by being better communicators. Mastering the instruction provided in *Leadership Communication* will take leaders of all types a long way toward being a transformational leader. It will help them develop and project the positive ethos and other leadership communication capabilities they need to achieve positive results for themselves, for their organizations, and for their community.

Application 1.1 Assessing Leadership Communication Abilities and Establishing an Improvement Plan

To complete the following self-assessment, you should reflect on your level of experience and expertise in each of the areas and on the roles you currently play in which improved leadership communication abilities would help you be more successful. If you need help in defining the areas or understanding what specific topics would be included in each, you may want to refer to and complete the comprehensive self-assessment provided in Appendix A—Checklist of Overall Leadership Communication Ability before completing Part 1.

Part 1

Using the following assessment table, score your own abilities in each of the general leadership communication areas and then answer the questions that follow it.

Score	Leadership Communication Area
	Ethos, credibility, leadership image (how you are seen by others)
	Audience analysis
	Communication strategy
	Written communication
	Oral communication
	Visual communication
	Emotional intelligence: dealing with Your own feelings
	Emotional intelligence: interacting with others
	Coaching and feedback
	Cross-cultural literacy
	Team communication and dynamics
	Internal, employee communication
	External relations

1 = Need lots of work here
2 = Need some work here
3 = Acceptable, but could be stronger
4 = Very good abilities, close to leadership communication level
5 = Excellent abilities, leadership communication level achieved

1. What do you consider your greatest leadership communication strengths?

2. What do you consider your greatest leadership communication weaknesses?

3. What leadership communication roles do you currently play and which areas of leadership communication are most important in them?

Part 2

Answer the following questions to help you develop your goals before moving to the plan in Part 3:

1. What communication leadership roles would you like to play in the future (at your organization or in your career overall)?

2. What are your short-term and long-term leadership communication improvement goals?

3. What new skill do you want to work on first, second, third, etc.?

4. What barriers do you anticipate having to overcome to reach your improvement goals?

5. How long do you think it will take you to achieve your goals?

6. How will you know you are succeeding?

7. How will you obtain feedback?

Part 3

In Word or Excel, create a table or grid similar to this one to develop your personal leadership communication plan. Using a table or grid format will help you track your progress more easily. Be sure to make your goals and action steps specific.

Improvement Goal	Action steps to achieve goal	Deadline	Method to measure success

**Application 1.2
A Question of
Ethics**

Answer the questions for each of the following scenarios and be able to explain your answer and rationale for coming to the conclusion that you do.

1. You have to travel to New York for a conference. Your company will cover your food expenses and has given you the option of taking a per diem of $75 or submitting itemized receipts ($75 maximum per day). Since you know the cheap places to eat in New York, you know that you will come out with money in your pocket if you take the per diem, so you do. Is this ethical or not?

2. Your close friend and colleague tells you that she is going to take the per diem and pocket the extra money in the scenario in #1. What should you do, if anything? Should you report her?

3. As a researcher, you prepare research reports for your company. The company has a rotating work schedule, which allows you to work three days at the office and two at home. Since you are a very fast worker, you are able to complete the research and write the two required reports in three days at the office, so you regularly enjoy a four-day weekend. Is this right or wrong?

4. You regularly use the Internet to shop and buy gifts. During the workday, you spend your down time looking for good deals and doing your shopping while at work. Is this ethical or not?

5. You have a friend who sends you political cartoons and jokes attacking political parties, governments, and leaders through e-mail at work. You sometimes forward these to your friends. Is this right or wrong?

6. A good friend of yours has applied for a job at your company and has given your name as a reference. At previous jobs, your friend has had problems with poor performance, but you really like him and would find him fun to be around at work. Do you give human resources a positive reference for your friend or not?

7. Your company policy states that you cannot accept gifts of more than $50 value. One of your best clients offers you tickets to a professional soccer match worth $150. Since you really want to attend the game and do not want to offend the client, you accept the tickets. Is this right or wrong?

8. As part of a team developing a new software product, you discover that a teammate accepted an expensive gift from your Japanese partner while in Japan working out the details of your agreement to bring the product to market. Do you report the teammate to management or not?

9. You are a member of a hiring committee for a nonprofit organization, focusing on environmental issues. The committee has narrowed its search down to the "perfect candidate." However, when one member performed a Google search of her name, he found pictures and some personal confessions in Facebook that he found very offensive. He feared that her "questionable judgment," as he called it, could hurt the organization's fundraising efforts. Is hiring her or not an ethical question?

10. One of your employees has a personal blog. Apparently, he uses this blog regularly to lambast his fellow workers, pointing out their flaws and mocking their mistakes. Another employee found the blog and has brought it to

your attention, noting that she is offended by his behavior. Is speaking to him about his blog ethical?

Source: *Items 1, 3, 4, 6, and 7 are modified versions of scenarios from Barbara A. Wilson's study "Predicting Intended Unethical Behavior," presented at the Association for Business Communication convention 2004. Deborah J. Barrett at Rice University created the other scenarios for class discussion.*

Application 1.3 Defining Transformational Leadership: A Communication Profile

Find an example of someone you consider to be a transformational leader and write a communication profile that includes the following information:

1. The individual's name, title, current position, and relationship to you. Explain if you know the person personally or professionally; if you do not, explain why the person interests you.
2. Your rationale for selecting him or her. Include why you have selected this person and why you think he or she is a good example of transformational leadership.
3. Your sources of information. How have you learned about the person?
4. A video (a link) or some other example of the person's communication abilities.

Be prepared to discuss your selected leader and show the video if instructed to do so.

Notes

1. De Pree, M. (2003). *Leading without Power*. San Francisco: Jossey-Bass.
2. Mintzberg, H. (1973). *The Nature of Managerial Work*. New York: Harper & Row; Eccles, R. G., and Nohria, N. (1991). *Beyond the Hype: Rediscovering the Essence of Management*. Boston: Harvard Business School Press.
3. Ready, D. A., and Conger, J. A. (2003). Why leadership development efforts fail. *Sloan Management Review* 44, No. 3, pp. 83–88.
4. Smith, B. N., Montagno, R. V., and Kuzmenko, T. N. (2004). Transformational and servant leadership: content and contextual comparisons. *Journal of Leadership & Organizational Studies* 10, No. 4, pp. 80–92.
5. For more on transformational leadership, see Burns, J. M. (1978). New York: Harper & Row; Bass, B. M., and Avolio, B. J. (1993). Transformational leadership: A response to critiques. In M. M. Chemers and R. Ayman (Eds.), *Leadership Theory and Research: Perspectives and Directions*. New York: Free Press. Smith, Montagno, Kuzmenko (2004); Pounder, J. S. (2008). Transformational leadership: Practicing what we teach in the management classroom. *Journal of Education for Business* 84, No. 1, pp. 2–8.
6. Bass B. M. (1985). *Leadership and Performance Beyond Expectations*. New York: Free Press; Bass, B. M. (1996). *New Paradigm of Leadership: An Inquiry into Transformational Leadership*. Alexandria, VA: U. S. Army Research Institute for the Behavioral and Social Sciences; Bass, B. M. & Avolio, B. J. (Eds.). (1994). *Improving Organizational Effectiveness through Transformational Leadership*. Thousand Oaks, CA: Sage Publications; Smith, Montagno, Kuzmenko (2004).
7. Greenleaf, R. K. (1977). *Servant Leadership: A Journey into the Nature of Legitimate Power and Greatness*. Mahwah, NJ: Paulist Press; Spears, &

L.C., Lawrence, M. (Eds.). (2002). *Focus on Leadership: Servant Leadership for the 21st Century*. New York: John Wiley & Sons.

8. Conger, J. A. (2004). Developing leadership capability: What's inside the black box? *Academy of Management Executive* 18, No. 3, pp.136–39.

9. Avolio, B. J. (1999). *Full Leadership Development: Building the Vital Forces in Organizations*. Thousand Oaks, CA: Sage.

10. Bowman, G. W., Jones, L. W., Peterson, R. A., Gronouski, J. A., and Mahoney, R. M. (1964). What helps or harms promotability? *Harvard Business Review* 42, No. 1, pp. 6–18.

11. Original idea for a diagram of the field of communication and their overlap is from: Shelby, A. N. (1993), Organizational, business, management, and corporate communication: An analysis of Boundaries and relationships. *Journal of Business Communication*, 30, No. 3, pp. 241–67.

12. Roberts, W. R., Trans. (1954). *The Rhetoric and Poetics of Aristotle*. New York: Random House, p. 25.

13. Roberts (1954), p. 90.

14. Roberts (1954), p. 91.

15. Kouzes, J. M., and Posner, B. Z. (1993). *Credibility: How Leaders Gain It and Lose It, Why People Demand It*. San Francisco: Jossey-Bass.

16. Roberts (1954), p. 25.

17. Conger, J. A. (1998). The necessary art of persuasion. *Harvard Business Review* 76, No. 3, p. 88.

18. Bamlund, D. C. (1962). Toward a meaning-centered philosophy of communication. *Journal of Communication* 12, pp. 197–211.

19. Cialdini, R. (2001). Harnessing the science of persuasion. *Harvard Business Review* 79, No. 9, pp. 72–80.

20. Conger (1998), p. 87.

21. Butler, J. K., and Cantrell, R. S. (1984). A behavioral decision theory approach to modeling dyadic trust in superiors and subordinates. *Psychological Reports* 55, pp. 19–28.

22. Bass, B. M. (2004), The ethics of transformational leadership. In J. Ciulla (Ed.), *Ethics: The Heart of Leadership,* 2nd ed. Westport, CT: Praeger.

23. Podsakoff, P. M., Niehoff, B. P., Moorman, R. H., and Fetter, R (1993). Transformational leader behaviors and their effects on followers' trust in leader, satisfaction, and organizational citizen behaviors. *Leadership Quarterly* 1, pp. 107–42.

24. Kouzes and Posner (1993).

25. Solomon, R. (1998). Ethical leadership, emotions, and trust: Beyond "Charisma." In J. B. Ciulla (Ed.), *Ethics: The Heart of Leadership*. Westport, CT: Quorum Books.

26. Roberts (1954), p. 25.

27. Bass, B. M., and Steidlmeier, P. (1999). Ethics, character, and authentic transformational leadership behavior. *Leadership Quarterly* 10, No. 2, p. 186.

28. Ethics Education in Business Schools, AACSB Task Force Report 2004.

29. National Business Ethics Survey 2007, Ethics Resource Center.

Chapter 2

Leadership Communication Purpose, Strategy, and Structure

The direction-setting aspect of leadership does not produce plans; it creates vision and strategies.

John P. Kotter, "What Leaders Really Do," *Harvard Business Review*

Inspiring leaders are very clear on what they are trying to say. . . . If you want to inspire, you have to find the words. Carl Rogers described this in terms of two translations— from an awareness of what you're experiencing or feeling that translates into thoughts, and then the translation of those thoughts into words.

James G. Clawson, "The Inspirational Nature of Level Three Leadership," *Inspiring Leaders*

Chapter Objectives

In this chapter, you will learn to do the following:

- Establish a clear communication purpose.
- Develop a communication strategy.
- Analyze audiences.
- Organize written and oral communication effectively.

Leaders need to consider their purpose, strategy, and structure early in the communication process. Strategy consists of two actions: (1) determining the purpose, goals, or vision of what we want to achieve and (2) developing how best to achieve the purpose, goals, or vision. When developing a communication strategy, we first determine exactly what our goal or purpose is in communicating with our audience, and then we decide how best to accomplish that purpose and connect with that audience.

Communicating with anyone inside or outside an organization without stopping to develop a strategy and analyze the audience could keep us from connecting with that audience and potentially harm both us and the organization. In short, not developing a strategy could prevent messages from reaching audiences as we intend. Exhibit 1.2 in Chapter 1 demonstrates the numerous interruptions that can hinder our message arriving as we intend and explains that leadership communication necessitates anticipating the interruptions. A sender can eliminate many of the interferences or barriers to successful communication by taking time to develop a strategy and understand the audience.

In this chapter, you will learn to apply communication strategy to achieve your communication goals, whether those goals involve a fairly narrow communication activity, such as an e-mail sent to apply for a job or a presentation to explain your findings in a research project, or are part of a larger communication event, such as a merger or crisis that involves multiple communication channels. Effective communication strategy allows you to anticipate and more likely avoid the barriers and, therefore, eliminate the interferences that could prevent your messages from reaching your target audiences.

Effective leadership communication depends on your thinking and planning strategically, understanding your audience, and structuring your communication for different situations, delivery methods, and audiences to ensure that you connect with your audience and deliver your intended message. You will learn to establish a clear communication purpose, develop a strategic leadership communication plan, analyze audiences, and ensure that your message is logically and appropriately organized for the different audiences you will encounter, whether participating in an online or offline discussion, delivering a presentation, or creating written correspondence or reports.

Establishing a Clear Purpose

Leaders recognize that communication has consequences. To ensure that those consequences are what we intend them to be, we first need to establish a clear purpose for each communication activity in which we engage. What do we want our audience to know as a result of reading our e-mail, following our blog, subscribing to our Twitter, or listening to our presentation? What is our message for them? What do we want them to do?

In professional communication, we usually have one of four overall goals:

- **To inform**—transferring facts, data, or information to someone.
- **To persuade**—convincing someone to believe or act in a certain way.
- **To instruct**—instructing someone in a process, procedure, or policy.
- **To engage**—involving someone in a collaborative exchange of ideas.

Sometimes we may simply want to transfer information and are expecting no response or action as a result, but most often leadership communication is action-oriented. We want the receivers to respond, to follow up, or to do something in response to our communication. To ensure that their responses or actions conform to our expectations, we need to be very clear about our specific purpose.

Clarifying the Purpose

Breakdowns in communication frequently occur because we have not taken enough time to articulate a clear purpose. If we initiate the communication, the purpose emerges from our own thoughts and ideas, and we may need to generate the ideas to make the purpose clear and support it. If we are responding to a message sent to us, the sender's message may influence our purpose and determine our response. If we are setting up regular communication through online channels, we need to ensure that the purpose of that channel is clearly communicated to those who will subscribe or follow.

In some cases, the purpose emerges easily. For example, if we need to tell our team that we are planning to introduce a new product, our purpose is to **inform** them of our decision and explain the product. However, if the product represents a radical departure from our company's current strategy or core business, our purpose becomes more complex: now, we need to **persuade** them that the decision is a good one, which may require us to analyze the advantages and disadvantages and gather support for our argument before we share our decision with them. We may even need to establish an in-depth rationale that the decision is valid, which means we should spend time generating ideas and clarifying the advantages and disadvantages so that we can clearly and concisely state our purpose as well as the reasons behind it.

In other cases, the purpose may evolve over time. For example, if we start a corporate blog, our initial goals may be to **inform** and **instruct** people about our products or offerings. However, as we gain followers, we may prefer to **engage** them in conversations that can have a direct impact on the types of changes we want to make in our product or organization.

Whatever our approach, in this phase of developing a communication strategy we should not be concerned with organizing or editing our communication. Rather, we should focus on making our purpose clear to ourselves and/or our team, which may not even involve beginning to create the communication itself. We need to turn off the computer, put our phones on silent, and let the ideas flow.

Finally, we need to remember that clarifying our purpose is an iterative process; once we start on the next step, we may revisit our purpose and edit it.

Generating Ideas

Once we determine our specific purpose, and sometimes while we are determining it, we can begin to come up with supporting words and ideas and explore our thoughts about the subject. In addition, we may need to make sure that our ideas are complete, particularly if our communication is complex. In the previous example of introducing a new product, we would want to explore the pros and cons of introducing the new product before we attempt to persuade our product team that it is a good idea.

In this stage of developing communications, it is essential that we free up the creative side of our brain to think about our purpose and capture all our ideas quickly. We should not try to create and correct at the same time; the corrective impulse interferes with the creative one and often shuts down creativity entirely. We need to turn off the internal censor and let the ideas flow. Try one of these four methods to help you and your team generate ideas:

1. Brainstorming

Brainstorming in this context is conducting an internal discussion with ourselves, recording the subject and any ideas related to it as they occur to us without concern for merit, order, or logic. We might look for the pros and cons, for instance, or attempt to isolate the main topics and list all examples that come to mind. In this type of individual brainstorming, we would want to follow the same rules applied in any well-facilitated group brainstorming session:

- Write down your purpose or overall idea.
- Using free association, list all the words or phrases that come to mind related to the purpose.
- Remember, no idea is a bad idea, so suspend evaluation and turn off the internal censor.
- When you run out of ideas, look back over your list to see if any of the ideas already recorded inspire other ideas.

Some people find that a time limit helps push their thinking; others find that it hinders them by adding an element of stress. Do what works best for you.

2. Idea Mapping

Idea mapping, also called mind mapping, is similar to brainstorming in that we attempt to generate as many ideas as possible related to our

EXHIBIT 2.1 Generating Ideas through Idea Mapping

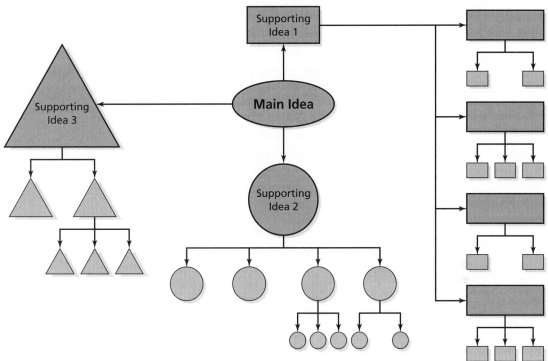

main topic; it differs in that, instead of a list of ideas, we create a visual representation of our ideas. We first write our main topic in the middle of the page, represented by the oval in Exhibit 2.1. Then, we write down all the ideas that come to mind in relation to this idea, starting with the most general and working outward.

If you find that this more visual form of idea generation works for you, you may want to designate different shapes for different kinds of ideas, but you should not let the visual design slow you down. Again, you must avoid filtering, editing, or evaluating and let your mind roam freely from topic to topic.

What you produce may appear random, although patterns will start to emerge that will help you refine your topic and hone in on what it is you really want to say. You can then draw similar shapes around related ideas or color-code them. Later, you can go back and better organize your idea map, possibly regrouping some topics and removing others. The goal is to create an exhaustive page of ideas and thoughts that support your main idea. Then, you might move to a new page to start collecting the facts and data for each of the supporting topics, represented by the smaller shapes in Exhibit 2.1.

Note that a real idea map will probably appear more random and chaotic than this example, but that is as it should be. The goal is to generate ideas and to attempt to be complete in doing so, not to create a neatly drawn diagram.

3. The Journalists' Questions: Who? What? Why? When? Where? How?

Another useful tool to help us generate ideas is the journalists' questions of who, what, why, when, where, and how. Journalists use these questions to generate ideas for a story. This approach is particularly useful when working with policy, process, and procedural topics.

For instance, if we were writing an e-mail describing a change in policy, we would want to establish the following:

a. To whom does the policy apply?
b. What exactly is the policy? What has changed?
c. Why is the policy in place? Why have the changes been made?
d. When does the policy take effect?
e. Where would people needing more information obtain it?
f. How would they obtain it?

4. The Decision Tree

The decision tree is a way to break a topic into its parts, so that we can see how the subtopics relate and whether we have the right support and enough support (Exhibit 2.2). It resembles idea mapping but is more structured and depends on an internal question-and-answer dialogue to be most effective. For example, if we were creating a presentation to persuade our organization that it should design and launch a new educational software package, our argument might be as demonstrated in Exhibit 2.2.

It may help you to use this approach if you think of it as a dialogue, beginning with the main topic, "ABC should design and launch

EXHIBIT 2.2
An Example of a Decision Tree

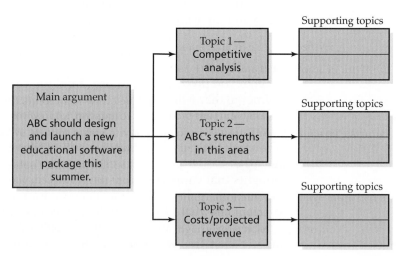

a new educational software package this summer." This assertion leads to a series of "why" questions. The answers become the supporting topics. The why answers are (1) because no one else is competing in this space, (2) because we have the internal capabilities to design and launch the product efficiently and effectively, and (3) because the costs would be low and the revenue potential high. Then, in developing the supporting topics, you would provide the data and facts for each of these. Once you have finished with the decision tree, you will probably have a very complete argument and will be ready to develop the communication strategy to deliver it.

Connecting Thinking and Communicating

Using these methods of generating ideas can help us clarify our purpose and our thinking. Our thinking and our communicating are intertwined and clearly dependent on each other. If our thinking is muddled, our communication will be; if our communication is muddled, it is probably because our thinking is as well.

In "Clear Writing Means Clear Thinking Means . . . ," Marvin H. Swift demonstrates the connection of clear thinking to clear writing and presents a very instructive example of how the relationship of writing and thinking might work when drafting a memo.[1] Here is the first draft of the memo:

First Draft of the Memo

To: All Employees
From: Samuel Edwards, General Manager
Subject: Abuse of Copiers

It has recently been brought to my attention that many of the people who are employed by this company have taken advantage of their positions by availing themselves of the copiers. More specifically, these machines are being used for other than company business. Obviously, such practice is contrary to company policy and must cease and desist immediately. I wish therefore to inform all concerned—those who have abused policy or will be abusing it—that their behavior cannot and will not be tolerated. Accordingly, anyone in the future who is unable to control himself will have his employment terminated. If there are any questions about company policy, please feel free to contact this office.

Source: Swift, M. H. (1973). Clear writing means clear thinking means . . . *Harvard Business Review*, January–February, p. 59. Used by permission of Harvard Business School Publishing, all rights reserved.

Notice that the tone in this first draft is accusatory and angry. The writer isolates himself from his audience and refers to the employees as "the people who are employed by this company." With his subject line, "Abuse of Copiers," and the statement that employees will be "terminated," he creates a negative tone, making it doubtful that anyone would feel "free" to contact his office with questions.

If his purpose is to inform the employees of the problem, he has done that; however, if he thinks, as a leader should, about how best to motivate his followers, or as in this case, his employees, this memo would not accomplish his purpose. It would not create cooperation or support for him, the company, or the policy. Instead, it could alienate him from his employees and cause resentment.

As Swift discusses, when the writer wrote the first draft, his emotions were clouding his thinking. He was not thinking clearly and his writing shows it. After considerably more thought, particularly about how his audience would perceive his message and how he wanted them to respond, he rewrote his memo several times to yield the final version.

The Final Draft of the Memo

To:	All Employees
From:	Samuel Edwards, General Manager
Subject:	Use of Copiers

We are revamping our policy on the use of copiers for personal matters. In the past, we have not encouraged personnel to use them for such purposes because of the costs involved. But we also recognize, perhaps belatedly, that we can solve the problem if each of us pays for what he takes.

We are therefore putting these copiers on the pay-as-you-go basis. The details are simple enough . . .

Source: Swift, M. H. (1973). Clear writing means clear thinking means . . . , *Harvard Business Review*, January–February, p. 60. Used with permission of Harvard Business School Publishing, all rights reserved.

In this final version, he is showing much more consideration for his audience and thinking about how best to motivate them. It does a much better job of accomplishing his purpose. His positive tone is more effective than the negative tone of the first draft. He now uses "we," which brings him and the employees together. The style is also more concise and the content clearer. He is no longer isolating himself from his employees and projecting a threatening, punitive image. He has assumed a positive ethos. This version will achieve the results he intended—to stop the misuse of the copiers—without alienating his employees.

This example also demonstrates one test you can use to see if your purpose is clear—the use of an effective subject line (or a title in a longer document or presentation). A subject line should capture the purpose of your memo or e-mail and set the tone. Notice the difference in the negative "Abuse of Copiers" and the more neutral "Use of Copiers." If you find yourself struggling to create a subject line that clearly reveals your intention in an e-mail or a memo, or a title that specifically tells your audience the purpose of your report or presentation, then your purpose may not be clear in your own mind. If it is not clear to you, it will certainly not be clear to your audience.

This example illustrates the importance of clarifying your purpose before communicating it to others. It underscores that clear thinking about purpose as well as the audience yields clearer, more effective communication. Your purpose establishes the direction you want to go and the results you intend to achieve with your messages, which sets the stage for you to develop a strategy to accomplish those results.

Determining Communication Strategy

Once we have clarified our purpose, we are ready to engage in the more tactical side of communication strategy. Effective communication—whether a simple e-mail, a complex report, a meeting, or a presentation—requires going beyond clarity of purpose to the plan for accomplishing our purpose, the second essential step in any good strategy. At this point, communication strategy shifts to determining how to achieve our communication objectives within the context surrounding the communication.

Considering the Communication Context

All communication occurs in a context of interrelated conditions that surround it. Leadership communication never exists in a vacuum. As we define our purpose and develop our strategy, we need to recognize the context in which the communication occurs. Before we create any form of communication, we need to stop and assess our context. The following questions should help in that assessment:

1. What else is going on in the world, industry, distribution channel, or organization that will affect how the audience will receive this communication?
2. Where does the communication fall in the overall flow of communication—first or last?
3. What has happened before and after?

4. What are the organizational implications?

5. What are the people implications?

6. What does the audience know or believe about the context, compared with what the sender knows or believes?

7. What are the audience's expectations of this communication channel?

8. What are the cultural differences I should consider?

Understanding the context is essential to helping us ensure we create and develop our messages, so that our audiences listen to and accept them as we intend. Our audiences can be easily distracted by the noise around them, causing them to misunderstand our message, reject it, or miss it entirely. For example, in times of economic turmoil, any mention of cost-cutting measures can cause employees to become anxious and worry that their jobs may be in jeopardy, even if the company has no intention of letting anyone go. That does not mean the company cannot send the message, but it does mean it needs to word the message to reassure the employees as much as possible.

A specific example of a disconnect between the context and the messages occurred a few years ago, when a company announced the layoffs of a large number of its employees at the same time that is was promoting its high-profile golf tournament. When the company met with the employees to announce the layoffs, the employees angrily pointed to the company's spending money for the tournament. The management team was unprepared for such a response, since they had not considered the context of the tournament as they developed their announcement.

The employees' anger carried over into the public domain, causing the community to question the company's integrity and hurting its business and reputation for years following the event. In today's environment, this anger could have spilled over into employees' blogs and Twitter accounts and other social media, creating a buzz that would be difficult for the company's public relations and marketing teams to quell—a high price to pay for not considering context.

Leaders need to be sensitive to what is going on around them and consider the contexts of the messages they send; otherwise, they risk their messages' getting lost and perhaps alienating their audiences to such an extent that they will have difficulty regaining their attention and trust.

Using a Strategy Framework

Our strategic communication planning can be complex or simple, but we should approach it with a clearly defined method, ideally one that calls on our analytical skills, just as we would call on these skills for any problem we needed to solve. The Communication Strategy Framework (Exhibit 2.3) illustrates an approach to establishing a communication

EXHIBIT 2.3
Communication Strategy Framework

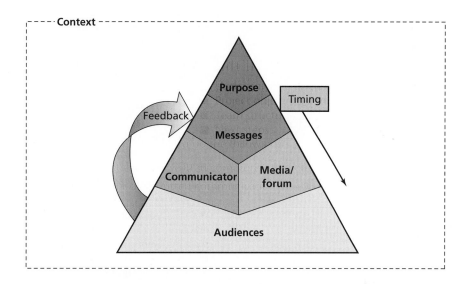

strategy that will ensure that we consider all of the angles and anticipate any issues that might emerge to interfere with communicating the message we want to deliver.

We need to consider each of the components in the framework: the purpose, messages, media/forum, timing, and communicator. At the base are our audiences, the foundation on which all of these other strategy components rest. Audience analysis is critical to any communication strategy and is so important that the next section of this chapter discusses it at length. In addition to analyzing our audience, we need to devise a method for assessing the impact of our communication on our audience through a feedback loop.

Using a framework helps us develop the "how-to" side of our communication strategy. We can and should use it for all types of communication activities before we send any messages, even in day-to-day communication, but it is particularly important in complex, critical situations, such as mergers and acquisitions, crises, and major change programs.

Exhibit 2.4 provides representative questions we should ask in analyzing each of the strategy components in the framework.

Our purpose guides the direction of our communication strategy, and in an organizational context, that purpose should link directly to the overall strategy. We may have one overall purpose or many, depending on the complexity of the communication situation. We may also have several messages that have to be tailored to different media and target audiences. Our overall purpose and overarching message should be consistent from group to group; however, the emphasis, the submessages, and the expected reactions may differ from audience to

EXHIBIT 2.4
Key Questions in Developing a Communication Strategy

Component	Key Questions to Ask Yourself
Purpose	What is my objective or what do I want to accomplish? Do I have different but related purposes for different audiences? How does my purpose relate to and support the organization's strategy?
Message	What is my overall message? How do I formulate my message to make it acceptable to my audience(s)? What do I expect others to do because of my message? What are my supporting messages? Do they differ for each audience?
Medium/Forum	What is the most effective means or channel for reaching each audience (e-mail, blog, memo, letter, meeting, speech, podcast, etc.)? Do I need to consider costs, logistics, or other practical matters in selecting my communication medium or forum?
Communicator	Am I the best person to deliver the message? If not, who should deliver the message(s)? Who would be the most credible or otherwise effective communicator for different messages or audiences?
Timing	Does timing matter? If so, when should the message(s) be delivered and in what order?
Audiences	Who are my primary audiences? Secondary? Accidental? What are their interests in this situation? What are their stakes in the outcomes? How will they be affected by my messages? How should I ask for feedback from this audience?
Feedback	How will I determine if my audience is receiving my messages as I intend? How will I measure or assess the impact?

audience. For example, investors may applaud a merger of one company with another, yet employees may be fearful and unhappy.

In addition, with more complex communications, such as those that affect the entire organization, the organization may need different communicators for different audiences and messages, and it will need to select the spokespersons carefully. In a merger or acquisition, for instance, both organizations will have several communicators and slightly different messages for the different audiences. The communicator could include the chief executive officer, chief financial officer, and chief public affairs officer, as well as the entire management team, area supervisors, and local representatives.

EXHIBIT 2.5   Example of Communication Strategy Analysis for a Merger (portion only)

Target Audience	Medium	Purpose	Message	Communi- cator	Timing
Investment community	Meetings/ Internet	Inspire confidence in company's stability and value	A strategic move designed to make both companies stronger	CEO	Day of announcement
Local media	Press conference/ Blogs	Generate positive public opinion and allay any fears of changes in their services	Good for the local economy and the people of the community	CEOs of both companies	Day of announcement
National media	Press release/ calls/ Internet	Generate positive public opinion and reassure potential investors	Good move for the industry, sound financial move, etc.	Public affairs official	Day of announcement
Employees (acquirer)	E-mail/ IM/ meetings	Keep good employees from leaving and reassure all that the company is stable	Good for all employees, creating stronger company, secure future for all	CEO, senior management team	Right after announcement
Employees (acquired)	E-mail/IM meetings	Keep good employees in place and make them as comfortable as possible	No layoffs, no major changes will occur (only if this is true)	CEO, senior management team	Right after announcement

Keep in mind as well that employees *will* become spokespersons for your organization; they will carry messages to others through e-mail, social networking sites, personal blogs, and the like. Part of any communication strategy should include proactively managing these messages and planning to respond to them.

Exhibit 2.5 illustrates how an organization might use the framework to develop a strategy for communicating a merger. It represents an excerpt from an actual strategy developed for a merger between two major high-profile companies. The complete communication strategy in this case consisted of several pages of an Excel spreadsheet containing over 25 different audiences and messages and with the timing broken down to minutes before and just after the merger announcement.

Creating an Action Plan

If preparing for a major communication event, or any communication that will reach multiple audiences and affect an entire organization, you will want to develop your communication strategy through an overall action plan similar to the one illustrated in Exhibit 2.6. The major phases of the strategy development and implementation are

EXHIBIT 2.6
Three-Phased
Communication
Action Plan

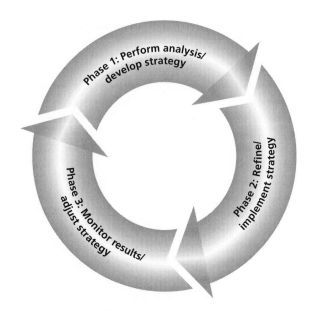

Phase 1: Perform analysis/develop strategy

Phase 2: Refine/implement strategy

Phase 3: Monitor results/adjust strategy

analysis, implementation, and assessment. The illustration suggests that the process is iterative, since you will probably find that you need to make adjustments once you begin to implement the strategy.

In Phase 1, you should use the strategy framework or a similar analytical tool to guide the analysis and frame the strategy. You then develop and communicate the plan. Finally, you monitor the impact and assess the success or failure of the communication strategy.

The previous merger example represents a portion of a much larger plan resulting from the analysis performed in Phase 1. Then, in Phase 2, the messages were transmitted to the identified audiences through the appropriate medium. In Phase 3, the organization conducted a survey to determine how well the merger messages had been received, so that they could adjust the approaches if necessary. For more about how you might develop a complex communication strategy, see Chapter 11 on change communication and employee communication in Section 3 of this text.

To summarize, effective communication depends on clarifying the purpose; developing a thorough, thoughtful communication strategy; and having an action plan for more complex communication.

Analyzing Audiences

Analyzing an audience is fundamental to any communication strategy, since the characteristics of audiences will determine the approach and shape the targeted messages. As the communication strategy framework illustrates, audience is the foundation on which all of the other

EXHIBIT 2.7
Audience Expertise Table

Source: Table created based on information from Houp, K. W., Pearsall, T. E., & Tebeaux, E. (2000). *Reporting Technical Information*, 9th ed. New York: Oxford University Press. Used by permission of Oxford University Press, Inc.

Audience	Medium	Purpose	Approach
Layperson/ nonexpert	Magazine article Newsletter Pamphlet Blog, Twitter	To entertain To inform To engage	Make interesting and practical Give background Define terms Use narratives and analogy
Executive	E-mail Memo Presentation Report	To inform To persuade	Focus on decision making Keep simple Be honest and direct Give conclusions and recommendations early
Expert	Journal article Report Professional network/ blog White paper	To inform	State the how and why Present limited background information Use language of the discipline State inferences and conclusions Cite numerous references
Technical	Reports Procedure Professional/ network/blog White Paper	To inform To instruct To persuade	State the how and why Provide limited background information Keep practical/avoid theory
Combined (diverse)	E-mail Memo Report Blog Twitter	To inform To instruct To persuade	Avoid technical language and jargon Use sections, divisions, and headings Define terms/limit technical information to appendixes Keep prose clean, concise, and simple

components in the framework rest. A leader addresses many different audiences, making it difficult to generalize about what approach to use in all circumstances; therefore, we need to analyze our audience in every communication situation and should approach each audience as unique. Four approaches to analyzing an audience are (1) by expertise, (2) by decision-making style, (3) by medium, and (3) by organizational context.

By Expertise

Exhibit 2.7 demonstrates approaching audiences by analyzing their levels of expertise. The exhibit shows the different media, purposes, and approaches to use with the different levels of knowledge and experience of audiences to ensure that they are receptive to the messages.

Research on how organizations learn has found that companies consist of communities of practice.[2] Communities of practice are groups that have common interests or a common knowledge base and interact frequently. The group could be a work group, a team, a function, a department, or even a company.

Individuals within a community of practice have a common knowledge base and usually a similar level of expertise. For example, the industries in which an organization functions will share knowledge and expertise, although within each of the organizations, individuals will have different specific areas of focus and greater depth in one area. In the energy industry, the exploration geologists, the petroleum engineers, and the geophysicists within a company may differ in degrees and in fundamental understanding of the science within their industry, but they have a common vocabulary and some shared knowledge and can be communicated with effectively using similar language and media—that suggested in the "Expert" and "Technical" rows in Exhibit 2.7, for instance.

In a university setting, the departments represent communities of practice; however, the professors and students within the departments are not limited to the knowledge represented in one subject area, and an approach to communication to professors in engineering could safely be used with professors in biology, or the approach used with professors of history could resemble that used with professors of English. Again, most likely we would want to approach them as Exhibit 2.7 suggests we approach experts and technical people.

When joining an organization early in our career, we usually join fellow experts, and we learn to communicate using the jargon of that discipline. As we move up in an organization, we begin to communicate more with individuals outside our area of expertise and our audiences become broader, more diverse, and less technical. The result is that we have to shift our approach to one we would use with a combined or nonexpert audience.

Leaders need to communicate to audiences with a range of expertise from the layperson, or nonexpert, to the technical or highly specialized individual. Taking time to think through these different levels of audience expertise and interests before or even as we develop our documents and presentations will help us ensure that our audiences understand and accept our messages.

By Decision-Making Style

When we seek a decision from our audience, we want to consider their decision-making style to ensure that we use a communication approach that is persuasive to them. In a *Harvard Business Review* article, Gary A. Williams and Robert B. Miller provide one useful approach to analyzing decision-making styles and argue that "persuasion works best when it's tailored to five distinct decision-making styles." Their research indicates that "more than half of all sales presentations

EXHIBIT 2.8 **Decision-Making Styles**

Style	Characteristics	Communication Approach
Charismatics	Talkative, captivating Easily intrigued by new ideas Make decisions based on information, not emotions	Begin with bottom line Focus on results Present straightforward arguments Use visual aids
Thinkers	Intelligent, logical, academic Impressed by arguments supported by data Tend to be risk averse Need time to come to their own conclusions	Openly communicate any concerns up front Have lots of data ready Provide all perspectives Be prepared to go through methods Be prepared for silence
Skeptics	Demanding, suspicious of every fact Aggressive, almost combative style Need to trust someone to believe their ideas Don't like being challenged or made to look uninformed in any way	Build credibility in yourself and your ideas by enlisting the help of someone they trust Emphasize the credibility of your sources Make arguments as concrete as possible, using specific examples
Followers	Cautious, responsible Risk averse Prefer innovative applications of proven solutions Make decisions based on track records, theirs or others'	Present proven methods, references, and testimonials Show how the idea is safe yet innovative Use case studies Present options Provide details
Controllers	Logical, unemotional, sensible, detail-oriented, analytical Abhor uncertainty and ambiguity Focus on the facts and analytics of an argument	Carefully structure your argument Provide details from experts Don't push too hard Provide the facts and leave them to decide

Source: Adapted and reprinted by permission of Harvard Business Review. From "Change the way you persuade," by G.A. Williams & R.B. Miller, 80 (5), pp. 65–74. Copyright © 2002 by Harvard Business School Publishing Corporation; all rights reserved.

are mismatched to the decision-maker's style."[3] Exhibit 2.8 explains the styles they identify.

In any situation, internal or external to an organization, knowing how the audience makes decisions will help us target our messages appropriately. We should try to anticipate our audience's response, considering very carefully what they will do after reading what we have written or hearing what we have to say. We should try to adopt the audience's point of view, assume the "you attitude." What is it that they need to hear to agree with our message? What will appeal to them? What will help them make the decision we want them to make?

By Medium

It is important to consider an audience's expectations for communication based on the medium through which they receive that communication. For example, employees may not expect to respond directly to the CEO if she sends an e-mail through a distribution list but may feel very differently if the same CEO puts a post on her blog. Likewise, customers interacting with our organization's Twitter accounts expect to be able to carry on online conversations if they desire, so we should be prepared to answer any tweets we receive if we interact through that medium.

By Organizational Context

It is also helpful when analyzing our audiences to consider the organizational context. Where are they, what do they know, and what do they need to know? When we communicate professionally, we are communicating within an organizational context. Whether the communication is simple or complex, we need to think carefully about organizational relationships and how they affect motivation. The questions in Exhibit 2.9 are designed to help not only determine who our audience is but also understand better what motivates them in a particular organizational context.

While most often communication may be too rapid to allow us to answer all of these questions every time we send a message, and in many cases our familiarity with the audience will minimize the need for analysis, with any important correspondence or report we should at least be able to articulate very clearly our purpose in writing to them

EXHIBIT 2.9
Questions to Clarify Audience and Organizational Context

1. Does the communication respond to a previous communication or particular request? If so, what? Where is this communication in the overall flow of communication?
2. What is the organizational context for this communication?
3. Who are the primary audiences (the persons who will act) and who are the secondary audiences? Who might be an unintended or accidental audience?
4. If they are the decision makers, what motivates them and how do you best persuade them?
5. If they are not the decision makers, what is their relationship to the decision maker?
6. How much do they know about the subject? What do they need to know?
7. What do I expect them to do in response to this communication?
8. How do I expect them to feel?
9. What do they have to gain or lose by accepting my ideas/recommendations?
10. How will this communication affect the organization?
11. Overall, what do I expect to happen as a result of this communication?

and our expectations of the audience as a result of this communication. This clarity of purpose combined with a good sense of our audience supports any successful communication strategy.

Organizing Communication Effectively

Once we have clarified our purpose, conducted our audience analysis, and created a strategy, we are ready to select the best structure for organizing our communication as the audience will see or hear it. The organization of our communication needs to be part of our early thinking and planning because the audience and our relationship to them determines how best to deliver our messages. We may use a rough outline, decision tree, or other device to organize our thinking as we develop our ideas, but we need to stop and ask if that structure is the best way to communicate this message to this audience.

Structure depends on purpose, messages, audience, and strategy. For instance, if our purpose is to persuade a hostile audience, we might want to begin indirectly, saving our main message or recommendation for the end. If we are addressing a decision maker who needs to see details before making a decision, we may want to present the facts upfront. If we are in a culture where relationships are valued more than results, we might want to begin by talking about general, nonbusiness topics before introducing the main subject of the communication. If, however, our audience consists of typical, busy U.S. executives, we will need to get to the main subject quickly, right upfront, or we risk losing their attention and trying their patience.

In thinking about our communication, we need to adopt the perspective of the audience and select and organize our information specifically for them. If we used the decision tree or idea mapping to develop our ideas, we already began to organize them and have selected and discarded some information. We can now shift to focusing on the logical ordering of our writing or speech for the audience.

In the case of text messages, instant messaging, and microblogging, we may not need to organize every outgoing message that carefully. However, we still need to ensure that any message sent through these and other social media fit into our overall plan for the structure and usage of those media. In other words, we need to organize our approach, even if we do not always need to organize our immediate message fully.

You may find the following questions helpful to determine the best approach to organizing your communication:

- What is the most effective way to open communication with *this* audience?

- How should I arrange the information I provide to ensure that the audience will follow the discussion easily, understand the main ideas, and be receptive to the information?
- What is the most effective way to end this communication?

Our audiences are busy, just as we are, and will be much more likely to respond positively to a blog post, an e-mail, or any other communication if we use the following guidelines:

- Get right to the main message.
- Stay on topic.
- Establish relevance to them.
- Organize the communication to be immediately accessible and relevant to their decision-making process.

How you open your communication will depend on audience analysis. The general rule for professional communication, however, is that **our purpose for writing or speaking usually comes first.** Background information is included only if we need it to establish a context for our communication or our relationship to the problem addressed. Likewise, we should place our recommendations at the beginning unless we have a specific reason for delaying them. If we delay the conclusions or recommendations until the end, many readers will go looking for them anyway, and listeners will become impatient waiting for them. Our audience wants to know immediately why we are writing or speaking to them. Therefore, with most business audiences, we need to deliver our main message immediately.

How we organize our communication once we move into the body of our discussion will depend on our analysis of our audience; however, the logic of the entire document or presentation, as well as that of each section of it, should be obvious to anyone. Our argument should be so logical that anyone can follow our reasoning and understand why one point follows another.

Selecting Organizational Devices

Usually, we use one or more of the following methods to organize individual sections and even the entire document or presentation:

1. **Deduction** (general to particular)—conclusions or recommendation, then the supporting facts, arguing from general principles to specific situations.
2. **Induction** (particular to general)—supporting information, facts that build to the conclusions or recommendations.
3. **Chronological**—first, second, and so forth, used to describe a process or procedure or relate events in the order they occurred as a narrative.
4. **Cause/effect**—because of X and Y, Z happened; a powerful and common form of analysis.

5. **Comparison/contrast**—similarities, then differences.
6. **Problem/solution**—explanation of the situation or problem, followed by ways to solve it.
7. **Spatial**—relationships of steps, pieces, or items to each other.

Frequently, the structure of our communication is either deductive or inductive. If deductive, we begin with an overarching argument or general principle, and then we provide levels of facts grouped logically by topic to support our major assertion. If inductive, we present our facts or groupings of facts first and build our argument from point to point, ending with a "therefore" and our conclusion.

Using the Pyramid Principle

In *The Pyramid Principle*, Barbara Minto illustrates how to structure an effective discussion in a business context by applying classical deductive and inductive logic.[4] The approach can be very helpful in ensuring that an argument is logical, complete, and effective in reaching different types of audiences in all contexts.

The Pyramid Principle emphasizes the "top-down" approach to organizing and presenting a message. It consists of one overarching summary statement, with levels of support linked in a dialogue (answering why, what, or how) below it. This dialogue is similar to the approach we use to create a decision tree to generate ideas. We start with our conclusion or recommendation at the top and then work through the levels of support, testing each level to make sure it answers "why," "what," or "how" for the level above it (Exhibit 2.10).

EXHIBIT 2.10 Example of a Pyramid

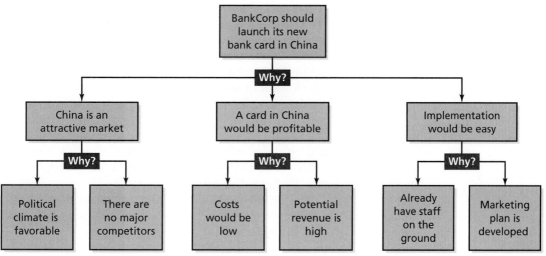

The Pyramid Principle is governed by the following rules:

1. The pyramid must be Mutually Exclusive, Collectively Exhaustive (MECE). That means that the topics at each level should not overlap with each other and that the evidence to support each should be balanced and as complete as necessary and reasonable.
2. Each level must summarize the ideas grouped below it.
3. The "ideas in each grouping must always be the same kind of idea."[5]
4. The "ideas in each grouping must always be logically ordered."[6]

Placing the levels in a sentence is helpful to test the logic and flow of a pyramid-structured argument. The sentence should make sense, flow easily, and be parallel. For example, for the pyramid in Exhibit 2.10, the sentence would read

> BankCorp should launch its new bankcard in China because China is an attractive market, a card in China would be profitable, and implementation would be easy.

Using the Pyramid Principle helps us structure a complete and logical argument. As we create the pyramid, we can easily see gaps in our evidence, establish the balance of our argument, and determine if each level logically supports the next. We can see if we have too much support for any one topic and not enough for another. A pyramid also makes it easy for us to see that each level of our argument clearly and logically supports the level above it and that we have not duplicated support under any of the topic boxes. In addition, drawing a pyramid helps if we are working with a team to create a document or presentation. With all topics and supporting details visually displayed, we can easily divide the topics into tasks, avoid duplication of effort, and determine quickly where the team needs to do more analysis.

Creating a Storyboard

Another technique for working out and mapping the structure of a document or presentation is a storyboard. A storyboard is particularly useful when working in a team to prepare a presentation. It allows everyone to see the logical flow and encourages each team member to imagine the individual graphics needed to support each idea. It also helps in dividing these pieces up for completion by the individual team members (Exhibit 2.11).

This storyboard contains what is called "ghost" slides, which suggest the content without actually showing it. They work well in helping us select the types of charts that would best support our conclusions and work particularly well with a team, making it easier to divide the slides up across the team members as they complete the data gathering necessary to fill in the information.

EXHIBIT 2.11
**Example of a
Storyboard for a
Presentation,
Video, or Podcast**

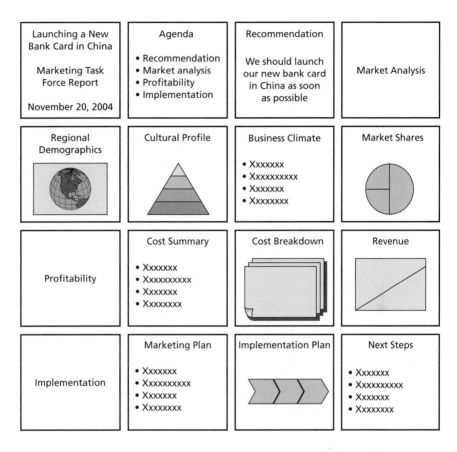

Ensuring a tight, logical organization for any communication is an important step in creating documents and presentations that deliver our intended messages to audiences so that they are receptive to them. Using a plan or map of the argument, whether a pyramid, an outline, a decision tree, or a storyboard, will strengthen simple messages and is essential in more complex communication. We should always establish a logical structure and think carefully about the organizational devices that will work best with our different audiences.

This chapter has focused on clarifying messages and developing a communication strategy, both essential skills for anyone wanting to master leadership communication. In addition, the chapter has illustrated how best to generate and organize ideas, so that they will reach different audiences as intended. Applying the principles and guidelines in this chapter to all the types of communication discussed in the remaining chapters of the book will help ensure that whatever type of communication activity involved will more likely accomplish the purpose and result in the action the sender of the message desires, which is the hallmark of effective leadership communication.

<table>
<tr><td>

Application 2.1
Communicating
Bad News

</td><td>

The Case: Superior Foods Corporation Faces a Challenge

On his way to the plant office, Jason Starnes passed by the production line where hundreds of gloved, uniformed workers were packing sausages and processed meats for shipment to grocery stores around the world.

Jason's company, Superior Foods Corporation, based in Wichita, Kansas, employed 30,000 people in eight countries and had beef and pork processing plants in Arkansas, California, Milwaukee, and Nebraska City. Since a landmark United States–Japan trade agreement signed in 1988, markets had opened up for major exports of American beef, now representing 10 percent of U.S. production. Products called "variety meats"—including intestines, hearts, brains, and tongues—were very much in demand for export to international markets.

Jason was in Nebraska City to talk with the plant manager, Ben Schroeder, about the U.S. outbreak of bovine spongiform encephalopathy (mad cow disease) and its impact on the plant. On December 23, 2008, the U.S. Department of Agriculture had announced that bovine spongiform encephalopathy had been discovered in a Holstein cow in Washington State. The global reaction was swift: Seven countries imposed either total or partial bans on the importation of U.S. beef, and thousands of people were chatting about it on blogs and social networking sites. Superior had moved quickly to intercept a container load of frozen Asian-bound beef from its shipping port in Los Angeles, and all other shipments were on hold.

After walking into Ben's office, Jason sat down across from him and said, "Ben, your plant has been a top producer of variety meats for Superior, and we have appreciated all your hard work out here. Unfortunately, it looks like we need to limit production for a while—at least three months, or until the bans get relaxed. I know Senator Nelson is working hard to get the bans lifted. In the meantime, we need to shut down production and lay off about 25 percent of your workers. I know it is going to be difficult, and I'm hoping we can work out a way to communicate this to your employees."

The Assignment

After reading the Superior Foods case, complete the following actions.

1. Clarify your purpose(s) for communicating with the employees at the Nebraska plant. Consider what the employees will want to know and how they will need to feel about Superior Foods.
2. Use one of the idea-generation approaches introduced in this chapter to determine your primary messages.
3. Draft a message to the employees, paying very careful attention to the organization and presentation method.

Source: Case developed by Beth O'Sullivan and assignment by Deborah J. Barrett, Rice University, 2004. Used with permission.

</td></tr>
<tr><td>

Application 2.2
Developing
Communication
Strategy

</td><td>

The Case: Spree Cruise Lines

At 9:00 a.m. on Monday, Tara Hoopes, manager of corporate communications for Spree Cruise Lines, arrived at her office at Spree's corporate headquarters to find several messages already in her inbox. The New Orleans city attorney,

</td></tr>
</table>

Mike Litke, had contacted several people at corporate headquarters, suggesting that the company may be liable for damages to two buildings close to where their latest cruise vessel had launched, and people in the company wanted to know how to approach discussing the situation with him and others.

Please call the investor relations office at ext. 3620—need to discuss the upcoming shareholder meeting.

Please call the City Attorney in New Orleans—she's claiming that several small, historic buildings incurred foundation and mortar damage yesterday. Thinks it might have been caused by vibrations from the *Sensation* leaving.

The 750-foot *Sensation* had set sail from New Orleans on Sunday afternoon, bound for a five-night cruise to Cozumel and Cancun. Tara checked the statistics on the vessel and its itinerary:

- Built in 1984, cruising speed 20 knots, gross tonnage 50,000, slated for dry-dock repairs in several months.
- Carrying 1,200 passengers on board, mostly U.S. Americans, about 35 percent under age 35, 40 percent between the ages of 35 and 55, and the remainder senior citizens.
- Staffed by Captain Hernan Galati, Chief Engineer Scotty Ferguson, and veteran Cruise Director Ned Carnahan. Additional staff on board: 650 crew members representing 20 countries.
- Cruising to Cozumel with a Sunday departure, followed by a day at sea on Monday and arrival in Cozumel on Tuesday morning. On Tuesday night, was scheduled to depart for Cancun, docking there all day Wednesday before returning to New Orleans on Friday.

Tara reached for the phone just as it rang. Ned Carnahan and Captain Galati were on the line. Before she could tell them about the full situation in New Orleans, they presented her with some problems of their own.

Sunday Night Aboard the *Sensation*

Ron and Marilyn Nelson stood on the stern deck, enjoying the view. It had been an exciting day, watching the huge ship dwarf the buildings on shore as they departed New Orleans. They had already explored the ship, delighted to find an Internet café, a sushi bar, two pools, and the rock-climbing wall. They had listened carefully to the announcements over the ship's public address system and had skimmed the *Spree Fun*, the ship's newsletter, which listed a wide array of excursions to book before their arrival on shore. As they had waited in line to book their excursions, Marilyn noticed the weather maps hanging on the wall in the main deck lobby.

"Looks like a tropical storm over in the Bay of Campeche," she noted.

"Don't worry," Ron said. "This is a huge vessel, and its engines are strong enough to outrun any storm!" Ron was an ocean engineer by trade, and he was an authority on anything that floated on or happened under water. He added, "We're on vacation—let's enjoy it!"

They booked a catamaran sail/snorkel trip and a horseback-riding excursion to visit the Mayan ruins at Tulum, leaving plenty of time for shopping in Cozumel and Cancun.

Now, standing on the stern of the vessel, there was no evidence of a storm. Ron and Marilyn watched the two wakes made by the twin engines—frothy white foam that trailed from the ship into a moonlit sea. They went down the back staircase into a quiet, unused bar and lounge area. The glassware on the metal shelving was clinking together loudly, making an eerie echo across the room. Other parts of the ship were noisy with the voices of excited passengers, but as they passed into the quiet cigar lounge, they could clearly hear a loud, rhythmic bumping sound. Ron remarked, "There is something wrong here; it sounds like the dual engine props aren't synchronized."

Later that night, Marilyn could not sleep. It seemed that the vibration was getting worse and the plastic grids over the lighting system in the cabin were rattling loudly. Concerned, she got up and went to the Internet café to check information about cruise ships. Were they meant to make so much noise? She chatted with a couple of friends online, who told her that they hadn't had noise like that on their cruises, which only worried worry her more. Finally, she posted to her Facebook status: "Listening to the loud vibration on the *Sensation*—been going on for hours. Should I be worried?" Responses began coming in quickly, and soon Marilyn's network was re-posting the news in other places. The buzz had begun.

In the Captain's Quarters

At 6:00 a.m. Monday morning, Scotty Ferguson, chief engineer, knocked at Captain Galati's door. He said, "Sir, the propulsion unit running the left engine prop won't hold up—we've got to shut it down. Running it could result in permanent damage, but we might have to restart if we need the full 20-knot engine speed to outrun the storm later in the cruise."

"Scotty, are you sure?" asked the captain. "It will take us three days to reach Cozumel if we travel on half power. And we'll have to skip Cancun and turn right around to get back to dock by Friday. The guests have already booked their on-shore excursions. Let's get Ned up here."

Ned, the cruise director, grumbled to himself as his stateroom phone rang. He thought to himself, Just one last cruise on this old ship; corporate promised I could move to a European route if I just finished this one last cruise. He spoke briefly with the captain and told him he would be right up.

On his way to the captain's quarters, he thought about what Captain Galati had told him, and his mind worked quickly—I think we'd better call Tara at corporate, tell the passengers, refund or reschedule all the on-shore excursions, monitor the Internet café to see how many people have already contacted travel agents to disembark in Cozumel—and what about that storm?

Even though passenger tickets clearly stated that itinerary changes could occur and that Spree would reimburse only $30 per person, it was Ned's job to keep the passengers happy—not to mention what this could mean for

Sensation's future marketing plans. He was already calculating the financial impact to the cruise line and he couldn't help wondering if the minor engine troubles on the last cruise hadn't been properly repaired.

Tara's Phone Call

"Hello, Tara, we've got a delicate situation here," Ned said.

Captain Galati interrupted, "We have to shut down one engine immediately; I know the passengers will be upset, but the integrity of the ship is my first concern."

"Of course, Captain," Tara said. "Tell me what's going on."

They reported the damage to the engine's propulsion system and their decision to shut down one engine and reduce their cruising speed to 10 knots. The arrival into Cozumel would be delayed; rather than arriving at 9:30 a.m. on Tuesday, they would most likely arrive at 4:00 p.m. To ensure a timely return to New Orleans by Friday, they would have to depart Cozumel at 2:00 a.m. Wednesday, skipping the Cancun destination altogether and cruising straight through.

Tara's cell buzzed; her boss had sent a text. "Check Twitter buzz on *Sensation*—we have a problem." A quick search showed her that the passengers were aware of the potential problem already; they'd been buzzing about it all night. And then there was the city attorney.

Tara thought for a moment. "Ned, Captain Galati, we have a bigger problem than you might realize. Your passengers have already been talking to friends and family about the noise, and people on shore are getting worried. The city attorney here is also suggesting that our ship may have damaged some buildings as it left port. There's a lot at stake for Spree here. I think we'd better talk about how best to approach the situation."

The Assignment

1. Identify all of the key audiences for the communication surrounding this incident. What do you know about each of them? Are there other audiences linked to this audience, either as secondary or "future" audiences?
2. Answer the following questions about the audiences identified in question 1.
   a. What is the message you want to send to each key audience?
   b. What information does the audience *already know* and what information do they *need or want to have* about the situation?
   c. How does this audience feel at this point and how would you like them to feel at the conclusion of the situation or after receiving your communication?
   d. How will you motivate or persuade them to accept your messages?
3. Develop a communication strategy considering the following questions:
   a. What are your key objectives for this communication? (Consider personal as well as departmental and corporate objectives.)
   b. Who is the best spokesperson to deliver this message and why? What other people could serve as spokespersons?
   c. What is the best channel, or medium, to use to communicate with this audience? Also consider the option of using several channels for these communications.

d. When is the best time to communicate the information?

e. Are there cultural or other contextual considerations you should keep in mind?

f. How will you know if your communication has been successful?

Source: Spree case and assignment developed by Beth O'Sullivan, Rice University, January 2004. Updated by Sandra Elliott, April 2009. Used with permission.

Application 2.3 Using the Pyramid Principle to Organize an Argument

Use the Pyramid Principle to structure an argument based on the facts provided here. First, establish an assertion at the first level in answer to the following question: Should AmeriHotels build a new, upscale hotel in Metroburg, near a new major downtown convention center and sports arena? Second, identify at least three primary supporting ideas. Third, group the facts under the supporting ideas.

1. No other hotels exist within walking distance of Metroburg's new convention center or the sports arena.

2. Experts predict a downturn in hotel bookings for at least the near term (one to three years) and possibly longer.

3. No restaurants exist outside of the convention center or sports arena, and the restaurants that do exist within the convention center offer "fast food" only.

4. Members of several ethnic groups and other local residents, many of whom had residences displaced by the convention center and sports arena developments, may oppose building permits.

5. The new convention center is in a high-crime area.

6. There are three other four-star, upscale hotels in the vicinity (within a short driving distance) of the new convention center.

7. The city of Metroburg has obtained funds for park and landscaping efforts in the area.

8. Studies indicate that businesses thrive in the areas surrounding large urban convention centers and sports complexes/arenas, particularly in the accommodations/dining sectors.

9. Some statistics indicate a high correlation between sports arenas in large urban areas and increased numbers of outside visitors who stay overnight.

10. The city of Metroburg has committed to increased police presence/patrol in the area.

11. AmeriHotels has a spotty record concerning minority hiring and relationships.

12. Last year, AmeriHotels adopted a new vision statement promising that the company would make diversity and community-based hiring a top priority.

13. AmeriHotels has experience building in inner-city locations.

14. AmeriHotels has asked its followers on Facebook and Twitter for their thoughts, and the response has been generally positive.

15. One group, the Alliance for Inner City Development, has openly posted videos to its Web site in which members of the local community say they will be priced out of their homes and will be forced to leave.

16. There is land near the new convention center and sports arena available for purchase and development.

17. Property values in the Metroburg downtown area have skyrocketed in the last year.

Source: This pyramid exercise was adapted from an exercise originally designed by June Ferrill, Rice University.

Application 2.4 Using the Pyramid to Structure an Elevator Speech Project Update

We should always have an elevator speech (a succinct but meaningful summary) ready that we can deliver when we are asked unexpectedly by a team leader or supervisor to update them on our progress. It is also frequently used in business plan competitions and in real situations with venture capitalists, for example. The pyramid is a very useful device for structuring any short presentation you are asked to deliver, whether a summary of the research you are doing or a project in which you are involved.

1. Think of some research you are doing or a project in which you are involved or have just completed, and create a very brief (one-minute) bottom-line summary of it, using the pyramid as your stucturing device.

2. Pretend someone has asked how your research or project is going.

3. Find a partner; give him or her your summary.

4. Now, give each other feedback and do it again.

Notes

1. Swift, M. H. (1973). Clear writing means clear thinking means. . . . *Harvard Business Review* January–February, p. 60.

2. Wenger, E. (1998). *Communities of Practice: Learning, Meaning, and Identity.* Cambridge: Cambridge University Press. Also, see Wenger, E., McDermott, R., and Snyder, W. M. (2002). *Cultivating Communities of Practice.* Boston: Harvard Business School Press.

3. Williams, G. A., and Miller, R. B. (2002). Change the way you persuade, *Harvard Business Review*, 80 (5), pp. 65–74. Copyright © 2002 by Harvard Business School Publishing Corporation; all rights reserved.

4. Minto, B. (1996). *The Pyramid Principle: Logic in Writing and Thinking.* London: Minto International.

5. Minto (1996).

6. Minto (1996).

Chapter 3

The Language of Leaders

To say language is everything to a leader is no understatement. It's a fact.

Tom Peters, Management consultant and author of *In Search of Excellence.*

Just as an artist works from a palette of colors to paint a picture, the leader who manages meaning works from a vocabulary of words and symbols to help construct a frame in the mind of the listener.

Gail T. Fairhurst and Robert A. Sarr, *The Art of Framing: Managing the Language of Leadership*

Without the right words, used in the right way, it is unlikely that the right actions will ever occur. . . . Without words, we have no way of expressing strategic concepts, structural forms, or designs for performance measurement systems. In the end, there is no separating action and rhetoric.

Robert G. Eccles and Nitin Nohria, *Beyond the Hype: Discovering the Essence of Management*

Chapter Objectives

In this chapter, you will learn to do the following:

- Achieve a positive ethos through tone and style.
- Communicate clearly and concisely.
- Follow the language rules that matter.
- Edit and proofread your own writing more effectively

Leaders lead and inspire others to action through their effective use of language. In *The Art of Framing: Managing the Language of Leadership*, Gail Fairhurst and Robert Sarr argue that "leadership is a language game, one that many do not know they are playing. Even though most leaders spend nearly 70 percent of their time communicating, they pay relatively little attention to how they use language as a tool of influence."[1] The introduction to this text discussed how leaders use language as a tool of influence every day. Their ability to influence their audience positively, overcoming barriers to effective communication, is the essence of leadership communication.

The goal of this chapter is to help you create a positive ethos through the effective use of language—the use of the right words in the right way through the right communication channel to achieve the outcome you intend. The language we use creates our ethos. If we are unsure and lack confidence in our writing or speaking abilities, our choice of words, our style, and our tone will reveal it. If, on the other hand, we are confident in our ability to use the language of leaders, that confidence will resonate in our words and enhance our influence with all our targeted audiences.

In one of the best and most concise books on style, *The Elements of Style*, E. B. White says, "Every writer, by the way he uses the language, reveals something of his spirit, his habits, his capacities, his bias. This is inevitable as well as enjoyable. . . . No writer long remains incognito."[2] And no speaker does, either. We reveal who we are through our use of language. For instance, in the following speech given a few years ago by the then CEO of Pennzoil, Hugh Liedtke, during a legal battle between his company and Texaco over a company they were both seeking to buy, reveals his ethos:

> There is perhaps a greater question involved [than the legal details]. It turns on the crucial point of integrity in our industry.
>
> It's one thing to play hardball. It's quite another thing to play foul ball. Conduct such as Texaco's is not made legal simply by protestations that the acts involved were, in fact, legal. All too often such assertions go unchallenged, and so slip into some sort of legal limbo, and become accepted as the norm by default. In this way, actions previously considered amoral somehow become clothed in respectability.
>
> Pennzoil's litigation challenges this mindless slip into acceptability. We seek to test the acceptable standards of behavior in our industry.
>
> A contract is a contract. We used to say that in the oil industry, business was done on a handshake. Should it now require handcuffs?
>
> . . . We believe that integrity is more than just a word. It is a standard of conduct in a world perhaps gone slipshod. Our industry was built on that standard, and Pennzoil will continue to make every effort to see to it that this standard is upheld.[3]

From this short portion of his speech, without knowing anything about Mr. Liedtke, you have formed opinions about his ethos. His language suggests an ethos of confidence, honesty, dedication to his company and his industry, and a rather folksy and down-to-earth quality, with his baseball metaphor and comment about business being done on a handshake.

Since this was a prepared presentation to his stockholders, Mr. Liedtke may have had some help from a speechwriter, as CEOs quite often do for important speeches, although he was well known for his communication abilities and for writing his speeches himself. Speechwriter or not, the words would have to be natural to him, or he would not have sounded sincere. Overall, Mr. Liedtke creates a positive ethos and influences his audience to trust him and follow him. He presents himself as a leader—through the use of clear, confident, resonant language.

Leaders want their audiences to perceive a positive ethos in their tone, to see them as confident, and to trust and believe them. This chapter begins by discussing how you can achieve a positive ethos through your writing and speaking style, which your audience perceives as your tone. It provides ways to make your style more concise and, by doing so, to ensure that you sound more forceful and confident. It then highlights the language of persuasion, reviews the correct use of language expected in leadership communication, and concludes by providing techniques to help you to edit your own work.

Achieving a Positive Ethos through Tone and Style

To project a confident tone when we speak and when we write, we need to possess confidence not only in our knowledge on the subject but also in our ability to capture the content in the right words used in the right way. We want to sound confident and speak with authority; at the same time, in some channels, we want to sound approachable and open to conversation

The words we select and how we decide to combine them in sentences create our style; our audience perceives that style as our tone, and through that tone, they make assumptions about our ethos and our objectives. The tone, or what our readers perceive as our attitude toward them or toward the subject, influences the success of our message and inspires others to believe in us and our vision. For transformational leaders, it is crucial to know how best to use language for positive impact and to avoid a style that creates any negative responses in their audiences.

How Style Can Impact Audiences

We want to be clear and crisp in our language yet not sound too harsh or brusque, as the sample e-mail illustrates in Exhibit 3.1. As you read this e-mail, ask yourself what kind of ethos the writer is projecting. What are the connotations of the language? (Note: The example e-mails,

EXHIBIT 3.1
Dismissal E-mail with a Harsh, Uncaring Tone

To: John Smith <jsmith@bskya.com>
From: J. T. Cole
Subject: Layoff

Dear John:

Effective with the close of business on Wednesday, May 10, 2008, your job will be abolished and no further work will be authorized on that position.

Your support and assistance of B-Sky Airlines in its sales efforts have been most appreciated.

Sincerely,

James T. Cole

Director of Reservation Sales

cc: Personnel file
     Employee
     Original mailed to home address.

memos, letters, and so on in this chapter were written as you see them here. The names and dates have been changed, but the rest of the content is as it appeared in the originals.)

The e-mail in Exhibit 3.1 shows no concern for the audience. It begins with the harsh statement that John's job has been "abolished" and then ends with an attempt to soften the brutal effect by thanking John for his "efforts." The thank-you seems insincere and even out of place in this otherwise cold, bad-news note. One element of style that contributes to the distancing, uncaring tone is the use of passive voice sentence constructions: "will be abolished," "will be authorized," and "has been most appreciated." These distance Mr. Cole from his audience and from the actions. In addition, that this message was sent in an e-mail makes the tone seem even more uncaring.

Imagine the difference if he had written the following sentences instead:

> As of May 10, 2008, I will abolish your job and authorize no more work on your position.

and

> I appreciate your support of and assistance at B-Sky Airlines in its sales efforts.

The first would be too direct; besides, it is unlikely Mr. Cole has made this decision. It is a decision people above Mr. Cole have made, so selecting a direct, active style in the opening sentence would not

EXHIBIT 3.2
Rewritten
Dismissal Letter

B-Sky Airlines
121 no. 20th Bld.
Newyork, 10021

Dear John:

As you know, B-Sky has encountered extremely difficult financial times over the last few months. We have done everything we can to keep the airline functioning as in the past so that we can serve our public and keep all of our employees employed. Now, however, we have come to a point where we must make some difficult decisions. The most difficult decision is having to let some of our people go. Regrettably, your department is one that we must cut. Therefore, as of May 10, 2008, we will no longer authorize work in your department.

Your severance package will include the following. . . .

We all regret that the layoffs are necessary. We value your department and your individual contributions to B-Sky Airlines. We appreciate your sales efforts over the years and wish you the best for the future.

Sincerely,

James T. Cole
Director of Reservation Sales

make this e-mail more effective. The letter in Exhibit 3.2 delivers the same message with a better ethos.

The message has not changed—John is still out of a job—but at least Mr. Cole has shown some concern and seems sincere in his regrets and in his appreciation. Since it is a bad-news letter, the indirect style is more appropriate. In addition, the words selected in the second version create a more positive ethos for Mr. Cole. Finally, sending this harsh message as a letter would make Mr. Cole appear to be taking more effort with his communication, which could also help some in delivering such bad news.

The letter in Exhibit 3.3 is also a rejection letter with a problem in tone. In this case, a student received it from the U.S. House of Representatives when he applied for a summer internship. How would you feel if you received it?

The opening to this letter is probably acceptable. It is direct and expresses some regret. The second paragraph, however, alienates the reader and makes the sender seem foolish. To admit that a decision is "arbitrary" makes it sound as if it had no basis in logic, as if they drew

EXHIBIT 3.3
Rejection Letter with an Alienating Tone

One Hundred First Congress
U.S. House of Representatives
Committee on the Budget
Washington, DC 20515

March 8, 2009

Blakeman Brown
6500 South Main
Houston, TX 77030

Dear Blakeman:

Thank you for applying to the Budget Committee Republican staff for an internship. I am sorry that we will not be able to accept you to our program this summer.

We had several dozen applicants. However, we have room for only two interns this summer. Our selections process, therefore, was fairly arbitrary in light of these odds.

Again, thanks for applying.

Sincerely,

Martha Phillips

the names out of a hat. In fact, the wording may distort the writer's intentions and may be inaccurate.

These examples, as well as the Liedtke speech, illustrate how important the words are that we choose to convey our messages.

Determining Our Own Style

In a classic *Harvard Business Review* essay on style, "What Do You Mean You Don't Like My Style?" John Fielden illustrates and analyzes the different styles that a business writer might use in response to a letter from a business acquaintance. The sender (Frank Scalpel) has asked the receiver to serve on a committee. His serving on this committee could be perceived as a conflict of interest, since it could place the receiver in the position of evaluating his own company's proposals to automate the hospital's information flow. However, it is not clear if Frank is aware of the potential conflict or if he is simply being careless and not thinking that the receiver's company might be submitting a proposal that the committee would then be reviewing.

Fielden includes four possible responses to the letter, all reprinted in Exhibit 3.4. As you read each one, think about the tone and the perceived ethos of the sender, and ask which of these responses most resembles what you think of as your own style.

EXHIBIT 3.4
Responses to Frank's Letter

Source: Reprinted from Harvard Business Review. Fielden, J. (1982). What do you mean you don't like my style? May-June, pp. 1–8. Copyright 1982 by Harvard Business School Publishing Corporation; all rights reserved.

Response 1

Mr. Frank J. Scalpel
Chairman, Executive Committee
Community General Hospital
Anytown, U.S.A

Dear Frank,

As you realize, this litigious age often makes it necessary for large companies to take stringent measures not only to avoid conflicts of interest on the part of their employees but also to preclude even the very suggestion of conflict. And, since my company intends to submit a proposal with reference to automating the hospital's information flow, it would not appear seemly for me to be part of an evaluation team assessing competitors' proposals. Even if I were to excuse myself from consideration of the XYZ proposal, I would still be vulnerable to charges that I gave short shrift to competitors' offerings. If there is any other way that I can serve the committee that will not raise this conflict-of-interest specter, you know that I would find it pleasurable to be of service, as always.

Sincerely,

Response 2

Dear Frank,

Your comments relative to your respect for my professional opinion are most appreciated. Moreover, your invitation to serve on the hospital's data processing evaluation team is received with gratitude, albeit with some concern.

The evaluation team must be composed of persons free of alliance with any of the vendors submitting proposals. For that reason, it is felt that my services on the team could be construed as a conflict of interest.

Perhaps help can be given in some other way. Again, please be assured that your invitation has been appreciated.

Sincerely,

(continued)

EXHIBIT 3.4
(continued)

Response 3

Dear Frank,

Thank you for suggesting my name as a possible member of your data processing evaluation team. I wish I could serve, but I cannot.

XYZ intends, naturally, to submit a proposal to automate the hospital's information flow. You can see the position of conflict I would be in if I were on the evaluation team.

Just let me know of any other way I can be of help. You know I would be more than willing. Thanks again for the invitation.

Cordially,

Response 4

Dear Frank,

Thanks for the kind words and the invitation. Sure wish I could say yes. Can't though.

XYZ intends to submit a surefire proposal on automating the hospital's information systems. Shouldn't be judge and advocate at the same time!

Any other way I can help, Frank—just ask. Thanks again.

Cordially,

What is the tone of each response in Exhibit 3.4? What is the projected ethos of the writer? Which writer appears more confident and at ease with himself? In addition to asking yourself which one is closest to your natural style, you should also ask which one of these you might use even if not your usual style, and which would you never use. Answering these questions will help you get a sense of your own style and the tone that is typical of your writing.

Every person has an individual style. It is your voice; it is the "you" that your reader perceives and your "natural" style and tone. However, if the situation justifies it, you might adopt any one of these styles, although Response 1 and Response 4 are probably a little far from a style you would consider using. Most people would probably see the first response as too formal and stilted, the second too passive, and the fourth too casual.

Most businesspeople select Response 3 as closest to their own and as preferable for the situation. Although it is a good letter, it contains some problems with tone in the second paragraph in the context of the case. Since Frank's motivations are unknown and we do not want to offend him, we would not want to say "naturally" or "you can see." These words imply that Frank knows he is asking the receiver to do something questionable. This implication, in turn, casts doubt on Frank's ethics and could result in a loss of face that would damage his relationship with Frank.

If you would select Response 3, the one most other business people would select, you are probably already using the style usually found in professional communication. You may use this style consistently for this kind of communication, most likely varying it only slightly when the situation calls for a different tone, such as when communicating with a close friend or family member. Often, we are not even that aware of the tone we project, although we should be.

In today's professional environment, the numerous channels we have available make selecting the appropriate style for communication more complex. For example, again, realizing that the tone in e-mails often seems more impersonal and indirect than we might intend, what tone should we use to respond if a colleague sends us an overly pushy e-mail asking us to help her land a position in our company? How should we respond if our manager sends us what sounds like an angry text message, given that text messages are so abbreviated that they can sound harsher than intended? How should we respond if a competitor posts a blog entry challenging our business practices, or should we?

As we can see, using the language of leaders effectively involves more than just an understanding of traditional styles of communication; tone, word choice, and style are influenced by changing communication technologies.

After looking at the examples provided in this chapter, you should realize how your ear detects tone in writing and speaking without your even being aware of doing it. You should apply the same scrutiny to hearing your own tone that you applied to analyzing the tone in the previous examples. You should read what you have written out loud and practice a presentation aloud or, even better, record what you plan to deliver and play it back to yourself. If you are still not sure how you sound, you should ask others to read what you have written and listen critically to your tone.

We need to know how others perceive the language that we use, our tone. The more we can anticipate the audience's response and hear how we sound to others, the better able we will be to control our tone and use it to influence our audience. Being aware of our style and tone moves us one step closer to developing our leadership style and a positive ethos.

EXHIBIT 3.5
Guidelines for
Creating a
Positive Ethos

1. Do not try to imitate someone else's style. Although you can adjust your tone slightly to different situations, you do not want to move too far away from your natural voice. If you do, you risk sounding artificial and perhaps superficial.
2. Read what you have written aloud to hear how you sound, and if something is particularly sensitive, ask the opinion of another person before you send it.
3. Never send something out when you are angry or upset. Always wait until you have control of your emotions and can select your language carefully. This guideline is *especially* true with instant communication channels, such as e-mail and instant messaging.
4. Be careful in your use of complex language or "thesaurusitis," finding a word in a thesaurus and using it because it is a "big" word when a simple one would be better, for example, saying "utilize" instead of "use," "obfuscate" for "confuse," or "appellations" for "titles."
5. At the same time, be careful of your use of shortened words and phrases. "LOL" may be generally understood these days, but it's not appropriate to use in professional e-mails. Remember, abbreviations can carry different meanings to different people in different cultures or contexts.
6. Use strong verbs and avoid passive voice unless you have a specific reason to use it (see discussion below).
7. Select a positive over a negative construction when possible. For example, say, "We will begin implementing the changes you recommended on January 22" instead of "We will not be able to implement your recommended changes before January 22."
8. Avoid using too many modifiers or empty words, such as "sort of," "kind of," "possibly," "thing," or too many "ly" words in particular.
9. Be careful in the use of qualifiers, such as "in my opinion," "I think," "I believe," "probably," and "I feel." They can make you sound too unsure of yourself and hesitant.
10. Eliminate fillers, such as "you know," "uh," and "um" from your speech.
11. Avoid "up speak," making statements sound like questions.
12. Be careful with the use of jargon (see discussion below). Use it only when it is the best way to say what you want to say and when you know for sure the audience will understand it

Although we never want to move too far away from our natural style, since to do so will make us sound insincere, we may need to change it some for different situations and techology. We can learn from specific techniques leaders use to make our language more powerful and to improve our ethos, developing an ethos that signals to our audience that we know what we are talking about and can be trusted. Exhibit 3.5 provides some guidelines for creating a positive ethos in writing and speaking.

To test your style, try stepping back and looking critically at something you have written. Put yourself in the shoes of your audience. Ask yourself, "How do I come across?" "Is there confidence in my tone?" "Do I project a positive ethos?"

Using the Language of Influence

If we follow the guidelines to creating a positive ethos, we will see the impact our language will have on our audiences. As discussed in Chapter 2, in professional settings we are usually communicating with four primary purposes in mind: (1) to inform, (2) to persuade, (3) to instruct, or (4) to engage. Often, however, even when communicating to inform or instruct, we are also attempting to influence or persuade others. That's what transformational leaders do.

We use our ability to influence when we negotiate an agreement or sell something, but we also use it to convince others to believe in our visions. We influence others in everyday situations, such as to persuade someone to hire us or give us a promotion, to obtain support for our recommendations, to argue for the validity of our research findings, and even to sway our colleagues to go to lunch at our favorite restaurant.

Our style influences and persuades others, and our tone, the way our audience interprets our style, affects their perception of us. When we engage others in our blogs or exchange text messages with friends or colleagues, the undercurrent often is one of influencing others to believe as we do, to do as we do. This capability to persuade even informally is crucial for transformational leaders, and as discussed at length in Chapter 1, our ethos as created by the language we use can be the most persuasive tool we have.

The next section will provide some guidance on improving your ethos even more by making your style persuasive, forceful, and concise.

Communicating Concisely

Being concise in our writing and speaking has become even more essential to communicating effectively in a professional setting today: If we do not deliver our message in a few words, we risk losing our audience, especially in the instant communication channels that have sprung up all over the Internet. In addition, we can risk muddling our message, since concise witing is usually more lucid and clear. Clear writing tends to be direct, to the point, and free of jargon, pomposity, and wordy constructions.

Again, looking at Mr. Liedtke's speech, he says, simply, "A contract is a contract" and "We believe that integrity is more than just a word."

He could have said, "Contracts are legal documents that are meant to be obeyed" or "It is believed by most people that integrity means being trustworthy and honest." If he had, his presentation would not have been as powerful, and his ethos would not have been as positive. His sentences are very concise, containing only the words he needs to deliver his meaning. Additional words would dilute that meaning.

Unfortunately, early education and a steadily growing focus on standarized testing may have negatively influenced some of our writing habits. In the past, teachers often gave writing assignments that specified a certain length. As a result, we may have counted words, added fillers, and used complicated language to meet the required length, when what we should have been doing was saying the most with the fewest and simplest words possible. Instead of looking for what the French call "le mot juste" (just the right word), we chose bigger, more impressive words and wrote sentences full of deadwood—words that could and should be removed because they are meaningless.

To achieve conciseness in professional writing, we often need to break old habits of wordiness that we do not even realize we have. Writing concisely requires practice and a critical eye for our own style, as well as an understanding of how others view that style in various channels.

To help you make your writing more concise, this section offers a series of guidelines. *These guidelines are not rules on style,* because "rules" suggests "right" or "wrong." The guidelines only demonstrate what is *usually* preferred when communicating as a leader.

Once we begin to master our own leadership style and develop our voice, we may find that we need to break away from stylistic guidelines because the guidelines hinder the delivery of our message or interfere with the rhythm of our prose. In other words, we have a good reason to do so. We may want to be wordy or even purposely vague at times. We may want to write in passive voice or begin a sentence with "there is."

The meaning we intend should guide our choice to write or speak as seems best to us. We will simply want to ensure that carelessness or haste is not the reason for our wordiness. As the French philosopher and mathematician Blaise Pascal wrote years ago, when he apologized to a friend for writing such a long letter, it takes much longer to write something short than to write something lengthy. He wrote, "I have made this [letter] longer, because I have not had the time to make it shorter."[4]

The following 10 guidelines will help you achieve greater conciseness and a style that is more direct and forceful.

1. Avoid the overuse of the passive voice—the actor should usually come first in the sentence.

Passive Voice	Active Voice
The report was written by the committee. (seven words)	The committee wrote the report. (five words)
Object action actor	*Actor action object*

Choose the active voice unless you have a specific reason for using the passive, such as the following:

- You want to protect the actor in the sentence.
- You are not sure who is responsible for the action.
- The actor is unimportant.
- The company style, discipline style, or some other mandate dictates otherwise.

The lesson here is to use the passive voice because you intend to use it, not out of haste or carelessness.

Beware of using grammar/style checkers to determine if you are using passive voice. While they can be useful in flagging passive construction, they cannot distinguish between past tense sentence constructions and passive voice; therefore, they will often label a sentence passive when it is not. See Appendix B for a discussion of voice and tense.

2. Avoid overusing expletives, such as "there is" or "it is"—watch for the "it is . . . that" construction, in particular.

Construction with Expletives	Nonexpletive Construction
There is one manager at BDC who is not very efficient.	One manager at BDC is not very efficient.
There are two fundamental issues in the area of effectiveness that the team must analyze first.	The team should analyze two fundamental issues in the area of effectiveness first.

Use your meaning and emphasis to guide your use. For instance, in the second example, the emphasis shifts from the issues to the team, when you may want to highlight the issues.

3. Avoid the use of prepositional idioms.

Idioms to Avoid	Concise Replacements
due to the fact that	because
during the time that	while
for the purpose of	to
for the reason that	because, since
if the conditions are such that	if
in order to	to
in the event that	if
in the area of	in
in the case of	in
in the interest of	for
in the nature of	in
in the region of	around
next to	by
on the top of	on, above
over and above	beyond
with regard to	regarding
with the purpose of	to

While usually these idioms are unnecessary, you may want to use them to ensure clarity, particularly if your writing will be translated into other languages, or you may decide that the rhythm of your prose necessitates their use. Again, use them intentionally, not out of carelessness.

4. Avoid the overuse of relative pronouns—"who," "which," and "that."

Unnecessary Relative Pronouns	Sentences without Relative Pronouns
Mr. Bigelow is a man who never misses a meeting.	Mr. Bigelow never misses a meeting.
The documentation which was written by Joan Browning is helpful.	Joan Browning's documentation is helpful.

5. Avoid the repetition of words and ideas.
Look at the following introduction and conclusion from a one-page letter:

> We on the board of the United Way were disheartened by the statement you made yesterday. We feel that there is a grave **misunderstanding.** If this **misunderstanding** is not cleared up, it will harm both the needy and the unity we are all trying to foster in the community. I wish to have a personal meeting with you to clear up this **misunderstanding** immediately.
>
> If this boycott is carried out, the needy will suffer. Organizations such as the Red Cross, the Boy Scouts, and Catholic Counseling, all badly in need of contributions, will suffer. If we can iron out this **misunderstanding,** all these worthy charities will benefit. Solving this **misunderstanding** is in all of our best interests. This **misunderstanding** will also harm the unity that we are trying to bring to El Paso. All of the races and religions of the community must live in harmony. We must not let this **misunderstanding** polarize the community.

Obviously, a misunderstanding exists, but the needless repetition weakens the effect of the letter. The writer needs to think a little deeper to give the argument substance. Needlessly repeating words and ideas suggests shallow thinking and careless writing.

The following example, based on the policy statement discussed in Chapter 4, illustrates a common type of repetition found in lists:

> In order for an employee to qualify for reimbursement, the employee must satisfy all of the following requirements:
>
> (1) **Employee must** be of production foreman level or higher or the rank of secretary or higher.
> (2) **Employee must** enroll in a state-accredited institution in courses at the college or graduate level.
> (3) **Employee must** complete the course with at least a "C."

If you find you are repeating the same words at the beginning of each item in a list, you need to move the repeated words into the introductory sentence. Usually, you can set up the list so that you start each item with an active verb, which will make your writing more direct and forceful; see the following example:

For employees to qualify for reimbursement, they must

- **Be of production foreman level . . .**
- **Enroll in a state accredited institution . . .**
- **Complete the course with at least a "C."**

Excess verbiage can be very irritating to your audience, so you should try to make every word you write and speak significant. You should repeat words or ideas only to emphasize an important message or to create a particular rhetorical effect. For instance, you usually want to state your primary message and the main supporting topics in both the introduction and the conclusion of a presentation, and if some discussion intervenes in a document, you may find that you need to restate your main message later.

At the same time, do not be *too* concise. For example, one-word responses to e-mails are often read as dismissive or abrupt, perhaps even angry. Consider the context of your writing and determine if repetition of a key concept is imperative to the ethos.

6. Do not overuse descriptive words, particularly adverbs (-ly words).

The first version sounds insincere and exaggerated in addition to being too wordy.

Ineffective Use of Words Ending in *-ly*	Example with *-ly* Words Removed
I personally felt that the CEO's wonderfully articulated presentation decisively swayed the stockholders in his favor.	The CEO's presentation convinced the stockholders.

7. Avoid weasel words—ambiguous, noncommittal words, such as the following.

almost	different	like	special
as much as	elements	look	things
aspect	feel	manner	up to
basis	field	situation	virtually
can be	help		

8. Be aware of jargon (language used in particular disciplines) and other kinds of gobbledygook.

Legal documents are full of jargon, creating the perception that lawyers are always talking only to other lawyers, or as cynics might say, legal language perpetuates the need for more lawyers:

> *The aforementioned documents for the application of the captioned corporations for a Certificate of Authority to Transact Business in Texas are enclosed.*

The legal profession is not alone in the tendency to use jargon; all professions use the language of their discipline. Writers and speakers create problems anytime they continue to use the specialized language of their discipline when communicating with others outside their discipline. For example, engineers, IT professionals, accountants, and investment bankers should feel comfortable using the language of their group with their group but not when writing or speaking to those not of the same profession.

The higher up you move in an organization or the more you communicate to the public on your organization's behalf, the more diverse and less specialized your audience becomes. As an organizational leader, you are addressing all employees, external stakeholders, and the general public. Jargon can make portions of your audience feel excluded or lead to their misunderstanding your message.

Jargon is so widespread in most professions that you probably find it handy shorthand and use it daily without realizing it, but you need to learn to avoid it. In fact, a number of Web sites have emerged dedicated to fighting the overuse of business jargon in particular. They provide lists of jargon, translations of jargon terms, and even ways to avoid jargon.

One site provides the following passage as a way to test your recognition of business jargon, and it offers $100 to the first person to e-mail a one-paragraph summary of 150 or fewer words explaining clearly what this company does. It asks readers to answer the following questions:

- How many examples of jargon can you find in the excerpt below?
- What do you think this company does?

Unicorp: Dedicated to Excellence

One of Unicorp's corporate objectives is to develop strategic relationships with key customers and be recognized for our ability to deliver services of superior value. This competitive advantage will be achieved through continued focus on our core competencies, management attention to the development of operations and process management excellence in all parts of our business, the identification and application of best processes, and continued attention to direct and indirect cost management. The focus on core competencies will promote the concentration of knowledge in select areas consistent with the tenets of Unicorp's strategic plan, Unicorp 2000. Management's attention to operations and process management excellence in all business areas will be achieved through the continued expansion of our management and technical staff, as well as through consistent application of corporate quality programs such as benchmarking and continuous improvement, leading to the establishment of Unicorp's superior business processes in each core competency. Finally, continued attention to direct and indirect cost management will enable Unicorp to offer customers a superior, value-added package of high-quality service at a competitive price.

Source: www.westegg.com/jargon.

To combat the overuse of business jargon, the authors of *Why Business People Speak Like Idiots* created a software program called *Bullfighter,* which works similarly to a spell-checking program to rid your documents and PowerPoint presentations of jargon. You can download a free copy of the program at www.fightthebull.com.

Although we all use jargon, we need to be sensitive to its use and abuse. Jargon is a particular problem in international settings, where it can cause miscommunication. If we recognize that jargon has its place and use it only with audiences who share our cultural and business contexts, we will be safe. We need to be careful, however, that we do not let jargon become our only way of sharing information because our communication will seldom be clear if we do.

9. Avoid nominalizations (turning verbs into nouns by adding –*tion*)

Nominalization Example	Active Verb Example
The product management team will perform an investigation of the marketing strategy.	The product management team will investigate the marketing strategy.

Your communication will be much more powerful if you avoid nominalizations and use active verbs whenever possible. Review your sentences to determine if you have, in fact, selected the most appropriate words to serve as the verbs.

10. Avoid redundancies.

The redundancies in Exhibit 3.6 are more common in speech than in writing, but you should be careful to avoid them in both. This guideline warrants a few words of caution, however:

- You do not want to become so obsessed with cutting redundancies that you hinder your natural voice or flow. The result can be choppy, disjointed prose.
- Occasionally, the rhythm of your prose or the need to translate your communication into another language may necessitate your using redundancy.

The list in Exhibit 3.6 should make you sensitive to common redundancies so that you can avoid them or at least be more aware of how often you hear them and use them. In Exhibit 3.6, only the words in bold are needed to convey meaning.

As George Orwell in "Politics and the English Language" says, "If it is possible to cut a word out, always cut it out." Our goal should be to keep all our communication as short and simple as possible and eliminate everything that is not relevant and necessary.

EXHIBIT 3.6
Popular
Redundancies

actual **experience**	difficult **task**	mutual **cooperation**
advance **planning**	direct **confrontation**	**my** personal **opinion**
advance **warning**	**during** the course of	old **antique**
all meet together	**each** and every	one and the **same**
alongside of	**either** and/or both	pair of **twins**
and **moreover**	end **result**	past **history**
as **for example**	established **fact**	**period** of time
at 12 **midnight**	**few** in number	personal **friend**
at 12 **noon**	final **end**	**plan** ahead
at about	foreign **imports**	**postponed** until later
at **some time** to come	grand **total**	**raise** up
basic **fundamentals**	**I** myself personally	**reason** is because
but however	**introduced** for the	**reason** why
but **nevertheless**	first time	**refer** back
chief **protagonist**	**irregardless** (not	**remand** back
climb up	even a word)	**repeat** back
close **proximity**	**is** now **pending**	**return** back
combine together	**lift** up	**revert** back
commute back and	major **breakthrough**	rough **rule of thumb**
forth	mass **media**	**sufficient** enough
complete **monopoly**	**may** possibly	sworn **affidavits**
consensus of opinion	**merge** together	true **facts**
continue on	most **equal**	usual **custom**
definite **decision**	most **unique**	when and **if**
different **kinds**	mutual **agreement**	**whether** or not

In addition, you should use the simple word over the complex in most cases. For example, look at how complex, exaggerated language can destroy the beauty and effectiveness of the familiar Christmas poem, "The Night before Christmas":

> Twas the nocturnal segment of the diurnal period preceding the annual Yuletide celebration, and throughout our place of residence, kinetic activity was not in evidence among the possessors of this potential, including that species of domestic rodent known as *Mus musculus*. Hosiery was meticulously suspended from the forward edge of the wood burning caloric apparatus, pursuant to our anticipatory pleasure regarding an imminent visitation from an eccentric philanthropist among whose folkloric appellations is the honorific title of St. Nicholas.

> Source: Parady by GIMS; otherwise, author unknown. Original by Clement Clarke Moore or Henry Livingston.

This passage exemplifies "thesaurusitis." It demonstrates the danger of selecting the complicated over the simple. In leadership communication, we want to apply Henry David Thoreau's dictum on life: "Simplify, simplify, simplify." Simplifying our language will allow us to connect more easily with our audience and help them perceive the positive ethos we hope to project.

To conclude this section on conciseness, wordiness can indicate careless communication. Beyond carelessness, our audience may also interpret wordiness or the use of complicated language as deception or purposeful obfuscation. The resulting lack of clarity can even suggest that our thinking is careless, superficial, and imprecise or that we are too busy or do not care enough about our audience to take the time to make our communication clear and concise. It takes time to find "le mot juste," but doing so will improve our ethos and our ability to connect with and influence our audience.

Writing for Social Media: Additional Considerations

Blogs, social networks, collaborative workspaces, and even microblogs have become inundated with corporate presences. If we are involved in writing for social media, we should keep three additional guidelines in mind:

1. Be honest and enter the space humbly.
   The social media space is filled with people declaring themselves experts in everything from logistics to search engine optimization. We will not win followers by insisting we are among them; we must prove our expertise first.
2. Say something meaningful.
   We prove ourselves worthy of being read by saying something that adds to the conversation already going on in the network. Listen to what others are saying, and add when and where you can.
3. Don't be *too* concise.
   Tweets that overuse shortened words or "me too" comments do not represent a strategic use of language. We should use the space strategically to help develop a conversation.

Following the Language Rules that Matter

A concise and confident style and an appropriate tone contribute to a positive ethos. In addition, studies have found that the correct use of language affects ethos as well: Beason writes that "[grammatical] errors create misunderstandings of the text's *meaning,* and they harm the *image* of the writing (and possibly the organization to which the writer belongs . . .). Errors affect a person's credibility as a writer or employee."[5]

Most audiences are surprisingly adept at detecting errors in writing or speaking, and many can be harsh and unforgiving. Errors in grammar, spelling, and mechanics may cause an audience to characterize the speaker or writer as hasty, careless, indifferent, uninformed, ignorant, stupid, or poorly educated or as a faulty thinker, a poor oral communicator, or someone who is not a detail person—to the detriment of the ethos of the individual and the organization.[6] As one investment banker wrote in the previously referenced study,

> The banking industry is more or less thought of as being a perfect industry. . . . And we try to do everything right, and I guess it bothers me if we present something on a piece of paper that is not . . . as near perfect as it can be. If I'm going to write you a letter, then my image went out in the letter, or my company's image. My bank's image needs to be nearly perfect, and a grammatical error, I think, would be offensive to some of my customers.[7]

The letter in Exhibit 3.7, sent by a vice president to a placement center director and the deans of a major university, reinforces the importance of being very careful in your use of language. For a leader, correct use of the English language is crucial. Our credibility as a leader, our ability to represent ourselves and our organization, and our ethos all depend on using language carefully. Careless errors are potentially damaging to a company: As Leonard and Gilsdorf found in their research, "Usage errors in business messages can cause misreading[s] that carry a high price. (Not all business messages with potential legal or financial consequences get reviewed by editors and legal counsel.) Error-prone writers might, for example, inadvertently obligate themselves or their firms financially, compromise themselves or their firms ethically, or erode their own and their firms' credibility."[8]

The rules that govern the English language are numerous; however, some are more important than others and, according to survey findings, matter more than others in contemporary professional communication. What follows is a brief overview of the rules that matter to professionals today and a guide to *traditional U.S. English business grammar* (as opposed to journalism or other contemporary usage).

If you see yourself as very strong in English grammar, you can skip the short review provided here. If you are unsure, you might want to pause before reading the next section to complete the "Usage Self-Assessment" (Appendix C). If you suspect you need more review or have forgotten some of the terminology used in discussing grammar, you should read Appendix B ("The Business of Grammar").

This section emphasizes rule violations or errors that can cause misreading or suggest that the writer is careless or not well informed: in other words, the rules that affect ethos. The principle that governs this review of the rules is that it is better to be safe and follow traditional business grammar than to adopt what we see or hear in other contemporary settings, particularly in the media.

Even in more casual communication, such as responses on blogs or social networks, we should follow the basic rules, since anything we

EXHIBIT 3.7
Letter to
Placement Center
Director and
Deans

Dear Jerry, Martin, and Susan:

I am pleased to tell you that shortly I will be extending offers for positions to two of your graduating students. A colleague and I interviewed 20 students on campus and brought four in for follow-up office interviews. Without exception the students were bright, articulate, and well prepared analytically. The comments back from my colleagues following the office interviews were glowing about the students' abilities and personalities.

That is the good news.

The bad news is that some of the students have serious problems on paper, specifically in writing their cover letters and resumes. One candidate is getting his MBA at "The Univesity of XXX." One worked at "Merill Lynch." One doesn't know the difference between "perspective" and "prospective." The examples are endless. Everyone makes mistakes, and that's part of being human. However, I would think that students' resumes and cover letters would be a place where they would do more than spell-check—they would carefully read line by line; they would ask their friends or Placement Center advisors to review the documents, etc.

I eliminated some strong candidates from consideration because of errors, but others slipped through my review. I will not let that last part happen again. In the future, I will eliminate from my review any candidate with these kinds of errors, without regard to their experience. I'm sure that is the approach that most recruiters take anyway, which brings me to my core point:

As an alumna who spends a great amount of her personal time working to advance the university's recognition, I am gravely embarrassed to think that these kinds of errors are circulating throughout the business community. I do not buy the story that these students should be responsible for themselves. They should be responsible for much more than that—representing the school and their alumni as well as themselves. I am more disappointed than you know that this is not the case. I am not sure how best to communicate my concerns to the students, but I am confident that among the three of you, the correct approach will be taken.

Best regards,

Lauren

Lauren LeBlanc
Vice President of Investments

put in writing can be easily copied or forwarded. You may find some of the rules more conservative than those you have learned in the past or observed in some business settings or in the media. The goal is to prepare you as a leader to make educated choices. You will be prepared to choose to ignore a rule rather than violate it from lack of knowledge.

Surveys of executives and of members of the Association for Business Communication have identified the types of errors that business professionals find most bothersome.[9] Exhibit 3.8 lists the top 20 types of errors executives find most distracting. The second column contains the sentences used in the survey to illustrate the errors; the third column, possible corrections.

These errors bother professionals the most because they suggest that the writers are being hasty and careless. The errors in the top 10 are also the types of errors that can cause the reader to misinterpret or fail to understand the meaning. These errors fall into three primary clusters of grammar and usage rules all leaders should know:

1. Punctuation
2. Pronouns
3. Sentence structure

The following sections discuss the important rules within each of these clusters, which if mastered will allow you to avoid most of the mistakes in Exhibit 3.8.

The Power of Punctuation

Why does punctuation matter? It allows us to follow the complete thoughts embodied in sentences and distinguish between them. Punctuation makes reading easier if used correctly and can lead to misreading if used incorrectly. Look at the challenge of sorting out the writer's meaning in the following passage, for example:

> That that is is that that is not is not that that is not is not that that is that that is is not that that is not is not that it it is.[10]

Believe it or not, with the proper punctuation, this passage makes perfect sense (see endnote 10 for the answer). Of course, this example exaggerates the issue, but it makes the point that punctuation has power, some marks having more than others. (If you want additional information on correct usage of punctuation marks beyond this brief review, see Appendix B.)

The strongest marks of punctuation are the **end marks** (? ! .), and the weakest are **commas (,)** and **dashes (—),** with the **colon (:)** and **semicolon (;)** resting somewhere in between in terms of their power to separate two independent clauses or complete sentences.

EXHIBIT 3.8   **Top 20 Most Distracting Grammatical Errors**

Type of Error	Example Sentence with Error	Corrections (in bold)
1. Sentence fragment	Although the Department of Transportation has implemented rules making it legal for employers to test an employee for drugs if he or she works in the airline, trucking, gas pipeline, or maritime industries. and Small companies suffer in a tight labor market. One of their problems being that they can't compete for qualified personnel.	Although the Department of Transportation has implemented rules making it legal for employers to test an employee for drugs if he or she works in the airline, trucking, gas pipeline, or maritime industries, **many still do not test their employees.** and Small companies suffer in a tight labor market, **one** of their problems being that they can't compete for qualified personnel.
2. Unpunctuated parenthetical expression [interrupter]	When the time came for the representatives to sign the contract **however** the bid was withdrawn. and The chair fired five department heads **among them Jerald Destefano.**	When the time came for the representatives to sign the contract, **however,** the bid was withdrawn. and The chair fired five department heads, **among them Jerald Destefano.**
3. Run-on sentence	He focused all his energies on his personal goals he never wavered from his chosen path.	He focused all his energies on his personal **goals; he** never wavered from his chosen path. or He focused all his energies on his personal **goals, and he** never wavered from his chosen path. or He focused all his energies on his personal **goals and never** wavered from his chosen path.
4. Faulty parallel structure	Most people he encounters are impressed by **his calm manner, meticulous attire, and being ambitious.**	Most people he encounters are impressed by **his calm manner, meticulous attire, and ambition.**
5. Dangling modifier	**Looking very tired and worn,** a decision was finally reached by the committee.	Looking very tired and worn, **the committee finally reached a decision.**
6. Apostrophe in plural noun	Signs at the lot instruct motorists to park between the **line's** and not back into any parking space.	Signs at the lot instruct motorists to park between the **lines** and not back into any parking space.

(continued)

EXHIBIT 3.8   (continued)

Type of Error	Example Sentence with Error	Corrections (in bold)
7. Comma splice	Only 1,000 new full-time jobs will be **created, management** will fill the remaining 9,000 positions by urging part-timers to apply for existing full-time positions.	Only 1,000 new full-time jobs will be **created; management** will fill the remaining 9,000 positions by urging part-timers to apply for existing full-time positions. Or Only 1,000 new full-time jobs will be **created. Management** will fill the remaining 9,000 positions by urging part-timers to apply for existing full-time positions.
8. Use of reflexive pronoun when objective case is needed	After lunch, the chair introduced Jameson and **myself** to the assembly.	After lunch, the chair introduced Jameson and **me** to the assembly. *Use object pronoun. Apply the "us" test.*
9. Use of "less" for a count noun	After the recession, Textron rehired **less** technicians than Puritan Mills did.	After the recession, Textron rehired **fewer** technicians than Puritan Mills did.
10. Use of nominative case pronoun in compound indirect object	The vice president directed my associate and **I** to submit reports to the executive committee.	The vice president directed my associate and **me** to submit reports to the executive committee. *Use object pronoun. Apply the "us" test.*
11. Use of "between" for more than two	The three buyers talked **between** themselves and decided to use the same vendor.	The three buyers talked **among** themselves and decided to use the same vendor.
12. Adverbial clause as complement to linking verb	The reason I fired him after two years with our company **is because** he was incompetent.	I fired him after two years with our company **because** he was incompetent.
13. Its/It's confusion	Specific Dynamics claims that **it's** agreement with our company has been violated. and As McAuliff pointed out, **its** a good thing that the auditors talked to the department before making the findings public.	Specific Dynamics claims that **its** agreement with our company has been violated. and As McAuliff pointed out, **it's (it is)** a good thing that the auditors talked to the department before making the findings public.
14. Use of adverb "badly" with state-of-being verb "feel."	The accounts supervisor felt **badly** yesterday.	The accounts supervisor felt **bad** yesterday.
15. Misspelling of "principle"	I voted against the provision as a matter of **principal.**	I voted against the provision as a matter of **principle.**

(continued)

Type of Error	Example Sentence with Error	Corrections (in bold)
16. Lack of apostrophe in possessive noun	Our **firms** performance has been excellent.	Our **firm's** performance has been excellent.
17. Starting a sentence with "But"	A recent IRS effort attempted to scan tax returns. **But** because the scanner could not decipher the taxpayers' handwriting, the process ended up costing more than the manual method.	A recent IRS effort attempted to scan tax returns, **but** because the scanner could not decipher the taxpayers' handwriting, the process ended up costing more than the manual method.
18. "Which" used to refer to entire preceding clause	Customers find it hard to locate the store, **which** affects business.	Customers find it hard to locate the store, **a serious problem that** affects business.
19. Use of plural pronoun to refer to singular noun	Auto retailers on the Internet let **the buyer** configure a vehicle to **their** taste and see the firm price of the car **they** want.	Auto retailers on the Internet let **the buyer** configure a vehicle to **his or her** taste and see the firm price of the car **he or she** wants. or Auto retailers on the Internet let **buyers** configure a vehicle to **their** taste and see the firm price of the car **they** want.
20. Use of plural verb with either/or subject structure	**Either** the vice president **or** the marketing director **are** going to the reception as a company representative.	**Either** the vice president or the marketing director is going to the reception as a company representative.

Source: for first two columns is Leonard, D. & Gilsdorf, J. (2001). Big stuff, little stuff: A decennial measurement of executives' and academics' reactions to questionable usage elements. *Journal of Business Communication 38(4)*, 440. Reprinted by permission of Sage Publications. Column three (corrections) has been added by this text's author.

To use end marks, colons, and semicolons correctly, you need to recognize independent clauses (see Appendix B—"The Business of Grammar" for more on clauses and sentences). Identifying independent clauses will help you avoid creating fragments, run-on sentences, or comma splice errors (types of errors #1, #3, and #7 in Exhibit 3.9).

The following chart illustrates what marks can and cannot do between independent clauses.

Independent Clause	Strongest	Independent Clause	Usage
1. Mary balanced the books	? ! .	John paid the bills.	Acceptable
2. Mary balanced the books	;	John paid the bills.	Acceptable
3. Mary balanced the books	:	John paid the bills.	Acceptable
4. Mary balanced the books	—	John paid the bills.	Not acceptable
5. Mary balanced the books	,	John paid the bills.	Not acceptable
	Weakest		

Depending on intonation, you could read sentence one in the chart as a question, an exclamation, or a simple sentence, and the second independent clause could be a separate sentence as well. The use of the semicolon in sentence two would be correct, since the sentences are independent but clearly similar in length and structure. The use of the colon in sentence three would not be typical, but it is also acceptable. Sentences four and five, however, are not correct, since the dash and the comma are too weak to separate the two independent clauses.

Confusion often occurs over what to do with the marks in between the two power positions of the end marks and the commas—the **colon (:)** and the **semicolon (;).**

Colons

The **colon** is used to introduce lists or to signal that what follows explains or elaborates what has come before. It creates a sense of anticipation. The sentence that follows demonstrates the use of a colon to introduce a list:

> The officers of the European organization are as follows:
> President—Gini Puccini, Rome
> Vice President—Andreas Jung, Berlin
> Secretary—Jorge Borges, Madrid
> Treasurer—Josephine Willingham, London

Note that placing the colon between a verb and its objects is incorrect and should be avoided, even though it is common in modern usage. You should not write the following:

> The officers of the European organization **are:**
> President—Gini Puccini, Rome
> Vice President—Andreas Jung, Berlin
> Secretary—Jorge Borges, Madrid
> Treasurer—Josephine Willingham, London

The following sentence shows the use of the colon to signal that what follows explains or develops what has come before:

> "To be, or not to be: that is the question."—Shakespeare, *Hamlet*

Semicolons

The **semicolon** is used to separate closely related independent clauses not joined by a **coordinating conjunction (and, or, but, for, so, yet, nor);** to separate independent clauses joined by **conjunctive adverbs (accordingly, also, besides, consequently, further, however, moreover, nevertheless, then, therefore, thus, etc.);** or to separate a series of phrases or clauses containing numerous commas.

The following famous quotation demonstrates the use of the semi-colon when ideas are closely related and parallel in structure:

> "Ask not what your country can do for you; ask what you can do for your country."—President J. F. Kennedy

The following sentence demonstrates the use of the semicolon with a conjunctive adverb:

> Susan was well prepared for her interview; however, she still did not get the job.

If the conjunctive adverb is used as an interrupter, it would not need a semicolon before it, but it would need commas around it, which is Type of Error #2 in Exhibit 3.8. See the following example:

> Being well prepared for her first interview, however, did not help Susan to get the job.

The following shows the correct use of the semicolon in a sentence with many commas:

> The organization has scheduled the next round of office photos for the following dates in these locations: May 20, 2009, Miami, Florida; August 25, 2009, Johannesburg, South Africa; and Sydney, Australia, November 15, 2009.

Dashes and Commas

You should avoid using dashes (—) to separate two independent clauses. In fact, you should use the dash sparingly, if at all, in more for-mal writing, although you might want to use it to set off a parentheti-cal expression. Such usage signals that the information within the dashes is important or necessary. For example, in the following sen-tence, the sentence needs the information set off by dashes to have meaning:

> The works of three major writers—Ben Franklin, Shakespeare, and Sir Walter Scott—are the source of most common sayings.

Like the dash, commas are too weak to separate two independent clauses, but commas can be used to set off a parenthetical expression. They can also be used to separate two independent clauses if helped with a coordinating conjunction:

> Mary balanced the books, **and** John paid the bills.

Commas after Introductory Phrases

Always place a comma after an introductory clause beginning with a subordinating conjunction (after, although, as, because, before, during, even though, if, since, than, though, unless, when, where, whereas, etc.). Also, it is best to place commas after introductory phrases even if they are short. Doing so makes it easier for your reader to read your sentences:

> From a humble beginning, Marion Manufacturing Company has grown to be an enormous multinational corporation.

A comma should always follow an introductory absolute phrase:

> The surveys completed, we were ready to start analyzing the results.

Commas with Items in a Series

Contemporary usage (journalism, in particular) has led to the demise of the comma before the "and" with items in a series. For example, people write "The flag is red, white and blue." Leaving out the comma, however, can create ambiguity and cause misreading; therefore, it is safer to follow traditional usage and place a comma before the **and.** For example, look at the problem created by leaving the comma out in the following sentence:

> Maria says that she joined the Peace Corps because of her parents, Mother Teresa and Gandhi.

As written, the sentence is saying that Mother Teresa and Gandhi are Maria's parents, which we can safely assume is not the intended meaning. And look at the change in meaning in the following example:

> The steering committee recommended that they start their analysis by looking at the following departments: personnel, benefits and insurance, production, human resources and social services.

or

> The steering committee recommended that they start their analysis by looking at the following departments: personnel, benefits and insurance, production, human resources, and social services.

In the first sentence, it is not clear if "human resources and social services" is one department or two; thus, the comma is needed to avoid confusion.

Your decision to use a comma or not should be based on your being absolutely sure that omitting the comma does not change the meaning or leave the possibility of misreading. Going through this reasoning, however, requires more time and energy than just placing the comma before the **"and"** anytime you have items listed, which is the most appropriate choice for business and technical writing.

When writing for other than business audiences, however, you need to be flexible and sensitive to their conventions; for instance, since journalists do not use the comma, when writing journalistic copy or for the news media, as in press releases, you may want to omit the comma, but you should test the meaning.

Commas with Nonrestrictive Clauses

Use commas with nonrestrictive clauses (meaning that they can be removed from the sentence without changing the meaning). Clauses beginning with **that** are restrictive, but clauses beginning with **who** or **which** may be either restrictive or nonrestrictive, so you must ask yourself "If I remove the clause, will the sentence still make sense?" For example, look at what happens when you remove the clause from the following sentence:

The data **that accompany the report** came from his database.

Without the bolded clause, it is not clear what data the writer means. Therefore, the clause is necessary (restrictive) and does not require commas around it.

Contrast the following—

The analysis, which includes his formulas, accompanies the report.

The clause provides additional information, but the information that the analysis "includes his formulas" is not necessary to understand the meaning of the sentence.

Commas with Dates and Time

In the United States, dates are usually written in the following way:

June 4, 2009

instead of

4 June 2009

Again, follow the customs of the country in which the documents are created or in which the organization's main office is located. If you do use the month, day, year order, you need a comma after the day. If, however, you use only the month and the year, you do not need a comma; thus, the following is correct as written:

June 2009

The use of 6/4/09 (month, day, year) is acceptable in informal settings only and should be used with caution with international audiences, since it could be read as April 6, 2009.

Apostrophes

Apostrophes are added with an "s" to nouns to show ownership; "'s" is added to singular and plural nouns not ending in "s"; plural nouns ending in "s" take the apostrophe alone in most cases, although the pronunciation usually determines when to add the "s" as well. Apostrophes are also used to create contractions (can't, don't, etc.). Apostrophes are not used to create possessive forms of personal pronouns (hers, **not** her's; its, **not** it's) or in plural nouns when not possessive (Type of Error #6 in Exhibit 3.8).

You will also still see the apostrophe used before an "s" after numbers, acronyms, and abbreviations—for example, "MBA's" instead of "MBAs" or "1990's" instead of "1990s." Although most modern guides to usage say to omit the apostrophe here, technically, either is correct as long as leaving the apostrophe out does not cause a misunderstanding. For instance, "As" looks like "as" when you might mean "A's," as in "I expect to make "A's." Whichever option you choose, be consistent.

Parentheses

Parentheses are used in pairs to set off interrupting information in a sentence when dashes would give the information too much emphasis and commas might lead to misreading. Note: The period is placed inside the parenthesis if the entire sentence is parenthetical and outside if not; see the discussion of apostrophes for an example.

Quotation Marks

In the United States, quotation marks should always be placed outside periods and commas; inside semicolons and colons; and inside or outside (depending on the context) question marks and exclamation marks. In other countries (for example, Europe, Canada, and Australia), the comma and period are placed outside the quotation marks, so you will need to follow the custom of the country in which the document is written or the country that serves as the headquarters of the organization.

."	,"	**Always correct**
";	":	**Always correct**
"?"	"!"	**Depends on the sentence**

Even if the construction seems illogical to you, as in the following example, the rule in the United States remains the same.

> Shing-Hwa expects to make good grades in all of her classes; even in Economics 598, she expects to make an "A."

Ellipses

The ellipsis is defined as "three spaced periods." Please note the word "spaced." That means that you literally hit the space bar key before, between, and after each period; thus, it should look like . . . and not ... or...when you use the ellipsis in a sentence, which is not the way Microsoft Word wants to treat it. If you use the ellipsis at the end of the sentence, then you should use four periods, with no space before the first period. The ellipsis indicates that the writer has omitted some words from a direct quotation, although it is usually not needed at the beginning of a direct quotation if you have worked the quotation into your prose:

> William David Thoreau, an American Transcendentalist, wrote that, when you hire people to work for you, you should not hire someone "who does your work for money, but him [or her] who does it for love of it."

The ellipsis should not be used as you see writers sometimes use it (particularly in e-mail) to suggest they have more to say but are not taking the time right now to say it. In other words, they are using the ellipsis to mean "in addition" or etcetera. This usage is careless and even irritating to the reader, so you should avoid it. Also, note the use of brackets [ ] to indicate that words are inserted in the direct quotation.

The Correct Use of Pronouns

The rules for the use of punctuation will help you avoid some of the mistakes in the top 20; however, some of the sentences in Exhibit 3.8 contain grammatical mistakes that deserve some discussion. The first and one of the most frequent and an important mistake in contemporary usage is the misuse of personal and indefinite pronouns (Types of Errors #8, #10, and #19). See Appendix B—"The Business of Grammar" for a discussion of the correct use of all types of pronouns.

Personal Pronouns

A personal pronoun (see the following table) refers to a specific person or thing mentioned previously (antecedent) and must agree in person and number with that antecedent.

Subject Pronouns	Object Pronouns
I, we	Me, us
He, she, it	Him, her, it
You	You
They	Them
Who	Whom

Subject pronouns perform the action in the sentence, and object pronouns receive it:

> Tomas and I will meet you in the conference room at 10:00 a.m.
>
> Please divide the money between Katya and me.

You should use object pronouns following prepositions (between, to, from, among, over, under, etc.). One way to test for whether to use "I" or "me" is to substitute "we" or "us." In the second sentence above, for instance, you would not say, "Please divide the money between we." Therefore, you know that you should use "me."

In the first sentence, you might be tempted to use "myself" instead of "I," but this usage is incorrect. Although the first person reflexive pronoun—"myself"—is frequently misused to replace "I" or "me," such reflexive pronouns are very seldom used in English. They have a very specific meaning—an action that reflects or comes back to the subject:

I will do the work myself.

Do not use "myself" just because you are unsure whether to use "I" or "me"; instead, take the time to test if "we" or "us" is appropriate, and then you will know which first person pronoun to use.

Indefinite Pronouns

Indefinite pronouns do not refer to any particular person or thing—for example, "anybody," "everyone," and "something" (see Appendix B for a complete list).)

Be very careful with agreement in number—singular or plural—when using indefinite pronouns. They often cause mistakes in pronoun antecedent agreement—for example,

You should say, "Everybody must file his or her report."

Not "Everybody must file their report."

If you are unsure, you can use the verb test: "Everybody is" or "Everybody are"?

Collective Nouns

You should be aware of a cultural difference in the treatment of pronoun reference to collective nouns, such as "board," "committee," "corporation," "department," and "company." In the United States, collective nouns are usually thought of as singular and take singular verbs and pronouns. For example, in the United States, a company is treated as singular and is referred to by "it," as in the following example:

Brown & Partners, LLP, is considered successful in its market area.

In other countries, such as Great Britain and Australia, a company is treated as plural, which means the preceding sentence would read

Brown & Partners, LLP, are considered successful in their market area.

As with other differences across countries, you should usually follow the conventions of the country in which the company has its headquarters.

Effective Sentence Structure

Sentences are traditionally said to convey a complete thought; that is, they make a meaningful statement. (See Appendix B for more on sentences.) While most writers (or speakers) recognize sentences and would make few mistakes when constructing them, some common errors do occur frequently in professional writing that have ended up in the top 20 mistakes to avoid. In fact, two of the errors in Exhibit 3.8 (Types of Errors #4 and #5) are in the top 10. The discussion that follows is to help you avoid these types of errors.

Parallelism

Parallelism means that the listed words, phrases, or clauses within your sentences or the sentences themselves (as in a list of complete thoughts in a PowerPoint slide) are alike in structure. Parallel structure makes your sentences easier to read, gives your writing balance and rhythm, and creates greater efficiency in your prose. The preceding sentence is an example of parallel structure; note the repeated verbs—"makes," "gives," and "creates"—are alike. Now, look at the following sentence, which is not parallel:

> The committee recommends that we ask all registrants to sign up by 5:00 p.m., the day of the race, complete all forms online, payment should be by credit card, and they should have their numbers pinned to the front of their shirts.

Look at how much easier the following version is to read:

> The committee recommends that we ask all registrants to sign up by 5:00 p.m. on the day of the race, complete all forms online, pay with a credit card, and pin their numbers to the front of their shirts.

The following illustrates the use of parallel structure in a bulleted list:

> When negotiating, the following actions are essential:
> - Identifying interferences to effective communication
> - Developing a communication strategy and analyzing your opponent
> - Recognizing effective influencing and persuasive techniques
> - Learning the specifics of the culture with which you will be negotiating

Anytime you have a list of bulleted items, as you frequently will in a PowerPoint presentation, you should be very careful to maintain parallel structure for all the items.

Dangling Modifiers

A dangling modifier is one that does not clearly or logically refer to the subject or object to which it is connected. Usually, it occurs at the beginning of a sentence, and the subject of the clause following it cannot logically perform the action described:

> Worrying that the titles would not align correctly, the template was adjusted.

Obviously, the template was not worried; some unnamed person was. The sentence should read as follows:

> Worrying that the titles would not align, the designer adjusted the template.

Sexist Language

Leaders should avoid sexist language. Sexist language shows a bias, or preference, toward one gender over another, often by implying exclusion of the nonpreferred gender. Using "man" or "he" all the time is not appropriate in most environments, particularly in the workplace. The issue creates problems when using English because the English language does not provide easy alternatives for the singular masculine and feminine pronouns; therefore, you will often need to rewrite sentences to make your subjects plural so that you are not locked into using "he" or "him."

For instance, instead of saying,

> Everybody must pay his income tax.

You can say,

> Taxpayers must pay their income taxes.

or

> All Americans must pay their income taxes.

Of course, it is not always so easy to avoid sexist constructions, but you should take care that you do not offend anybody. In some situations, however, it is difficult to find a totally inoffensive construction that avoids doing violence to the language.

Since the 1960s, attempts to find substitutions for "he," "him," and "his" have led to rather awkward replacements:

1. **He or she, him or her, he/she, him/her,** or **his/her.**
2. **S/he** (no equivalent has been created for **him/her** or **his/her**).

The first replacement ("he or she") is grammatically correct and is sometimes the best alternative; however, it becomes rather awkward when overused and interrupts the flow of the language. The second replacement has received negative response, since it looks so strange and is impossible to pronounce, so it should be avoided.

Again, trying to make the antecedent plural, as in the previous taxpayer example, is usually your best choice. Remember, although some people are now intentionally using a plural pronoun to refer to a singular antecedent to avoid the problem, you should *never do so*. You are better off being perceived as slightly sexist than being perceived as illiterate. To write *"Everybody* should pay *their* income taxes" is still considered *substandard* and probably always will be, since it violates a basic grammatical rule about agreement of pronouns and the nouns to which they refer. See Appendix B for a discussion of indefinite pronouns and collective nouns.

The Use of Ms.

"Ms." is a convenient and well accepted way to address a woman of unknown marital status; however, if you know the marital status, you may use Mrs. or Miss if you are sure that your audience prefers to be addressed that way. Follow your audience's lead, if possible. If the individual has written to you and signed her letter "Mrs. Brown," then address her as "Mrs. Brown" when you write to her.

A Note on Letter Salutations

When you are not sure of a woman's marital status, use "Ms." in the salutation of letters. If you are unsure of the sex, then use the first and last name:

Dear Leslie Smith:

If you do not know the name, address the person by position:

Dear Customer:
Dear Managers:

Never begin a letter with "Gentlemen:" or "Dear Sir:"
You may also remove the salutation and just use a subject line, although you should use this as a last resort:

Expert Computer Systems
2920 Main Street
Houston, TX 77002
Subject: Defective Computer Parts

Or use an attention line:

Expert Computer Systems
2920 Main Street
Houston, TX 77002
Attention: Computer Parts Department

The Use of Words Ending in "Man" or other "Guy" Words

The suffix "-man" has been replaced by "-person" in words such as "chairman," although in many cases complete substitutions have been offered.

Thus, "chairman" has become "chair"; "mailman," "letter carrier"; "policeman," "police officer"; and so forth. You only need to consider these changes in general references; if you know the subject is male, you can use the masculine form of the word.

In addition, you will want to avoid using "you guys" in most professional settings. Although a popular expression, right up there with "you all" in some parts of the United States, it should be avoided (as should "you all," for that matter, but for different reasons) to ensure you do not offend a large portion of the population—females.

Editing and Proofreading Techniques

Editing is an important skill that requires discipline and practice. It is particularly difficult to edit our own work. Many communicators are not sure what they need to watch for besides the obvious typos and spelling. However, mostly we just do not take (or have) the time to edit or proof our own work.

Editing involves reviewing presentations, documents, and all other written communication to see if they are clear, concise, and correct. Often, editing means reading closely to see if another word would work better or determine if we have fallen into passive voice or some other wordy construction.

Proofreading occurs after editing. It is reading the communication closely to identify errors in usage, grammar, spelling, or formatting.

We should engage in editing or proofing only after we have completed the content and feel certain that we have included all of the information we plan to include. It is particularly important to avoid editing or proofing in the idea-generation stage of communication, since to do so will hinder creativity and thinking.

The following provides a few guidelines on editing and proofreading your own work:

1. Do not proofread as you compose. Proofread after you think you are finished.
2. Try to put some time between when you write something and when you proof it.
3. Know what errors you tend to make or overlook, and watch for them in particular.
4. Watch for common trouble spots, such as transposed letters, confused words, pronoun/antecedent disagreement, dangling modifiers, and misused apostrophes. Also check for lack of consistency in presentations, in particular.
5. Proof using a hard-copy instead of on the screen whenever your communication is important or complex. We tend to miss

EXHIBIT 3.9
Checklist to Review the Use of Language in Your Own Work

Style and tone
☐ Appropriate tone, not too informal or formal, not potentially offensive for selected audience.
☐ No use of inappropriate jargon or abbreviations.
☐ Concise (not wordy, verbose, or containing passive voice constructions).
☐ No overuse or misuse of modifiers (e.g., "ly" words) or other qualifiers ("I think", "I believe", "I feel", etc.).
☐ No diction problems (wrong or poor word choices).
☐ No unclear or awkward sentence or phrase constructions.
☐ Overall, clear, concise, and confident.
Usage (top 20) and proofreading
☐ No usage or grammar errors.
☐ No punctuation errors.
☐ No spelling errors.
☐ No typos or other proofreading errors.

mistakes on the screen. If writing a comment, text, or tweet, consider using a text editor to compose; then review before copying and sending.

6. Finally, proofread the document and each slide backwards to catch typos and spelling errors. Actually start at the end of the page and sentence and work your way to the beginning. When we proof our own work, we tend to read what we think we have written instead of what is actually on the page. By reading backwards, our eyes are forced to **focus on** each word.

Most important, we should take the time to read back over our writing even when sending a text message or e-mail; while it is more difficult to see our mistakes on a screen, particularly on handhelds, we will see many of the errors and avoid looking careless.

The checklist in Exhibit 3.9 should help in reviewing the use of language in our own work. Combined with Exhibit 4.14 in Chapter 4 on reviewing written communication, it provides a very complete approach to editing and proofreading our own work.

Making Computers Work for us

Computers have clearly made creating documents and presentations much easier, but they have also caused us to make mistakes; therefore, they deserve a few caveats on their use. In particular, we need to watch for the following common problems:

1. Jumping into writing a document without adequate planning.
2. Seeing only the screen version, causing us to lose sight of the document as a whole.
3. Relying too much on spell-checkers, when they can catch only some of the mistakes.
4. Depending on grammar-checkers, when they are extremely limited in what they can correct.
5. Proofreading on the screen, thus missing many typos and other errors.
6. Moving words and phrases around easily, causing us to leave in extra words and omit necessary ones.

We will improve our writing and avoid many of the preceding problems if we follow these guidelines:

1. When using the computer for idea generation, recognize that what we enter at this brainstorming stage seldom qualifies as a final version ready for our audience because it will probably lack coherence or clear organization. We should not let the desire to get it just right or to organize the ideas at this stage slow down the composition. Instead, we should use the computer to overcome writer's block and get ideas down quickly; then go back through and organize them.
2. Take advantage of features such as word search to look for common redundancies, wordy expressions, unclear references with "this" and "that," or words you may tend to misuse, such as "affect."
3. Experiment with different formatting to see what makes the document more accessible and readable. For letters and basic documents, Microsoft Word has templates we can use. However, since the spacing and text font selected are not always the most effective, we may want to do our own formatting, perhaps postponing it until after having entered all of the text.
4. Recognize the limitations of spell-checkers, but always run them to catch careless errors; just do not expect the spell-checker to find all mistakes. It will not catch "there" and "their," for instance.
5. Be wary of style/grammar checkers. The English language is too complex and irregular for a style/grammar checker to recognize what is right or wrong in many cases. For instance, style checkers often label past tense sentences as passive voice. Thus, unless the writer knows grammar rules and best style practices well enough to determine

when the style/grammar checker is incorrect, it can be more dangerous to use one than not. In fact, in addition to missing many major errors, these checkers tend to add errors. We should rely on a grammar checker only to highlight possible mistakes and must know what to follow and what to ignore; otherwise, we will add more mistakes than we will correct.

6. Do the final proofreading from a hard copy, not on the computer screen, whenever possible. When not doing so, as when using IM or sending text messages, at least slow down long enough to read back over what you have written before sending.

With longer, more formal documents or any important one, we might want to have someone else look over our work to provide the "fresh eye" that leaders sometimes need. We need to remember that audiences will connect us to what they see written, and while most audiences may overlook an occasional slipup, errors in the use of language can harm us and our company.

In conclusion, this chapter has provided instruction in creating a positive ethos through the use of the language of leadership. To convince others, we need to communicate confidently and reflect an appropriate tone in all that we write and say. We need to be concise and ensure that our language is clear, crisp, and meaningful. We need to recognize the power of language to persuade others; at the same time, we accept the responsibility to be honest, logical, and ethical and never misleading or manipulative. Finally, we need to avoid careless grammatical and usage errors and take the time to edit and proofread our communication to ensure it is clear and correct.

As leaders, we manage meaning for those who follow us by the words we select and the way we put those words together to create sentences. The more control we have over the use of language, the greater our influence and our ability to lead.

**Application 3.1
Passive Voice**

Try your hand at recognizing and changing the passive voice constructions in the following sentences. First, underline each passive voice construction; then, rewrite the sentence, making it active. Be prepared to discuss why the passive might be the better choice in some of the sentences.

1. An order for 5,000 T-shirts was placed by the Student Association.
2. Requests for class transfers will be accommodated if the request is made in person, the receipt of payment for the class is shown, and a $1 processing fee is paid.
3. Data were selectively collected to allow computation of the unique ratios utilized by "corporate raiders" in assessing a buyout candidate.
4. Detailed information on filling out the form is presented forthwith.
5. It has been decided that your proposal does not follow the RFP guidelines as outlined and, therefore, it must be rejected.
6. To implement the policy, a memorandum will be issued to all management personnel in my division.

**Application 3.2
Conciseness**

Eliminate the unnecessary words in the following sentences:

1. We are in receipt of your expense report, but due to the fact that it contains errors, we need to discuss it with you as soon as possible.
2. Per your e-mail, we are sending you the report in regard to our analysis of the Patrick Co. reengineering project.
3. Please be advised that, as of January 10, 2009, we will no longer authorize work on the Javia account.
4. To ensure that the optimal conclusions will be drawn, it is absolutely essential for you to ensure the analysts are given any and all data that are necessary for effective completion of the analysis assigned to them to complete.

**Application 3.3
Positive
Messages**

Rewrite the following sentences to make the messages positive:

1. Please don't waste ink and paper. Don't print PowerPoint in anything but pure black-and-white format.
2. I cannot meet with you before Monday to discuss the report, so you should not wait for my approval to create the final version.
3. We are not hiring any new employees until the next quarter earnings are available. Please do not contact us until then.
4. I don't think it will be too much trouble to change the policy as long as no one disagrees with the changes.
5. Our market presence was weak internationally, so we have launched a new marketing campaign in Bolivia, Italy, and India.
6. Our refineries do not release dangerous particles into the air.

**Application 3.4
Parallelism**

Rewrite the following sentences to make them parallel:

1. Highland Services offers friendly, fast responses to all customers, our technicians are professional, and lowest cost is our goal.
2. To persuade your audience, you must:
   - Consider the audience's motivation.
   - Include your bottom-line message early.
   - The strongest arguments should come first.
   - Key points summarized at the conclusion.
3. The team gave the following reasons for not completing the project on time:
   - Unrealistic time allotment.
   - Major computer problems.
   - They lacked the necessary data.
   - The team just did not get along at all.

**Application 3.5
Usage and
Mechanics**

The following paragraph contains usage and mechanical errors. Correct the errors in the space provided within the passage. Sentences may contain more than one error or none.

(1) Group leaders must prepare the program agendum and should distribute it at least several days before the meeting. (2) They should also ensure that the group have a satisfactory place to meet. (3) A designated conference room or a suitable substitute. (4) If the meeting is a formal conference and has a number of people which are not acquainted leaders should place name cards on the table in front of each persons chair. (5) Having started the meeting, name cards make discussion easier. (6) Once the meeting has started, discussion leaders must keep it moving. (7) Each of the members have to assume the same responsibility. (8) A group sometimes drifts off course into trivial and unrelated matters, therefore, leaders must guide them back to the central problem. (9) Though leaders must have kept the group process moving, they must often be careful about revealing their own position. (10) This has been of great importance to my colleagues and I. (11) We recognize that a high status person for example a company president, can cut off discussion by revealing their own view to clearly.

**Application 3.6
Use of Language
Overall**

After you have read the following e-mail from Mr. Thompson, answer the questions below. Note: Again, this note was actually sent.

1. How do you like the way the e-mail looks—letterhead, formatting, and the like?
2. Does the e-mail's appearance influence your response to it? How?
3. What mistakes in usage do you notice?
4. Are there any expressions that Mr. Thompson uses that bother you in particular? What are they, and why do they bother you?
5. How do you feel about Mr. Thompson? Do you like him? Do you trust him? Why or why not?
6. What would you change about the way the e-mail was written?

To: Mr. Robert Browning, General Partner
From: Charles J. Thompson, Jr
Subject: Follow-up

Hey Rob. . .

We're in receipt of your good letter of July 20, 2009, and it's good to hear from you again... Good to learn that you're doing well. As for myself, still trying desperately to 'Catch-up' after having returned this past Monday, from a very enjoyable vacation. All this past week has been devoted to 'Wading thru papers', which I am sure you fully understand...since you wer Golfing in the California all week!

The purpose of our letter to you today is to get your response as to the 'Common-denominators' 'which are prevalent in the acquisitions you've made thus far, in relationship to the types of situations you are desirous of pursuing at this time...

I am seeking to 'Get a handle' on the main points of your acquisition thrust in order that we may approach your needs more intelligently, and therefore ultimately aid/be beneficial and/or instrumental with such needs...

Look to hear from you with this written documentation in order that we PRESS ON in your behalf...

I'm out of here for the entire week of 20th for NCN in Chicago, and look to hear from you as soon as possible...

Rob, that's the news from the Thompson Tower.

With the Best of Regards, I remain

Very truly yours,
Charles J. Thompson, Jr., President
Executive Consultants, Inc. - *"Where True Consultants Meet Worthy client's Needs"*
P.O. Box 44296
New York, NY 11201
Phone 917-562-7471
Fax 917-733-1234
cjt@eci.com
www.ECI.com

Notes

1. Fairhurst, G., and Sarr, R. (1996). *The Art of Framing: Managing the Language of Leadership*. San Francisco: Jossey-Bass.

2. Strunk, W., Jr., and White, E. B. (1959). *The Elements of Style*. New York: Macmillan, p. 53.

3. Petzinger, T., Jr. (1987). *Oil and Honor: The Texaco-Pennzoil Wars*. New York: Berkley Books, pp. 271–72.

4. Blaise Pascal, Lettres provinciales, Letter 16. Pascal's quotation in French reads: "Je n'ai fait celle-ci plus longue que parce que je n'ai pas eu le loisir de la faire plus courte."

5. Beason, L. (2001). Ethos and error: How business people react to errors. *College Composition and Communication* 53, No. 1 (September), pp. 33–64.

6. Beason (2001).

7. Beason (2001), pp. 56–57.

8. Leonard, D., and Gilsdorf, J. (2001). Big stuff, little stuff: A decennial measurement of executives' and academics' reactions to questionable usage elements. *Journal of Business Communication* 38, No. 4, p. 440.

9. Hairston, M. (1981). Not all errors are created equal: Nonacademic readers in the professions respond to lapses in usage. *College English* 43, pp. 794–806. Results based on a survey of 101 professional people, asking them what usage and mechanical errors bothered them the most. Leonard, D., and Gilsdorf, J. (1990). Language in change: Academics' and executives' perceptions of usage errors. *Journal of Business Communication* 27, pp. 137–58. Results based on a survey of 133 executive vice presidents and 200 Association for Business Communication members. In 2000, Leonard and Gilsdorf repeated their survey, but they changed the format slightly. Instead of the categories of lapses used above, they used a scale ranging from "most distracting" to "least distracting." The survey respondents totaled 64 executives and 130 academics. They found that the usage errors that "distracted" both the executives and the academics were very similar to those they had found in their 1990 survey. They also found very little difference between the two groups.

10. Ravenel, W. B., III. (1959). *English Reference Book*. Alexandria, VA: Newell-Cole, p. 143. With added punctuation, the passage reads as follows: That, that is, is. That, that is not, is not. That, that is not, is not that, that is. That, that is, is not that, that is not. Is not that it? It is. For similar punctuation challenges, see Barrett, D. J. (1986). From "Thinking Man" to "Man Thinking": Exercises requiring problem-solving skills. *Activities to Promote Critical Thinking*. Urbana, IL: National Council of Teachers of English.

Chapter 4

Creating Written Leadership Communication

Developing excellent communication skills is absolutely essential to effective leadership. The leader must be able to share knowledge and ideas to transmit a sense of urgency and enthusiasm to others. If a leader can't get a message across clearly and motivate others to act on it, then having a message doesn't even matter.

Gilbert Amelio, president and CEO, National Semiconductor Corporation

More and more, the ability to speak well and write is important. You know, writing is not something that is taught as strongly as it should be in the educational curriculum. So you're looking for communication skills. . . . I think this communication point is getting more and more important. People really have to be able to handle the written and spoken word.

Richard Anderson, CEO, Delta Air Lines. *New York Times* interview with Adam Bryant, 2009

Right now, your customers are writing about your products on blogs and recutting your commercial on YouTube. They're defining you on Wikipedia and ganging up on you on social networking sites like Facebook. These are all elements of a social phenomenon—the groundswell—that has created a permanent shift in the way the world works.

Charlene Li and Josh Bernoff, *Groundswell*. Boston: Harvard, 2008.

Chapter Objectives

In this chapter, you will learn to do the following:

- Select the most effective written communication medium.
- Create individual and written communication.
- Interact with social media effectively.
- Organize communication content coherently.
- Conform to expectations in correspondence.
- Include expected contents in reports.
- Format professional communication effectively.

Professional written communication falls into one of two broad types: (1) correspondence (text messages, e-mails, blog posts, memos, and letters) and (2) reports (including proposals, progress reviews, performance reports, and research documentation). Through their correspondence and reports, leaders assert their influence in a wide range of organizational settings. Leaders write correspondence several times daily. They also write different kinds of reports, from complicated studies and white papers with recommendations and pages of analysis to shorter progress reviews.

Audiences carry with them certain expectations when they receive and read the various genres, or types, of written professional communication. In addition, they judge the leadership qualities of the writer. The audiences ask: Is the message clear? Is the argument logical and complete? Is the tone appropriate? Has the writer been careless in the content or use of language? Problems in any of these areas can prevent our messages from reaching our audiences as we intend.

The inability to create clear and coherent written communication has hindered countless careers. Even something as apparently innocuous as an internal e-mail can hurt us and our organization. For example, an e-mail discussed in this chapter damaged a midwestern CEO's reputation and resulted in a substantial dip in his company's stock price. Once we are in a leadership position, our communication becomes far-reaching and public, with the power to change the entire direction of our organization. By recognizing the importance of every written communication we create, we begin to appreciate the importance of making sure we approach the writing of all of it with utmost care, from the simplest text messages and e-mails to the most complicated reports.

This chapter focuses on helping you create written leadership communication that accomplishes your communication purposes. Chapter 2 emphasized that leadership communication depends on establishing a clear purpose, developing a communication strategy, analyzing an audience, and ensuring that we use the most effective organizational structure. This chapter will begin by applying these principles to creating written communication. In addition, this chapter discusses how to make all types of written communication coherent to our audiences and explains the relatively new world of social media, providing a strategy for approaching the most common types as a leader. It concludes by emphasizing achieving coherence by using a logical structure and effective organization and by making sure our documents conform in content and format to the expectations in the typical professional settings.

Selecting the Most Effective Communication Medium

As with any effective leadership communication, we need to clarify our purpose, analyze our audience, and develop a communication strategy before we put pen to paper or fingers to the keyboard to create a document. We have a number of options to consider when selecting the best document medium.

When writing, people generally reply in kind: For example, if someone sends us an e-mail, we send an e-mail back, or if someone sends us an instant message (IM), we respond via IM (or, if the request is complicated, we ask the person to call or e-mail). When we are initiating the chain of communication, the usual communication practices of the organization will probably guide our choice of medium. If the organization uses IM or e-mail for everything, then we will as well.

If we have complete freedom to select the medium and are not limited by the previous chain of communication or the practices in the organization, we should select the medium best suited for the context and our message. Exhibit 4.1 lists some of the advantages and disadvantages of each written medium to help in deciding which is the best to use in different situations.

Creating Individual and Team Written Communication

Once we have developed our strategy and selected the most appropriate medium, we can then create and perfect our written communication. Whether we are creating our communication alone or in collaboration with a team or other group, having a plan will help us be more productive and streamline the creation process considerably. This pre-work is even important for writing in social media; we should make a plan before entering the space.

EXHIBIT 4.1 Advantages and Disadvantages of Each Written Medium

Medium	Advantages	Disadvantages
Blogs	• Personal and somewhat casual • Reaches a large audience • Easily shared	• Still a new medium; standards have not been set, and expectations are unclear • No way to ensure that the message reached the intended audience • Easily shared
Tweets (Microblogging)	• Immediate and casual • Easily shared • Fosters conversation and collaborative thinking	• Because it is so immediate, can be sent without thoughtful consideration • Still a new medium; standards have not been set, and expectations are unclear • Easily shared
Social Network Post (Facebook event, wall post, etc.)	• Reaches "fan" base, so fosters viral spread of message • Fosters collaboration and conversation	• Limited audience • Easily overlooked • Potential for negative social backlash
Text message	• Fast, easy, immediate	• Too abbreviated for more complex or sensitive communication
E-mail	• Fast, immediate • Easily distributed to one or many • Creates a permanent electronic trail	• Easily distributed to the world, accidentally or on purpose • Discoverable in litigation • Formatting sometimes lost in transmission
Memo	• Usually considered informal and for internal use • Creates a permanent paper trail • Allows writer to control layout	• Slower than e-mail • Thought of as more informal than a letter • Creates a permanent paper trail
Letter	• More formal, reserved for external use primarily • Creates a permanent paper trail • Stands out from the crowd • Allows writer to control layout	• Slower than e-mail • Creates a permanent paper trail
Discussion outline	• Informal • Tends to encourage discussion	• May be seen as too casual and even careless unless positioned effectively
Chart pack or deck	• Can be informal or formal depending on the setting • Easy to create effective data charts	• Usually requires discussion in person or at a minimum text explanation to accompany it
White papers	• Usually seen as more informal than a report with a focus on educating and providing information usually through electronic channels • Often used by businesses, particularly high-tech, to promote products, services, ideas	• Seen by many now as a sales tool, thus causing some to question purpose and not see them as always trustworthy • Commercial use has weakened credibility as a source of new ideas or as example of thought leadership
Reports	• Usually viewed as formal • Allow fuller discussions and analysis of subjects • Come in numerous shapes and sizes (see report table below)	• Are seldom read in their entirety • May require additional time and effort to compile and to format

Creating Individual Written Communication

Exhibit 4.2 provides a phased approach to follow if working alone, from the initial steps of establishing purpose and strategy to the final step of producing a completed document. Approaches to creating written communication differ from person to person. Some people work best from an outline, while others feel more comfortable using the idea mapping or brainstorming techniques discussed in Chapter 2. We should find the approach that works best for us, realizing that we will be more productive if we follow some sort of step-by-step plan.

Ideally, we should go through each step in order, making sure that we leave all editing until the final phase. One of the greatest barriers to idea generation is editing while writing or creating. The brain cannot be creator and critic at the same time. The purpose and strategy affect content, organization, format, and style. They will, of course, govern how we approach the process and how we complete it.

Our purpose will usually be clear by the time we reach Phase 2, although sometimes we may find that we start writing the draft before we know exactly where we are heading. Sometimes we simply need to get words on the page or screen to help the ideas flow, and as they do, we gain greater clarity in our message. For example, when sending e-mails, we may write a few sentences that we end up deleting once we realize what we really want to say. If we find we are hitting a writing block, we may need to go back to brainstorming or mind mapping to free up our ideas.

Creating Team Written Communication

Leaders often manage the process of document and presentation creation within a team setting. Doing so effectively requires preplanning and a clearly defined approach. Without a plan, team document and

EXHIBIT 4.2
Individual Written Communication Creation Process

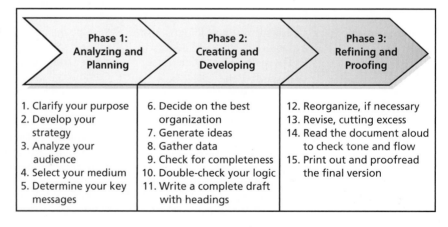

Phase 1: Analyzing and Planning	Phase 2: Creating and Developing	Phase 3: Refining and Proofing
1. Clarify your purpose 2. Develop your strategy 3. Analyze your audience 4. Select your medium 5. Determine your key messages	6. Decide on the best organization 7. Generate ideas 8. Gather data 9. Check for completeness 10. Double-check your logic 11. Write a complete draft with headings	12. Reorganize, if necessary 13. Revise, cutting excess 14. Read the document aloud to check tone and flow 15. Print out and proofread the final version

presentation creation can involve extra work and yield lower-quality results. Teams use one of two ways to divide the tasks: (1) single scribe or (2) multiple writer. Both of these approaches can be managed online with such applications as Google Docs or other collaborative workspace. For instruction in these two approaches to dividing up the work across a team and using Google Docs to collaborate on team work, see Chapter 10.

Interacting with Social Media

More and more, leaders are expected to interact in the social media space. A recent Rosetta study (2008) states that 59 percent of top retailers have a fan page on Facebook, for example.[1] Forbes.com, in fact, recommends that even CEOs should use social networks and Twitter.[2] Through blogs, Twitter accounts, Facebook profiles, and professional networking sites, leaders project their ethos and interact with their company's varied audiences, often without the assistance of a marketing or PR team, and often without direction, which can be risky.

Social media are changing the face of communication across all industries, even finding their way into political campaigns. For example, U.S. President Obama used social media, such as Facebook, YouTube, and Twitter, very effectively in his election, communicating easily and frequently with his constituencies and leaving most of the other candidates constantly playing catch-up. In fact, some say his "victory demonstrated that platforms like YouTube and Twitter could transform electoral politics."[3]

While some corporations are slower to accept these new media, most realize they must. Domino's Pizza is just one of many corporations recently who faced a scandal facilitated by the Web. Many are realizing the value and the importance of Web 2.0. They are finding that "social software can be used to boost productivity" and as Web 2.0 evangelists say, "it can facilitate an open-ended corporate culture that values transparency, collaboration and innovation. Most important, it can be an effective way to build a customer-centric organization that not only communicates authentically but also listens to customers and learns from that interaction."[4]

It is important for us to consider carefully how we want to approach social media and how we wish to present ourselves in these very public, constantly changing spaces. The following sections outline some of the best strategic practices for using two of the most popular forms of social media—blogs and microblogs—and recommend strategies for understanding the different uses of language in these spaces.

Setting up a Professional Blog

The list of companies, blog posts, and Web sites devoted to providing advice on how to create a professional blog is extensive and will change quickly, we can be sure, but the following are a few available, as of the publication of this book:

www.presentationzen.com/
www.tompeters.com/
http://msmvps.com/blogs/tohlz/
www.pptblog.tlccreative.com/
www.visualbeing.com/
http://pptideas.blogspot.com/

A review of many of these top-visited sites shows some commonalities in the guidelines for using blogs:

1. Define your purpose before you begin.
   Denise Wakeman from www.buildabetterblog.com echoes the sentiment of many when she suggests that you need to ask—and answer—a critical question before you begin blogging: Why will your blog exist?[5] She notes that, to answer that question, you will need to know the audience you want to attract, your goals for the blog, and what others are already writing. Chapter 2 on leadership communication strategy can help you with this step.

2. Be involved in the conversation.
   Most lists of tips for blogging include a statement much like this one from Alan Johnson: "The opportunity to interact with your readers is one of the most important things which makes blogging special in the first place."[6] If you only post and never respond to your audience, you will lose the audience. Blogs are designed to foster conversation, so make conversation happen!

3. Give credit.
   According to Darren Rowse, one of the best-known bloggers on the Internet, one of the quickest ways to ruin your reputation as a blogger is not to give credit to and link to others when you use their ideas. In fact, he warns that not giving credit and properly linking can get your blog banned from some search engines.[7] In addition, many professional bloggers have noted the value of linking to others as a means of building their own readership and getting involved in the larger blogosphere.

4. Make it different.
   Blogs can go wrong quickly when they are used as simply another marketing tool. Matthew Fraser and Soumitra Dutta of Forbes.com warn that "new media require new ways of doing business" and note that the real value of blogs and other social media is their ability to foster collaboration and create new channels for interacting with key stakeholders openly and honestly.[8] Any blog you create should be a mix of the personal and the professional—

one that comes naturally to you and is still good for your organization.

5. Keep writing.

Professionals bloggers in many different fields warn that the quickest way to doom a blog is to take a break and stop writing. As you define your purpose, put together a time line that includes when you will post, when you will review and comment on responses, *and* when you will read others.

Once we have a strategic plan in place, we need to consider our strategic approach to language on our blog as well. Blogs are usually more casual in tone and style than other professional writing, but standard rules still apply; we should be generally correct and positive in our language and avoid all the pitfalls discussed in Chapter 3 and later in this chapter. Likewise, the rules that apply to e-mail and other electronic communication also apply to blog posts; we should open meaningfully, establish context, provide only the details we need, and close with grace.

Creating a Microblog Plan

Microblogs, such as Twitter and Friendfeed, have exploded recently. As of March 2009, Twitter was growing at an overwhelming 1,382 percent and included more than 7 million accounts in the United States alone.[9] Many companies, from media networks to manufacturing firms, have created Twitter accounts to keep those interested up to date on their activities. Many organizations monitor Twitter to keep abreast of the social "buzz" about their company or brand, and some enterprising companies, such as Comcast, have reached out across these networks to improve their brand and customer satisfaction.[10]

Approaching these microblogs, however, can be overwhelming, and many people have noted their capacity for taking over their time. It is important, then, that we approach writing microblogs from a strategic perspective. Once again, Chapter 2 of this book can help in identifying your purpose, goals, audience, and strategic framework, but without a clear approach to this relatively new communication channel, it is easy to flounder.

Many people have made recommendations for how to approach Twitter. One of the most succinct and clear strategies, however, comes from Nicole Nicolay (@nik_nik, http://activerain.com/blogs/niknik) from *My Tech Opinion*. The following steps summarize her approach, and the complete article can be found at the link found in the citation.[11]

1. Select check-in times; don't check it all day, every day.
2. Determine what kind of tweets you want to include, based on your goals for your Twitter account. Nicolay recommends five types of tweets and offers suggestions.

3. Create your tweets and post them to a tool (such as Twutter or TweetLater) to automate their delivery.

4. Interspace these with spontaneous, interesting items worthy sharing.
   Source: Nicole Nicolay. www.mytechopinion.com. Used with permission.

It is worth mentioning that the language of micoblog posts is, by necessity, much shorter than other forms of professional communication. However, we should still carefully consider the style and tone of our posts, as well as their readability. And once again, each microblog site has its own expectations of how and what we can post; before we begin putting out our messages, we should become familiar with these general rules of conduct.

Organizing the Content Coherently

The initial stages of creating written communication can be rather messy, particularly the idea-generation stage. When we are generating ideas, we are engaged analytically, which means we are breaking things apart and probably even free associating as one idea leads to another. Once we have exhausted the sources of ideas, we move into the stage of organizing them to present them to others. A professional audience expects order and logic in a document; they expect it to make sense to them, to be coherent.

To "cohere" means to hold together, which is what we want our communication to do. We want the pieces—sentences, paragraphs, and sections—to conform to a systematic arrangement or plan that is logical and apparent to readers. Chapter 2 covered different approaches to organizing a document or a presentation and the dependence of an organization on communication strategy and audience analysis. This section focuses specifically on creating coherence in written communication by organizing the content and including the content expected by professional audiences.

For social media, our posts, comments, tweets, and the like should "cohere" as well—to a central theme or idea. Think of the entirety of a blog or profile on a social network as a "document" that defines the writer as a professional in that space.

Organization and Content

Chapter 2 discussed how organization depends on purpose, audience, and strategy and explained some of the options for organizing our communication. We need to anticipate our audience's response and stay focused on our purpose. We will want to select the organizing device, such as deductive, inductive, or chronological, that best matches our purpose and content.

In some cases, the type of document will dictate the organizational structure. For instance, if we are describing a process or procedure, we will usually use a chronological structure, taking our readers through each step in turn. In a proposal, however, we might use any number of logical structures—including deductive, problem solution, comparison and contrast, and cause and effect—to organize the document or sections in the document. These different structures will be applicable, despite the similarity of the informational content from one proposal to another.

The logic of the entire document, as well as that of each section, should be obvious to our readers. We want the logic to be so clear and the organization so tight that no one wonders, "Where did that come from?" Although they are useful references, too frequent use of the following expressions in a report may signal that the organization needs to be stronger: "As mentioned or discussed earlier," "Returning to point A again," or "In the previous section."

In a professional setting, particularly in the United States, we usually want to organize our document deductively, stating our main message, conclusion, or principal recommendation directly at the very beginning of the document and proceeding through secondary arguments and supporting information. We might select inductive organization if communicating in different cultures or if we have a hostile or resistant audience and decide it is best to take an indirect approach by explaining and presenting our evidence before stating our main message or recommendation.

Again, traditional outlines, storyboards, decision trees, and the Pyramid Principle are effective techniques for organizing a document. We should anticipate our readers' questions and attempt to organize the document so that we answer the questions as they would occur to the audience.

Opening with Power

In the opening, most of the time we should begin strongly by quickly stating our main message, but we need to let our analysis of our audience guide us on how to begin. We may want to begin indirectly for the following reasons:

- To establish the context for the communication if it is complex and a part of a chain of communication.
- To include a more gentle opening with some appropriate pleasantries if our audience's culture would expect it.
- To provide some information to soften the bad news we must deliver.
- To explain the reasoning or logic if we have complicated information to deliver.
- To explore an idea or posit a topic for discussion in social media spaces.

Again, we should use our analysis of the audience to determine how best to begin, but in most cases, we should try to state our main point as early as possible in our document so that the reader knows our reason for writing.

In the first paragraph of most professional correspondence, we need to establish the context briefly before the purpose. For example, if we are responding to an e-mail sent to us, we might begin as follows:

Dear Mara:

In response to your e-mail of October 5, on setting up a meeting to discuss progress on the Zinex account, I would like for you to set up a team meeting for next Monday, October 10, at 10:00 a.m. . . .

Starting by stating our purpose ("I would like for you to set up a team meeting for next Monday, October 10, at 10:00 a.m.") without the context ("In response to your e-mail of October 5, on setting up a meeting to discuss the progress on the Zinex account") would make the exact meeting topic we have in mind ambiguous for Mara. While the company may be small enough and the number of clients small enough to make ambiguity unlikely, it is always best to make the exact context clear in the opening of most correspondence.

If the correspondence is longer, we might need to prepare the reader for what is to come by listing the topics covered as well. Then, we address the topics in the order introduced, using headings to set off each major section. To expand on the previous example, for instance, we might begin as follows:

Dear Mara:

In response to your e-mail of October 5, on setting up a meeting to discuss progress on the Zinex account, I would like for you to set up a team meeting for next Monday, October 10, at 10:00 a.m. In the meeting I have three primary objectives, which I discuss below: (1) progress, (2) issues, and (3) next steps.

We would then include a discussion of each of these topics, using the topics as our headings.

We can remember to include the expected opening in professional communication, if we keep the CPF acronym in mind:

C = Context—What is the impetus for the communication? What surrounds it that could influence it?

P = Purpose—Why am I writing? What is my reason?

F = Foreshadowing—What is coming in this communication and in what order? What should readers expect to see as they read it?

The next example demonstrates a very indirect opening to a letter. In fact, it is so indirect we cannot even be sure what the writer's purpose is in writing to Ms. Watson.

Dear Ms. Watson:

This past weekend I watched the Florida Golf Classic on television and was impressed by the show of support for the tournament. Obviously, the senior golf tour has progressed to a serious competitive level, and I applaud your efforts in having a part in the evolution. I am an avid fan of all sports, especially golf, and am happy to see greats such as Arnold Palmer and Jack Nicklaus continuing to play competitively. I know that your organization has only 10 people who work directly on the tournament, yet you have made the Classic the second largest on the tour, in terms of prize money. This status is quite an accomplishment, and I would certainly enjoy contributing to the effort to make the Classic the most recognized tournament on the senior tour.

The amiable, rambling opening paragraph leaves us wondering about the purpose and asking, "So what?" By the end of the paragraph, we may have determined that the writer wants to apply for a position, but we cannot be sure. The writer could be asking about donating money or volunteering in some way.

In the second paragraph, this job applicant finally makes the purpose clear:

Joanne Brownstone, who held an internship in public relations in your organization last year, spoke enthusiastically of her work with the tournament. She suggested that I contact you about an internship, since my current studies in business administration and my involvement in the sports field would contribute to your efforts in planning future tournaments and events.

This paragraph would have made a much better opening to the letter. The applicant establishes a context for writing (the source of the information about the possible internship opportunity) and then states the purpose of the letter (to apply for an internship).

In leadership communication, it is particularly important to make sure we deliver our main message early. We want to start our letters, memos, and e-mails fast and get to the point quickly, providing only enough background information to establish the context. Getting to the point quickly demonstrates greater respect for the busy reader on the receiving end. The reader must know within the first couple of sentences why he or she is receiving this communication or should consider reading this post.

We can check whether we are getting to the point directly by applying the "so what?" test. Broadcasters used this test in the past. They would ask themselves, "Am I saying anything to which my listeners could say so what?" The "so what?" test works well to remind us to think about the value of the information we are providing to the reader. We do not want our readers to say "so what?" to anything we write.

Developing with Reason

We should aim for the same directness and brevity in the discussion or development section of our documents as we do in our introduction. Again, we will want to apply the Mutually Exclusive, Collectively Exhaustive (MECE) test.

We need to test our logic by making sure that our supporting topics do not overlap and that we have provided adequate justification for each one. MECE also suggests a balance to the sections in the amount of information provided for each one. If, for instance, we find that for one topic we need several pages and for another only a short paragraph, then we need to reassess our topics and consider grouping that short one with another or breaking the longer section down into several distinct topics. Once we know we have the right topics and can develop each topic adequately, we should feel comfortable that our discussion section will appear reasonable to our audience.

In solving many of the problems that we tackle in professional settings, we collect more information than we can or should present to our audience. We need to be carefully selective in the information we include in our discussions. We want to include only what is necessary to support our message and further our goal. We must avoid the inclination to include all of the analysis simply because we or our team has done it. We should select only the data that are necessary to make our point, and place other relevant information in an appendix or attachment.

If we are unsure of the importance of certain information, we should probably leave it out or consign it to an appendix. Most of our audiences are more interested in our interpretation of the data than in seeing the data, so we should be particularly careful to be selective. Again, we should ask, "Can anyone say 'so what?' to this?"

Finally, once we know the content is logically organized and reasonable in its balance, we want to consider how to make it accessible to our audience. We can make the document easy to read by formatting and carefully using headings and bulleted or numbered lists. We will want to use meaningful (message-driven) headings and avoid long paragraphs. We want our readers to be able to easily scan our document and locate what they want to read.

Most people read documents selectively, which means they go to the section that is of most interest to them or that is relevant to their department or function. Studies have shown that very few business-people read a longer document from cover to cover. Researchers found that most decision makers read the executive summary, but only 60 percent read the introduction and conclusions, and only 15 percent read the discussion or main body.[12]

We should avoid lengthy paragraphs and long sections of discussion between headings, finding places in a long paragraph to break it up into shorter paragraphs and use headings and lists. Also, we need to provide clear transitions from idea to idea within paragraphs and between them. It is fine to have one-sentence paragraphs. In fact, it is better to have shorter paragraphs, particularly in e-mails, since the added white space makes them easier to scan.

The policy statement in Exhibit 4.3 illustrates a poorly organized, lengthy paragraph. Notice how difficult it is to follow the logic and how tedious it is to read. In fact, we would probably avoid reading it if it came across our desk.

Before turning to a reorganized and reformatted version, look closely at the policy statement in Exhibit 4.3 and think about how to reorganize and reformat it. As with most policy statements or procedures, this statement could be restructured using the journalist's questions of who, what, when, where, and how.

Reorganizing and reformatting the policy statement makes it much easier to read (Exhibit 4.4). Readers can now scan the reorganized and reformatted policy quickly and find what they need to know. This example illustrates the importance of organizing documents into a logical structure, as well as the value of headings in making that logic clear and in helping the audience read the prose quickly.

Closing with Grace

Once we have taken our audience through our discussion, we should end as quickly and directly as we began. We should, however, provide a sense of polite, unrushed closure. Traditional academic writing

EXHIBIT 4.3
**Example of a
Poorly Organized
and Formatted
Policy Statement**

Training Division Policy #4503.11

This policy applies to all employees except Production Division employees below the rank of supervisor and clerical employees below the rank of Junior Administrative Assistant. In order to encourage personnel to develop greater professional competence in their respective fields and to prepare for professional advancement, personnel registering in credit courses at the college or graduate level in state-accredited institutions of higher education will be reimbursed for the direct costs of tuition, registration fees, and required course textbooks and other materials upon successful completion of such instruction. Certification that the college course will contribute to the employee's professional growth will be provided by the employee's direct supervisor and countersigned by the supervisor's direct superior unless the supervisor be at the rank of vice president or higher. Successful completion is defined as completion with the grade of C or higher (or equivalent). Costs of travel and costs of nonrequired materials such as paper and clerical help will not be reimbursed. Submission to the Training Division of receipts for all expenses, approval of the direct supervisor that the course fulfills the requirements of this policy, and documentation of successful completion are required before reimbursement through the Training Division budget. Supervisors are encouraged to allow released time for personnel to enroll in credit college courses for professional development when departmental or divisional schedules permit. Released time is encouraged only when scheduled meetings of credit college courses occur during regular working hours. If possible and necessary, personnel may be required to make up working time outside normal working hours. If the credit college course can be taken outside the individual's normal working hours, no released time should be given. To receive reimbursement, personnel should submit Training Division Form 4503B to the Training Division in accordance with the instructions on that form.

requires closings that restate or summarize what has already been said. A letter, a memo, a post, or an e-mail is too short to require such repetition of ideas, so their conclusions should call for action, mention contact information or follow-up arrangements, anticipate any problems, and/or offer a courtesy closing (Exhibits 4.5. and 4.6).

In a longer document, we may want to summarize our main points very briefly, and depending on the type of report, we may end with our conclusions or recommendations. However, it is usually more effective to have stated our conclusions or recommendations up front and end with next steps or implementation plans.

EXHIBIT 4.4
Example of an Effectively Organized and Formatted Policy Statement

ABMC's Policy on Reimbursement of Educational Expenses
Training Division Policy 14503.11

The purpose of ABMC's Policy on Reimbursement of Educational Expenses is to encourage its employees to develop their professional skills and prepare for advancement through the completion of college-level courses. The following outlines who is eligible, what is covered, and how to file.

Who Is Eligible

All product division employees above the level of supervisor and clerical employees above the level of junior administrative assistant are eligible for the reimbursement.

What Is Covered

The following are the expenses covered under this policy:
- Direct costs of tuition
- Registration fees
- Required texts and other required materials

Travel costs and costs of general school supplies, such as paper and pens, are not reimbursable.

How to File

To file for reimbursement, take the following steps:

1. Obtain certification that the course will contribute to your professional growth from your direct supervisor, countersigned by his/her superior (if your supervisor is a vice president, the countersignature is not necessary).
2. Register for the course at a state-accredited institution of higher learning.
3. Complete the course successfully (a minimum grade of "C+" or equivalent).
4. Submit the following to Sam Gates, Training Division Office, Building C, Room 209:
   - Training Division Form 4503B
   - Proof of successful completion of course(s)
   - Certification from supervisor
   - Receipts for all expenses

Note that classes should be taken outside of working hours. If the class is offered only during working hours, release time may be allowed as divisional schedules permit; however, you may be required to make up missed time.

If you have any questions or need help, call Sam Gates (Ext. 9933).

EXHIBIT 4.5
Sample
Transmittal
Letter

Global Communication Services
6108 Martin Lane
Houston, TX 77000

December 11, 2009

Ms. Kerith Karetti, CEO
Hamill Brothers, Inc.
2708 W. 43rd Street
New York, NY 10036

Dear Ms. Karetti:

We have enclosed our final draft of the marketing analysis you requested. We have enjoyed working with your team to identify the potential to expand your product into Asia. In the report, we have provided not only the analysis of the market but also some ideas on how you might move ahead.

Our analysis indicates a tremendous opportunity for your company, and we suggest you move forward in developing a complete marketing plan as soon as possible. We believe you and your team are positioned to move quickly using this analysis as your launching point.

If we can be of any further help as you move into this project, please let me know. We always enjoy working with your group and look forward to continuing our relationship in the future.

Sincerely,

Janette Zuniga

Janette Zuniga
Senior Managing Director

Enclosure: Final Marketing Analysis to Determine Expansion Opportunities in Asia

EXHIBIT 4.6
Sample Memo

Date: February 2, 2010
To: All marketing team members
From: Alan Zhang, scribe this week
Subject: Meeting notes with next steps from February 1 meeting

As our team decided, we want to keep notes of our meetings and send them to each other weekly. As the scribe this week, that task fell to me. Therefore, I am sending you a summary of the meeting organized into the two main topics that we discussed: (1) making team meetings more effective and (2) organizing our team tasks. Please review this memo and let me know before 8:00 a.m., Wednesday, February 10, if I need to add anything and resend these before our next meeting.

Making Team Meetings More Effective

We decided that we can definitely make our meetings more effective. Some of the methods we discussed were as follows:

- Schedule more face-to-face interactions, but keep a "get it done and make it productive" attitude
- Agree to meeting times and maintain communication lines regarding availability
- Designate a leader for every team meeting
- Distribute an agenda with 24 hours' notice
- Follow up all team meetings with minutes that express decisions and agreed-upon next steps

Organizing Tasks More Effectively

We also discussed ways to organize our tasks more effectively. We came up with two actions:

- Create a team action plan with tasks and responsibilities allotted to specific members
- Divide up tasks according to project phases

We ran out of time, so we will be continuing this discussion at our next meeting.

Establishing the Next Steps

Our next step is a phone conference Wednesday at 11:00 a.m., to discuss the progress on the marketing project and to finalize our approach to organizing our work more effectively.

I look forward to our next meeting and again, if I left anything out of this summary, please let me know by Wednesday morning, so that I can send out a revised version before our conference call. You can reach me at x6785 or through e-mail at zhangA@swiftly.com.

Conforming to Content and Formatting Expectations in Correspondence

We will determine the actual content of our letters, memos, e-mails, and text messages based on our purpose, strategy, and audience, but these types of professional communication carry some expectations of what we should include. In addition, we want to use a format that follows standard professional writing conventions, which are designed to make our documents accessible as well as attractive. Good formatting reveals and supports the organization, as the rewritten version of the policy statement in Exhibit 4.4 demonstrates. Format is important in helping our audience see the structure and logic of our documents and in making it easy for them to skim or read selectively.

This section illustrates the formatting of typical types of correspondence (e-mails, memos, and letters) and provides information about and examples of the standard content we will want to include. In particular, it provides guidelines for e-mail, since it has become such a common medium for professional communication and is often used ineffectively.

If a company or organization does not have a style guide for the formatting of letters and memos, we should follow the conventions included in most business writing handbooks and in college dictionaries. The examples provided here follow these conventions.

Blogs and social networks also create expectations. For example, Facebook status updates are usually three lines or less, and Twitter forwards usually include "re-tweet" info (RT@ and the original Twitter account name). It is best to skim the content of any social media space and become familiar with these expectations before beginning to interact.

Letters and Memos

Most businesspeople today prefer the block format for letters, illustrated in the sample letter of transmittal (Exhibit 4.5), with a simple "Sincerely" to close the letter.

Memos should include all the preliminary elements of date, to, from, and subject (avoid "re" unless it is used by your organization). The following are two warnings about memos:

1. Make sure the subject line captures the "so what?"—the purpose for writing—very specifically.
2. Repeat that purpose in the first sentence of the memo (see Exhibit 4.6).

E-mails and Other Electronic Communication

E-mail has rapidly become the most frequently used medium for professional and personal communication. It is also the most common use of the Internet. Daily e-mail usage is projected to hit 10 trillion person-to-person e-mails, excluding SPAM, by 2010.[13] Although we still send and receive printed letters and memos, they are becoming rarer and are often transmitted as e-mail attachments rather than as hard-copy. E-mails follow a format similar to that of a memo, but they have some special guidelines we should follow to ensure that they are effective.

Likewise, electronic communication in many forms has boomed in recent years. Companies use wikis to collaborate, IMs to ask quick questions, corporate intranet blogs to share information with employees, and more. The basic rules that apply to e-mail apply to these forms of electronic communication as well.

Subject Lines and Post Titles

The subject line or post title takes on tremendous importance, since it usually determines if our audience will read further. We should take special care to craft subject lines and post titles that tell recipients why they should read our message.

Look at the following, for example. Which would you open if they came from your peers?

Subject: For your information

Subject: Forward: Forward: Forward: Funny!!!!!!!!!

Subject: Reminder

Subject: Agenda for Tomorrow's Meeting

Subject: How are you?

And which of the following intranet blog posts would you read?

Title: My Saturday

Title: Moving Forward with New Strategies

Title: Hating Life Right Now

Title: More Info from Last Week!

Title: Upcoming Policy Changes

The context of the e-mail or post will influence our inclination to read it. For example, when our boss, instead of a peer, sends an e-mail, we will probably open it, no matter what the subject line says because what he or she has to say is important to our job, our career. Most of us do not have time for communication that is not directly related to us or for communication that requires no action on our part, as is suggested by "for your information," and few of us have the patience or interest to open forwarded messages, since they are often mass-mailed and include jokes or lame examples of someone else's sense of humor. And, of course, often they are SPAM and can contain viruses.

If we do not have the power of our position to inspire others to respond and read our e-mails or posts, then we need to ensure that the subject line or title captures the audience. Think of it as the title of a book or the caption from an article. What will make us take that book off the shelf or click on that caption in the *New York Times* online?

Tone and Content

We also need to be particularly careful with the tone and content of our e-mails. A harsh tone will be perceived even more harshly in an e-mail than in a hard-copy memo because people expect e-mails to be informal. We need to be extra cautious about what we say in an e-mail because receivers can easily forward them to the world. Even if e-mails are not sent to unintended audiences, they still become a permanent, easily accessed record.

The e-mail in Exhibit 4.7 provides an example of the damage a harsh message in electronic format can do. The CEO of Cerner, a midwestern computer company, actually sent it to his management group. The capitalization, the formatting, and all the content are exactly as written by the CEO, altough his name has been changed.

McCutcheon sent this e-mail to his 400-member management team on March 13, and by March 21, it had made its way across the Internet. Shortly afterward, it appeared in its entirety in the *New York Times,* and Cerner's stock dropped by 22 percent.

If we compare this e-mail with the first version of the copier memo discussed in Chapter 2, we see some similarities. Both were written when angry feelings clouded rational thinking. Fortunately, the writer of the copier memo realized before he sent it that he needed to reconsider his approach. The CEO of Cerner did not, and with the speed of the Internet, his message went global, and his company suffered because of it. This example serves as a warning for everyone using e-mail: we need to think carefully about all possible audiences and the possible repercussions of the communication before hitting "send."

Legal and Other Potential Issues

Given the importance of e-mail, IMs, and other electronic communication in the workplace, it is surprising people still take them so lightly. For example, a *Business Wire* article states,

> E-mail, the electronic equivalent of DNA evidence, is playing an increasingly common role in workplace lawsuits and regulatory investigations. A primary source of evidence in high-profile discrimination, sexual harassment, and antitrust claims, e-mail is regularly used to bolster cases, embarrass organizations, and damage reputations. A new survey of 1,100 U.S. companies reveals that 14% of respondents have been ordered by a court or regulatory body to produce employee e-mail, up from 9% just two years ago.[14]

EXHIBIT 4.7
Cerner CEO's
E-mail to His
Managers
(reprinted exactly
as it appeared
when it was sent
with errors
uncorrected)

From: McCutcheon, Bill (name changed)
Sent: Tuesday. March 13, 2001 11:48 a.m.
To: DL ALL MANAGERS
Subject MANAGEMENT DIRECTIVE: Week #10_01: Fix it or changes will
be made
Importance: High

To the HQ_based managers:

I have gone over the top. I have been making this point for over one year.

We are getting less than 40 hours of work from a large number of our
HQ_based EMPLOYEES. The parking lot is sparsely used at 8 a.m.;
likewise at 5 p.m. As managers—you either do not know what your
EMPLOYEES are doing; or YOU do not CARE. You have created
expectations on the work effort which allowed this to happen inside
MWCC, creating a very unhealthy environment. In either case, you have a
problem and you will fix it or I will replace you.

NEVER in my career have I allowed a team which worked for me to think
they had a 40 hour job. I have allowed YOU to create a culture which is
permitting this. NO LONGER.

At the end of next week, I am plan to implement the following:
1. Closing of Associate Center to EMPLOYEES from 7:30 a.m. to 6:30 p.m.
2. Implementing a hiring freeze for all HQ based positions. It will require
   Cabinet approval to hire someone into a HQ based team. I chair our
   Cabinet.
3. Implementing a time clock system, requiring EMPLOYEES to 'punch in'
   and 'punch out' to work. Any unapproved absences will be charged to
   the EMPLOYEES vacation.
4. We passed a Stock Purchase Program, allowing for the EMPLOYEE to
   purchase MWCC stock at a 15% discount, at Friday's BOD meeting. Hell
   will freeze over before this CEO implements ANOTHER EMPLOYEE
   benefit in this *Culture*.
5. Implement a 5% reduction of staff in HQ.
6. I am tabling the promotions until I am convinced that the ones being
   promoted are the solution, not the problem. If you are the problem, pack
   your bags.

I think this parental type action SUCKS. However, what you are doing, as
managers, with this company makes me SICK. It makes sick to have to
write this directive.

(continued)

EXHIBIT 4.7
(continued)

[MWCC e-mail continues]

I know I am painting with a broad brush and the majority of the HQ based associates are hard working, committed to MWCC success and committed to transforming health care. I know the parking lot is not a great measurement for 'effort', I know that 'results' is what counts, not 'effort'. But I am through with the debate.

We have a big vision. It will require a big effort. Too many in HQ are not making the effort.

I want to hear from you. If you think I am wrong with any of this, please state your case. If you have some ideas on how to fix this problem, let me hear those. I am very curious how you think we got here. If you know team members who are the problem, let me know. Please include (copy) Sarah in all of your replies.

I STRONGLY suggest that you call some 7 a.m., 6 p.m. and Saturday a.m. team meetings with the EMPLOYEES who work directly for you. Discuss this serious issue with your team. I suggest that you call your first meeting tonight. Something is going to change.

I am giving you two weeks to fix this. My measurement will be the parking lot: it should be substantially full at 7:30 a.m. and 6:30 p.m. The pizza man should show up at 7:30 p.m. to feed the starving teams working late. The lot should be half full on Saturday mornings. We have a lot of work to do. If you do not have enough to keep your teams busy, let me know immediately.

Folks this is a management problem, not an EMPLOYEE problem.

Congratulations., you are management. You have the responsibility for our EMPLOYEES. I will hold you accountable. You have allowed this to get to this state. You have two weeks. Tick, tock.

Bill. . . . .
Chairman & Chief Executive Officer

The evidence of the detrimental effects that follow when an internal e-mail or other electronic communication finds its way to external audiences through the Internet, let alone the potential use in litigation, should encourage people to approach all electronic communication cautiously. Messages sent through electronic media can seriously hurt an organization's reputation and hurt the individual who sends them.

The misuse of e-mail can result in employees' being fired; in fact, it has: "According to a survey just completed by the American Management Association and the ePolicy Institute, over half of the companies they surveyed in the United States have fired workers for inappropriate usage of e-mail or the Internet. Of the companies surveyed, 43 percent are monitoring e-mail and 45 percent are tracking other Web activities."[15]

Many observers feel that e-mail, blogging, Facebook, IM, and other computer-mediated communication have led to poorer written communication abilities, despite some growing evidence to the contrary.[16] However, it is interesting that in some cases the opposite is happening, as more and more people are using writing as their primary way of communicating and connecting to others through their PDAs and computers. Text messaging and IM, in particular, are rapidly gaining in popularity, moving from informal communication between friends to media common in professional communication. By the end of 2013, the Gartner group estimates that 95 percent of workers in leading global organizations will be using IM as their primary interface for real-time communication.[17]

When e-mail first emerged, hurried writers were sometimes careless about how they composed their e-mails. Perhaps because of its easy use or the perception of being informal, e-mail seemed to encourage carelessness. We used to see spelling mistakes, usage errors, inappropriate capitalization (particularly the annoying use of all caps and all lowercase), and overall poor formatting—all mistakes people are not as likely to make in a printed memo or letter, and seem less likely to make today. E-mail seems to have crossed over into the mainstream of "proper" businesss communication and now has rules on its use; thus, people seem to be a little more careful when composing e-mails.

Specific Guidelines for IM and Text Messages

Forms of electronic communication other than e-mail are still seen as "ruleless" to some extent. Therefore, careless writing has somewhat worsened with the advent of companywide IM systems, such as Microsoft Communicator, and many of the mistakes found in e-mails in the past are now found in IM and text messages, perhaps because these media are so easy to use or perhaps often we are writing in less than optimal conditions, while standing waiting for the Metro or walking down the street, for example.

Many of the guidelines for e-mail apply to IM and text messages; however, the number of words is usually limited so much that our writing becomes telegraphic. The shorthand language we use in IM may not be understood in professional contexts and, therefore, should be used with caution. For instance, the message on the cell screen at the left would be unintelligible to most professionals today. Might it be acceptable in the future? Perhaps, but for now, when we use text messaging or IM in a professional setting, we should use complete words and sentences and proofread our message before sending it. The message on this cell phone from one professional to another would probably read as follows:

John,

Send me an IM re the money ASAP.

I am out of the office tomorrow.

Thank you.

Bill

No doubt electronic communication can be an extremely effective tool for sharing information and fostering collaboration, but it deserves as much care as any hard-copy writing, perhaps even more, since it can be shared much more easily with the world. At a minimum, we should avoid the following blunders, identified as the 10 most common mistakes of business e-mail correspondence, in our electronic communication in most cases:

Ten Most Common Mistakes of Business E-Mail Correspondence[18]

1. Unclear subject line.
2. Poor greeting (or none at all).
3. Unfamiliar abbreviations.
4. Unnecessary copies (CCs).
5. Sloppy grammar, spelling, and punctuation.
6. All caps in the message.
7. No closing or sign-off.
8. Rambling, unformatted message.
9. Unfriendly tone.
10. No clear request for action.

Source: Leland/Customer Service for Dummies; copyright © 2000. This material is used with permission of Wiley Publishing, Inc., a subsidiary of John Wiley & Sons, Inc.

The bottom line on all forms of electronic communication is to treat it with care. Take the time to write well, paying attention to organization and format as well as style and tone. Tone is especially important, since it is very easy for our audience to misinterpret our intention in an e-mail.

Reading our writing aloud, and even reading it to someone else, if the subject is sensitive and we want to ensure that we will not offend the audience or come across as negative, harsh, or insensitive can help us catch problems with tone. In fact, if the content is sensitive, you might want to reconsider electronic communication as your medium.

Overall, we need to take the time to proofread all our electronic documents, printing out the most important ones, since it is very difficult to see mistakes on a computer screen, PDA, or phone. Finally, we should not be misled into thinking that our audience will overlook carelessness just because they view a medium as informal. Although most readers are a little more forgiving with electronic communication, many are not. Carelessness of any sort can hurt a career; as we have already seen, an insensitive or careless e-mail could result in our ending up in *The Wall Street Journal* or *New York Times*.

Including Expected Content in Reports

Professional audiences also have expectations for longer documents and reports. The type of report, the company style, and the industry standards often dictate content and organization. Leaders in organizations write reports that inform, instruct, or persuade. Often, they team up with or supervise others in writing these reports. The reports may be long or short, formal or informal. They may even tell a story; for instance, the report might first include an overview of the current situation, then discuss the details that have complicated the situation, and finally suggest a resolution or recommendation to improve the situation.

Although many reports serve multiple purposes, such as informing and persuading, Exhibit 4.8 lists typical types of leadership communication reports organized by their primary purpose.

One type of report students may create not listed in Exhibit 4.8 is a case report, frequently used in undergraduate and graduate business and executive training programs. For case analysis and report contents, see Appendix D.

A Formal Full-Length Report

When the different types of reports in Exhibit 4.8 are formal, they include the contents outlined and discussed later in this section. Most full-length formal reports conform to the content and sequencing pattern in Exhibit 4.9.

A formal full-length report should have a table of contents. If the report is delivered electronically, the table of contents should contain hyperlinks to the sections of the report. The table of contents reveals the organization of the report. It allows readers to see the overall content and select the sections relevant to their needs and interests. The two examples in Exhibit 4.10 illustrate a poorly created table of contents and then a more effective one. The first example does not suggest any form of organization or grouping of ideas; it appears to be a random list of topics. The second example, although containing too little information, at least suggests some logic in organization.

EXHIBIT 4.8   Purposes and Types of Leadership Communication Reports

Purpose	Report Type	Focus of Content
Inform	Progress	→ Outlines the status of the tasks in a project, including work completed, work remaining, and anticipated delays (see typical contents below). → Sometimes includes analysis for discussion or preliminary conclusions for testing with audiences.
	Financial	→ Includes financial performance for reporting purposes, such as to the SEC for public companies (for example, 10-Ks and 10-Qs).
	Sales/ marketing	→ Provides the sales achievements and figures for a standard period of time (a week, month, or quarter). → Often includes sales prospects and projections and could focus on market trends, positioning, and product development.
	Operational	→ Varies across industries and companies, but may include overall operational/project performance or compliance to regulations, such as health, safety, and environmental.
	Meetings (minutes)	→ Provides a summary of the major topics discussed. → Usually includes date, attendees, old business, new business, and action items.
	Research/ investigative	→ Reports on the results of research and often provides recommendations on actions. → Includes investigative research, analysts reports, benchmarking.
Instruct	Procedure	→ Explains the steps to be completed to accomplish some goal. → Usually presents the actions in chronological order.
	Policy	→ Summarizes the organizational regulations or guidelines that govern employee behavior.
	Performance appraisals	→ Documents the quality of an employee's work with the intention of creating needed legal records and providing feedback to improve performance.
	Request for Proposal (RFP)	→ Provides guidelines on the information to include in a proposal.
Persuade	Annual	→ Reports on the financial performance of an organization with the intent of influencing external and internal constituencies, primarily investors and analysts. → Frequently includes a company's mission, vision, accomplishments, and plans.
	Feasibility	→ Argues that an approach or idea will work; recommends action. → Usually focuses on economic, technical, and cultural aspects.
	Proposals	→ Seeks acceptance for a product, service, or potential solution by defining the needs and benefits (see typical contents below). → Often responds to an RFP and is seen as a sales document that is legally binding.
	Business plans	→ Discusses all of the important components of a business or business idea, including value proposition, feasibility, and profitability. → Follows standard content expectations, such as those provided by the Small Business Administration.

EXHIBIT 4.9
Formal Report
Content

Content	Purpose
1. A Letter or Memo of Transmittal or Preface	Sets the stage for the report and is usually addressed to the decision maker. It should identify the purpose of the attached report, may provide highlights of the content, and always ends with a statement of what the writer expects the receiver to do next in response to the report. It will also contain contact information for the sender. Exhibit 2.5 is an example of a letter of transmittal.
2. Cover	Contains a title that captures the "so what" of the report. Usually contains the sender's name and the receiver's, as well as the date.
3. Title Page	Contains the same information as the cover, but may also contain a short abstract or descriptive summary of the report contents.
4. Table of Contents	Lists all important sections of the report (see examples below). It will usually list the main headings and second-level subheadings from the discussion section.
5. Executive Summary	Summarizes the main idea(s) from the body of the document, including conclusions and recommendations. Generally, approximately 10 percent of the discussion section length; however, it must be long enough to capture the central content of the report, so it may need to be longer than 10 percent. See discussion below.
6. Introduction	Provides context for the report, including any information the reader needs to understand the background and impetus for the report.
7. Discussion	Differs from report to report (see discussion of proposals and progress reviews below). It contains the developed content or argument organized logically.
8. Next Steps, If Appropriate	Outlines actions you expect the reader to take in response to the report as well as any follow-up actions you may be taking as well.
9. Appendix	Contains any data or other support for your report that is too lengthy or detailed for the discussion section. It may also contain qualifications, any graphs or diagrams not needed in the body of the document, and examples of survey instruments. Note: Any item included in an appendix must be mentioned by number in the report and then included in the order referenced.

EXHIBIT 4.10
Examples of Table of Contents

Example of a Poorly Organized and Poorly Formatted Table of Contents

Contents

Example of a More Effectively Organized Table of Contents

Table of Contents

If a report contains numerous graphs or data charts, we may need to include a list of figures, with their page numbers, following the table of contents (see Chapter 6 for guidelines on creating and using graphs).

Including Exhibits in Reports

Many types of documents contain exhibits, from memos to letters to reports. An exhibit (table, graph, diagram, and the like) should never be inserted into documents without some discussion of its contents and relevance or without being assigned a number and given a title, whether it is inserted directly into the text or placed in an appendix.

Exhibit Placement

It is best to insert an exhibit as close as possible to the text that discusses it, which means that most of the time we should embed it in our document so that it follows closely after any discussion of it, rather than in an appendix. At times, however, the exhibit may supplement our message but not be immediately necessary to the understanding of it, in which case we may place it in an appendix at the end of the document.

Exhibit Labels

We should assign a number and provide a title for each exhibit inserted in our document or attached in the appendix. Exhibits are always numbered consecutively. We must reference the exhibit by its number in our text discussion just prior to its appearance. If placed in an appendix, exhibits will need numbers and titles as well, and they should be in the order of their reference in the body of the document.

Handling Research Information in Reports

Professional reports usually include information that we have obtained from primary research (through surveys, interviews, experiments, or direct observation) or secondary research (which is research using published materials in books and on the Web). We need to ensure we handle both carefully, fully documenting our methods for primary research and our sources for secondary research and placing correct citations within our documents. Electronic versions of research information should include links to the original material whenever possible.

If we have used information that we gained by reading what others have said or written, we must include notes and a bibliography or list of sources cited at the end of the report just before the appendix. The notes can be parenthetical, placed at the bottom of the page or slide, or listed at the end of the document just before the bibliography. Report writers should follow a standard guide for documenting sources, such as *The Chicago Manual of Style,* the *Publication Manual of the American Psychological Association* (APA style guide), or the *MLA Style Manual.*

Since Web research is sometimes not well documented, we may not be sure how to reference it. First, we will want to verify its reliability as a source. Most reliable Web sources will indicate an author's name, an article or book title, and publishing information, such as the publishing company and date, or the author or group's affiliation with a university or professional or research organization. If information is cited inside another Web source without any of this information, it is our responsibility to trace back and locate the original source. If we cannot find one, we should be suspicious about the realiability of the information and will probably not want to use it. Once we get back to the original source, that is the bibliographical information we should use, with the full URL that takes our audience to the exact location.

Remember that anything we read on the Web and use in our report must be documented unless it is clearly common knowledge. Our citation will need to include the complete URL so that the reader can go to the exact source. Using the home page address alone is not sufficient anytime the site provides links to other pages within the Web site.

For example, the following is an incorrect Web reference to a direct quotation:

> Since 1980, Bain's clients have outperformed the S&P 500 index by a 3 to 1 margin. This success is not serendipitous, but a natural result of the approach that Bain takes to consulting, which always considers maximization of shareholder value (www.bain.com).

The correct method for handling the same reference follows:

> "Since 1980, Bain's clients have outperformed the S&P 500 index by a 3 to 1 margin. This success is not serendipitous, but a natural result of the approach that Bain takes to consulting, which always considers maximization of shareholder value" (http://205.134.84.25/bainweb/about/expertise/expertise_capability.asp?capability_id+56).

Since the reference is rather cumbersome, we can use an abbreviated version in the body of our document and then place this complete reference in the bibliography.

Today, resource tools, such as Zotero, can help us keep track of our online references by pulling the entire contents, a snapshot of the first page, or at minimum, a link to it into one easily organizable and accessible database. In addition, Zotero will create a complete citation for us to insert into our documents following whatever style manual we use.

As a reminder of what needs to be credited within the body of a document, the rules are as follows: *All words or ideas of others and all copyrighted, published, or Web information* we use in our documents, if taken word for word and placed in quotation marks or if paraphrased (written in our own words), must have the references placed immediately after each idea, quotation, or paraphrased statement (parenthetically or with a note number). This citation refers to the complete source information—author, title, city, publisher, date, pages—in either the footnotes or endnote or in the bibliography entry at the end of the document.

We cite our sources for three primary reasons:

1. To acknowledge, give credit to the person(s) who discovered or originated the idea.
2. To show that we have done our homework and researched the topic carefully to see what others have had to say or write about it.
3. To allow our readers to find the source of the information.

Being careful to give proper credit—identifying a source of information as the source—is part of the integrity of the individual using the information. Not giving proper credit is considered plagiarism, a serious violation of ethical conduct in most cultures and a violation of copyright laws in most countries.

Proposals and Progress Reports

Since proposals and progress reports are two of the most common leadership communication reports with expected content that is specific to each, the following sections outline the typical contents with a discussion of each major section.

Proposals

A proposal can be written as a formal report with a letter of transmittal, an executive summary, and the like, or it may be presented as a formal letter. Whichever format is appropriate for the communication situation, a proposal will include the sections described in Exhibit 4.11.

Remember a proposal is a sales document designed to convince someone of an idea or approach, and even us. In addition, it is considered a legally binding document for the sender and the person receiving and accepting it, thus the need for an acceptance clause, which is often included at the end.

Progress Reports

Progress reports are common in professional settings. They may be presented formally as reports or more informally as memos or e-mails. They allow us to highlight progress on a project or task and, if appropriate, to showcase our work. They usually include the following sections:

1. Introduction.
2. Project description.
3. Work completed.
4. Work in progress.
5. Work remaining.
6. Overall appraisal of progress.

EXHIBIT 4.11
Proposal Contents

Section	Contents
1. Introduction	Sets the stage with a statement of the problem and background or establishes the context for the proposal by discussing appropriate company and industry background (more detailed background or industry research may belong in other parts of the document or in an appendix). The introduction should also include a general overview of the purpose of the proposal.
2. Needs and benefits	Provides a detailed discussion of the organization's current problem or issue and your assessment of its needs and then discusses how the proposed solution will meet the needs and be of value to the receiver.
3. Scope	Specifies the boundaries of your proposed work by answering the following questions: (1) What areas are included in the study and which are not? (2) What is the main focus of your work? (3) What specifically are you proposing to deliver?
4. Method and working relationship	Establishes your research methods or analytical approach with your plan for working with clients if appropriate. For example, do you plan to use a team and include members of the department or company on that team? The round-table document included in Chapter 4 includes an example of a team structure approach (Exhibit 4.3).
5. Task and time breakdown	Shows proposal phases and timing, specific tasks, deadlines, and responsibilities. Often a very detailed Gantt chart, Critical Path Method (CPM), or similar work plan is included in the appendix. Often includes a discussion of contingencies (other approaches or what you will do to keep on track if some "what ifs" occur).
6. Costs	States the fees or costs for completing the work. Often proposals will provide different approaches and price them on a scale from the highest to lowest cost.
7. Qualifications	Summarize your key background and experiences, profiling capabilities. A more detailed description of qualifications, such as descriptions of similar projects or evidence of special certifications, may be included in the appendix if necessary.
8. Acceptance clause	Requests a signature from the receiver to indicate acceptance of the proposal and agreement to pay if appropriate. An acceptance clause may appear at the end of a formal proposal or in the letter of transmittal.

A table often works best if the project consists of fairly simple tasks. It could be set up to include the following columns:

Task	Work Completed	Work in Progress	Work Remaining	Comments

Executive Summaries

Since the executive summary is so critical to a professional report, and since it is the section of the report that our readers will most likely read, it must accurately, yet concisely, summarize the major messages of the original document so that our readers understand the substance of our report without reading further. The executive summary is an independent document even though it includes only information discussed in the report. This independence means that, although it may contain a graph or other figure in support of the content, it should not reference graphs or figures in the body of the document.

Although an executive summary is typically no more than 10 percent of the length of the report, it may need to be longer to cover the content of the report adequately. It should include our major conclusions and recommendations and enough support to persuade our audience to accept both. The tone should be direct and the style concise without being too abbreviated. See Exhibit 4.12 for an example of an executive summary.

Formatting Written Communication Effectively

Formatting is important in creating a professional appearance for all of our written communication. It makes them accessible to our audiences and easier for them to read. Our goal with formatting is to create documents so that readers can easily skim them, find our key messages, and select what they want to read. The frequent use of headings and lists to break up the text, separate main ideas, and avoid long blocks of text will make our documents more inviting for the audience.

Effective headings show that we care about helping our audiences read what we have written. They can add to our ethos and to our ability to persuade our audiences, particularly if we use message headings to help pull our readers into our argument.

If we do not have a style guide to follow in our organization, then our documents should conform to the following business writing standards.

EXHIBIT 4.12 **Example of an Effective Executive Summary**

Executive Summary:
Determining the Relationship between CEO Compensation and Company Performance

In response to a request by Chris Moellar, President of Executive Recruiters (ER), Performance Consultants, Inc. (PCI) was hired to determine what measures Fortune 500 companies use to establish the compensation of their chief executives. In particular, Ms. Moellar wanted to know if the CEO's compensation correlates directly to the financial performance of the CEO's company.

Analytical Methods

To determine what drives the compensation of top executives, the PCI team selected CEOs from a representative sample of Fortune 500 companies. For these CEOs, we performed statistical analysis to determine whether CEO compensation is positively correlated to performance. The average compensation of the 100 CEOs in our study was $3.1 million, ranging from a low of $0.5 million to a high of $10 million. In assessing company performance, we used five-year return on investment (ROI) as our primary measure; the companies in our 100-company survey group reported a five-year average ROI ranging from ($.5) billion to $5 billion.

Performance Impacts Compensation

We found a definite relationship between the five-year ROI of a company and the total compensation that the CEO receives. Based on our analysis, the CEO compensation increases with every 10 percent increase in a company's ROI level (Exhibit 1). In addition, besides performance, we found only one other factor that significantly influences CEO compensation: age. The older the CEO, the more salary he or she received.

Exhibit 1 CEO Compensation Correlates Directly to Average Five-Year ROI

Recommendation

Based on PCI's findings, CEO compensation is directly related to company performance, but other factors, such as CEO age, also have an impact on compensation. Given our results, ER should continue to monitor company performance and use the 10 percent increments as the basis for your recommendations to your clients on compensation levels and on adjustments.

Layout

A letter or memo should follow the standard conventions illustrated in the sample letter and memo in Exhibits 4.5 and 4.6. Allow adequate margins, which usually means *at least* 1 inch on all sides. If we have letterhead, we will want to align the margins with it. We should never crowd the page, but we need to avoid placing only a sentence or two and a closing on the second page of a letter. Instead, we should go back and cut some words. Also, we need to avoid "widow" words, a single word at the end of a paragraph appearing on a line by itself.

A report format should be appropriate for the method of delivery to the audience. For instance, if it is to be bound, we will need to leave a larger left-hand margin. With all business correspondence and reports, we should allow plenty of white space for easy reading and a more attractive appearance.

Spacing and Alignment

Professional documents should be single-spaced with a double-space (the equivalent of a one-line gap) between the paragraphs and no indentation of the first line of the paragraph. Text should be fully aligned on the left but not on the right. Full alignment (or justification) causes gaps when the document is printed, making the text more difficult to read; therefore, we should avoid using it for letters, memos, e-mails, or reports. Many of the Microsoft Word templates for professional correspondence include full justification, so we have to override this format as the default. The only time to use full justification is in a brochure or other similar promotional material, which will be professionally typeset and printed.

The following table illustrates how to align text and how not to in professional correspondence and reports.

How Text Should Not Be Aligned: Fully Justified Right Edge	How Text Should Be Aligned: Ragged Right Edge
Text should be fully aligned on the left but not on the right. Full justification causes gaps when printed, making your text more difficult to read. Therefore, you should not use it for letters, memos, e-mails, or reports.	Text should be fully aligned on the left but not on the right. Full justification causes gaps when printed, making your text more difficult to read. Therefore, you should not use it for letters, memos, e-mails, or reports.

The spacing at the end of a sentence and the beginning of another depends on the style we are following; we can allow one or two spaces after the end mark, although skipping two spaces in correspondence and in most reports makes them easier to read. Microsoft Word lets users set as the default whichever spacing preferred, which makes it easy to be consistent and to follow personal preferences or the standards set by an organization for all written communication.

Font Type and Size

For legibility and case of reading in written communication, we need to use one of the traditional serif (the tails on letters) fonts:

Times New Roman

Palatino

Garamond

Times New Roman has become the preferred font and is used most frequently in business documents, but any of these will work in most cases.

The serifs help the eye move across the page, thus making pages of text easier to read; however, for charts in oral presentations and for brochures or other documents where the span of text is short, a sans serif font (such as Arial or Helvetica) is usually best. For online documents (e-mail, in particular), most people seem to prefer sans serif fonts, although experts are still debating which is better to use. Since screen resolution is poorer than the quality of hard-copy printouts of documents, the sans serif fonts are usually sharper and thus probably the better choice. On Web sites, we often see mixtures of fonts, with lengthy text inserts in a serif font and the titles and links in sans serif fonts.

The bottom line on fonts is to be consistent; in general, use serif fonts for correspondence and reports and sans serif for presentations and online correspondence.

A font size of 11 or 12 points is best for correspondence and reports. A smaller size is difficult to read and causes legibility problems when faxed, since faxes decrease the size of the type.

Headings

Headings are essential in all but the shortest of formal documents, and we should make frequent and logical use of them. The formatting of headings should conform to the standard expectations that govern the handling of headings, all of which reinforce the major rules of logic, consistency, and accessibility. Since the purpose of headings is to make it easier for the audience to access the information in written communication, we need to make all headings meaningful by capturing the "so what?"—the specific message of the text that follows. Headings should add to our written communication, not distract from it in any way.

The exact formatting varies from discipline to discipline, but traditional heading hierarchy generally follows formatting illustrated below:

Chapter or Other Major Heading
(bold, centered, may be a larger font)

First Subheading (flush left on a line by itself)

Text that follows the first subheading starts with a capital letter and appears one line below the heading.

Second Subheading (flush left with period after it). Text that follows the second subheading starts with a capital letter and appears on the same line.

1. Third Subheading. Period after it, the text would start two spaces after the period. Text that follows the third subheading starts with a capital letter and appears immediately after it.

In addition, make sure all the headings are grammatically parallel, using the same part of speech: for example, all nouns or all the same verb form, all infinitives (to + the verb constructions), all participles (*-ing* forms of the verb), or all command form verbs ("keep," "make," "use," etc.).

In professional documents, we rarely see all capital letters or large cap/small cap used in headings, since it makes the text more difficult to read and takes up more space on the page. In addition, underlining is used very sparingly; instead, most people use **bold** when they want to draw attention to a word or statement. Underlining cuts off the lower portion of letters, reducing the graphic appeal of the document, and suggests a hyperlink that may not exist.

All caps and underlining are both remnants from the days of typewriters, when people had fewer options to distinguish their text and headings, so in addition to making the text more difficult to read, they make it look rather old-fashioned.

The following examples illustrate the problems created by using all caps and underlining:

ALL CAPS SHOULD BE AVOIDED IN HEADINGS AND TEXT

AND SO SHOULD LARGE CAPS/SMALL CAPS

Stay Away from Underlining Completely, Since

Using It Cuts Off the Bottom of Descending Letters

Although computers make it easy to format text—allowing us to vary font size, style, and color—it is usually better to maintain the same style of font throughout a document. For example, we usually would not mix Arial font, or a similar sans serif font, with Times Roman, or a similar serif font, in correspondence or reports, although we might mix them in a brochure or Web site.

Instead of mixing font styles, we should use bold and increase the size of the font:

Avoid Mixing Font Styles	Use Bold or Larger Font Instead
Advantages (Arial)	**Advantages** (Times Roman 14)
Cost Advantages (Times Roman)	Cost Advantages (Times Roman 12)

Finally, the heading does not take the place of the text, just as a subject line does not take the place of an opening statement of purpose in an e-mail or a memo. We should start our discussion as if the heading were not there.

How Not to Use Headings	How to Use Headings
Nontransplant program: This program will use only dialysis treatment. Maximum transplant program: This option is the most cost-efficient and practical in my opinion.	**Nontransplant program.** The nontransplant program will use only dialysis treatment. **Maximum transplant program.** The maximum transplant program is the most cost-efficient and practical.

To summarize, when using headings, follow the principles listed here:

Principles for Creating and Formatting Headings

1. Keep headings short, meaningful, and consistent in style.
2. Make sure that all headings are parallel—the same part of speech.
3. Use the same font used in the rest of the section, but make it bold, larger, or centered.
4. Be consistent in handling capitalization (either initial cap each major word or only the first word; avoid capitalizing every letter).
5. Avoid underlining headings.

Remember, format a report for accessibility and appearance. Use headings to label the sections so that readers can find them with ease and the document looks good. Companies or disciplines may have style sheets or templates that dictate the format. If not, follow the guidelines discussed here and make sure the headings are logical and consistent and accomplish the overall purpose of making the document accessible to the reader.

Lists

Lists are formatted using bullets or numbers. One rule of thumb on the use of bullets is with more than five items in a list, we need to use numbers, since they make it easier for the reader to keep track. Punctuating the items depends on the logic of what we have written or on aesthetics; there are no hard-and-fast rules. We should aim for some form of consistency, but even that is not always necessary in a longer document. Some lists treat items as separate units, while others treat items as grammatical units.

Two Examples of Separate Item Lists

A proposal contains the following sections:
1. Introduction
2. Needs and Benefits
3. Costs

or

A proposal contains the following sections:
- Introduction
- Needs and Benefits
- Costs

A Sample List with Items Treated as Grammatical Units

A proposal contains
1. An introduction,
2. A section on needs and benefits, and
3. A section on costs.

Note that there is no colon after the word "contains," before the list. A colon should be avoided between the introduction to a list and the list unless the introduction is a complete sentence and includes the object of the verb, as in the following two examples. Keep the items grammatically parallel, introducing each item with the same part of speech.

Incorrect Handling of Listed Items	Correct Handling of Listed Items
When writing a formal report, you should perform the following: 1. Draft the report. 2. Establishing the format. 3. Design of the graphics. 4. Publication of the report.	When writing a formal report, you should perform the following: 1. Draft the report. 2. Establish the format. 3. Design the graphics. 4. Publish the report.

If we use bullets instead of numbers, as we frequently do in leadership communication, the same guidelines apply. The previous list might appear as follows:

When writing a formal report, you perform the following:
- Draft the report.
- Establish the format.
- Design the graphics.
- Publish the report.

Placing periods at the end of each item is a matter of taste and appearance; just be consistent. Either place periods at the end of each item, or after none of them.

EXHIBIT 4.13
Example of Headings and Footers

Negotiating Across Cultures

Xxxxxxxxxxxxxxxxxxxxxxxxxxxxxxxxxxxxxxxxxx
xxxxxxxxxxxxxxxxxxxxxxxxxxxxxxxxxxxxxxxxxx
xxxxxxxxxxxxxxxxxxxxxxxxxxxxxxxxxxxxxxxxxx
xxxxxxxxxxxxxxxxxxxxxxxxxxxxxxxxxxxxxxxxxx
xxxxxxxxxxxxxxxxxxxxxxxxxxxxxxxxxxxxxxxxxx

Xxxxxxxxxxxxxxxxxxxxxxxxxxxxxxxxxxxxxxxxxx
xxxxxxxxxxxxxxxxxxxxxxxxxxxxxxxxxxxxxxxxxx
xxxxxxxxxxxxxxxxxxxxx

Xxxxxxxxxxxxxxxxxxxxxxxxxxxxxxxxxxxxxxxxxx
xxxxxxxxxxxxxxxxxxxxxxxxxxxxxxxxxxxxxxxxxx
xxxxxxxxxxxxxxxxxxxxx

William J. Barnett   Page X

Headers and Footers

Documents of more than one page should contain a header or footer containing identifying information, such as the subject or writer's name plus the page number. A longer report often has both a header and a footer. Usually, one carries the name of the entire document and the other the section heading and page number, and sometimes the date. Again, we need to follow the standard guidelines of our discipline or the style guide of our organization. The following example of a page from a report is typical of the layout you will find in many organizations (Exhibit 4.13).

Written communication of all types is integral to leadership communication. We spend much of our day writing and reading text messages, blogs, e-mails, memos, letters, and various types of reports. This chapter has provided guidelines to help leaders become more proficient and more effective in creating documents of every sort.

The checklist in Exhibit 4.14 will help in reviewing our own writing to ensure the content, structure, and formatting are effective.

EXHIBIT 4.14
Reviewing Your Own Written Communication

Content
Opening
❐ "So what?" subject line (text, e-mail, memo)
❐ Clear, specific context in the opening
❐ Clearly stated purpose for writing
❐ Specific foreshadowing statement
Body of Discussion
❐ Specific, meaningful content to support each major point
❐ No breakdowns in logic
Closing
❐ Appropriate closing in last paragraph
❐ Contact information and/or next steps established in last paragraph

Structure and Format
❐ Well organized logical, coherent
❐ Adequate transitions between sentences and paragraphs
❐ Effective formatting, following professional standards for the medium used
❐ No globby (long) paragraphs
❐ "So what?" headings
❐ Effective use of lists and/or bullets

When using this checklist with the checklist in Exhibit 3.9 in Chapter 3, we have a very complete approach to reviewing our written communication from the details of language to the structure to the broader content and formatting covered here.

**Application 4.1
E-mail Subject
Line Exercise**

Read the following four scenarios and write a brief and complete e-mail subject line for each.

1. You are working on the budget for next year, and members of your department met last week to discuss all the changes. You need each member to provide you with his or her budget figures so that you can roll up the various subaccounts. The budget is due tomorrow, and you really need the members' input by 4:00 p.m. so that you will have time to complete your part of the work.

2. To streamline the processing of expense reports, your accounting office has adopted new software that will enable employees to scan receipts. The new software also streamlines the categorization of expenses and totals each category automatically. Employees should have their reimbursements more quickly and you will save hours in staff time. The new software is a bit tricky, though, and you need employees to come to one of three training sessions so that they will know how to use it. All sessions will be held over lunchtime, with the first on Tuesday, one on Thursday, and one next Monday.

3. Your company recently adopted and rolled out a new benefits plan. After the rollout, you received word that there is one new addition that was not included in your materials: a child care advisory service that helps employees locate quality, affordable child care for their family. You want to let the employees know about this new feature.

4. You are the head of the Information Technology Division, and your company will be implementing a new enterprise resource planning system company-wide over the coming weekend. Bringing the system online will entail a significant effort by your team together with the consultants, and you will need to shut down the system at 5:00 p.m. on Friday to get started. Since many people in your company work until 6:00 or 6:30 p.m., even on Fridays, and sometimes come in on the weekend, you need to inform everyone of the necessity to shut down the system at 5:00 p.m. on Friday. You believe this will enable your team to finish by mid-day on Saturday, with time to test and troubleshoot the system before Monday.

Source: Developed by Beth O'Sullivan, Rice University, March 2004. Used with permission.

**Application 4.2
Writing E-mails**

The Case: Refinery Managers Face Budget Challenges
You work for a major international petroleum company, and you find yourself in a difficult position. As the budget coordinator for a large business unit made up of several key refineries, you have noticed that costs are rising so quickly that the refinery sites may soon become uncompetitive.

To begin getting costs under control, your team analyzes the budget and finds that a major component of refinery costs consists of an "overhead" allocation of costs from site services managers, as opposed to direct refinery costs. The site services managers provide an array of critical services to each refinery, such as central maintenance, storehouse services, security, HSE (health, safety, and environmental) services, human resources, and training/development services. The costs of these services across the full business unit's refineries are combined in a centralized cost center; that cost is subsequently allocated among the various refineries that use these services.

Your team knows that you must find a way to cut these allocated costs, so you decide to hold a meeting to talk with the site services managers about the budget and how it can be reduced so that each refinery can maintain a competitive advantage as a site. Of course, it is also important that refinery operations are safe and secure, so all of the services provided play an important role in the successful operation of the refineries. However, you need to find out from the site services managers what items can be cut or reduced while minimizing the impact on people and assets at the business unit level; if certain items in the site services budget are true necessities, you need to have more information about what makes them critical to the business.

You have no direct control over the site services managers, although a component of their annual bonus comes from how well the various refineries perform, so you should think carefully about how you will ask them for information.

The Assignment

Draft an e-mail to the site services managers scheduling a meeting to discuss the budget (alternatively, you may choose to create a meeting request). Since you have no direct supervisory control, it will do little good to demand cuts; in fact, a demand to cut the budget might result in the loss of a service that matters most to you! Therefore, consider your strategy and your persuasive approach carefully as you prepare the e-mail. You may also consider whether to use a direct or an indirect approach to the memo. Remember to craft a clear and complete subject line for the memo, provide all the information they need to attend the meeting, and close with the next steps or how to contact you for further information.

In addition, consider what you might want to send to your audience to help prepare them for the meeting. Include a list of the attachments you would include with this e-mail, along with a brief explanation of why you would include each one.

Source: Developed by Beth O'Sullivan, Rice University, March 2004. Updated by Sandra Elliot, May 2009. Used with permission.

**Application 4.3
Creating an
Executive
Summary**

The Case: Merging Benefits at Huge Computer Company

Two major high-tech companies, Huge Co. (HC) and Computer Co. (CC), have recently merged to form Huge Computer Company (HCC) and are now starting to combine the operations of both. A key issue of the integration has been how to treat the benefit and retirement plans from the two companies—in particular, how to blend the plans for the software engineers, who are key to the continued success of the new company. Read the following case and write an executive summary of your key findings for the partner of the Human Resources Consulting firm.

Two Companies—Two Cultures

HC has been an industry leader for the past 20 years in both hardware and software. HC is a large company, with an employee base of about 22,000 in four countries. Its corporate culture is relatively formal: HC does things "by the book." About 3,500 software engineers work for HC, and all operate out of the Silicon Valley offices. The average tenure among the software engineers is 10 years. HC redesigned the software engineers' benefits package 2 years ago, based on their research in industry best practices. HC spends about $20,000 per employee on annual benefits but has done no surveys to determine employee satisfaction with the new benefit plan.

CC is a young software company headquartered in Austin, Texas. CC is known for its leading-edge developments and has risen to the top over the last seven years. In fact, *CORP. Magazine* recently recognized CC as one of the "Top 100 Companies to Work For in the U.S." Its corporate culture still has a casual, collegiate feel and its business practices are highly flexible, stressing the need for creativity and innovation. CC has about 8,000 employees, including 2,000 software engineers. Gaining access to those engineers was one of the key reasons for the merger. CC spends about $26,000 per employee on annual benefits. CC has had essentially the same benefits package for six out of its seven years of existence.

A Consulting Team Gathers Information on Benefits

Although technically the two companies have been combined into one company, they are still operating independently and are just starting to combine their workforces. The COO of the new entity has hired your consulting firm to assess the current plans of both companies. It is her goal to develop a blended system that represents the best features of both benefit plans and a plan that will be well received by software engineers in both groups.

To learn more about the retirement and benefits plans at both companies, your team decides to interview HR managers and departmental managers at both companies. For both HC and CC, you want to gather information on the following topics:

- The strengths and weaknesses of current benefits programs and areas for possible improvements.
- An assessment of how well the current plan meets the needs of the software engineers.
- Each company's perceptions of the plans of the other company.
- Key areas software engineers will be concerned about regarding the adoption of a common benefits plan.

Your team holds several interviews, from which you gain managers' perceptions and information on both of the existing plans. Notes from two interviews are included here.

Notes from the Interview of the Computer Co. Benefits Manager

Date: February 17, 2010

Interview Objective: Obtain the CC manager's perspective on the merger of benefit plans between HC and CC and on the perceived strengths and weaknesses of both

Interviewee: Mariel Salinas, Benefits Manager at CC

Interviewers: Two of your team members

Background: The benefits manager, Mariel Salinas, has six years of experience in human resources and joined CC three years ago. Her previous employer was a cutting-edge advertising agency, and she feels that the way CC treats its employees is very consistent with what she experienced at her former job. Both industries depend on their "human capital" to achieve success; rewarding creativity and independence is critical to the company's performance.

When Mariel came to CC, she initiated a benchmarking study to review the hiring and benefits practices of the top 50 technology companies to familiarize herself with the industry. She also discovered that CC is way above average on granting stock options and way below average on employer contributions to 401K plans. In addition, the results showed that CC has earned a reputation as one of the top 100 best working environments in the country because of flexible hours and benefits options.

Quotes from the interview:

About Benefits at CC

"Our company is comprised primarily of younger workers. They focus more on perks like vacation packages, on-site concierge, and the company fitness center. They aren't really worried about retirement packages, dental insurance, or life insurance."

"To meet our employees' diverse needs, we use a 'cafeteria plan' approach. That means we supply an à la carte system of point-based options. Employees can distribute their points to the categories of benefits that appeal to them. As a result, every employee has a different benefits package, but the dollar values are consistent."

"I think one of the weaknesses of our benefits and retirement program is the lack of long-term focus on retirement. The interests of our employees would be better served if they were a little more focused on their future."

"Several employees have complained that our vision plan doesn't include Lasik eye correction surgery, but you know, I think that's over the top. I'm not sure that we should focus too much of our attention on that sort of thing, or we'll soon be paying for all kinds of cosmetic surgery!"

About Benefits at HC

"HC was included in a benchmarking study that we did, but that was three years ago. And they have revamped their benefits program since then."

Notes from the Interview of the Computer Co. Benefits Manager (continued)

"When we did the study, the problems HC had were tremendous. In fact, I think they may have revamped the system when they got the benchmarking data. The worst part of their program was how it didn't even begin to compete with the other benefits packages. In fact, if their employee base wasn't so old and set in their ways, they would surely have moved on to a different company by now. . . . "

"No, I guess I'm not too familiar with their current system. I've heard rumors, but I don't really know how it works. I guess the strength of their program is that it must work for their people. Retention at HC is very good. But their employee base has such a different demographic from our software engineers."

On Merging the Benefits

"I am very concerned that the people in charge might decide to use HC's benefits system, since they have so many more employees than we currently have on our system. And I'm guessing that their program is less expensive. The problem is that our system is so much better. It's nationally recognized as being progressive and friendly to our employees. But since HC recently redid their program, we'll probably get stuck with their way of doing things."

"I think the employees are most concerned that the merger is going to rob them of the innovation and flexibility they've come to expect around here. In addition, I'm afraid that changing the benefits system will send a negative signal to our folks that the HC system and employees are more valuable in this merger relationship. I anticipate a huge attrition problem."

Notes from the Interview of the Huge Co. VP of Human Resources

Date:	February 17, 2010
Interview Objective:	Obtain the HC perspective on the merger of benefit plans between HC and CC and on the perceived strengths and weaknesses of both
Interviewee:	Adam Nagami, VP of Human Resources for HC
Interviewers:	Two of your team members

Background: Adam Nagami has been in the Human Resources business for 20 years, having started his career as a junior HR analyst at HC. He has "grown up" with the company and prides himself on keeping current with trends in HR. As the current VP of Human Resources, he directed the redesign of the HC benefit and retirement plan two years ago and feels that it is now an excellent plan. Although he did not survey the employees to assess their level of satisfaction with the plan, he based his changes and recommendations on industry "best practices" and what he felt was most appropriate for HC's employee base.

Notes from the Interview of the Huge Co. VP of Human Resources (continued)

Quotes from the interview:

About Benefits at HC

"Our employee base consists of mostly people in their late 30s and 40s. Many of them have families and are focused on having good health benefits. They also care about long-term savings and we have active participation in our 401K program."

"As you know, we revamped our benefits and retirement programs two years ago, and so far, I haven't heard any negative feedback from our employees, so I haven't spent the time or money to conduct any surveys, but let me tell you about a few key features."

"We use a standard cafeteria plan that allows a choice between two types of medical plans and choices on coverage for life insurance and dental. We've also recently added a flexible spending account option to our plan—this allows for pretax dollars to be set aside to reimburse employees for items not covered by our regular plan—for example, they can use it to reimburse themselves for out-of-pocket medical expenses or expenses the plan wouldn't ordinarily pay for, such as eyeglasses or Lasik surgery. They can also use it for dependent care—for their children or older relatives—so it offers lots of flexibility."

On Merging the Benefits

"I don't know much about the CC plan, although I know it is highly ranked. I think that CC's software engineers are a much younger group and that they don't care that much about life insurance or reimbursement for care of elderly parents, but I think the key here is to show them the flexibility we can offer and help educate them about planning for their future. As they start families, they might appreciate some of our benefits. The combined company will now have almost 30,000 employees, so we can expect to negotiate some real economies of scale with our providers. I think if we can convince the CC engineers that our way is best, the transition will go quite smoothly."

The Assignment

As the head of the consulting team, you need to brief the senior partner on your findings so that he can then meet with the COO at Huge Computer Company. You need to synthesize the information from the interviews, consolidate your key findings, and *develop a one-page executive summary* comparing the key features of the plans and making any observations or recommendations you have about merging the plans. Remember that the senior partner may or may not read your full report, so any key findings and your recommendations need to be easy to access and understand.

Source: Case and exercise developed by Deborah J. Barrett, Beth O'Sullivan, and Beth Peters, Rice University. Used with permission.

Application 4.4 Rhetorical Analysis of a Transformational Leader's Communication

To help you identify the language and writing that characterize transformational leaders, for this assignment, you are to select and analyze a speech or written communication created by a person you see as a transformational leader. The analysis should include the following:

1. Name of the speech (occasion) or document.
2. Audience for the speech or document (actual and implied, if appropriate).
3. Stated and implied purposes (if different from stated purpose).
4. Rhetorical strategies and techniques, such as the use of any of the following (provide examples from the speech or writing):
   a. Figurative language (similes, metaphors, symbols, imagery).
   b. Appeals (to emotions, logic, ethos).
   c. Logical fallacies.
5. Style (provide examples from the speech or writing).
   a. Clarity and conciseness.
   b. Use of language, word choices (diction).
   c. Passive or active voice.
   d. Simple or complex sentences; short or long sentences.
6. Visual strategies and tactics.
   a. Format (layout, headings, paragraph length, fonts, etc.).
   b. Use of images (photos, graphs, diagrams, etc.).
7. Oral strategies and tactics (for speeches).
   a. Music.
   b. Volume.
   c. Speech patterns (articulation, intonation, emphasis).
   d. Other sound effects.

The objective of this assignment is to help you appreciate a leader's use of language for rhetorical purposes (usually to argue a point of view or persuade others). You should select the speech or written document carefully to ensure that it has enough depth or substance to allow close reading and analysis. You should plan to read or listen to it several times, looking deeply at how the individual selects words, composes sentences, and organizes thoughts.

Application 4.5 Creating a Twitter Plan

Review the case study in Application 4.3. Imagine that you have briefed the senior partner on your findings and, in a somewhat radical move, she has asked you to help the company put its finger on the pulse of social media. Specifically, she has asked you to open a Twitter account through which you can start sharing the news of how the company is changing and improving and start tracking what others are saying. Your assignment is to create a Twitter plan, outlining the types of posts you will create and the expected timing of the posts. Also, include in the plan at least two samples of the kind of posts you think will be helpful in building HC's reputation in the industry.

You might find that Chris Brogan's "50 Ideas on Using Twitter" has some ideas you can use: www.chrisbrogan.com/50-ideas-on-using-twitter-for-business/.[19]

Notes

1. http://adamhcohen.com/facebook-retailer-study-october08/.

2. Fraser, M., and Dutta, S. (2009). Yes, CEOs should facebook and twitter, Forbes.com. www.forbes.com/2009/03/11/social-networking-executives-leadership-managing-facebook.html.

3. Fraser and Dutta (2009).

4. Fraser and Dutta (2009).

5. www.buildabetterblog.com/2009/04/business-blogging-tip-whats-the-blogs-purpose.html.

6. www.dailyblogtips.com/5-blogging-traps-you-need-to-avoid/.

7. www.problogger.net/archives/2006/01/12/9-ways-to-screw-up-your-professional-blog/.

8. Fraser and Dutta (2009).

9. http://mashable.com/2009/03/16/twitter-growth-rate-versus-facebook/.

10. www.boston.com/business/technology/articles/2008/07/07/hurry_up_the_customer_has_a_complaint/.

11. www.twitip.com/make-a-tweet-plan-to-get-the-most-from-twitter/.

12. Dodge, R. W. (1984). What to Report, as quoted in Houp, K. W., and Pearsall, T. E. *Reporting Technical Information.* New York: Macmillan, p. 85.

13. IDC White Paper (March 2007). *The Expanding Digital Universe: A Forecast of Worldwide Information Growth through 2010*, p. 7, Figure 7.

14. *Business Editors New York Business Wire*, May 28, 2003.

15. Alboher, M. (2008). E-mail at Work: Some Basics. *New York Times*, February 23, p. 1.

16. Leonard, D., and Gilsdorf, J. (2001). Big stuff, little stuff: A decennial measurement of executives' and academics' reactions to questionable usage elements. *Journal of Business Communication* 38, No. 4, 439–75. See more recent work on the influence on IM in particular: Tagliamonte, S. A., and Denis, D. (2008). Linguistic ruin? LOL! Instant messaging and teen language. *American Speech* 83, No. 1, pp. 3–33; and the research of Pam Takayoshi and Christina Haas of Kent State at http:fpdc.kent.edu/center/staff/hassTakayoshi.html.

17. www.gartner.com/it/page.jsp?id=507731.

18. For more guidance on e-mail, you may want to go to www.albion.com/netiquette/index.html. Virginia Shea's *Netiquette*, which she defines as "network etiquette, the do's and don'ts of online communication," was one of the first sources to provide rules of Internet communication; her site still remains one of best of the many that are now available.

19. www.chrisbrogan.com. Used with permission of the author.

Chapter 5

Leadership Presentations

A speech or talk should be the oral projection of your personality, experience, and ideas.

James C. Humes, *The Sir Winston Method: The Five Secrets of Speaking the Language of Leadership*

A speech is like a symphony. It can have three movements, but it must have one dominant melody.

Sir Winston Churchill

Chapter Objectives

In this chapter, you will learn to do the following:

- Plan your presentation, including developing a communication strategy.
- Prepare a presentation to achieve the greatest impact.
- Present effectively and with greater confidence.

The skills of a leader are clearest when he or she is speaking—whether informally, with a few people around a conference room table or in a virtual meeting, or formally, standing before a large group or sitting in a Webcast delivering a prepared presentation. Much of the 70 to 90 percent of the time that managers engage in communicating is spent in conversations or presentations, either talking to others one-on-one or speaking in groups or to groups. According to Eccles and Nohria in their book *Beyond the Hype: Rediscovering the Essence of Management*, "Through their speeches and presentations, managers establish definitions and meaning for their own actions and give others a sense of what the organization is about, where it is at, and what it is up to."[1]

Through public speaking, individuals provide the innovative ideas that lead to change, participate in the dialogue that makes the organization

EXHIBIT 5.1
The Three "P's"
Approach to
Presentation
Development and
Delivery

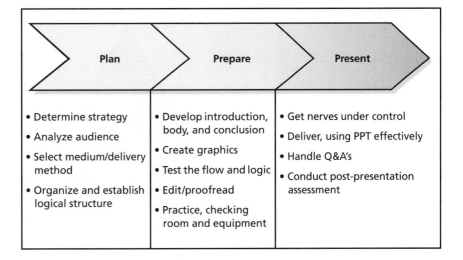

Plan	Prepare	Present
• Determine strategy	• Develop introduction, body, and conclusion	• Get nerves under control
• Analyze audience	• Create graphics	• Deliver, using PPT effectively
• Select medium/delivery method	• Test the flow and logic	• Handle Q&A's
• Organize and establish logical structure	• Edit/proofread	• Conduct post-presentation assessment
	• Practice, checking room and equipment	

grow, and bring attention to themselves and their abilities. As individuals move higher in the organization, their pronouncements become even more public and they spend greater amounts of time engaged in public speaking, whether internally to larger groups of employees or externally to the community. Therefore, leaders must master public speaking, becoming comfortable and confident in all kinds of presentation situations so that they project a positive ethos for themselves and their organizations.

This chapter applies the tools and techniques of previous chapters—determining the strategy, structuring communication coherently, and using language effectively—to the art of public speaking. The chapter will take you through each of the action steps in the Three "P's" process: planning, preparing, and presenting (Exhibit 5.1). The process provides an approach to developing presentations that will help you move through each step strategically so that you can deliver any type of presentation with confidence.

Planning a Presentation

In the planning phase of developing our presentation, we (1) determine our strategy, (2) analyze our audience, (3) select the medium and delivery method, and (4) organize and establish our logical structure.

Determining Strategy

Just as we clarify our purpose to write effectively, we need to define the purpose of our presentation clearly and specifically and develop a communication strategy using the communication strategy framework introduced in Chapter 2 and repeated below (Exhibit 5.2).

EXHIBIT 5.2
**Communication
Strategy
Framework**

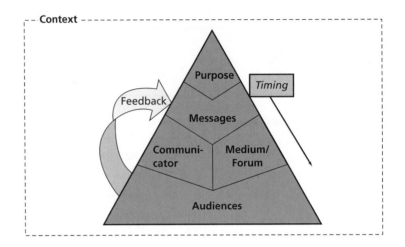

Context

In presenting, as in writing, we first need to consider the context for our presentation. What is most important about what is going on in our organization, in the local area or region, in our market or industry, or even on the broader stage—in the world—that will be first in the minds of our audience? There might be an event or something happening to which we might want to refer to help frame our presentation, or we might need to establish some background for our presentation to provide the context that the audience needs to understand our purpose. The more we can relate our presentation to what is on the minds of the audience, the more easily we will be able to garner their attention.

Purpose

We also need to establish a clearly defined purpose. What is most important for us to achieve in the presentation? What do we want our audience to do in response to what we say? These questions will lead us logically into the analysis of our audience.

Audience

The more we know about our audience, the more at ease we should be in presenting to them. At a minimum, for any presentation, we should be able to answer the following questions:

1. What is my primary purpose in delivering this presentation to this audience?
2. Who is my primary audience? Will there be secondary audiences affected by what I say?

3. What is motivating the audience to attend and how do I motivate them to listen to me?
4. What do I expect the audience to do as a result of hearing my presentation?
5. How do I expect them to feel?

Timing

We also need to consider the timing of the presentation. If, for example, we are presenting right after lunch, we may find our audience more challenging to engage. If we are first in the morning, we may need to deal with latecomers. If it is the end of the day, the audience's attention may be on leaving work for the day. Finally, if the presentation will be recorded and made available to others, the audience's attention will vary.

Feedback

We should think about obtaining feedback in all presentation situations so that we can measure our success in reaching the audience with our message and make adjustments in our presentation style or content if necessary. The first question is, is it feasible to obtain any feedback? And then the second is how best do we obtain it?

If we are face to face with our audience, we should be able to tell from their reaction to our presentation how they have received our message, but obtaining more structured feedback may be important as well. In fact, we may even want to build the feedback into our presentation by using audience response technology, which allows our audiences to respond in "real time." For example, many larger events make use of Twitter for real-time audience reaction, asking people to use a "hashtag" when posting about the presentation. Other such offerings, such as Poll Everywhere, use cell phones and IM technology to gather feedback. Such easily available audience response technology can be used in any setting—small meetings, large conferences, classrooms, and so forth—to determine opinions, measure understanding of concepts, obtain audience questions, or even conduct brainstorming.

Of course, the purpose of our presentation will shape the feedback. If, for example, we are presenting the quarterly performance to the board of directors, they will probably tell us what they think while we are presenting, and we will be able to discern their response by the questions they ask during and after the presentation. If we are presenting to analysts, they, too, will tell us how they feel about what we have said by their questions, and then we will see if we have succeeded in delivering our message by what they write.

If, on the other hand, we are delivering a presentation to a large group at a professional meeting or conference, the only feedback we receive might be the expressions on the faces of the listeners. This form of feedback is important and useful, however, and obtaining it requires our being actively enaged with our audience by establishing meaningful eye contact, which is important in all presentations, as discussed below.

Selecting the Medium and the Delivery Method

In developing a strategy for a presentation, we will choose from several options for the medium and the delivery method. Recognizing the advantages and disadvantages of each method helps in our selecting the right one for each situation (Exhibit 5.3). The presentation delivery methods compared here are assumed to be extemporaneous, a prepared presentation spoken without notes or text. It is very rare in professional situations to deliver a memorized presentation or to read a prepared speech, although occasionally speakers will read their presentations at technical conferences or use teleprompters at large trade shows and conventions.

The three most common types of professional presentations—the round-table, the stand-up presentation, and the impromptu—are discussed here.

Round-Table Presentations

The round-table presentation method has become increasingly popular for professional settings. Using this delivery method, we sit at the table with our audience and deliver a prepared document instead of standing up in front of our audience to deliver the presentation.

The typical round-table is an interactive exchange between the presenter and the audience. Round-table presentations encourage discussion and tend to be less formal than stand-up presentations, although they require as much or even more preparation on the part of the presenter. To deliver a round-table presentation effectively, we need to feel so comfortable with the content that the audience's questions, interruptions, or desire to jump to the end of the document do not throw us off course. Also, we must be very familiar with the content on each page so that we do not need to look down at it too much.

We select the round-table approach anytime we want to achieve one of the following:

1. Encourage an informal, interactive discussion.
2. Receive input from audience members.
3. Build consensus or gain agreement on conclusions or recommendation.

EXHIBIT 5.3 **Advantages and Disadvantages of Each Delivery Method for Oral Communication**

Delivery Method	Advantages	Disadvantages
Stand-up without visuals	• Allows flexibility in delivery of content • Makes you appear confident • Makes it easier to connect with audience and establish rapport	• Requires careful preparation and comfort with content • Means keeping close track of timing, particularly if questions are allowed
Round-table	• Allows for interactive discussion • With printed presentation pack, appeals to auditory and visual audiences • Makes it easier to establish real contact with audience	• Makes it more difficult to control flow of discussion • Seems more informal than stand-up presentation • Presents some delivery challenges
Stand-up with computer projection	• Allows some flexibility of delivery • Provides visuals to support your messages • Appeals to both oral and visual audience preferences	• Calls for comfort with the technology and creates dependence on it • Requires backup plan • Makes it harder to keep audience focused on you
Stand-up with overheads	• Allows some flexibility of delivery • Provides visuals to support your messages • Appeals to both oral and visual audience preferences	• Seems old-fashioned • Limits what you can do with graphics • Poses some potential technical problems
Stand-up with flipcharts/white boards	• Offers complete flexibility • Encourages discussion • Eliminates technical problems • Allows easy recording of audience contributions	• Takes presenter away from audience when writing on boards • Makes presenter appear less prepared • May be difficult to read
Videoconferencing	• Allows interaction across time and space • With chart pack, can appeal to auditory and visual audiences	• Delays in voice transmission cause some distraction • Limits what you can do with visual aids • Makes it difficult to establish rapport • Poses potential technical problems
Phone conferencing (conference call)	• Allows interaction across time and space	• Limits what you can do with visual aids • Makes it difficult to build rapport • Causes loss of body language cues
Webcast	• Allows interaction across time and space • Allows for a variety of visual aids • Can be used to foster collaboration • Easy to gather feedback	• Limits audience interaction and eliminates visual cues • Relies heavily on presenter's vocal skills • Can feel impersonal • Audience easily distracted

4. Check the accuracy of facts or identify sources of missing facts.

5. Uncover and resolve major issues.

6. Present a lot of information in a short amount of time.

Delivering a Round-Table Presentation

Most of the principles that apply to stand-up presentations also apply to round-table discussions, but round-table presentations differ in the handling of the materials and in the delivery:

1. We hand out the presentation pack to the group before we start, which means we will need to control the situation by guiding the audience through the pack and by keeping them focused on the page we want to discuss.

2. Since the audience has a printed copy of the presentation in front of them, we can usually place more information on a page than we would with an overhead or computer-projected presentation, although we need to be careful not to overcrowd the page.

The delivery of a round-table presentation should follow the same guidelines used for any good presentation; however, we need to be even more aware of the importance of establishing and maintaining eye contact. It is very easy when sitting at a table with a document in front of us to look down instead of up, so we need to make sure we are so well prepared that we do not need to look down at the page after turning to it. We should be looking up and at our audience most of the time.

When we deliver a round-table presentation, the following guidelines will help to control the pace and flow of the discussion:

1. Direct the audience to the specific page.

2. State the major message of the exhibit (which should be captured in the chart title).

3. Explain any legends, symbols, abbreviations, or acronyms.

4. Guide the audience through any complex diagrams or graphs.

5. Allow the audience time to scan the page.

6. Be flexible and responsive to the discussion.

7. Provide transition before turning to the next page.

8. Watch own body language and be sensitive to theirs.

Whenever we deliver a round-table presentation, we need to be very careful to give our audience enough time to skim the page, and be alert to their body language. If they need time to think about what we have given them, we should not feel that we must keep talking: Silence is OK. In fact, in many cultures, it is expected and valued. Finally, we need to remember that we want to encourage discussion and welcome questions as we present.

Formatting a Round-Table Presentation Handout

The round-table presentation pages resemble the slides in a stand-up presentation except for the following:

1. The pages are numbered; otherwise, you would not easily be able to tell people which page you were discussing.
2. The page may contain more information than a slide for a stand-up presentation.
3. A smaller font (even 12-point) is appropriate.

We may elect to use a chart pack with only the graphs included, but it is usually better to create an entire presentation, with cover page, agenda, and appropriate text, as well as the graphs, since people often pick up the packs without having the opportunity to hear the presentation. The round-table presentation pack should be complete enough that anyone picking it up will understand the main messages. Exhibit 5.4 demonstrates selected pages from a typical round-table presentation pack.

Stand-Up Extemporaneous Presentations

One of the most popular delivery methods for professional presentations is still the stand-up extemporaneous presentation. It can be the most effective form of presentation if structured and delivered correctly. Stand-up extemporaneous presentations offer four major advantages over any other method. They allow us to

1. More easily control the flow of the presentation.
2. Maintain eye contact and rapport with our audience.
3. Make adjustments based on the audience's response.
4. Appear confident and knowledgeable.

Delivering effective extemporaneous presentations means speaking without relying on external promptings, such as reading from our computers or from notes. We must resist the temptation to memorize the presentation or to write everything down because, if we do, we will sound unnatural and will be unable to adjust easily, should we need to vary the presentation. On the other hand, we also need to resist the other extreme of not having any notes because, no matter how experienced we are, we may need to refer to them for supporting information or numbers.

In most presentation settings today, we will have our laptop computer in front of us with the audience seeing a projected presentation on a large screen behind us. This arrangement allows us to face our audience but glance at our laptop without breaking eye contact for more than a few seconds. We do not want to look at our laptop screen too much, however, since doing so will decrease our eye contact with

EXHIBIT 5.4   Selected Pages from a Typical Round-Table Presentation Pack

**Establishing a Marketing Plan
for Brown & Peterson**

Round-Table Discussion Proposal
Presented by
L&B Consulting Firm

February 15, 2010

Today's Discussion

❒ Our understanding of the current situation

❒ Study objectives and proposed approach

❒ Suggested team structure and our capabilities

❒ Outstanding questions and next steps

2

**Our Understanding of Your
Current Situation**

❒ Offices in Houston; Dallas; Los Angeles;
London; Paris

❒ Three primary practices: litigation, business,
and government

❒ Specializing in areas such as energy, taxation,
labor and employment, corporate, real estate,
and finance

❒ Brown & Peterson (B&P), along with its peers,
is caught in the transition in the legal profession
from no marketing or self-promotion to need
to establish marketing campaign and
public profile   3

**The Largest Law
Firms by Revenue**

$ Millions

Brown &
Peterson

Davis &
Jimenez $67   Johnson
$92   & Smith
                $243
        $177
Kramer $231
& Mattee   James &
                                Connelly

Source: *Lawyer Reports*, July 7, 2009.   4

(continued)

our audience and make us appear less confident. If a laptop or similar smaller computer screen is not available for us to see but we have a podium or table nearby, we will probably want to print out our presentation in handout version of two to six slides per page. That way we can glance down to see where we are, yet not have to turn the page each time we change slides.

Impromptu Presentations

Many of the presentations we deliver in a professional setting are impromptu, which means we are called on to deliver them without

EXHIBIT 5.4   (continued)

Success factors

❑ Total revenue

❑ Number of attorneys

❑ Courtroom wins

❑ Recognition for speaking and writing

❑ Membership on law school faculties

❑ Bar pass rates and percentile rankings

❑ Ability to attract and retain top recruits

How do you leverage your critical success factors to build corporate reputation?

5

Project Objectives

❑ Obtain a better understanding of B&P's competitive market

❑ Establish profile of B&P's current image, reputation, and market perception

❑ Determine the firm's value proposition, other key messages, and target audiences

❑ Develop a marketing communication plan and materials to reach target audiences

❑ Define ongoing communication needs

Establish and maintain a highly respected, recognizable public image for B&P

6

Summary of Proposed Approach

Areas of focus	Competitive analysis	Brand identity/image research	Niche capability building	Ongoing communication
Action items	• Identify competitors • Establish benchmarking criteria • Perform basic competitive research • Develop survey • Conduct surveys • Assess promotional materials	• Profile current image/market perception • Identify gaps • Determine value proposition and messages • Identify audiences	• Define practice area capabilities • Create materials to illustrate niche capabilities • Identify niche audiences	• Determine communication marketing needs • Link plan with other initiatives • Define individual communication responsibilities • Establish ongoing communications program
		• Develop communication plan • Create marketing materials • Establish media campaign • Identify other public relations opportunities		
Timing:	October–November	December–February		February–March

10

Potential Team Structure and Responsibilities

Steering Committee
• Managing Partners
• X Consulting Firm

• Guides strategy development
• Ensures link to firm's strategy

Team Leaders

B&P Team • Partners • Associates • PR Director	Core Team (L&B) • Deborah Davis • Kelly Jones • Michael Smith	Additional Resources • Other partners • B&P personnel • Other specialists
• Provides information • Works with Core Team on plan	• Manages process • Performs analysis • Develops plan • Creates materials	• Supplies additional information and expertise

Project Team

11

Questions

❑ Will we have access to previous relevant research, such as the X Consulting Firm findings?

❑ How accessible will partners and associates be for interviews and fact finding research?

❑ Will B&P be able to free up resources to participate in team problem solving?

❑ How much in the way of promotional materials has already been completed?

❑ What will a successful strategic corporate image campaign look like in your eyes?

14

Immediate Next Steps

❑ Determine B&P's success factors

❑ Establish scope of competitive analysis and benchmarking

❑ Identify target audiences

❑ Develop interview guides and targets

❑ Collect all previous research and complete gathering of promotional materials

❑ Assemble the B&P team

❑ Formally launch the engagement

15

much, if any, warning. For example, we may find ourselves in the elevator with a superior who asks how the project we are leading is coming along. This is the classic "elevator speech," in which we only have the time the elevator takes to go between floors to answer the question.

We can prepare for these kinds of encounters by making frequent mental or written notes of the project status, noting the major messages of greatest interest to our audiences. Essentially, we prepare ourselves for the elevator speech by anticipating that it will occur and periodically formulating the key message—the "so what?"—to convey the status of the project, the preliminary findings, or a brief summary of the analysis.

Of course, at times, we are called on to speak impromptu without benefit of any preplanning or strategizing. In those cases, the following techniques will help you perform more effectively:

1. Do not rush into speaking. Take a deep breath and gather your thoughts. A few seconds of silence will not bother anyone, not even in virtual presentations.
2. If appropriate, start by giving your name or by saying something informal to break the ice, such as a positive comment about the surroundings or the people joining the Webcast.
3. If appropriate, refer to something that a previous speaker said, but again be positive.
4. Think very simply of the primary message you want to deliver and isolate only a couple of supporting topics.
5. State your message and your supporting topics before you dive into details, and then go back at the end and repeat the main points.

We will become more comfortable with impromptu presentations the more we do them, so we should practice them frequently even if it means creating a bunch of topics, putting them in a bag or an envelope, and drawing one out daily in our own office or at home (see the impromptu exercise at the end of this chapter for a few suggested practice topics).

Establishing a Logical and Effective Structure and Format

The organization, or structure, of a presentation proceeds from the needs and interests of the audience, our purpose, and the demands of the subject matter. When we start to outline or map out our presentation, we will refer first to the analysis of our audience to determine the most effective structure. We need to ask ourselves the following questions:

1. Do we want to start with our recommendation and then present the data to support it (direct approach)?
2. Do we want to present the facts and lead to the conclusion (indirect approach)?

In most situations, it works best to state the conclusions or recommendations first and then provide the supporting data; however, if the culture would expect a more indirect approach or our audience will be resistant to our conclusions or recommendations, then we may want to build our argument by presenting the evidence first. We need to think carefully about which pattern will work best with this audience. Then, we consider the nature of our subject matter and our overall purpose to develop a logical structure for the body of our presentation that will appeal most effectively to our audience.

Also, if we are presenting on a controversial topic and some audience members are opposed to our view or approach, we will want to prepare a refutation and place it either in the body of the presentation or at the beginning. To ignore the opposition completely may cause some to question our objectivity and the validity of our analysis.

Although it is usually better to work the refutation into the body, if we know our audience may be so focused on the opposition to our argument that they will not listen to anything we have to say, we may want to address it in our opening. However, we will not want to spend too much time on the refutation in the introduction, since doing so could sidetrack the audience from our major argument. Another option is to leave any mention of opposing views to the Q&A, but although no one may bring it up, we need to be prepared if they do. By leaving the opposing views to the the Q&A, we risk someone making so much of the opposition that it weakens our argument.

As we map out our preliminary plans for the organization of the presentation, we need to keep in mind that, in a speech, the audience cannot go back and look at the preceding message, as they can in a document. We thus need to make sure that each point is logically related to the ideas that precede it and the information that follows and that we use adequate, even obvious, transitions from point to point. Also, in a presentation we need to use repetition more than we would in writing, particularly in the body and conclusion, since an audience's memory is short and attention span fleeting.

In the initial stage of creating and organizing a presentation, we need to establish the format, and since most presentations routinely use PowerPoint templates, we should select one that meets our needs and helps support our message. In fact, we may want to create a ghost pack—a pack that establishes the format and contains the slides we think we are going to use, even if only an idea exists at this point. A ghost pack can be particularly useful for a team because the team can easily assign each section or chart to a specific team member. The storyboard in Chapter 2 serves as an example of a ghost pack (Exhibit 2.11). The ghost pack establishes the format and layout as well as the preliminary outline for the presentation.

Preparing a Presentation to Achieve the Greatest Impact

After we have analyzed our audience, developed our communication strategy, and determined the overall structure, we are ready to start preparing the presentation. The preparation consists of developing the introduction, body, and conclusion; creating the graphics; testing the flow and logic; editing and proofreading; and practicing.

Developing the Introduction, Body, and Conclusion

Modern expectations for good presentations have not changed that much from the expectations of the past. What the ancient Greeks taught about the introduction, the body, and the conclusion is as applicable today as then—in fact, maybe even more applicable, considering our short attention spans and poor listening habits.

Therefore, for almost every presentation, skilled presenters follow this traditional rule:

Tell them what you are going to tell them.

Tell them.

Then, tell them what you have told them.

If the presentation is very, very short, we may be able to avoid repeating our topics at the beginning and the end; however, doing so is always helpful for our audience. For a longer presentation, it is essential for the audience to hear the messages repeated. Most audiences will pay more attention to the introduction—particularly if we provide a hook (that is, something that captures their attention and establishes what is in it for them) and to the conclusion than to the middle or body (Exhibit 5.5). In a longer presentation, we want to keep reminding the audience of our main arguments and drive them home strongly in the conclusion. We can be sure we will gain the full attention of every listener when we utter the magic words "And in conclusion."

The Introduction

The introduction to our presentation starts as soon as we stand up and start walking to the podium or front of the room. We will want to take

EXHIBIT 5.5
Audience's
Attention in a
Presentation

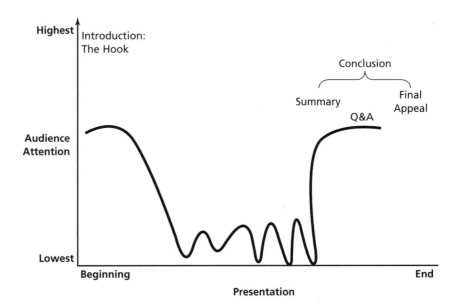

command of ourselves and the situation the moment we stand up, and we need to be aware that our posture and the way we carry ourselves will affect the audience's perception of us before we even start to speak.

After we have established our presence in front of the room, we will want to arouse interest and create a positive atmosphere for the presentation. Numerous options exist for how to start a presentation. We can start with a fact, a quotation, an example, an -anecdote, a question, or a reference to the occasion or something else in the context of the presentation. We can start with humor if it is appropriate to the occasion and if we are absolutely sure it will not offend anyone. It is usually better, though, to tell a humorous anecdote rather than a joke.

What we do not want to do is joke about our subject or apologize for being unprepared; it destroys our credibility and diminishes everything that we say afterward. We should be prepared, or we should not be there. We need to remember that we are addressing fellow human beings with similar interests and problems who have come to hear us because they expect us to say something meaningful. We want to start quickly, get to the point, and establish a positive relationship with our audience.

We should introduce our overall message and each of our supporting topics, saying something like "I am going to cover (1), (2), and (3)." Then, we can discuss each of these supporting points in order and say in the conclusion "I have covered (1), (2), and (3)." For the opening to a presentation, remembering the CPF acronym is again helpful:

C = Context—What is the impetus for the presentation? What surrounds it that could influence it?

P = Purpose—Why am I delivering this presentation? What is my reason?

F = Foreshadowing—What is coming in this presentation and in what order? What should the audience expect to hear as they listen to it?

If we used the Pyramid Principle or wrote out a storyboard, we should have a tight, logical story that flows easily from slide to slide. We can test the presentation logic by creating a one-sentence summary that includes our overall message and supporting topics. If we can create a meaningful, logical sentence, then we probably have a logical story to tell. This story will serve as the guide to the creation of our agenda slide for the presentation.

If using visual aids, such as slides, we can use them to help cue the audience to the structure and main messages of our presentation. In addition to telling them what we will discuss, we will show the audience an agenda or a today's discussion slide or, if appropriate for our topic, the framework or model around which our presentation is organized.

The agenda page may be a few bullet points of the main sections of the presentation. The agenda page could be a list of topics or it could capture our story, which we will present using a narrative structure. Our first bullet would summarize the current situation, the next one or two would discuss the complication, and the last would suggest a resolution. Even if our agenda slide does not actually contain this story word for word , the audience should at least be able to determine what the story is by looking at our bullet points.

An agenda, or setup, slide should be concise but meaningful. Our agenda slide should not contain a list of all of our slide topics; such a laundry list suggests a poorly organized presentation. Also, we should avoid using the following words as bullet points on our agenda: "Introduction," "Conclusion," and "Questions." These take up space without communicating anything to our audience. Every bullet should capture a "so what?" Exhibit 5.6 shows the dos and don'ts of agenda pages.

The Body

The body of the presentation, which usually accounts for 80 percent, should be concise and focused. The effective presenter will follow a storyboard or similar outline or plan, judiciously selecting the main points and being careful not to overwhelm the audience with too much

EXHIBIT 5.6   Examples of Agenda Pages for a Presentation

How Not to Do an Agenda	How to Do an Agenda
Today's Agenda	**Today's Agenda**
■ Introduction ■ Understanding of current situation ■ Competitive analysis ■ Niche capabilities ■ How you measure your success ■ Project objectives ■ Overview of approach ■ Proposed approach ■ Team Structure ■ Next steps ■ Conclusion ■ Q & A	■ Understanding of current situation ■ Project objectives and approach ■ Team structure and our capabilities ■ Next steps

detail. Keep in mind that our audiences only want to see what is relevant to them and, in some cases, what we can do for them. Beware of anything in the presentation to which the audience can say, "So what?" Elaborate on each main point with specific examples or explanations accompanied by graphics when appropriate (see Chapter 6 for information on when and how to use graphics effectively).

Throughout the presentation, we will want to provide transitions to lead from one topic to the next and one graphic to the next and make sure that our presentation is so well organized and logical that, when we move from topic *a* to topic *b*, no one could question why we are doing so. This clear structure is especially true for any presentation that will be delivered over the Internet, since the audience may face a short delay between the visual and auditory elements of the presentation. Again, it is usually best to organize a presentation directly, giving the conclusions and recommendations first, with the facts to support or illustrate it woven through the body of the presentation. However, as discussed previously, the organization depends on our audience analysis and our communication strategy.

The Conclusion

The conclusion to a professional presentation will usually include a summary of what we have said by going back over the main points and reinforcing them. If we are using visual aids, we may want to show the audience a summary slide that highlights our main messages. We may even want to bring the agenda slide back at this point, although for a short presentation that would not be necessary. The conclusion may also contain the recommendation if we did not make it in the opening or if we presented it in the beginning but think it useful to repeat it at this point.

Effective presenters do not just stop talking or say, "Well, that's all" in their conclusion. Also, they do not just trail off. We must remember that this is our last chance to deliver our message, and we should make the most of it and go out strong. The tone should be energetic and forceful. We need to work on the conclusion as much or even more than on the introduction and body.

If our presentation includes a Q&A section, we should include a conclusion (usually as a slide) that summarizes the main points before moving into the Q&A, but then after the Q&A, we should also provide a brief restatement of our major message. This summary statement is important in bringing the audience back to us; it allows us to address any concerns the questions may have raised and to ensure the audience leaves with our message on the top of their minds, not the last questioner's message. Of course, often audiences will start to leave immediately after the Q&A; therefore, we need to be prepared to regain control and to pull them back in to listen to our final words.

Creating the Graphics

No question, graphics can add to a presentation. Many people are better able to take in and process information presented visually rather than orally. Adding graphics to a presentations helps us reach everyone. Further, several categories of information—including quantitative, structural, spatial, and highly complex—can be conveyed more efficiently and effectively in visual rather than auditory form.

We do, however, want to be selective in the use of graphics. Unfortunately, graphics are sometimes overused or misused. The result is a presentation in which the graphics offer more distraction than support, making the presentation appear to be all show and no substance. Since the next chapter discusses when to use graphics, which graphs to use, and how best to design graphics using PowerPoint, the only point to be made here is that presenters should use graphics when possible, but use them with care.

Testing the Flow and Logic

We should take time after planning and preparation and before practicing to ensure that our presentation flows smoothly and that it is logical. We should test the flow by telling the story of our presentation aloud to ourselves and to someone else. Can we tell the story in a couple of minutes? What are the main messages? Do they flow logically from one to the other? After this test, we may find that we need to go back and do some reorganizing, but it is worth the time. A presentation has to be clearly logical to the audience or they will not stay with us.

Editing and Proofreading

The final form of a presentation should be clear, concise, coherent, correct, and confident. Once the presentation starts, we cannot go back and correct the slides or take back slips in what we have said. If we are using visual aids, we will need to edit and proofread them very carefully.

In the editing process, we should first look at each slide title and make sure it is meaningful: Does it capture the "so what?" of the chart below it? Also, we should look at how much we might be able to cut from bullets without losing the meaning. We will want to make them as concise as possible, but not so concise that they no longer say anything.

Finally, we should proofread each slide carefully, looking for consistency in title placement, font type and size, and margins. We need to remember that mistakes are magnified on a slide. Therefore, it is worthwhile printing our slides and going over each one, reading from the bottom to the top. Then, we will want to project each slide and look at it on the screen. Finally, if we plan to provide handouts of our slides, we should preview the printed version in pure black and white to ensure margins work and no text is lost off the edges of the slides once printed.

Practicing to Facilitate Effective Delivery

Practicing a presentation is often the key to delivering it successfully in front of an audience. All presenters need to find a practice method that works for them and make sure that they allow time for it.

Giving the Presentation Out Loud

Just going over our presentation in our mind is not sufficient. Most of us need to go through our presentation at least twice out loud. It is best to try to recreate the speaking situation as closely as possible, in the scheduled location and with the same equipment. Also, we should practice at least once in front of a mirror, being sure to speak aloud. Practicing in front of a mirror allows us to see ourselves as others see us and gives us a chance to see how well we are establishing eye contact. Even better is to video ourselves, or to deliver the presentation to friends and listen to their feedback.

It is particularly important to set time aside for a group practice when delivering a team presentation. Practice is the only way to establish smooth transitions from speaker to speaker, to ensure all sections are complete and coherent, and to judge the timing accurately.

Checking the Room and Setup

When delivering a presentation using any form of technology, it is particularly important to check the room ahead of time if at all possible. We want to be familiar with the equipment and the layout before we present. In some circumstances, it may be possible to adjust the layout or setup to accommodate our specific needs. In other cases, we may have to make adjustments to our own plans to accommodate the room.

We will want to load our presentation onto the computer hard drive and make sure it projects as intended. This test is particularly important because computer projectors often alter the colors of slides, and we need to see them exactly as they will appear when we present them to ensure that there are no distortions. Also, it is a good idea to check the size of the font for the particular room, making sure the person sitting in the very last row can read the bullet points and see the graphics easily.

The same strategy applies for any virtual presentation software we use, such as LiveMeeting or WebEx. When possible, we should test the environment ahead of time with a partner to ensure that the connection speed is adequate and that our visual aids do not need to be altered.

Timing

For most professional presentation settings, we will be speaking under a time constraint. It is very important to obey the time limits. If we are allowed to go overtime, we may finish our talk, but we risk irritating the audience. If we are stopped before we finish, we lose the chance to reiterate our main ideas and to end strongly.

Also, we should prepare for the inevitable, organizing our presentation so that we can adjust it if it needs to be shortened. One approach is to build in two or three examples to support each main point and then cut them back to one or two if we see we are short on time. Another approach is to cover the most important points first, but that can lead to an anticlimactic presentation in which we lose our audience toward the end, so this approach should be used with caution.

Finally, to ensure the timing is right, we will want to practice our presentation with a timer and keep the presentation a little under the required time limit. When it comes to time limits, we must be prepared, be flexible, and anticipate the unexpected.

Presenting Effectively and with Greater Confidence

When it comes time to present, we will need to concentrate on our delivery style, focusing particularly on our eye contact, stance, speech, and overall effect. We will want to appear comfortable, confident, enthusiastic, and professional. Since much of the success of our presentation will be determined by how our audience perceives us right at the beginning, we should be prepared to establish our expertise and our value to the audience immediately and maintain that positive ethos throughout.

Getting Nerves under Control

Public speaking is often cited as one of humankind's greatest fears, and everyone has advice about how to overcome nervousness when presenting, from practicing some yoga deep-breathing exercises to pretending everyone in the room is naked. Some techniques are more reliable than others.

The advice often given to professional athletes before they perform is to visualize their success. Sports trainers teach the athletes to see the moves they are making and imagine themselves serving that ace, making that goal, or hitting that home run. All of us have to find what works best for us.

The most important method for overcoming nerves is to be well prepared. If we know our subject, have our story down pat, and are prepared for whatever the situation may throw at us, we will not be as nervous.

Nervousness is not all bad. It releases adrenaline, which catalyzes the energy that usually enhances performance, so a little nervousness is good. Too much, however, can hurt our credibility.

If suffering from too much nervousness, it may help to put the presentation into perspective if we remember that the audience is human and, most of the time, forgiving. We are the only ones who will notice most mistakes (a typical audience hears only a small portion of what a presenter says and remembers even less). Our attitude will shape the audience's attitude. If we are at ease, they will be at ease. Sometimes it helps to take a few deep breaths and to think of something pleasant. We need to be natural, be ourselves.

It helps if we are able to laugh at ourselves. A smile, if the situation is appropriate, will go a long way toward helping us relax and connect with our audience. It relaxes our face muscles and makes us appear more at ease with the audience.

If nervousness makes us forget what we are planning to say while speaking, a technique called "shirttailing," repeating what was just said, may help us recall our words. The audience will think we are doing it for emphasis, and it should trigger the next idea in our head.

Most important, we need to focus on the audience and not on ourselves. We need to find that friendly face (and there will be one) and establish eye contact with him or her. Although we should make sure we look at the rest of the audience as well, we can keep coming back to the friend. If possible, it helps to get into the room ahead of time and start to establish a rapport by chatting with the audience. If we can "get out of ourselves" and worry more about the audience, we will not be nervous, and our overall performance will be much more effective. We need to remember, it is the ability to connect with the audience that makes a great presenter.

If, however, presenters find that they cannot get their nerves under control, they may want to try some of the newer virtual reality exposure

(VRE) therapy, a conditioning technique using software that is being applied to overcome phobias, such as fear of flying, fear of heights, and fear of public speaking. Although VRE is fairly new and only a few tests have been conducted to see how well it will work for public speakers, the early results suggest some success.[2]

Eye Contact

When leaders present, they seem to connect with everyone in the audience. If we are in their audience, we feel as if they are talking to us personally. They do this by looking at different people in the audience for a few seconds and actually establishing eye contact with them. Depending on the cultural expectations, our looking directly in the eyes of as many of our audience members as possible will suggest confidence as well as an interest in them. We do need, however, to be sensitive to cultural differences, since some cultures consider looking someone directly in the eye offensive, in which case our eye contact may need to be glancing and indirect.

Presenters want to avoid a rapid eye movement approach, in which they glance quickly from person to person, since it makes them appear unfocused and nervous. Also, it is better not to stay locked on one person too long, since it will make that individual uncomfortable. Every speaker tends to favor one side of the room; therefore, we may need to concentrate on ensuring that we do not neglect half of the people we are addressing.

Good speakers really look at the people in their audiences, not over their heads or out the window. Presentation trainers sometimes advise presenters to look at people's foreheads instead of in their eyes; however, people can tell where we are looking, and by not looking people in the eyes, we are not establishing a connection with them.

Finally, we need to be careful not to look down at our notes or read from them; we should only glance at them as necessary (although, again, if we are well prepared, we will not need many reminders). We should only glance at our computer screen briefly as well, and never turn our back to our audience to look at the slide screen.

Stance and Gestures

Our stance and our posture reflect our attitude toward our subject and our audience and reveal our confidence. Someone who has his or her head down with shoulders slumping appears unsure or distracted. To project confidence and establish a positive ethos, we want to stand straight and tall and look out at our audience. Usually, we will want to assume an open stance with our feet shoulder-width apart and our weight evenly distributed. Our goal should be to maintain a comfortable, relaxed stance, appropriate to the situation.

We should use our hands as we would in a conversation, although if we tend to move them too much, we may need to be more restrained when presenting. Usually, people look and feel most natural if they bend their arms, keeping elbows at their sides.

We should avoid pointing or gesturing at our projected slides. Instead, we should use the features in PowerPoint to highlight the areas of the slide on which we want the audience to focus. If we find ourselves in a situation that requires pointing to the screen, we should be careful not to turn our back. Instead, we should move back even with the screen, face the audience, and gesture to our side.

Also, since few people are steady enough to hold laser pointers completely immobile and positioned exactly over what they want to highlight, it is better to avoid using them.

If possible and appropriate, it is best to come out from behind a podium. The podium creates a barrier between us and our audience, and establishing a rapport with them will be easier if we remove the barrier. We usually do not need to stand in one place unless the space in the room is limited or our movement might make our audience uncomfortable. In a large room, in particular, we may need to walk toward the audience and maybe even from one side of the room to another to connect with the entire audience. We want to be careful that our walking is purposeful and not random pacing.

If rocking is a problem, and presenters are having trouble breaking the habit, they might try practicing by standing in a box or a garbage can, as strange as it may sound so that they become aware of where their feet are and that they are moving. Tennis coaches sometimes use this technique to teach beginners where to place their feet when serving.

Here are some common problems with stance that we will want to avoid:

Common Problems with Stance and Gestures to Avoid

1. Slouching or assuming a similar informal stance more appropriate to the company picnic than the boardroom.
2. Leaning to one side.
3. Pacing up and down or around the room too much.
4. Clasping our hands in front or behind us.
5. Standing with our hands on our hips.
6. Gripping the podium until our knuckles turn white.
7. Gesturing too much or when not appropriate or natural.
8. Fidgeting with keys, pens, a pointer, a tie, and the like.
9. Rocking or shifting our feet.
10. Leaning on the podium or sitting on the table.

Few presenters realize exactly what they are doing or how they are moving when they present, so the best way to see what we *actually* do in front of an audience and not what we *think* we do is to have someone videotape our presentations. All of us are amazed at what we do.

Sometimes we find that we are better than we think, which builds our confidence.

If presenters are not happy with how they appear when they present, they will want to isolate what they are doing wrong or badly so that they can work on eliminating it as they practice. To help isolate the nonverbal problems, it will help to watch the video without the sound, focusing on the hand and body movements. Also, playing the video in fast-forward will highlight repeated gestures; although the movements are exaggerated, such visualization will help us see what we are doing more objectively.

Although all leaders want to develop their own leadership presentation style, it may help to watch some good presenters. How do they stand? How do they move? What gestures do they use? We may want to try some of their techniques that seem to work particularly well.

With YouTube, we have all kinds of examples of presentations at our fingertips. The 2008 political season provides a wealth of good and bad examples. For example, go back and look at Hillary Clinton's or Sarah Palin's presentations at their parties' conventions. With both, we see individuals skilled at connecting with their audiences. They both appear very natural and sincere, and both create very positive ethos for themselves.

Voice and Speech Patterns

Most of our individual speech patterns have been established by the time we are five years old; however, we can make changes if we need to and if we are aware of what we are doing and what we need to change. Common problems occur in articulation, pronunciation, inflection, rhythm, volume, and the use of fillers, such as "uh" or "um."

The key to changing our speech patterns is knowing what we do now, and a recording is the best way to find out. If we are working with a video, to hear our speech patterns, we should not watch the video, only listen to it. Often, we are not even aware of how many fillers we use, for example, so by listening only and not watching, we pay more attention to them and realize how dependent we are. Counting the fillers ourselves or having someone else count them, as they do in Toastmasters, can be a real eye-opener for many of us. Often, just being aware of the use of fillers helps us cut back on the number of them we use.

Effective leaders speak clearly so that the audience can understand them. They speak loudly enough for the people in the back of the room to hear them. They pause between sentences and use few, if any, fillers. They sound confident, which comes from making statements and avoiding "up-speak," an inflection that occurs if we emphasize the last word of a sentence, as we do when asking a question.

We should try to observe the following guidelines for the vocal qualities of our delivery:

1. Speak to the last row in the audience, but raise the volume naturally. If we have to strain to be heard, then we need to use a microphone. If we are delivering using voice over internet protocol (VOIP) or teleconferencing, we should speak at a natural volume.
2. Articulate clearly, making sure to pronounce all important syllables, particularly the last.
3. Do not talk too fast. Build in pauses between main ideas and be careful not to run ideas together.
4. Vary the rhythm and pitch appropriately to avoid sounding monotone. Our voice should reflect the enthusiasm we feel for the topic and the energy that generates. Relaxing our face muscles and smiling will often help.
5. Either avoid the words that tend to cause pronunciation problems or practice them until able to say them perfectly 10 times in a row.

For leaders, the ability to present will be an important part of whatever position they hold. As emphasized throughout this discussion of delivery, watching ourselves on video and objectively observing how we look and sound is the best way to become aware of bad habits or mistakes in delivery so that we can improve and become the strong and confident speaker that a leader needs to be.

Delivering Effectively with Visual Aids

The good techniques for delivery using PowerPoint, overheads, or other visual aids vary little from delivering a presentation without aids. we want the audience to focus on us, so our goal should be to make the handling of our visual aids as unobtrusive as possible. In particular, we need to be aware of our eye contact, stance, voice, transitions, and timing. In addition, we need to test the projection or display equipment and any other technology (for example, remote control, speakers, or microphones) ahead of time.

Eye Contact

The need to maintain continuous eye contact becomes a problem for presenters who are accustomed to looking at the projection or laptop screen. We should look at our audience, not back at the projection screen or down at our laptop. We should seldom look back, although we may need to glance at the screen occasionally to ensure the right slide is up if we do not have a monitor in front of us.

Our goal should be to maintain our eye contact with our audience at all times. If we turn our back, we lose this contact, and our voice will be less audible, since we will be projecting at the screen instead of out toward the audience. In most presentations, our delivery should proceed as if there were no projected images behind us or in front of us.

Stance

We should assume a firm stance and position ourself so that we are facing forward and have easy access to whatever device we are using to change our slides. We need to make sure we do not block the screen from the view of the audience in any part of the room. There is no one best place to stand, since it will depend on the layout of the room. In the interests of good rapport, we should position ourselves as close to our audience as possible and not next to the screen, which is usually located too far from the audience.

Voice

We should be careful to maintain our volume. Presenters have a tendency to let their voices fade when they move to change slides. We should finish our thought on the current slide and complete our introduction to our next slide; then, stop talking for a second and change to the slide we have just introduced. Volume goes along with eye contact. If we maintain strong eye contact, we are more likely to maintain the right volume of sound also; it is when we look away from the audience that we are most likely to drop our volume.

Transition

We want to make the transition from slide to slide as seamless as possible. One technique is to introduce each slide before showing it. Most presenters wait for the slide to appear and then start talking about it almost as if they do not know what is coming up until they see it. For a much more effective transition, we should introduce the topic, which should be the "so what?" or main message, of the next slide before it appears. Displaying our slide only after we have introduced it will help make us appear more confident and our presentation flow more smoothly.

If we are delivering a Webcast or other virtual presentation, it is good practice to pause a second or two when moving to a new slide or application. From time to time, we should also note for the audience where we are in the slide or application, since our audience may face a delay.

Timing

We should practice with our slides to ensure we do not have too many for our allotted time. The rule of thumb is to allow at least two to three minutes per slide. We should be careful to give our audience time to absorb complex graphic information and be prepared to walk our audience through it if necessary. Also, it is better not to use the automatic timing in PowerPoint; it is next to impossible to make it match the timing of the presentation exactly. Having the slides advance ahead of the presenter or even behind will be distracting to the presenter and to audience.

Technology

If possible, we should always check the technology and the room in advance and make sure we know how to use it and that everything is working. We should also see how our presentation projects. Are the colors as we intend? Are the font sizes large enough for the audience to see all text from the back of the room? Sometimes projectors distort our colors, and we need to adjust them before we present. We will want to see where the screen, the projector, and the computer are positioned so that we will know where to stand to establish eye contact and the best rapport with our audience. Also, we will probably want to load our presentation onto the computer we are using instead of running it from a disc or thumbdrive. The same applies for any virtual delivery solution; we should test it beforehand.

Even if all the technology checks out, we will want to come prepared, in case technical problems occur, so we should always bring handouts as a backup, and never rely on computer projection to work flawlessly. It may falter in some way or fail entirely. We need to be prepared to handle any situation.

Handling Q&A

It is not unusual for presenters to spend more time preparing for the question and answer session than for the presentation itself. Effective handling of Q&A requires thorough preparation, careful listening, and the humility to say, "I do not know, but I will find out for you."

Presenters control the presentation content, but they never know what questioners might ask. At that now famous analyst conference call shortly before Enron collapsed, Jeff Skilling, then Enron's CEO, delivered his prepared remarks effectively; but when faced with hostile questions, he lost his poise and called one persistent questioner an obscene, derogatory name that received more media attention than his prepared remarks.

Leaders manage Q&A sessions by being prepared, even overprepared, particularly for the difficult questions. They anticipate all questions and prepare answers just in case. They also practice staying in control of the topics and of themselves.

When we are presenting with a team, all participants should work out a plan, stipulating who will answer which types of questions. If the presentation is formal, team members should position themselves at the end of the presentation to indicate which members are ready to answer the questions. During the Q&A session, the following tips will help in managing the audience:

Tips for Handling the Q&A Session

1. Determine and announce the timing of questions before starting the presentation. If delivering a virtual presentation, consider having a moderator gather questions during the presentation, and use those questions to begin the Q&A session.
2. Listen very carefully to the question.
3. Repeat the question or paraphrase it for the sake of ensuring you understand it and so the audience can hear it. This technique also provides that some time for formulating an answer.
4. Keep answers short and simple: Answer the specific question; then stop. Avoid talking too long or going off on a tangent.
5. Do not try to bluff your way through an answer. It is better to say very politely, "I am not sure I have an answer for that question at the moment, but I will find out for you."
6. Move away from any questioner who tries to isolate you in a two-way–conversation so that you break eye contact with him or her and reestablish it with the rest of the room.
7. Handle difficult questions or multilayer questions by answering them as completely as time allows and in the order they are asked, but be prepared to say, "I will be glad to discuss this question in more detail after the presentation."

After answering the last question, we will want to make sure to repeat our main message so that we control the way the presentation ends. Rather than letting the audience leave with the answer to the last question in their minds, we want them leaving with our main message in their minds.

Overall Effect

Ultimately, our ethos determines the overall effect of our presentation. A leader must project a strong, positive ethos in all presentation situations. Our credibility, knowledge, and integrity must be without question, or we will lose our audience, no matter how logical our presentation may be. We want to appear poised and confident.

The best way to project a positive ethos is to believe in what we are saying and to be fully prepared. As obvious as it may sound, nothing will take the place of preparation. To deliver an effective presentation, we must be prepared. Some guidelines suggest spending one hour in preparation for each minute that we will be presenting. While that may be too much in some cases and would certainly need to be modified depending on the type of presentation and our knowledge of the subject, it suggests emphatically how important it is not to neglect or underestimate preparation time. The success of our presentation and, in the long run, our career may depend on it.

In summary, to appear confident and project a positive ethos when presenting, we need to do the following:

1. Focus our energy on our audience.
2. Create and maintain rapport.
3. Adopt a secure stance.
4. Establish and maintain eye contact.
5. Project and vary our voice.
6. Demonstrate our messages with gestures.
7. Adjust our pace of delivery based on the audience response.
8. Relax and be ourselves.

**Application 5.1
Oral
Presentation
Self-Evaluation**

Videotape one of your presentations, and then use the following form to assess it. You should watch the video three times: (1) Watch with the sound turned off to focus on body movements and delivery; (2) listen without watching so that you can hear what you really say; and finally, (3) watch and listen. In addition, if you have a problem with fillers, you might want to listen one additional time to count the "uhs."

Needs Work Average Good Excellent	
Delivery	**Strengths:**
Leadership image _____ • Confidence • Stance & movement • Approach & departure from podium	
Gestures _____ Eye contact _____ Fillers (uhs, etc.) _____ Energy level _____	**Areas to improve:**
Voice, articulation, _____ language, grammar • Tone • Volume • Pauses • Rate/pace • Fillers • Articulation • Language usage	**Strengths:** **Areas to improve:**

Needs Work	Average	Good	Excellent	
Content and organization				**Strengths:**
Introduction _____ (context, purpose, & topics)				
Organization _____ (coherence & logic)				
Knowledge & _____ control of content				**Areas to improve:**
Conclusion _____ (summary of main points)				
Graphics				**Strengths:**
Quality of graphics _____ (conforms to graphic basics—simple, easy to understand)				
Ability to present _____ **charts & graphics effectively** (introduce before showing, walking audience through them if needed)				**Areas to improve:**
Effectiveness of _____ **chart titles** (capture meaning of the chart)				

Overall presentation and improvement plans:

1. What was the best part of your presentation? Why?

2. What are key areas to improve?

3. How do you propose working on improvement areas?

4. How will you measure your progress in these areas?

**Application 5.2
Practicing
Impromptu
Presentations**

Select a couple of the topics from the following list and practice delivering a three-minute presentation on them. Allow yourself two to four minutes of preparation time for some of them, but also practice reading them and then starting to talk with no preparation.

1. Discuss the most memorable event in your life.
2. Select a TV show and discuss its merits.
3. Discuss why cats make better pets than dogs or the other way around.
4. Discuss why some movie or book is great.
5. Discuss why exams are or are not a good measure of a student's learning.
6. Describe the most challenging task you have ever completed and how you accomplished it.
7. Discuss how communication technology, such as cell phones, PDAs, or blogs, is changing the way people communicate.
8. Discuss the value of working as a volunteer.
9. Discuss the primary considerations for determining which university to attend.
10. Select a hobby and discuss its merits.

**Application 5.3
Developing a
Round-Table
Presentation**

Huge Co-Revisited

Review the circumstances surrounding the Huge Co. merger with Computer Co. presented in the application section of Chapter 3. Assume the role of the head of the consulting team that has interviewed the human resources managers at both Huge Co. and Computer Co. You have been asked to develop a round-table presentation to deliver to the senior partner and two new consultants who will be joining the project team. Consider the need for background information as well as the synthesized information from the interviews, and create the ghost pack for the round-table presentation.

**Application 5.4
Transforming a
Round-Table
Presentation for
Virtual Delivery**

After you developed the round-table presentation material for Application 5.3, you discover that the senior partner will not be able to join you and the two new consultants for your presentation. She requests that you create a virtual meeting instead. Considering this new development, revisit your materials from the application and make any changes necessary.

Notes

1. Eccles, R. G., and Nohria, N. (1992). *Beyond the Hype: Rediscovering the Essence of Management.* Boston: Harvard Business School Press, pp. 47–48.
2. Anderson, H. V. (2003). A Virtual End to Stage Fright. *Harvard Management Communication Letter* (January).

Chapter 6

Graphics and PowerPoint with a Leadership Edge

Charts are an important form of language. They're important because, when well conceived and designed, they help us communicate more quickly and more clearly than we would if we left the data in a tabular form.

Gene Zelazny (2001), *Say It with Charts*

Presentations largely stand or fall depending on the quality, relevance, and integrity of the content. The way to make big improvements in a presentation is to get better content.

Edward Tufte (2003), *The Cognitive Style of PowerPoint*

Chapter Objectives

In this chapter, you will learn to do the following:

- Recognize when to use graphics.
- Employ fundamental graphic content and design principles.
- Select and design effective data charts.
- Create meaningful and effective text layouts.
- Make the most of PowerPoint as a design and presentation tool.

Leaders need to know how and when to use graphics. Graphics improve presentations and documents, particularly if the material is primarily quantitative, structural, pictorial, or so complicated that it can be illustrated more efficiently and more effectively with a visual aid than with words alone. Graphics will contribute to the success of our oral and written communications. Most people are more visually oriented today than in the past, and they expect and respond to graphics in presentations and printed documents. Even though it is a cliché, the expression "a picture is worth a thousand words" conveys a powerful truth. People respond to visuals. In fact, research has proven that presentations with visual aids are 43 percent more persuasive.[1]

Leaders use visuals that are integral to the communication of their intended meanings and not ones simply added for show. When selected appropriately and designed carefully, graphics embody and carry the meanings that create our message. Since nearly all word processing, spreadsheet, and presentation programs available today make it possible to create visual content, adding graphics to presentations and documents has become increasingly easier. However, the ease of use has also led to gratuitous and poorly designed graphics and presentations with flash but too little content.

In addition, since most of us create our own presentations and we do not have the training that a graphic artist would have, we may end up with less than optimally designed slides. Edward Tufte condemns Power-Point, arguing that its "cognitive style routinely disrupts, dominates, and trivializes content."[2] However, PowerPoint and presentations created in similar programs can and do contain solid content and can and do communicate content effectively—but only if the content is solid to begin with and if the slides conspire fully in communicating the speaker's message.

Used appropriately, graphics and PowerPoint can provide a leadership edge, that is, the ability to influence the audience positively. Knowing how to deliver messages effectively with words and pictures is a powerful combination, and developing even a basic understanding of the principles of graphic design can provide an advantage.

This chapter will focus on when and how to use graphics effectively, provide some basic guidelines for designing effective graphics, and deliver some guidance on designing and presenting PowerPoint slides, both in person and over the Internet.[3]

Glossary of Terms Used in This Chapter

- **Visual Aid**—object, picture, drawing, diagram, graph, table, and the like included in a presentation to help the audience understand the message.
- **Graphics**—visual designs, drawings, diagrams, tables, or graphs, intended to support, explain, illustrate, or clarify a presenter's message. Note: When Zelazny says "charts" in the opening quotation, he means graphics as defined here.
- **Graph**—representation of numerical information in a line, bar, or pie graph or similar conventionally scaled depiction of data.
- **Slide**—used in PowerPoint or similar presentation programs to define the separate pages in a presentation, even though technically they are not intended to be shown with a slide projector, but using computer projection.
- **Chart**—page in a presentation, can be text or graphics, often used interchangeably for "slide."
- **Pack or Deck**—hard-copy collection of slides/charts intended for support and as handouts in stand-up or round-table presentations.

Recognizing When to Use Graphics

Graphics should never be gratuitous; they should always be purposeful. They should add to the content of the presentation or the document. For presentations, in particular, graphics should supplement the content and never detract from it. They are not meant to replace the speaker.

Specifically, graphics should serve the following purposes:

1. Reinforce the message.
2. Provide a road map to the structure of a presentation.
3. Illustrate relationships and concepts visually.
4. Support assertions.
5. Emphasize important ideas.
6. Maintain and enhance interest.

Reinforce the Message

Reinforcing the message means that the chart captures and emphasizes the main ideas expressed by the speaker. Recognizing that many people are visually oriented, we can help our audience to remember more of what we say if we reinforce our words with visuals. Although we do not want to overuse text charts, even a simple one can help reinforce our message and can be absolutely essential when presenting material over the Internet. We need to ensure, however, that what is on the screen is consistent with what we are saying. A common problem in presenting with word charts is that the speaker says something very different from the words projected on the screen. This discrepancy causes the audience to be confused: Do they listen to the speaker or read the screen?

Presenters need to keep in mind that the words on the screen should echo what they say. They may paraphrase or expand on the words, but they should not say anything that diverges too far from what is displayed. Also, they should never simply read from the screen. After all, the presenter should know the subject matter well enough to speak about it without reading.

Presenters may also want to use graphic charts to reinforce their message. For instance, if the message is that sales are down, presenters can reinforce that message with a line graph showing how much and over what length of time. If the message is that the company needs to be involved in community outreach, they might show pictures of some community efforts currently underway, such as inner-city cleanup or Habitat for Humanity.

The bottom line is that we should always think of ways to use charts, whether verbal or graphic, to help our audience remember our message.

Provide a Road Map to the Structure of a Presentation

Using a text chart to establish the agenda or discussion topics is one very common method of establishing a road map to the structure of a presentation. One common mistake, however, is to list all or most of the slide titles on the agenda chart (see Exhibit 5.6). This laundry list of topics does not suggest the "structure" of the presentation. In fact, it can suggest a lack of structure, an aimless stringing together of ideas. Instead, we should use the agenda slide to reflect the logic of our presentation, using the Pyramid Principle or other structuring device to help us group our slides into like ideas, so that the agenda tells the story in miniature. In other words, we should think of the agenda as an executive summary with only the headings included. Then, we will create an effective agenda slide that our audience will more likely remember.

If our topic is complex, we might want to use a structural graphic as a road map for our presentation. For instance, in the discussion in Chapter 5, a graphic was used to set up the steps in developing and designing a presentation. We could use the same graphic to introduce each section in the presentation, thus keeping the entire framework in the audience's mind as we introduce the specific pieces in the presentation (Exhibit 6.1). When we use a framework or even a text slide to set up the entire presentation and then each of the major sections, the slide serves as a tracker, a slide designed to help our audience keep track of where we are in the presentation.

If we decide to use a framework, we need to be careful that it is not so complex that our audience gets lost in it or that our presentation is so short that repeating the same graphic becomes tedious.

EXHIBIT 6.1 **Using a Framework as a Road Map for a Presentation**

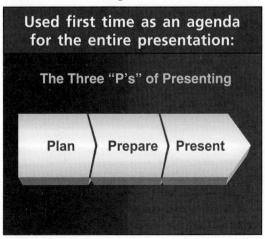
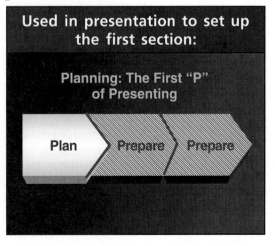

EXHIBIT 6.2 **Misusing a Framework as a Tracker on Each Slide**

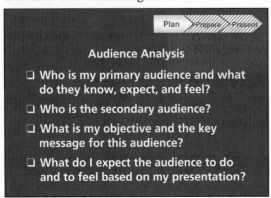

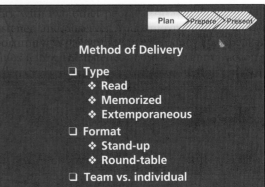

Some presenters take a tracker too far, placing a small version of it on every slide in the presentation. It is best to avoid using a tracker in this way, since it diminishes our workspace and must be so reduced that, to our audience, it will only be a distraction that adds little, if any, meaning (Exhibit 6.2).

There are two exceptions: We may want to use this type of tracker if we are presenting a process flow in which the audience must be reminded of the whole to appreciate the parts, or we may find such a tracker helpful in a longer Web presentation.

Illustrate Relationships and Concepts Visually

Graphics usually work better than words to help an audience understand relationships and concepts. For example, the triangle used in Chapter 2 to introduce strategy is a concept graphic. It shows how all of the components of a communication strategy connect to the others, build on them, and influence them with audience analysis as the foundation for every other component above it.

Exhibit 6.3 is a concept chart designed to show the relationship among the components of an individual communication development plan. The framework shows the individual development at the center, with the team experiences and group instruction influencing the development from the top and the bottom. Framing the development on each end are the beginning self-assessments with an improvement plan and then the post-assessments with reflection to measure the improvement results. The presenter could use color and shading for each arrow and PowerPoint's building capabilities to introduce the components one at a time so that he or she could make

EXHIBIT 6.3   Graphic Showing Relationships

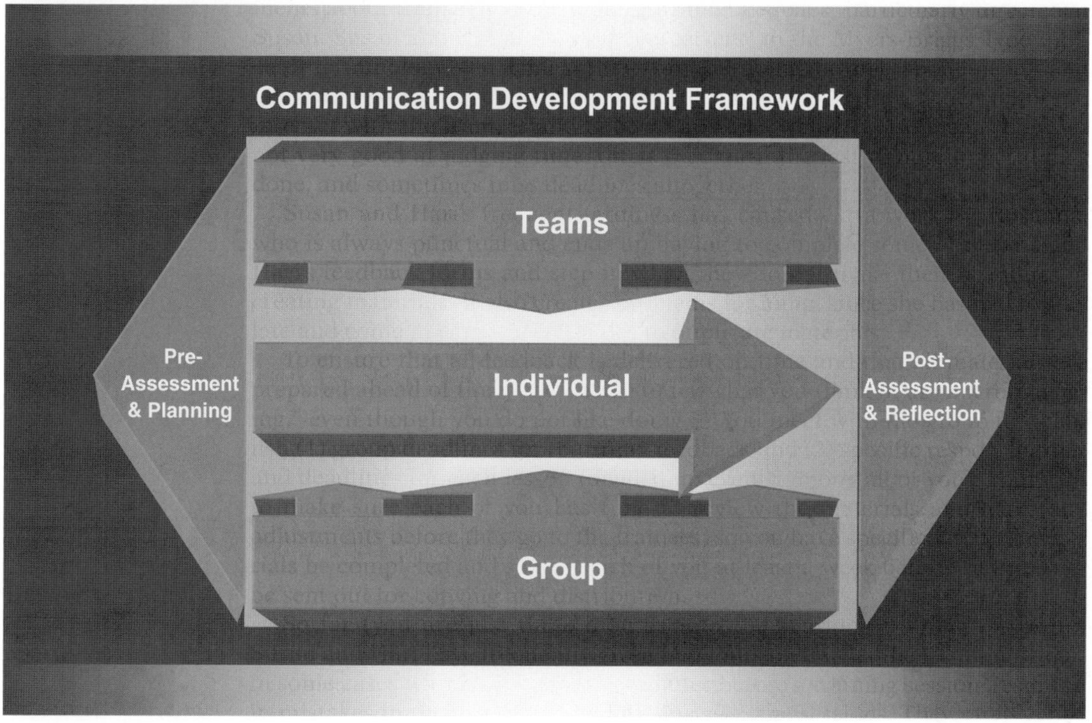

their meaning and their relationship to the other components clear to the audience.

Concept graphics are useful in clarifying ideas and in creating a mental picture for the audience. For instance, in Exhibit 6.4, a standard Microsoft clip art of a puzzle shows different approaches to problem solving. On one side, we have the "synthesizer," or the person who puts things together and sees similarities, and on the other, we have the "analyzer," or the person who takes things apart and sees differences.

Exhibit 6.5 illustrates a few of the most commonly used business concept charts. To see more examples of concept graphics, see Gene Zelazny's *Say It with Charts;* he dedicates an entire chapter to examples of visual concepts and another chapter to visual metaphors.

Support Assertions

Graphics to support assertions are often quantitative charts; however, we might use qualitative charts if we have based our assertions on interviews or open-ended surveys and want to show our audience quotations from our subjects. Exhibit 6.6 demonstrates a typical quantitative chart

EXHIBIT 6.4   Concept Graphic

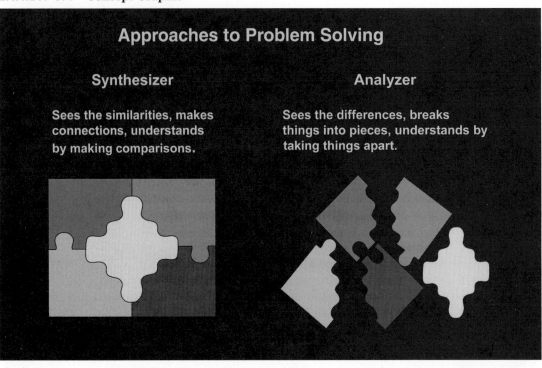

EXHIBIT 6.5   Common Concept Charts

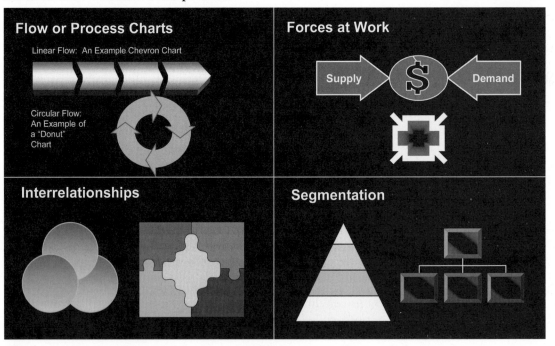

EXHIBIT 6.6
Example Quantitative Chart to Support an Assertion

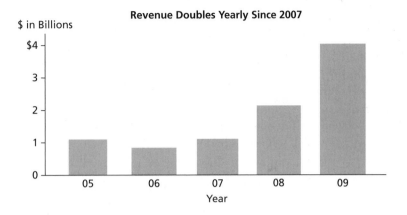

supporting the assertion that revenues have doubled each year since 2007. While this assertion is fairly simple and we could probably get away with making it orally, adding a graphic that shows the numbers improves credibility and can have a greater impact on the audience.

Exhibit 6.7 shows a qualitative chart created to support the assertion that communication is a priority in performance reviews. It demonstrates how we might use quotations from interviews to support our findings and overall conclusion.

EXHIBIT 6.7
Example Qualitative Chart to Support an Assertion

Communication Important in Performance Reviews at ABC	
Interview Findings	**Representative Quotations**
Employees beginning to realize communication is important in reviews.	• "My communication ability was highlighted as one of my main strengths in my performance review." • "My communication weaknesses kept me from receiving a good review."
Employees think communication is important to management.	• "Communication effectiveness seems to be a high priority to management in reviews now." • "This is such a bottom-line company, I was surprised management put so much value on what I see as a soft skill—communication."
Employees evaluated as "high" in communication effectiveness are rewarded.	• "Employees who are rated high on communication in reviews receive the promotions." • "No matter what kind of deal maker you are, only the good communicators rise to the top here."

Emphasize Important Ideas

All presenters hope that orally emphasizing the important points, and maybe even repeating them, will fix them in the audience's memory. Studies show, however, that audiences remember more of what they see than what they hear, although they do not retain much of that, either. To put it simply, as taught in one ancient Chinese proverb,

I hear and I forget;

I see and I remember;

I do and I understand.

The common English expression indicating understanding suggests the importance of the visual as well: "I see." Thus, if we want to emphasize important ideas, we should do so in words and in visual aids, whether using word charts or graphics.

Maintain and Enhance Interest

Using graphics to maintain and enhance interest requires a word of warning. Essentially, adding interest means introducing some variety in our slides and looking for ways to make our presentation graphically interesting; it does not mean throwing in wild colors, crazy cartoons, or superfluous animation just for the sake of doing so. As always, the most important rule for the use of graphics applies here: Graphics should add to the presentation and the presenter and not detract in any way. We should think about ways to make our presentations more visually appealing but approach the task with caution. For instance, a presenter using Exhibit 6.8 would probably get our attention but would run the

EXHIBIT 6.8
Example of a Graphic That Risks Going Too Far to Add Interest

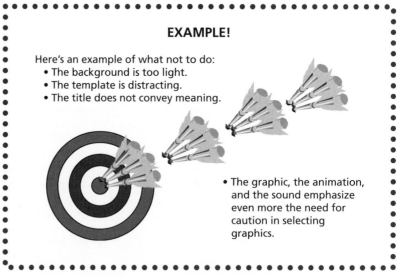

EXAMPLE!

Here's an example of what not to do:
- The background is too light.
- The template is distracting.
- The title does not convey meaning.

- The graphic, the animation, and the sound emphasize even more the need for caution in selecting graphics.

Note: Please see color version online at www.mhhe.com/barrett3e.

risk of our being so distracted by the graphics that we might not hear the intended message. If we imagine the darts flying into the target with a swooshing sound, we would probably feel that this chart goes too far to make a point.

If the presenter used this slide with others on presentations to reinforce a lesson in what not to do, it could be effective by its contrast to the previous charts as a bad example. People do seem to remember bad examples better than they do good ones. Also, it could accomplish the purpose of breaking up the purely instructional slides with something a little lighter. Such a poorly designed chart does, however, need the appropriate context to convey this message, which brings us back to the cardinal rule of using graphics: *Graphics should enhance the delivery of our message, not detract from it in any way.*

When preparing graphics for a Web presentation, it is especially important that we consider what kind of actions in a visual will help guide interest and what kind will distract. Since the audience will often only see the visuals we create, we need those visuals to highlight our key points well. Distracting animation, poor-quality images, and complicated slides can often work against us in Web presentations.

Employing Fundamental Graphic Content and Design Principles

This section focuses specifically on the content and design principles that we should follow whenever creating data or text charts for leadership presentations. For charts to add to the presentation, they should convey our messages clearly and effectively to our audience. In addition, they should be legible and designed so that they contribute to communicating our messages.

Conveying Messages Clearly and Effectively

The following guidelines apply to all data and text charts:

1. Keep charts simple *but* meaningful. Often, instruction in creating and using graphics will include the adage "Less is more," originally used by Ludwig Mies van der Rohe (1886–1969), an architect and designer who started the minimalist school. Effective leaders keep their graphs simple enough for their audience to understand easily, yet they also know that the graphs still communicate something. While we should strive for simplicity in whatever graphs we create or slides we design, we must avoid reducing the content on the slide so much that the meaning evaporates.

The content of slides, whether graphics or text, should not be mere decoration or embellishment. Empty pictures and hollow words add nothing and should not be part of the presentation. We should always ask ourselves: Is the graphic useful? Is it necessary? We have all sat through presentations with slides that were not much more than decorative pictures, objects, or cartoons that added little to the message. If the visual aid does not add to the presentation, we should cut it, no matter how attached we may be to the graphic or even how much time we spent creating it.

In *The Cognitive Style of PowerPoint* (2003), Edward Tufte argues that PowerPoint is so flawed that it is impossible to communicate anything meaningful using it; however, it is not the medium that is flawed—it is the users of it. Many of the standard presentation templates call on us to use few words and fairly simply graphics, but that does not mean that we cannot create a presentation that contains solid, thoughtful, and meaningful content. We simply need to make sure our message is clear in our own mind and then make every word and every graphic work for us in conveying our message. We need to remember *we* are delivering the main messages; the graphics are there to support us.

2. Include only one main message per chart or slide. If we have too many messages, we risk losing our audience. Often, we need to back away from the slide and ask ourselves the following questions:

- What am I trying to communicate?
- If the audience leaves with only one message from this slide, is it what I intend?
- Do all words support this message?
- Do the graphics support this message?

If we have too much information for one slide, we should continue the same message over onto subsequent slides, using the same chart title with the word "continued" at the end of it.

3. Make sure the chart title captures the "so what?" The title on the chart should clearly announce the main message or provide adequate information for interpreting any graphs. We have all heard others say that "the numbers speak for themselves." However, the significance of numbers is seldom transparent, and numbers can convey a range of potential messages. Therefore, simply putting a graph up, displaying some numbers, does not ensure that our audience will see them the way we do.

It is our responsibility as presenters to make sure the numbers are configured and displayed to carry the meaning we intend and that they cannot be interpreted otherwise. We can help ensure that our audience interprets the numbers as we do by putting a title on the slide that tells the audience the meaning of the numbers or other data we are showing them.

Selecting the Most Effective Colors

The right colors and fonts can make a difference in how effective our PowerPoint presentation is. Selection should focus on colors and fonts that show up best when a presentation is projected. Often, company logos determine colors and fonts; however, these are not always the best choices to make for entire presentations. To make effective decisions on colors, it will help you to know something about color psychology and graphic design. What follows provides some of both.

Selecting the color combinations for our presentations should not be arbitrary or simply based on personal color preferences. As with all aspects of our presentation, we need to consider our message and the image we wish to project. Knowing the colors most color specialists consider "right" for presentations can be useful, as can color psychology in general. For instance, knowing that too much of a vivid yellow causes fatigue and even aggravation and that cool shades, such as blues and greens, have a calming effect could be important in supporting our messages. In addition, we should be sensitive to the cultural associations for some colors to ensure that our colors do not deliver messages we do not intend.

The focus here is on selecting the colors that project best and promote legibility for the audience, as well as on how we can draw the audience's eye to our most important message by effectively using color.

For more information on the design aspects, the psychology, and the cultural associations of colors, see the following sources:

- The Color Voodoo publications (most of them can be purchased through their Web site, www.colorvoodoo.com, for under $30)
- www.colormatters.com
- www.infoplease.com/spot/colors1.html
- www.sensationalcolor.com/color-meaning-symbolism-and-psychology/
- www.lighthouse.org

The Lighthouse International site is particularly interesting, since it reminds us that many people have impaired sight and have trouble seeing colors. While only a few people may be completely color-blind, many have trouble with distinguishing subtle shades of colors.

For everyone, the greater the contrast the better when it comes to putting colors right next to each other in a presentation. Backgrounds and fonts that do not contrast sufficiently make the text difficult to read. Unless company colors dictate differently, it is usually better to stay with the traditional primary or secondary colors or their combinations for professional presentations and to avoid pastels.

The traditional color wheel (Exhibit 6.9) shows the primary and secondary colors that tend to work best in presentations. The color

EXHIBIT 6.9
Basic Colors and Contrasts

Source: www.lighthouse. org/colorcontrast.html. Used with permission of the author; Aries, Arditi, PhD, and Lighthouse International as the copyright holder.

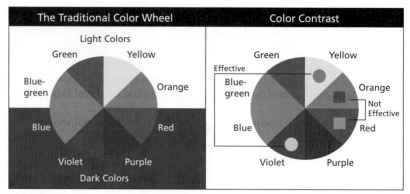

Note: Please see color version online at www.mhhe.com/barrett3e.

contrast chart shows how to select opposites for strong contrast. It also demonstrates what happens when colors of the same hue are placed next to each other; the red square on the orange slice and orange square on the red slice do not allow enough contrast for easy legibility and the squares may not be visible to some people.

The secret of effective color choices is not so much the choice of one color but the choice of one in contrast to the others used with it: "Most people—or at least those of us without an art background—don't understand that the colors they choose are not as important as the relationships they create. Some colors work together, others fight against each other. Establishing a sound relationship is key."[4]

We want the colors we select for our presentation to work together, not against each other. In addition, we want the sharpest contrast, since the sharper the contrast the greater the legibility

One principle of color relationships to keep in mind is that a lighter color appears to move outward and a darker color recedes; therefore, a lighter font shows up better on a dark background than a dark font on a white background. This color rule is particularly true in a room some-what darkened, as is usual with PowerPoint presentations. Notice what happens in Exhibit 6.10 when the background colors are changed.

Clearly, the greater the contrast, the easier it is to see the font—and the sharper the letters appear. Similar color contrasts should guide us in selecting colors for shapes and objects. In the two slides in Exhibit 6.11, when the AutoShape colors are changed, our eye is drawn to the rectangle in the center if it is lighter and to the arrows when they are lighter.

The message we intend to emphasize should determine the colors we use. If our main message is as the title suggests in Exhibit 6.11—the "forces" affecting the industry—then making the force boxes a lighter color will draw the audience's eyes to them. If, however, we intend to emphasize the industry's profit splits, then the colors in the first version

EXHIBIT 6.10
Color Contrast of Fonts with Backgrounds

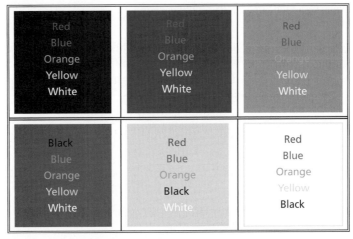

Please see color version online at www.mhhe.com/barrett3e.

EXHIBIT 6.11
Using Color to Direct the Audience to the Main Message

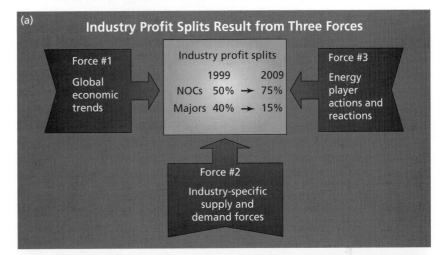

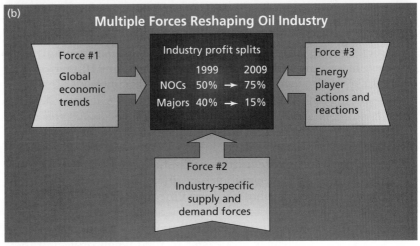

Note: Please see color version online at www.mhhe.com/barrett3e.

will work better, since the lighter color draws the eye and seems to project outward more. If the profit split is the main message, then the title for the first slide might be "Industry Forces Result in Dramatic Changes in Profit Splits."

In summary, when using colors,

1. Keep them simple and select colors that work well together.
2. Ensure that the colors are easy to see when placed against each other.
3. Check text color, in particular, to see that it contrasts with background colors sufficiently to be clearly legible.
4. Make sure the colors support the desired image and the intended message.

Also, light backgrounds in projected presentations usually create unnecessary glare, which becomes uncomfortable for the viewers. The same is true for Web presentations, since large amounts of white space on a computer screen can tire the eyes and make the presentation appear fuzzy, as Exhibit 6.12 shows. Finally, we should not forget to consider and, if possible, check the computer and the projection equipment that we will be using. With unfamilier and untested equipment, the safest background is black with a light font. The projector can distort the shading of any other color of background, causing too little contrast and even ugly color combinations.

Selecting the Most Effective Fonts

With computer presentations, recent studies have shown that a light font on a dark background (dark blue or black) is the most legible; however, for overhead presentations, a dark font on a white background projects better in most settings. Some font colors are difficult to read on some backgrounds. For instance, red fonts on a blue background result in fuzzy images (Exhibit 6.13).

Most presenters have been warned that the font needs to be large enough to be read from the back of the room in which they are presenting. Most of the time, a font 20 points or larger will work for the text within the slides; however, when possible, check the room setup to be sure. Titles require a larger font, but the default for titles in PowerPoint is usually larger than necessary and makes it difficult to have a title of any substance. In most settings, 28-point size for the titles works well. Of course, if presenting the slides over the Internet, we may be able to use a smaller font, but most experts still agree that anything smaller than 16 points becomes difficult to read, even on a computer screen.

Recent studies in readability have found that, in addition to the size of the font, the style matters as well. A sans-serif font (such as Arial) is cleaner and easier to read when projected than a serif font (such as

EXHIBIT 6.12
**Effects of a Light
Background on
Web Presentations**

Image on Presenter's Screen

WebTrends Products and Services

WebTrends Software	WebTrends on Demand
You own the software	Hosted version: no hardware or software to purchase
Requires IT and administrator resources	Lowers IT requirements for maintenance and administration
Can integrate with other data sources	Cannot integrate other data source (within product)
Can use standard Web server log files and/or SmartSource Data Collector (SDC) log files	SmartSource Data Collector log files only

Image on Audience's Screen

WebTrends Products and Services

WebTrends Software	WebTrends on Demand
You own the software: can load on any device you like.	Hosted version: no hardware or software to purchase
Requires IT and administrator resources	Lowers IT requirements for maintenance and administration
Can integrate with other data sources	Cannot integrate other data source, but requiree more effort
Can use standard Web server log files and/or SmartSource Data Collector (SDC) log files	Uses SmartSource Data Collector log files only

Times Roman), used for printed documents. Thus, the font of choice is a sans-serif font for projected and Web-delivered presentations (see Exhibit 6.12).

Capitalization is another element of font selection that we need to handle carefully. All caps should be avoided; using all caps makes the text difficult to read and gives the audience the sense that the presenter is shouting at them. Using initial caps on all words within bulleted lists also decreases readability. Finally, we should avoid underlining any words or text; it cuts off the bottom of letters and makes the words more difficult to read. Instead, it is better to use a larger font, bold, italics, or different colors for emphasis.

The bottom line is to make the font as easy to read and as comfortable for the audience as possible. The goal should be legibility, not simply aesthetics.

EXHIBIT 6.13   Examples of Poor Color and Font Selection

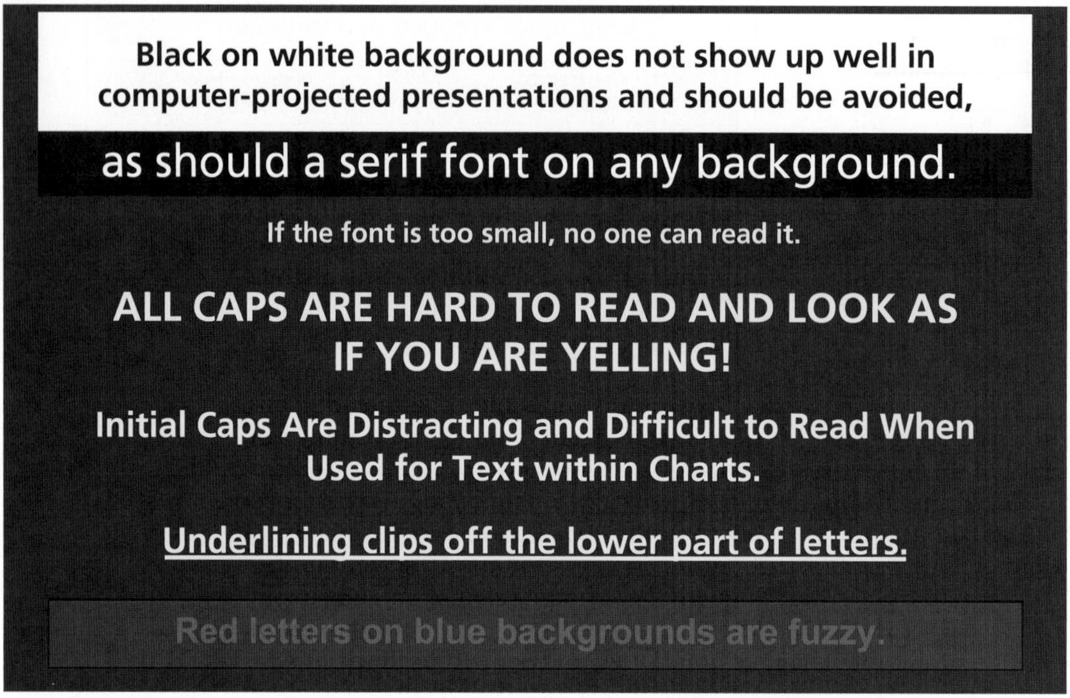

> **Black on white background does not show up well in computer-projected presentations and should be avoided,**
>
> ## as should a serif font on any background.
>
> If the font is too small, no one can read it.
>
> ## ALL CAPS ARE HARD TO READ AND LOOK AS IF YOU ARE YELLING!
>
> **Initial Caps Are Distracting and Difficult to Read When Used for Text within Charts.**
>
> **<u>Underlining clips off the lower part of letters.</u>**
>
> Red letters on blue backgrounds are fuzzy.

Note: Please see color version online at www.mhhe.com/barrett3e.

The following table is a summary of the guidelines for colors and fonts.

Guidelines for Using Colors and Fonts

1. Stay with the basic colors (primary or secondary).
2. Go for contrast in backgrounds and fonts and in AutoShapes or any objects or text placed next to each other.
3. For most settings, use a dark background (dark blue or black) for computer-delivered presentations.
4. Use a contrasting font, such as white, cream, yellow, or light gold, on dark backgrounds.
5. Use only a sans-serif font, such as Arial, in computer-projected presentations.
6. Make the font size at least 20 points for text and 28 points for titles (depending on the size of the room).
7. Do not use the following:
   - All caps in titles or text.
   - Initial caps except in titles.
   - Underlining.
   - Red fonts on blue backgrounds.

Selecting and Designing Effective Data Charts

For data charts to add to our presentation or document, we first need to clarify our message and then we can determine the type and content of the graph that will add to, support, or explain that message best. We may have someone to help design our graphics, particularly if we have reached a high level in an organization; however, we are more likely to end up designing our own graphics and creating our own PowerPoint. Even if we are lucky enough to have help, it is useful as we manage others and oversee the creation of our presentations to possess some knowledge of the best types of graphs, as well as the best designs, to ensure the clarity and accuracy of the different kinds of data we will be conveying to our audiences.

Edward Tufte, a Yale University statistician and author of several books on graphic design, provides the following best-practice guidelines for creating data charts:

Excellence in statistical graphics consists of complex ideas communicated with clarity, precision, and efficiency. Graphical displays should

- Show the data.
- Induce the viewer to think about the substance rather than methodology, graphic design, the technology of graphic production, or something else.
- Avoid distorting what the data have to say.
- Present many numbers in a small space.
- Make large data sets coherent.
- Encourage the eye to compare different pieces of data.
- Reveal the data at several levels of detail, from a broad overview to the fine structure.
- Serve a reasonably clear purpose: description, exploration, tabulation, or decoration.
- Be closely integrated with the statistical and verbal descriptions of a data set.[5]

Source: Tufte, E. R. (1983). *The Visual Display of Quantitative Information.* Cheshire, CT: Graphics Press, p. 13. Used with permission.

Tufte emphasizes that graphs should be carefully selected and designed to ensure that the meaning of the numbers dominates, not the method of analysis. The goal of the graph should be to aid the audience in understanding the data and our central message. Selecting the best type of graph for the type of information that we want to convey and then following a few basic design principles for graphs will help us communicate our message more effectively. Exhibit 6.14 demonstrates commonly used data graphs, explains when to select one or the other, and includes pointers on how to make them easier for our audience to grasp the content in a presentation.

EXHIBIT 6.14 **Selecting the Most Effective Graphic Format for Data Charts**

Type	Guide to Use and Design	Examples
Pie	• Compares proportions and relative amounts of components • Works well with nonspecialists or executive audience • Start with largest portion at 12:00 • Avoid legends; instead, place numbers inside and labels outside • Select outline around pie and between segments for printing	**Two Firms Have Highest Revenue** $ Millions Brown & Peterson Davis & Jimenez Johnson & Smith $67 $92 $243 Kramer & Mattee $177 $231 James & Connelly Source; *Lawyer Reports*, July 7, 2009.
Bar or column	• Conveys absolute value data, relative sizes, or close comparisons • Emphasizes differences • Works well with most audiences • Rotate y-axis label to horizontal position for easy reading • Keep space between bars smaller than width of bars • Avoid 3-D to allow easier lineup with numbers on y-axis	**Sales Increase Since Matrix** $in Billions $4 3 2 1 0 03 04 05 06 07 08 09 Year **Matrix implemented**
Line	• Demonstrates trends or interactions between variables • Good for showing movement over time • Useful for most audiences • Avoid legends; instead, place labels next to lines when possible • Rotate y-axis label to horizontal position for easy reading • Avoid using too many lines	**Global PC Market Share in Units** Percent 20 15 10 5 0 2004 2005 2006 2007 2008 2009 HP Dell Acer

(continued)

Knowing when to use graphics and the best graph to select helps ensure that the graphics add to our presentations and documents, but we also need to remember to consider the ethics of the graphics, particularly when using data charts.

EXHIBIT 6.14 (continued)

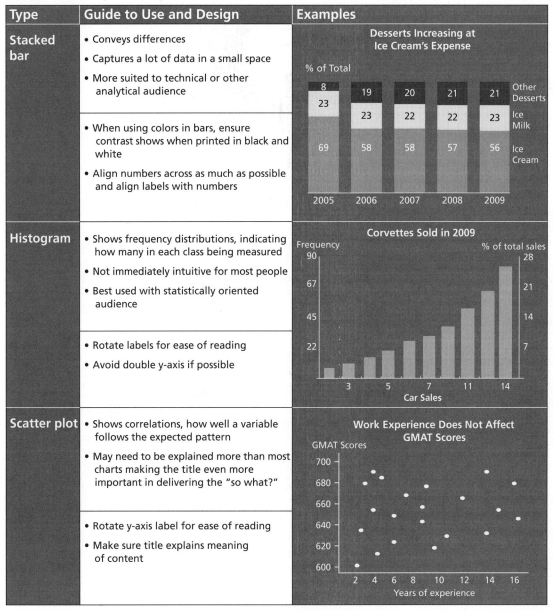

Type	Guide to Use and Design	Examples
Stacked bar	• Conveys differences • Captures a lot of data in a small space • More suited to technical or other analytical audience • When using colors in bars, ensure contrast shows when printed in black and white • Align numbers across as much as possible and align labels with numbers	**Desserts Increasing at Ice Cream's Expense**
Histogram	• Shows frequency distributions, indicating how many in each class being measured • Not immediately intuitive for most people • Best used with statistically oriented audience • Rotate labels for ease of reading • Avoid double y-axis if possible	**Corvettes Sold in 2009**
Scatter plot	• Shows correlations, how well a variable follows the expected pattern • May need to be explained more than most charts making the title even more important in delivering the "so what?" • Rotate y-axis label for ease of reading • Make sure title explains meaning of content	**Work Experience Does Not Affect GMAT Scores**

Ethically Representing Data

Tufte emphasizes the importance of the integrity of graphic representation of data: "Graphical excellence begins with telling the truth about the data."[5] Ethical leaders would not intentionally distort the data through manipulating the numbers or purposely designing graphs that mislead the audience. In addition, they should be careful that they do not confuse their audience or accidentally mislead them by using poorly designed graphs or incorrectly selected graphs or by taking or presenting information out of context.[6]

As we consider the type of graph to use, we should test the integrity of our graphics by asking the following questions:

1. Does the data set completely support the message I wish to convey?
2. Have I provided or will I be able to provide enough context for the data to be interpreted accurately?
3. Are the numbers accurate and depicted honestly and accurately?
4. Does the design distort or hide the data in any way?
5. Are all axes and data accurately and adequately labeled?

Overall, we need to make sure that our graphics add to the substance of our presentations and that they do not distort, distract, or confuse the audience in any way. We want to aim for meaningful and clear content, honest and accurate depiction, and simplicity. If we then select the most effective graph to demonstrate or support our message, the graphics should help us communicate more powerfully.

Creating Meaningful and Effective Text Layouts

Text slides are the staple for most presentations and, in fact, are often overused. They may seem fairly simple and straightforward from a design point of view; however, Exhibit 6.15 contains a few guidelines and examples (first bad and then good) to make text slides more effective. In addition to the guidelines and examples, Exhibit 6.15 also contains a few technical tips on using PowerPoint.

The goals with any text chart are to make it as readable as possible and to make sure that it contains meaningful content. Achieving both of these objectives is not always easy because to ensure legibility we must minimize the words, which means every word must count. With very complicated information, keeping the text concise yet meaningful can be a challenge. If we find it too difficult, then perhaps it is time to reconsider PowerPoint as the best medium to convey our information. We may want to use a handout or poster board or perhaps use a round-table format instead.

Determining what is the best medium should be part of our strategic thinking as we begin to prepare the presentation; however, sometimes we have moved far into the creation of the presentation before we realize that PowerPoint will not work for all of our information, in

EXHIBIT 6.15 **Guidelines for Creating Effective Text Slides**

The Guidelines and PPT Hints	The Bad Examples
1. **Do not put too many words on the slide,** as done on the slide at the right. You should not have too many bullets or too many words at each bullet. 2. **Do not have only one bullet or sub-bullet as a category**. If you do, you should rephrase your points or elevate your bullets. Thus, the single bullet below "Expansion Division" needs to be broken into two.	**Key Current Quarter Priorities** **Global Division:** • Maintain consistent price pressure against competition • Execute toward lower alternative targets • Implement new global/local philosophy **Technical Division:** • Use SWAT team and various Area projects such as ACE in So America and Thrust in Europe to impact customer acceptance of the Newline 2000 and families and increase channel sales out on Newline 2000, 2500, and 3300 • Analysts removed Newline products from problem watch in July; communications deliverables sent to Global Marketing groups worldwide **Expansion Division:** • Deplete Technical inventory by end of Q1 to pave the way for AMstart (launch AMstart with European mono availability in Q3; European and So American color models in Q4)
3. **Use hanging indents for text lists of more than one line.** **Technical Tip:** To create the "hanging" indent, it is easiest to make your ruler visible in <View> and then adjust the bullets. Each bullet level will adjust when you adjust one of them. 4. **Avoid having too many "widow words" (see right).** **Technical Tip:** To get rid of "widow" words, cut words, decrease font, or increase margins, but be careful to stay as close to a consistent font and margin as possible.	**Key Current Quarter Priorities** **Global Division:** •Implement new global/local philosophy the structure **Widows** •Work with Area divisions to increase/monitor attach rates **Technical Division:** ♦Use SWAT team and various Area projects such as ACE in So America and Thrust in Europe to impact customer acceptance of the Newline 2000 ♦Analysts removed Newline products from problem watch in July; communications deliverables sent to Global Marketing groups worldwide No hanging indent
The Guidelines and PPT Hints	**The Good Examples**

5. **Keep the text simple but present meaningful content**. Note the use of hanging indents and the spacing between the lines and between the bullets and the text.
 	
6. **Make sure all bulleted items are parallel in structure.**
	Key Current Quarter Priorities
	❏ **Global Division**
	  ❖ **Maintain consistent price pressure**
	  ❖ **Execute toward lower alternative targets**
	  ❖ **Implement new global/local philosophy**
	  ❖ **Increase/monitor attach rates**
	❏ **Technical Division**
	  ❖ **Improve customer acceptance of Newline**
	  ❖ **Achieve target market share**
	  ❖ **Increase channel sales on Newline families**

(continued)

EXHIBIT 6.15 (continued)

The Guidelines and PPT Hints	The Good Examples (continued)

7. **Use some variation in how you lay out the text (slide after slide of lists of bullets can get rather boring). See example.**
 	
Technical Tip: It is usually easier to create each column of text as one text box. In this example, "Division" is in the same box as "Global" and "Technical." You can control the spacing between the items to ensure alignment across columns, by using <Line spacing> in <Format>.
	Current Priorities by Division
	
	Division Priority Actions
	
	Global ❖ Implement global/local philosophy
	             ❖ Work with Area divisions to increase attach rates
	
	Technical ❖ Use SWAT team to impact customer acceptance of Newline families
	             ❖ Increase channel sales on Newline families to achieve market share

8. **Maximize the impact of your title slide.** In other words, communicate the main message and the who, what, and when. See good example to the right. **Technical Tip:** Use the title master for the first slide, so that you can format it differently from the rest of the presentation. Also, you will usually need to change the font size on PowerPoint title master. Use shadow fonts with care; check readability, since the shadows often make the letters look fuzzy. Selecting bold fonts is usually best.	**VIETNAM** **The Softer Side of Doing Business Successfully in Vietnam Today** Captures "so what?" Presented by VBT Team: Mary Smith Jin Nguyen Charles Johnson Lists team members Identifies audience To Area Division Staff September 8, 2010 Gives date
9. **Work the text and graphics together to convey the message as at the right.** **Technical Tip:** When using text with AutoShapes, it is better to create a separate text box than to link the shape and the text, which is the default in PowerPoint. That way, you can move the text where you want it easily and align it within an object and from object to object.	**Steps to Creating Charts** Determine the message Choose the comparison Draw the chart Adapted from Gene Zelazny, *Say It with Charts.*

which case we may want to use multiple media for the text charts and for the graphic charts as well.

Making the Most of PowerPoint as a Design and Presentation Tool

The focus of this section is on using PowerPoint as a tool to communicate our content more effectively. The major caveat in using PowerPoint, as with using any graphics in a presentation, is to recognize that the PowerPoint slides should enhance the presentation, not dominate it. No amount of flashy display can have the genuine impact of a meaningful, logical message delivered effectively.

Poorly designed slides, such as the one demonstrated in Exhibit 6.16, which was actually used at a board presentation, are responsible for much of the criticism and disdain for PowerPoint. This slide has too much "chart junk," or clutter (the zeros; unnecessary graphic elements, such as the background; and the 3-D effect). The 3-D effect and the legend make it difficult to read, the skyline in the background only

EXHIBIT 6.16   An Example of a Poorly Designed PowerPoint Slide

Note: Please see color version online at www.mhhe.com/barrett3e.

detracts from the message, and the axes are unlabeled. As a result, the slide is more distracting than useful in conveying a message.

The slide in Exhibit 6.16 is reproduced here as it appeared in a corporate presentation, with only the title changed to reinforce the message that, just because PowerPoint provides all kinds of graphic augmentation for presentations, it does not mean that we should use them. Examples such as this one have led some organizations to ban the use of PowerPoint, which is unfortunate; when used correctly, it can be a powerful and effective presentation tool. Its capabilities can help presenters in planning, preparing, and practicing their presentations, although its greatest strength is in the enhancements it provides to delivery.

It is not the aim of this section to teach the basic use of PowerPoint as a computer software program. The primary focus is on effective slide design in PowerPoint with the goal of making slides look better so that they communicate the content more effectively and provide the presenter a leadership edge.

The following discussions include guidelines on selecting and designing layouts and templates, inserting graphs, using animation, and delivering effectively using PowerPoint.

Focusing on Meaningful Content

Using the standard PowerPoint templates to guide content creation encourages the use of few words and fairly simply graphics. For more complex messages, most presenters will need to modify the templates; however, even keeping the templates as they are, the presenter can create solid, thoughtful, and meaningful content. Presenters need to make sure the message is clear and that every word communicates meaning and every graphic contributes to that meaning.

PowerPoint was not intended to be a replacement for thinking. It is a medium to help convey that thinking. Just as with any effective communication, the sender of the message needs to have something meaningful to say. The presenter creates the content and is responsible for ensuring that it is clear and meaningful. PowerPoint is simply a tool to deliver the content.

Therefore, we should develop our message and determine the content needed to support it. Then, we can select and adjust or create the template and layout to help deliver that message and content. We should not let the template dictate or limit our content. Doing so is misusing PowerPoint.

Using Microsoft's AutoContent Wizards and Content Templates

Some PowerPoint detractors blame the AutoContent Wizard, which was removed from newer versions of PowerPoint starting with 2007, for "dumbing down" presentations and creating presentations devoid of meaningful content. When Microsoft initially created the AutoContent Wizards, the creators saw the idea as "crazy" and the name as a joke. They knew (or certainly hoped) that presenters had their own content to put into the program, although after creating the AutoContent Wizards, they found that they did help those facing writer's block.

Of course, we cannot provide meaningful content if we simply use a template instead of thinking up the content. The AutoContent template may help inspire ideas, but the substance depends on our development of the ideas.

For example, look at what an AutoContent slide provides for a presentation on communicating bad news:

> **Our Situation**
>
> ◆ **State the bad news**
> ◆ **Be clear; don't try to obscure the situation**

Obviously, this slide contains no content. At most, the templates provide possible subject headings and suggestions on content, even though any thoughtful leader would question relying on PowerPoint to deliver highly emotional messages, such as the communication of bad news. Obviously, if leaders decided PowerPoint were the best medium, they would need to supply the content and would have to decide if the topics and order of them made sense for their organization and the message they were delivering.

In newer versions of PowerPoint, the AutoContent Wizard has been replaced by templates with some suggested content. However, again, the content is extremely limited. For example, in a presentation on teamwork, the first content slide after the title slide reads as follows:

> **Purpose and objectives**
>
> ◆ **State the purpose of teamwork**
>   **and objectives of this presentation**

Selecting the Layout and Template

If creating a new presentation, we may want to start with one of Microsoft's many design templates. Some of them conform to the graphic design and legibility guidelines contained in this chapter with little or no modification, but for many of them, we will need to darken the background to create enough contrast with our font and for more reliable projection of the colors (see the color discussion in the previous section), alter the font style and size, and personalize to ensure that our presentation represents our own personality or that of our organization, not a generic organization.

Many organizations have a standard template they ask their employees to use. These templates may not conform to the guidelines in this chapter but are the standard for the organization. If we work for an organization with a standard template, we will probably have to use it; however, when we can, we should still try to employ the standards discussed here.

The most common layout used in PowerPoint is the horizontal, or landscape. To create slides for a PowerPoint presentation, we do not need to make any changes in page setup, since PowerPoint defaults to the horizontal layout when we open the program. If we select "new presentation," we will see a white background with black font, which we could use to create a round-table, handout, or overhead presentation.

If we plan to use our slides in a stand-up projected or Web presentation *and* as a handout, we should create or apply a template with a dark background and light font; then, select "pure black and white" in the print options commands to print out a standard white background, dark font format (this will help avoid using up ink cartridges) for the hand out.

We will need to remember to select "pure black and white" in the print command window each time we print, however, since Microsoft does not let us select it as our default print mode.

Designing Original Templates

Designing our own or modifying one of Microsoft's templates is usually a better approach than using one of Microsoft's standard templates, since it allows us to create a design that reflects our organization's image or our own personality and sense of style or to reinforce or suggest our message.

Also, creating our own template suggests we are willing to take the time to personalize the presentation and that we are not simply pulling something off the shelf that others could use. Creating an original template will mean that the presentation will stand out, as we probably would want. Again, the template format should not detract from our

EXHIBIT 6.17
Example of a
Modified
PowerPoint
Template with
Logo Embedded

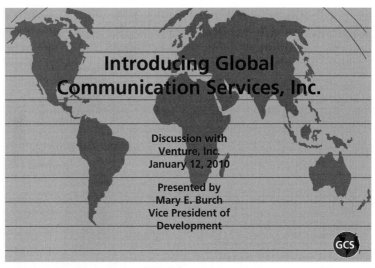

Note: Please see color version online at www.mhhe.com/barrett3e.

presentation or attract the audience's attention more than the message or the presenter. We will need to check our slides in slide view to ensure that the background does not overwhelm the foreground (any text or graphics).

One way to personalize a template is to select a simple picture or our organization's logo as the background. It should not be too complicated or showy, since a background that is too strong could overshadow the content on the slides, as is the case in the cityscape background in Exhibit 6.16.

Exhibit 6.17 provides an example of an effective background using a modified Microsoft template with the company's logo inserted.

Creating Documents Using PowerPoint

PowerPoint, although primarily a presentation package, can be used to create documents that include graphics as well. Again, PowerPoint defaults to the horizontal, or landscape, format, but we can select portrait if we are creating a report or other document that we intend for our audience to read rather than see in a stand-up presentation. A presentation can be converted to the portrait layout after created in landscape, but we may need to make some adjustments to the graphics to make them fit effectively in the new layout. Therefore, it is better to select portrait before creating slides or use the notes view instead, as illustrated in Exhibit 6.18.

We might select the portrait layout if we have a number of graphs and want to ensure that the explanations occur just above them.

EXHIBIT 6.18   **Example of a Report in PowerPoint—Portrait versus Notes View**

Portrait View	Notes View
The most important question for measuring the success of the communication program is the one that asks the students if they feel their communication skills have improved because of the program. As the chart shows, the students have self-reported improvement every year since 2006. If the 2006 number were adjusted to allow for the lower scores in sections taught by first-time instructors, the score for 2006 would be 88%. Clearly, the students realize and acknowledge that their communication skills have improved as a result of the program.	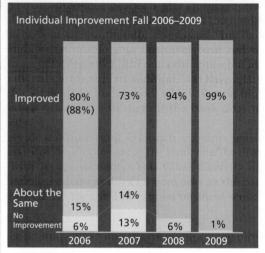

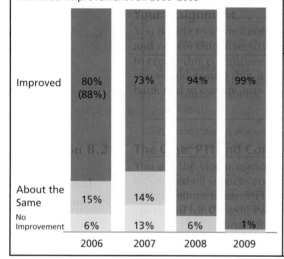

The most important question for measuring the success of the communication program is the one that asks the students if they feel their communication skills have improved because of the program. As the chart shows, the students have self-reported improvement every year since 2006. If the 2006 number were adjusted to allow for the lower scores in sections taught by first-time instructors, the score for 2006 would be 88%. Clearly, the students realize and acknowledge that their communication skills have improved as a result of the program.

Exhibit 6.18 shows an example of a page from a vertical report created in PowerPoint, using portrait view and notes view. For notes view, we simply select the notes format when printing the presentation for the audience.

Inserting Graphs and Other Objects

Many of the design faults that show up in PowerPoint presentations occur when people insert graphs or objects from other programs, Excel in particular. This section provides a few suggestions for avoiding and correcting the most common design problems. Exhibit 6.19

EXHIBIT 6.19
Poorly Designed Graph Inserted into PowerPoint from Excel

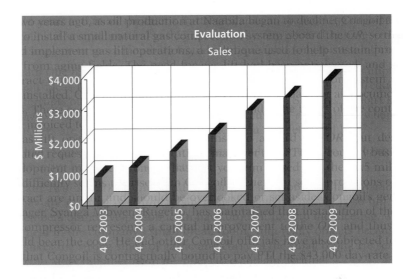

demonstrates a poorly designed graph for PowerPoint presentation purposes. Here are the problems:

- The chart has two titles, the one given in Excel and the one used in PowerPoint.
- Axis labels are not rotated to be read horizontally.
- Bars are too narrow; the space between should be smaller than the width of the bars.
- Use of 3-D makes reading the locations of the tops of the bars difficult.
- Chart junk clutters the exhibit: the zeros and the repetition of "4 Q" with each year.
- The background of the graph is not consistent with the background of the presentation.

Some of these problems could be corrected in Excel before importing the graph; however, it is often easier to correct them in Power-Point.

Our graphs should look as if they were part of the presentation, not pulled in at the last minute from Excel without concern for consistency in the formatting and clarity of the information being conveyed. Exhibit 6.20 shows the same graph reworked for projection in Power-Point. It is now simple, clean, and easy to read.

Although we end up with a graph that is more aesthetically pleasing, the main objective of these changes is legibility when the graph is projected. Taking the extra time to make our imported graphs easier to read and more attractive for a PowerPoint presentation is worth the effort; otherwise, our audience may think we are careless or not interested in their ability to read what we are presenting.

EXHIBIT 6.20
Corrected Bar
Graph Imported
from Excel

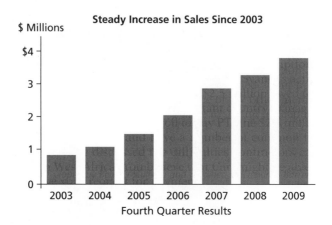

We can, of course, make the graph even more appealing by using color effectively and by following some of the design principles discussed previously, but the primary goal when adjusting any inserted graph or object should be to make it easier for the audience to get the message.

Using Animation

Animation is a great tool; however, it is easily overused and misused. The following guidelines will help presenters use animation effectively so that it adds to the impact of the presentation by supporting the main messages:

1. **Use animation only to control the delivery of the message or help the audience with the message.** We should think carefully about how we can use animation to control the delivery of our content. For example, if we want our bullets to appear when we talk about each one instead of all at once, we should consider how long we will spend on each bullet. If we are going to discuss each item separately at some depth and length, then it would probably be worth the effort and slight distraction to have them appear one at a time; however, if we are going to talk about all of the bullets in more general terms, it would be better to have all of them appear at the same time. The same principle applies for charts and graphs; if, for example, we intend to discuss one line on a line graph at a time, we might want to have each line appear as we discuss it, creating the line graph slowly as we share the information.

Although we should aim for one message on a slide, sometimes the overall message has several layers or pieces to it. For example, if we have a complex message, such as the one in Exhibit 6.11, we might want to use animation. When presenting this slide, we could use animation to control what the audience sees and when. We could bring in and discuss each arrow (force) while building to the total message of multiple forces reshaping the oil industry. Seeing the whole slide with all of the pieces in place at one time could confuse the audience. They might not know where to look, so we would want to control their attention by bringing in the pieces as we talk about them.

Finally, we should make our animation keystroke driven rather than automatic so that we can control the building of the slide.

2. Do not overuse animation or add it just because it is possible. It will only distract the audience and even irritate them. Think about the spinning logo people sometimes place in a corner of their slides or the moving Flash ads on Web sites. Our eyes go to the logo or object, no matter how hard we try to focus on the speaker or the other information on the page.

3. When animation is used to bring in text or AutoShapes, the text and shapes should appear or come in from the most logical direction and the shortest distance. For example, in Exhibit 6.11, the arrow at the left should come in from the left, the bottom arrow from the bottom, and the right arrow from the right. While this seems intuitive, we have all sat through presentations with objects flying in from all directions without rhyme or reason.

4. Avoid using several different animation techniques in one presentation. Decide on one or two main techniques and stay with them. Usually, the more conservative the better, which means the "appear" choice is often the best one.

5. Make sure to test the animation by running the presentation in slide view from beginning to end. In fact, even if we are not using animation, we should always review our presentation in slide view, since, for reasons unknown, animation will sometimes appear that we did not intend (suggesting gremlins do exist). We can usually get rid of these gremlins by checking the Animation Schemes and turning off "Apply to all" if it is selected.

As with all the design guidelines discussed in this chapter, we should use animation only if it adds to or helps us deliver our message.

Again, keep graphics simple, and design slides so that the audience can scan them easily and naturally. Also, although culture and preferred language will determine how someone reads (right to left or left to right), most now are accustomed to reading charts from left to right and top to bottom; therefore, we should consider the messages we want to emphasize when we design the chart. For example, most business and academic audiences expect to see a title at the top of the chart that tells them the major message. Make sure to take advantage of this expectation and do not bury major messages at the bottom or, even worse, in the midst of everything else in the center. Doing so risks its getting lost. If we must create a design contrary to an audience's natural reading inclination, we should be prepared to guide them to the portion of the slide where we want their attention. This kind of guidance requires that we practice with our slides, making sure we can provide this assistance in reading easily and smoothly without looking back at the slide in a stand-up presentation.

To summarize, when using graphics and PowerPoint, follow these top 10 guidelines:

Top 10 Guidelines for Using Graphics and PowerPoint for a Leadership Edge

1. Decide on the message, determine what information or data best support it, and then decide how best to show those data graphically.
2. Use graphics for the right reasons, such as to reinforce the message, to provide a road map to the presentation, and to support assertions.
3. Select the right kind of graph to illustrate the message.
4. Use integrity in selecting and designing all graphics, making sure any graphs do not distort the data.
5. Keep all graphics simple but meaningful. The graphic should make the message easier to understand, not more difficult. Make sure it is meaningful and actually says something.
6. Use a title (placed at the top of the slide) that captures the "so what?" of the slide so that the audience sees immediately the message the graph is communicating.
7. Create an original PowerPoint template or modify the standard ones Microsoft provides so that the presentation reflects the personality of the presenter or that of the presenter's organization.
8. Make the font size and any graphic images large enough for the audience to see, even from the back of the room.
9. Be careful with color selections; go for contrast but be conservative, remembering that color perception varies from person to person and color meaning varies from culture to culture.
10. Avoid overusing or misusing animation.

Finally, we should make graphics and PowerPoint work for us not against us, using graphics to support our message and PowerPoint as the tool it is intended to be. The presenter should be the focus of the presentation. The slides are there to aid us, not replace us. Used correctly, graphics and PowerPoint will provide a leadership edge and help us project a positive ethos.

**Application 6.1
Creating Graphs**

1. Review the quantitative data that follow. You will see that you can make several conclusions based on these data. What do you see? Select *one type of comparison* (part to whole, time series, etc.) and roughly sketch out a slide to support the conclusion you have drawn from the comparison. (You do not need to use all of the data.) Write a title for the slide that captures the "so what?" of the graph.

Sales Data for Gizmo Company Products ($000)*				
	Product A	**Product B**	**Product C**	**Total**
January	85	26	7	118
February	94	30	8	132
March	103	35	8	146
April	113	40	7	160
May	122	45	13	180
June	130	30	10	170

*You may assume that the profit margins on each product are similar.

2. Use the same process to analyze these data and sketch out a slide. Remember to write a title that tells the audience what you want them to conclude from the data.

Quench Beverage Company—Cola Sales Data for the United States and Mexico ($MM)				
	2002	**2003**	**2004**	**2005**
U.S.	24.1	40.0	37.5	47.4
Mexico	39.9	34.8	23.8	19.9

Source: This exercise was developed by Beth O'Sullivan and Larry Hampton, Rice University. Used with permission.

Application 6.2 Selecting and Designing Graphics Exercise

For each of the following topics, decide on the best type of graph to support the message and then design the graphic. Do these very quickly, sketching what first comes to your mind. Do not worry about being artistic; instead, capture your own creative ideas.

1. Over the last five years, Company A has outperformed its competitor, Company B (increasing revenue, decreasing costs).
2. GMAT scores are not related to grades in MBA classes.
3. Widgets yield the majority of WidCo's profit.
4. The bonus percentage depends on employee title and rank.
5. Four forces are driving industry growth.
6. The project consists of three phases.

Application 6.3 Exercise in Designing Visuals

Grab a pen, a pencil, or your computer and sketch the very first image that comes to mind for each of the following chart titles. The goal is to work very quickly and not to get caught up in making the lines straight or the graph or picture square or perfect in any way. Simply capture the message as best you can and don't over-think it.

1. The Web Site's Hits Have Quadrupled Since 2009
2. Apple's IPods Have the Largest Share of the MP3 Market
3. The Team's Project Will Advance in Three Phases
4. Houston's Airport System Ranks Fourth Nationally

5. The Age Distribution of the U.S. Population Differs Sharply from That of Developing Countries

6. Students Are Caught in the Crisscross of Decreased Scholarship Money and Increased College Costs

7. The Five Programs Are Interrelated

8. The Two Project Teams Must Interact for Better Results

9. The Task Forces Are Moving in Opposite Directions

10. The Range of Discounts Offered for the New PCs Varies Widely by Geographic Area

11. Forces at Work on the Faculty Will Result in the Restructuring of the Curriculum

12. The Development of Computer Viruses Follows a Vicious Circle

This exercise was inspired by my former McKinsey colleague, Gene Zelazny, in "Designing Charts for the Zen of It" in *Say It with Presentations* by Gene Zelazny (New York: McGraw-Hill, 2000). Thank you, Gene.

Application 6.4
Team Graphics and Oral Presentations

For this exercise, pretend you are in an investment group and your group has been selected to deliver an updated presentation on the company/division discussed in one of the following articles:

Nestle article
http://www.businessweek.com/investor/content/apr2009/pi20090428_699553.htm?chan=investing_investing+index+page_stocks+%2Bamp;+markets

Chrysler article (includes a video!)
http://www.businessweek.com/bwdaily/dnflash/content/may2009/db2009051_297080.htm?chan=top+news_top+news+index+-+temp_news+%2B+analysis

Zipcar
http://www.businessweek.com/technology/content/apr2009/tc20090430_383555.htm?chan=top+news_top+news+index+-+temp_technology

Although these *BusinessWeek* articles work well for this exercise, almost any article that includes financial performance data will work as well.

Your audience will consist of potential investors in the company, all of whom will be logging in to a Web presentation.

If you are not already working with a team, form a group of four or five people for this exercise. Each group will have 40 minutes to develop a 5-minute oral presentation that, since it will be delivered remotely, is heavily dependent on visual aids for communicating key ideas and maintaining interest. (Your team can choose who will present—not everyone needs to speak, although it is fine if you want everyone to deliver part of the presentation.)

Your presentation should convey the company's current situation and prospects. Your group may make an investment recommendation, if you wish, but you are not required to do so. You do not need to use all the data in the article, and you may add other information about the company (if it is from a reliable source).

Each group member should offer suggestions about what key messages to include in your visuals. The team then needs to agree on the "storyboard," that is, the ideas to be conveyed and the content and sequence of graphics.

Use the paper and the markers provided or your computer to create the visual aids you will use for your presentation. Of course, in the real world, you would have more time to make your visuals look professional. For today, you should focus on your story, capturing key messages, expressing them graphically, and presenting them effectively (remember to include an effective opening, strong transitions, and an effective closing for your presentation). Your visuals may include quantitative charts, diagrams, qualitative drawings, and word slides (where needed). Be sure to do the following:

- Include a title chart with the names of the group members and the company.
- Write a title that tells the main message of the presentation.
- Create "so what?" titles for each visual.
- Limit your content or "body" visuals to a number you can comfortably present in 5 minutes.

Source: This exercise was adapted from an exercise created by Beth O'Sullivan and Larry Hampton, Rice University. Updated by Sandra Elliot. Used with permission.

Notes

1. Vogel, D., Dickson, G., and Lehman, J. A. (1986). *Persuasion and the Role of Visual Presentation Support*. Study sponsored by the University of Minnesota and 3M Corporation.
2. Tufte, E. R. (2003). *The Cognitive Style of PowerPoint*. Cheshire, CT: Graphics Press. See Barrett, D. (2004). "The Power of PowerPoint." *Proceedings of the 2004 Association for Business Communication Conference* for a complete discussion of attacks on PowerPoint and a defense of it as a presentation tool.
3. PowerPoint is the primary presentation/graphics software discussed in this chapter because it has become a presentation standard, not to support or promote Microsoft and its products. All of the best practices presented would apply to any presentation or graphics software package.
4. Halverson, M. 3M Meeting Network—Choosing the Right Colors for Your Next Presentation, www.3m.com.
5. Tufte, E. R. (1983). *The Visual Display of Quantitative Information*. Cheshire, CT: Graphics Press, p. 53.
6. For examples of graphic distortion and how to avoid it and a discussion of visual ethics, see Tufte (1983); and Kienzler, D. S. (1997). Visual Ethics. *Journal of Business Communication* 34, pp. 171–87. For more on how data and statistics can be misused or quoted, see Best, J. (2001). Damned Lies and Statistics: Untangling Numbers from the Media, Politicians, and Activists.

Section 2

Organizational Leadership Communication

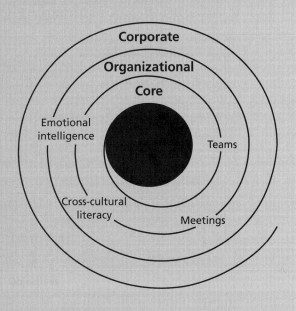

7

Emotional Intelligence and Interpersonal Skills for Leaders

You've got to have not just the business skills; you've got to have the emotional intelligence. . . .You have to have the emotional intelligence to understand what's right culturally, both in your company and outside your company.

Richard Anderson, CEO, Delta Air Lines *New York Times* interview with Adam Bryant, 2009

Emotional leadership is the spark that ignites a company's performance, creating a bonfire of success or a landscape of ashes.

Daniel Goleman, Richard Boyatzis, and Annit McKee (2001), Primal Leadership: The Hidden Driver of Great Performance, *Harvard Business Review*

Leaders are constantly communicating. . . . Their language goes beyond mere words. Body language, intuition, presence, accessibility—above all, behavior.

Max De Pree (2003). *Leading without Power: Finding Hope in Serving Community*

Chapter Objectives

In this chapter, you will learn to do the following:

- Appreciate the value of emotional intelligence.
- Take steps to increase your own emotional intelligence.

- Improve your nonverbal skills.
- Improve your listening skill.
- Motivate and mentor.
- Network to improve leadership connections.

Leaders need strong emotional intelligence and outstanding interpersonal skills. Recently, interpersonal skills have gained recognition under the name of "emotional intelligence."[1] Emotional intelligence, also often called emotional quotient, or EQ, is the capacity to identify and manage emotions in ourselves and in others. This understanding provides a foundation for our interaction with others and our ability to understand and relate to them and is often directly tied to an individual's success as a transformational leader.[2]

"Emotional intelligence" and "interpersonal skills" are sometimes used interchangeably, but a useful distinction is to see emotional intelligence as what is going on inside of us and interpersonal skills as emotional intelligence in action as we interact with others. Another way to think about the difference is to think of the relationship of emotional intelligence to interpersonal skills as we would the relationship of our IQ to our ability to demonstrate problem-solving acumen. Our ability to interact effectively depends on our emotional intelligence, which we display through our interpersonal skills.

Without emotional intelligence, leaders cannot communicate and connect with others effectively. Our emotional intelligence and interpersonal skills are judged by how well we interact with others, both verbally and nonverbally.

In addition, leaders' own emotional intelligence affects the climate and morale of the organizations and groups they lead: "'Emotions are contagious. Research shows that they determine 50% to 70% of the workplace climate; that climate, in turn, determines 20% to 30% of a company's performance.' What's more, EI accounts for 85% of what distinguishes the stars in top leadership positions from low-level performers."[3] Thus, the leader's emotional intelligence determines his or her success as well as the organization's culture and performance. For leadership communication, emotional intelligence is as important as the strategy, writing, and speaking skills included in the core of the leadership communication spiral, introduced in the first few chapters of this text.

The need for keen emotional intelligence becomes magnified when we interact with others in an organization, whether one-on-one, in groups, in meetings, or in teams; and it is this interaction that is the focus of the organizational communication ring of the leadership communication spiral. In addition, the advent of social media and networking sites has increased leaders' needs to learn how to interact with a broad, general audience in intelligent, thoughtful, and considerate ways.

Our successful interactions with others depend on communication: "The basis of any relationship is communication. Without communication—be it sign language, body language, e-mail, or face-to-face conversation—there is no connection and hence no relationship. The importance of effective communication skills to our Emotional Intelligence is crucial, and its value in the workplace is incalculable."[4]

While this entire book is dedicated to improving your leadership communication abilities, this chapter is devoted specifically to understanding emotional intelligence and developing the ability to uncover what Weisinger calls the "emotional subtext," which means getting below the surface of the words—in many cases, to the meaning beneath. This ability is essential to emotional intelligence. The first sections of this chapter discuss the value of emotional intelligence and how to achieve it; the later sections on nonverbal communications, listening, people development through mentoring and motivating, and networking focus on helping you increase your ability to understand the emotional subtext and demonstrate the interpersonal skills all of us need to be successful leaders

Appreciating the Value of Emotional Intelligence

An organization's culture reflects the emotional intelligence (or lack of it) of its leaders, and the leaders reveal that emotional intelligence through their communication ability and style. Think back to the example in Chapter 4 of the midwestern CEO who lambasted his managers in an e-mail because he thought the employees were not working long enough hours, citing the empty parking lot as one of his clues to the slacking workforce. What kind of personality does his e-mail reveal? What does it say about his attitude toward and relationship with his management team? What does it suggest about the company culture? The CEO's memo suggests emotional intelligence deficiencies, since he shows little concern for the emotions of his audience and little control of his own. He appears limited in his understanding of his audience and how best to motivate them.

The first version of the memo about the abuse of copy machines in Chapter 2 also exhibits limited emotional intelligence through its insensitivity to others and lack of awareness of how to motivate employees. The language in the first version, such as the use of passive voice ("It has recently been brought to my attention" and "Their behavior cannot and will not be tolerated"), and the threat ("Anyone in the future who is unable to control himself will have his employment terminated") suggest a culture that is authoritative and hierarchical, where management sits well above and separate from the employees. The language in the final version, however, suggests a company where the employees are part of a community with management: "We are revamping our policy. . . ."

Both of these examples show how the language that we use reveals the kind of leader that we are and the type of organization that we lead. Both are prime examples of how a deficiency of emotional intelligence can lead to communication mistakes, which in turn can lead to problems in the corporate culture and signal that cultural problems exist. All of the research into the importance of emotional intelligence demonstrates that possessing emotional intelligence is valuable to leaders personally and to the organizations they lead.

Understanding Emotional Intelligence

Reuven Bar-On, who developed the concept of emotional quotient in 1988, provides a technical definition of emotional intelligence. Emotional quotient (or intelligence) is emotional and social knowledge and the ability to

1. Be aware of, understand, and express yourself.
2. Be aware of, understand, and relate to others.
3. Deal with strong emotions and control your impulses.
4. Adapt to change and solve problems of a personal or a social nature.[5]

This definition suggests that emotional intelligence begins with the ability to identify and manage emotions in ourselves and in others, but it extends also to the ability to translate these emotions into actions that show flexibility and personal and social problem-solving ability. It implies that the actions should have a positive impact on others. Exhibit 7.1 contains a diagram that breaks emotional intelligence down into components similar to those Reuven Bar-On cites. It illustrates the

EXHIBIT 7.1 **Conceptualization of Emotional Intelligence**

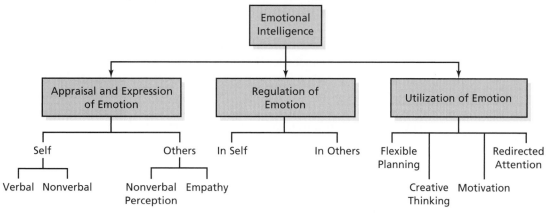

Source: Figure from Morand, D.A. (2001). The Emotional Intelligence of Managers: Assessing the Construct Validity of a Nonverbal Measure of "People Skills." *Journal of Business and Psychology* 16, No. 1, pp. 21–33. Figures based on Mayer, J., and Salovey, P. (1993). The Intelligence of Emotional Intelligence. *Intelligence*, pp. 433–42.

role of communication and the ways that emotional intelligence can be manifested.

The diagram in Exhibit 7.1 contains three branches of emotional intelligence: (1) the appraisal and expression of emotion, (2) the regulation of emotion, and (3) the utilization of emotion. Another way to think about these three branches is as they might be expressed or revealed: through communication, by control, and by action. Leaders demonstrate their emotional intelligence by appraising situations and other people and by expressing the appropriate emotions. In the left branch, the focus is on expressing ourselves verbally and nonverbally, as well as on understanding others by reading their nonverbal cues and by empathizing with them. The middle branch focuses on the control of emotions in the self and in others. The right branch deals with the manifestation of emotional intelligence in actions, such as planning with flexibility, thinking creatively, motivating others, and redirecting attention or energy when appropriate.

Consider the midwestern CEO again; his emphasis is on the self, what he feels, and what is in it for him—all part of the left side of the diagram. His e-mail suggests little empathy and little regulation of his emotions. In the end, his e-mail fails to suggest flexible planning, creativity, redirection, or motivation of his employees toward the actions he desires. Effective leadership communication depends on being able to analyze an audience and develop a communication strategy for the context, which includes the left and middle branches of the emotional intelligence tree in Exhibit 7.1. The CEO has fallen short here, which carries over into the failure to craft and deliver the messages that will inspire his employees to act as he wants. This example demonstrates how profoundly emotional intelligence influences our leadership communication ability, which in turn suggests our leadership style.

Connecting Emotional Intelligence to Leadership Styles

In *Primal Leadership*, Goleman, Boyatzis, and McKee argue that leadership styles fall into six broad categories: (1) visionary, (2) coaching, (3) affiliative, (4) democratic, (5) pacesetting, and (6) commanding. These last two may have a negative impact on the organization (Exhibit 7.2).

Any one of these styles might be effective in the right situation or in some cultures, although the authors' research demonstrates that pacesetting and commanding rarely work, particularly in the long term.

The style of communication will differ from leader to leader and from organization to organization, and the leaders will reveal that style by how they choose to communicate with employees.

The **visionary** leaders inspire others and would probably be very visible in the organization, speaking frequently in public internal forums, holding frequent meetings, sending out statements that motivate and provide guidance to all of the employees, and being accessible to their followers.

EXHIBIT 7.2 Leadership Styles in a Nutshell

Style	How It Builds Resonance	Impact on Climate	When Appropriate
Visionary	Moves people toward shared dreams	Most strongly positive	When changes require a new vision, or when direction is needed
Coaching	Connects what a person wants with the organization's goals	Highly positive	To help an employee improve performance by building long-term capabilities
Affiliative	Creates harmony by connecting people to each other	Positive	To heal rifts in a team, motivate during stressful times, or strengthen connections
Democratic	Values people's input and gets commitment through participation	Positive	To build buy-in or con sensus, or to get valuable input from employees
Pacesetting	Meets challenging and exciting goals	Often highly negative because frequently executed poorly	To get high-quality results from a motivated and competent team
Commanding	Soothes fears by giving clear direction in an emergency	Highly negative because so often misused	In a crisis, to kick-start a turnaround, or with problem employees

Source: Adapted and reprinted by permission of Harvard Business School Press. From *Primal Leadership: Realizing the Power of Emotional Intelligence* by Goleman, D., Boyatzis, R., & McKee, A. Boston, MA 2002, p. 55. Copyright © 2002 by Daniel Goleman; all rights reserved.

Visionary leaders are also often tapped to represent their organizations through blogs, social networks, or other social media interactions. These leaders are often those who inspire conversation, debate, and change in their fields.

Visionary leaders articulate a purpose and goals that appeal to those they lead. People believe in them and what they represent and want to follow them. An example from the political arena is U.S. President Obama. From the beginning of his campaign, he clearly articulated a vision and continues to do so now that he is in office. As Jack and Suzy Welch write in *BusinessWeek:*

> Let's start with vision, the thing without which a person simply cannot lead. And look, whether you like his politics or not, Obama's obviously got it. From the economy to the environment, education to health care, the President has articulated his goals to the nation.[6]

It is important to note that President Obama has been very involved in social media networks—from Facebook to Twitter to text messaging—to further both his election and his post-election goals. He may well represent the new face of visionary leadership in the Web space.

The **coaching** leaders would provide a strong, mentoring culture and probably place importance on training and development sessions and on management's responsibility for developing others. An example cited in *Primal Leadership* is David Ogilvy, founder of Ogilvy & Mather, one of the most successful advertising firms: "Ogilvy's leadership included a large dose of the coaching style: having a deep conversation with an employee that goes beyond short-term concerns and instead explores the person's life, including dreams, life goals, and career hopes."[7]

The **affiliative** leader would probably be involved in frequent interaction with employees and would walk the halls and be accessible, both one-on-one and in small groups. He would exemplify teamwork and collaboration. Joe Torre, the manager of the New York Yankees from 1996 to 2007, who coached the Yankees to 10 American League East Division titles, six American League pennants, and four World Series titles, is the example Goleman, Boyatzis, and McKee discuss:

> Such open sharing of emotions is one hallmark of the affiliative leadership style, which Torre exemplifies. These leaders also tend to value people and their feelings—putting less emphasis on accomplishing tasks and goals, and more on employees' emotional needs. They strive to keep people happy, to create harmony, and—as Torre did so well—build team resonance.[8]

The **democratic** leader would probably hold frequent meetings as well, but he or she would also survey employees and establish methods to obtain employee input. Democratic leaders are good listeners and very good collaborators. They are adept at including others in idea generation and problem solving. They recognize their own limits and willingly call on others to fill in the gaps in their expertise or experience.

Louis Gerstner, Jr., who was chair of IBM from 1993 to 2002, is considered such a leader. Coming in from outside of the computer industry, he openly and successfully drew on the expertise of those at IBM, while cutting $9 billion in expenses and laying off thousands and leading "a sensationally successful turnaround, charting a new strategic course for the company."[9]

Pacesetting leaders are hard-driving, constantly pushing the organization to excel. They are not likely to hold open forums with employees, choosing instead to make decisions on their own or with insider groups and communicating with employees when they have successful performance to celebrate or a new idea to push. They do not appear accessible to employees; therefore, open dialogue is unlikely.

The pacesetting style of leader "holds and exemplifies high standards for performance. He is obsessive about doing things better and faster, and asks the same of eveyone. He quickly pinpoints poor performers, and demands more from them, and if they don't rise to the occasion, rescues the situation himself."[10] The result is a highly competitive environment where employees compete against each other, soon becoming disenchanted and frustrated at feeling pressured to perform, no matter what the cost. This style of leadership may also lead to tense relationships with customers, now that blogs and social networks allow for robust interaction between the public and corporations.

An example is the leadership team at the top of Enron before its collapse, Ken Lay and Jeff Skilling, whose leadership turned Enron into the biggest wholesaler of gas and electricity. Skilling, who is now serving a 24-year prison term, exemplifies the pacesetting style in particular. He was well know as extremely hard-driving of himself and others. He demanded performance and perfection and would not tolerate anything less.

When entering the Enron building before the company collapsed in one of the largest corporate scandals in business history, visitors were greeted with monitors showing the stock price, which was constantly touted and used to push employees to perform. While for a business to emphasize the bottom line may not be all bad, Enron serves as an example of how the pacesetting leader's continued high pressure can be distructive, leading to disillusionment and perhaps bad decisions and even corruption.

The **commanding** leader lives by the motto of "Do it because I say so," according to Goleman, Boyatzis, and McKee. Both the e-mail of the midwestern CEO and first version of the memo on the abuse of copiers suggest a command and control leadership style, for example, and it seems clear these styles would not be effective in motivating employees in most situations.

However, commanding leadership may work temporarily in some situations if used judiciously—for example, when a major turnaround is needed or when facing a crisis. It might also be expected in cultures in which respect for authority dominates their decision making and way of working.

Jack Welch, former CEO of GE, supposedly exemplified the commanding style when he first took over at GE and needed to bring about a major turnaround. His firm and controlling top-down leadership style worked well at that time in the company's history, although he switched to a more visionary style soon after accomplishing the immediate need of the company turnaround.

In the four positive styles, the leader's tone would be receptive and open, whereas in the **pacesetting** and **commanding** styles, the tone would be closed and distancing. The pacesetting and commanding tones are suggested in the following: "It has been brought to my attention that some of you are abusing the copiers" versus the tone of "We should work together to achieve a pay-as-you-go policy."

A leader might vary his or her leadership style when the situation warrants it, but the ability to select the most effective style for different

EXHIBIT 7.3
Emotional Intelligence Domains and Competencies

Source: Reprinted by permission of Harvard Business School Press. From *Primal Leadership: Realizing the Power of Emotional Intelligence* by Goleman, D., Boyatzis, R. & McKee, A. Boston, MA 2002, p. 39. Copyright © 2002 by Daniel Goleman; all rights reserved.

Personal Competence: These capabilities determine how we manage ourselves.

Self-Awareness
- Emotional self-awareness: Reading one's own emotions and recognizing their impact; using "gut sense" to guide decisions
- Accurate self-assessment: Knowing one's strengths and limits
- Self-confidence: A sound sense of one's self-worth and capabilities

Self-Management
- Emotional self-control: Keeping disruptive emotions and impulses under control
- Transparency: Displaying honesty and integrity; trustworthiness
- Adaptability: Flexibility in adapting to changing situations or over-coming obstacles
- Achievement: The drive to improve performance to meet inner standards of excellence
- Initiative: Readiness to act and seize opportunities
- Optimism: Seeing the upside in events

Social Competence: These capabilities determine how we manage relationships.

Social Awareness
- Empathy: Sensing others' emotions, understanding their perspective, and taking active interest in their concerns
- Organizational awareness: Reading the currents, decision networks, and politics at the organizational level
- Service: Recognizing and meeting follower, client, or customer needs

Relationship Management
- Inspirational leadership: Guiding and motivating with a compelling vision
- Influence: Wielding a range of tactics for persuasion
- Developing others: Bolstering others' abilities through feedback and guidance
- Change catalyst: Initiating, managing, and leading in a new direction
- Conflict management: Resolving disagreements
- Building bonds: Cultivating and maintaining a web of relationships
- Teamwork and collaboration: Cooperation and team building

situations requires the emotional intelligence to assess the situation correctly and assume the style appropriate for the context and audience. It means understanding that leaders reveal their emotional intelligence in their words and their actions.

Exhibit 7.3 contains the "major domains" of emotional intelligence with their associated personal and social competencies, further illustrating how emotional intelligence can be manifested in interactions with others and in attempts to communicate with and lead them.

According to Goleman, Boyatzis, and McKee, no leader possesses all of these competencies, but "highly effective leaders typically exhibit a critical mass of strength in a half dozen or so EI competencies."[11]

Some competencies are certainly more important for effective leadership communication than others. These competencies are the focus of the remainder of this chapter, beginning with those included under self-awareness and self-management, moving through the relationship management competencies of developing others, and ending with increasing your social awareness by learning to network effectively.

Increasing Our Own Self-Awareness

The first step toward emotional intelligence is self-awareness. Socrates said, "Know thyself," yet as most thoughtful people realize, knowing the self is not easy. In his book *Emotional Intelligence at Work*, Hendrie Weisinger calls self-awareness "the foundation on which all other emotional intelligence skills are built" and says that self-awareness is an ongoing process.[12] He suggests that everyone exercise self-awareness at work by asking the following questions several times a day:

- What am I feeling right now?
- What do I want? How am I acting?
- What appraisals am I making?
- What do my senses tell me?

The self-assessment in Appendix A contains a number of questions relating to emotional intelligence. If you have not completed it, you might want to go back now and establish a baseline measure of your self-awareness and overall emotional intelligence.

Source: Popular image on the World Wide Web. Original source unknown.

Another way to become more self-aware is to take personality profiles, such the Myers-Briggs Type Indicator (MBTI) discussed here. You may want to visit the Emotional Intelligence Consortium Web site (www.eiconsortium.org), since it lists and contains links to some self-assessments of emotional intelligence and 360-degree feedback tools. You will also find a number of free resources available if you do a Google search for MBTI or "personality tests"; however, most of these resources will not provide a complete assessment or provide thorough feedback on the results, or they may solicit fees for more than the "free" tool provided. You should, of course, approach any of these solicitations with caution and check the credentials of the organization or administrator to ensure that you receive legitimate and complete presults

If you have never had the benefit of 360-degree feedback, or any feedback on your emotional intelligence, you will find such feedback provides different insight from personal assessments or personality tests. They allow us to see ourselves as others see us. For example, to others we may not be the lion we see in the mirror in the popular picture of the kitten looking in the mirror and seeing his reflection as a lion.

What is important to realize is that we can develop our emotional intelligence and by doing so improve our leadership communication ability, but we need to understand our strengths and weaknesses first.

Using Popular Psychological Profiles to Understand Ourselves Better

Psychological testing can help us gain insight into our behavior and how we interact with others, as well as how others interact with us. We can benefit from knowing ourselves better and identifying characteristics that may hinder our ability to interact effectively with others. With this knowledge, we can work toward modifying unproductive behaviors and perhaps, at a minimum, understand better why others respond to us as they do.

Numerous psychological profiling instruments exist for use by individuals and businesses. Three of the ones considered sound in their theory and applicability in a professional environment are the FIRO-B, the Five Factors, and the Myers-Briggs Type Indicator (MBTI). Each can assist us in understanding ourselves and others. Since the MBTI is the most widely used in business, with over 2.5 million tests administered in organizations across the world,[13] the discussion here focuses on the MBTI to illustrate how we might use a personality test to understand ourselves better and to manage others more effectively.

Using the MBTI

Katherine Briggs and Isabel Briggs Myers developed the MBTI using Carl Jung's concepts of personality types as the foundation for their personality assessments. Our individual personality type remains fairly consistent over time, although environmental influences can alter our responses slightly when we take one of the MBTI instruments

The MBTI consists of four dichotomies in 16 combinations. The dichotomies are as follows:

- Extravert (E) vs. Introvert (I)—indicates how we are energized.
- Sensing (S) vs. iNtuitive (N)—suggests how we take in information and interpret or understand the world.
- Thinking (T) vs. Feeling (F)—shows how we tend to make decisions.
- Judging (J) vs. Perceiving (P)—suggests our approach to life and work.

A person's type is indicated by a combination of the letters according to his or her preferences in each of these dichotomies. Exhibit 7.4 lists the characteristics common to each of the individual letter designations.

An individual type could be an ESTJ, INFP, or any other of the 16 possible combinations. The combinations, not just one of the letter labels, determine the personality type, although a letter may dominate.

EXHIBIT 7.4
Descriptors
Commonly Used
for Type
Indicators

How Energized		How Interpret/Understand	
Extravert	**Introvert**	**Sensing**	**iNtuiting**
Outgoing	Introspective	The five senses	The sixth sense
External	Internal	What is real	What could be
Breadth	Depth	Present	Future
Interactions	Concentration	Utility	Novelty
External events	Internal reactions	Facts	Insights
Expressive	Reserved	Tangible	Theoretical
Gregarious	Reflective	Actual	Fantasy
Multiple relationships	Limited relationships	Practical	Ingenuity
Speak, then think	Think, then speak	Specific	General
Do-think-do	Think-to-do	Analyzes	Synthesizes
		Methodical	Random

How Make Decisions		How Live and Work	
Thinking	**Feeling**	**Judging**	**Perceiving**
Head	Heart	Control	Flow
Objective	Subjective	Run one's life	Let life happen
Reason	Mercy	Set goals	Adapts
Laws	Empathy	Decisive	Wait and see
Firm but fair	Compassionate	Resolved	Flexible
Just	Circumstances	Organized	Scattered
Clarity	Humane	Structured	Open
Critique	Harmony	Definite	Tentative
Detached	Appreciative	Scheduled	Spontaneous
Analytical	Involved	Product focus	Process focus

The cartoon here illustrates how the types might differ, even in something apparently as simple as telling time. Starting with the man on the left and working across the characters, although we cannot identify all four letters of their types, we can infer that they most likely represent the following combinations within the types: SJ, NF, IN, EP. The SJ is very specific and decisive; the NF is general and focused on circumstances; the IN is concentrating and lost in thought; and the EP blurts out an answer without thinking and is not even sure what day it is. The cartoon demonstrates that even a small action can reveal something about the deeper personality of a person, although again, we should avoid jumping to conclusions and overgeneralizing about any type.

Leaders and Thinking vs. Feeling

Remember that no type profile or set of personality characteristics makes one person better than another. It just makes them different in

Source: Copyright © 1996–1999 Pat Marr.

important ways. Also, no type is necessarily a better leader, although studies have shown that certain types are better at some tasks than others. For example, those leaders with "Feeling" as their decision-making preference are better at some components of emotional intelligence, such as experiencing empathy and recognizing nonverbal cues, particularly facial expressions.[14] That does not mean that leaders with a "Thinking" preference cannot or do not use feelings to make decisions; it only suggests that their first inclination is toward logic and that they may need to work a little harder at drawing out their emotional intelligence than the "feeling" person does.

Legal Questions

Finally, organizational leaders need to understand the legal ramifications of such testing and the potential misuse of the information. You will want to check with your human resources or legal group if you are thinking of using the tests to help in team formation or dynamics, for instance, or to screen prospective employees, a widespread and growing use. A good source of information on the use of psychological tests in the workplace, including the legal issues, is Hoffman's *Psychological Testing at Work*.

Taking the MBTI

Many assessments, including versions of the MBTI, are available on the Web, although some require a fee and a psychologist to contact takers with the results. To appreciate fully the meaning of the MBTI or any other legitimate personality profile depends on understanding the assessment and its intentions; therefore, if you plan to take any psychology profile, you may want to consider talking the results over with someone licensed to give the test and reading some of the many books available on it. For instance, on the MBTI, you might find Otto Kroeger's *Type Talk at Work* helpful. It is particularly useful in relating the test to the workplace and in explaining how different types handle different jobs and team situations.

The Value of Knowing the MBTI

Knowing our colleagues' types can help us as a leader understand how they are motivated and how better to work with them. For example, if we are having problems with a member of our group missing deadlines or being late for meetings, knowing that he or she is a "Perceiver" helps us understand that his or her actions are not meant to be discourteous or disrespectful. We can then approach the behavior as a performance issue and provide feedback and perhaps coaching on the importance of better time management. That may not solve the problem completely, but if the individual performs well otherwise, we owe it to him or her and to our organization to recognize the inherent personality trait and respond appropriately to alter the undesirable behavior.

For Teams

Awareness of personality types can be advantageous in team settings. If we are working with a group of individuals who are not collaborating and seem to enjoy working apart solving problems rather than as a team, we might infer that they are Introverts and pair them up for specific tasks. If we have the opposite situation, a team of Extraverts and one Introvert who rarely contributes to the discussions directly but whom we know to be able to contribute, we can pull the individual into the discussions directly with specific requests or questions.

For Virtual Teams

More and more, companies are creating teams that are geographically diverse. These virtual teams have little to no face-to-face interaction, making emotional intelligence even more important. Understanding the personalities of those on a virtual team can help a leader guide them to success. For example, Extraverts on a virtual team will appreciate being able to lead discussions and present findings, whereas Introverts may prefer offline discussions and private feedback.

For Individuals

Using a personality profile can help in developing our self-awareness and understanding how best to interact with and manage others. As a result, it can contribute to personal development and to the dynamics of teams and even organizations. We need to keep in mind, though, that the profiles suggest how individuals are motivated and how they might approach certain situations; they do not predict behavior and certainly should not be used to create labels of individuals or even as ways to excuse a lack of performance of any type.

Developing an Approach to Improving Emotional Intelligence

After self-reflection and personality testing, can individuals really change their emotional intelligence? Goleman and others at the EI Consortium say "yes": "EI competencies are not innate talents, but learned abilities, each of which has a unique contribution to making leaders more resonant, and therefore more effective."[15] To do so requires that an individual be committed to change and willing to put in the effort. Goleman, Boyatzis, and McKee suggest the following steps "to rewire your brain for greater Emotional Intelligence":

Steps to Achieving Emotional Intelligence

1. **Who do you want to be?** Imagine yourself as a highly effective leader. What do you see?
2. **Who are you now?** To see your leadership style as others do, gather 360-degree feedback, especially from peers and subordinates. Identify your weaknesses *and* strengths.
3. **How do you get from here to there?** Devise a plan for closing the gap between who you are and who you want to be.
4. **How do you make change stick?** Repeatedly rehearse new behaviors—physically and mentally—until they are automatic.
5. **Who can help you?** Do not try to build your emotional skills alone—identify others who can help you navigate this difficult process.

Source: Reprinted from *Harvard Business Review.* From Primal leadership: The hidden driver of great performance. Goleman, D., Boyatzis, R., and McKee, A. December 2001. Copyright © 2001 by Harvard Business School Publishing Corporation; all rights reserved.

This approach calls on us, first, to assess our strengths and weaknesses; second, to obtain feedback from others on our strengths and weaknesses; third, to establish our goals; and fourth, to map out a plan to achieve those goals. At the heart of changing is the self-awareness that we need to change. Once we have that awareness, a vision of our destination and a plan to get there, we can improve our emotional intelligence.

According to Goleman, Boyatzis, and McKee "An emotionally intelligent leader can monitor his or her moods through self-awareness, change them for the better through self-management, understand their impact through empathy, and act in ways that boost others' moods through relationship management."[16] This section discussed developing self-awareness; the focus of the rest of this chapter is on the other side of emotional intelligence—relationship management through recognizing nonverbal communication, improving listening skills, developing others more effectively, and using networking to expand those relationships.

Improving Nonverbal Skills

The way we dress, walk, carry ourselves, stand in relation to others, use our hands, move our head, and change our facial expressions—all communicate to others. All of these are types of nonverbal communication, sending messages without using verbal language. As much as 65 to 93 percent of the meaning in communication is nonverbal.[17] Knowing something about nonverbal communication is clearly important for anyone wanting to improve his or her communication skills and is certainly important for any leader.

Nonverbal expressions are usually categorized into one of the following groups:

Categories of Nonverbal Communication

1. Appearance—looks, dress, grooming.
2. Paralanguage—vocal cues that accompany speech, such as volume, pitch, and rate.
3. Kinesics—body movements, such as gestures, posture, head movement.
4. Occulesics—eye movement, such as eye contact or looking away.
5. Proxemics—where you stand or sit in relation to others.
6. Facial expressions—smiles, frowns, sneers.
7. Olfactics—smells.
8. Chronomics—the way time is used.

All of these affect how we are perceived and how we perceive others, yet studies have shown that people in general are not very good at interpreting nonverbal behavior accurately.[18] In fact, it is only in judging facial expressions that we tend to be correct.

While the meaning of nonverbal communication involving body language differs substantially from culture to culture, researchers have identified six facial expressions that are consistently and universally interpreted across cultures: happiness, fear, sadness, surprise, anger, and disgust.[19]

We often misinterpret other nonverbal communication, imposing our thoughts on others instead of accurately reading theirs. Beyond the common facial expressions, nonverbal signals are so dependent on culture and context that we need to take great care in interpreting them.

In most cultures, the following are nonverbals that could hinder our being viewed positively by others; in other words, they hurt our ethos:

1. Smiling too often or when not appropriate can make us seem insincere or superficial, and not smiling at all can cause us to be seen as troubled or unapproachable.

2. Using gestures not consistent with our message—in other words, our body says something counter to the words we are saying—may cause others to question our honesty or veracity.

3. Standing or sitting small or crouching in our chair instead of standing or sitting up straight and confident will make us appear timid and unsure of ourselves.

4. Sitting back from the table instead of forward suggests we are not interested or engaged in the discussion. In negotiations, a common tactic is to mirror the movements of the other, which we tend to do unconsciously in many situations; however, we need to be careful how we use this tactic and be aware of how we are being perceived by others when we seem to mimic others or move too far from the ring of discussion.

5. Tilting our head to one side or the other can make us appear to be questioning the speaker, which, if we are, is appropriate.

6. Raising our eyebrows suggests questioning as well

7. Not maintaining eye contact in many cultures suggests that we cannot be trusted, whereas in others, it can be considered rude or aggressive.

8. Placing our computer or briefcase on the table suggests a lack of concern for others and if we open our laptop we are creating a barrier between us and the others, which could be appropriate in informal team meetings but in others could be considered inconsiderate and rude.

9. Looking down at our cell phone or PDA also suggests a lack of interest and will offend many.

10. Not touching web to web in a handshake can create a weak handshake where only the fingers touch, which we usually want to avoid. We should have a firm but not tight handshake (see the image below).

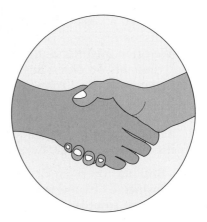

Developing a better understanding of nonverbal communication can help us in our communication with others and in our understanding of how they perceive our communications. The following are suggestions to improve nonverbal communication skills:

1. **Learn as much as possible about any culture in which you will be interacting.** Much of the meaning of nonverbal communication depends on culture; therefore, you need to know something about the culture of individuals before you can fully understand their nonverbal behavior. Edward T. Hall, one of the first to research and write about culture and nonverbal communication, says that, to understand people of a different culture, it is as important to know the nonverbal language (which he calls the "silent language") as it is to know the spoken language. He argues that most people, particularly North Americans, are not even aware of nonverbal language and its impact:

> Of equal importance is an introduction to the nonverbal language which exists in every country of the world and among the various groups within each country. Most Americans are only dimly aware of this silent language even though they use it every day. They are not conscious of the elaborate patterning of behaviors which prescribes our handling of time, our spatial relationships, our attitudes toward work, play, and learning. In addition to what we say with our verbal language, we are constantly communicating our real feelings in our silent language—the language of behavior. Sometimes this is correctly interpreted by other nationalities, but more often it is not.[20]

For example, many hand gestures acceptable in the United States are not acceptable in the rest of the world. Exhibit 7.5 illustrates frequently used U.S. gestures that should be avoided in most other parts of the world.

EXHIBIT 7.5
Common U.S. Hand Gestures and Their Meaning

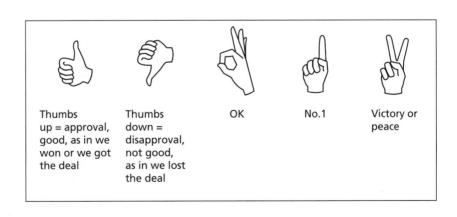

Thumbs up = approval, good, as in we won or we got the deal

Thumbs down = disapproval, not good, as in we lost the deal

OK

No.1

Victory or peace

The discussion of cross-cultural literacy in Chapter 8 will go further into some of the cultural differences, so for now, simply realize that nonverbal communication differs across cultures and misinterpreting it can result in serious miscommunication. Beyond the six universal facial expressions, few nonverbal signals carry the same meaning across all cultures. Therefore, anyone doing business with another culture must learn as much as possible about the role and use of nonverbal communication.

2. **Do not judge someone's actions out of context or leave the actions unexplored when important to you or the organization.** Remember that nonverbal behavior depends on context. What comes before and what will come after influence it. For instance, if someone walks past us in a corridor without speaking, we might assume that the person is irritated with us for some reason. We assign a meaning to the behavior that attributes an intention or motive to the other person.

However, the action could have any number of explanations. Perhaps the person is simply absorbed in thought or perhaps not feeling well. If the individual is in the midst of writing a report and thinking about the analysis and perhaps an Introvert as well, then the person may simply be absorbed in thought. If someone on the team that is writing this report has shirked his or her responsibility, then the person could be irritated with that individual, not us. Taken out of context, which includes past actions not observable in the present moment and perhaps unknown to us, we cannot know for sure, so any interpretation on our part is a guess, and again, we have greater confidence in our ability to interpret nonverbal behavior than is warranted much of the time.

If it is important for us to know the motivation for the person's actions, we need to ask. Too often, rumors and hard feelings grow in an office environment because people make assumptions based on nonverbal behavior.

3. **Develop an understanding of and sensitivity to nonverbal cues.** Notice, for instance, when what someone says seems to differ from how he or she is saying it, often a very reliable nonverbal signal. If the words and the body movement seem in harmony, then the person is comfortable with what he or she is saying. If, however, the movements seem exaggerated or forced, then the person may be uncomfortable with the audience or with the subject. Pay attention to facial expressions, volume, pitch, and pace of the voice. To practice being more sensitive to nonverbal communication, you might want to engage a group in role-playing exercises, videotape them, and then discuss the nonverbal communication that occurs.

4. **Assess your own use of nonverbal communication.** The best way to see ourselves as others see us is to videotape and watch ourselves. To focus on the nonverbal communication, we should watch the tape with the sound turned off. If we admire someone else's leadership image, then we should imitate the movements and behaviors we observe. While we never want to be false and never can or should move too far away from our natural self, modeling the movements of others and practicing them until they are natural for us can be helpful in breaking habits that we want to change. Confident speakers stand tall, establish eye contact, move with purpose, and use natural gestures to underscore or support their messages.

In addition to observing our body language, we should listen to ourselves giving a presentation, paying attention to our paralanguage (in this case, if on videotape, listen and not watch). Is our volume too loud or too soft? Do we talk too fast? Do we use fillers or allow meaningful pauses? Less skilled speakers often fill up any pauses with "uhs" or let each thought run right up into the next one. Skilled speakers, use silence effectively, allowing their audience to absorb their ideas, and never relying on fillers of any kind.

We need to pay attention to how we dress and use the space around us. If we want to be accepted by our peers, we must dress the part. If we want others to see us as the one in charge, we must arrange our space to suggest our authority. Even where we sit at a table sends messages to others. How we arrange our office and our desk says something about us as a person. While all of these external symbols can mislead, they do communicate, and a leader must be sensitive to them.

Nonverbal communication is as meaningful as spoken words, even more meaningful in many situations and cultures. Leaders must pay attention to it in any communication situation and strive to be more observant of the nonverbal signals people send.

Improving Listening Skills

Leaving listening out of any discussion of communication means leaving out at least 40 to 45 percent of the communication process.[21] Good listening skills are essential, and the lack of them hinders many people's careers. Most do not realize that good listening is hard work. According to Madelyn Burley-Allen in her book *Listening: The Forgotten Skill*, there are three levels of listening, with the highest level (Level 1) requiring more effort than people tend to expend:

Levels of Listening

Level 1—"Empathetic listening," where you refrain from judgment and listen with close attention, attempt understanding, and convey a sincere interest in the speaker's words.

Level 2—"Hearing words, but not really listening." Receivers pretend to hear and even respond; however, they do not understand the speaker's real intent because they are focusing on the words at a logical, nonfeeling level only.

Level 3—"Listening in spurts." Receivers tune in and out, hearing only part of what is said. They may even be pretending to listen when they are thinking about something else entirely.

While we should always aim toward maintaining our listening at Level 1, a number of barriers can interfere with listening, such as the following:

Common Barriers to Effective Listening

---

1. The speaker is talking about a subject of no interest to us or is boring. Although some blame for not listening falls on the listener, the sender carries responsibility as well.
2. We do not agree with the speaker; therefore, we do not listen to anything said or we think about counterarguments.
3. We may be more interested in what we have to say than in the other person. Extroverts easily fall prey to this communication breakdown.
4. We are distracted by other thoughts or by activities around us.
5. We have preconceptions about the subject or the speaker. Either we think we know what he or she is going to say before it is said, or we have already formed a judgment about the speaker or the content.
6. We respond emotionally to the words or ideas the person presents and, therefore, turn off our hearing to the rest.
7. We become so distracted by the person's delivery or something about his or her appearance that we shift our focus away from the words.
8. We only hear what we **want** to hear and fail to listen to anything else.

In addition to these barriers, we are so bombarded with noise every day that we become very good at filtering and hearing only what we want to hear. For example, we can have the radio on in the car and yet not hear a word the broadcaster is saying. Poor listening can easily become a habit, but it is one that must be overcome to succeed as leaders in any organization. Obviously, some breakdowns in listening are more difficult to overcome than others, such as an uninteresting speaker; however, everyone can become a better listener in all situations with some effort. The following chart provides 10 ways to improve your listening habits:

Ten Ways to Improve Listening Habits

1. Stop talking.
2. Stop thinking ahead to what you are going to say and turn off your own internal chatter.
3. Avoid multitasking (for example, talking on the phone while working at the computer or talking to someone in the room; attending to a lecturer while working at the computer).
4. Try to empathize with the speaker.
5. Don't interrupt, but ask questions if something is unclear.
6. Focus on the speaker closely, establishing eye contact if appropriate for the culture, but do not get in a "power stare."
7. Do not let delivery or appearance distract you.
8. Listen for ideas, not just for facts.
9. Listen with an open mind, not just for what you *want* to hear.
10. Pay attention to nonverbal cues and what is not said.

As a leader, it is not only essential to be a good listener, but you want others to see that you are listening. Exhibit 7.6 provides some actions we can take to signal that we are indeed paying attention to the other person and actually hearing what he or she is saying.

Again, good listening is not easy, but effective leadership depends on it. Therefore, we should work on our listening skills, just as we would

EXHIBIT 7.6

Using Verbal and Nonverbal Cues to Signal Listening

Source: Adapted from The Interactive Skills Program, Dalva Hedlund and L. Bryn Freedman, Cornell University Cooperative Extension Service. Retrieved from http://crs.uvm.edu/gopher / nerl/personal/comm/e.html.

Approach	Action
Nonverbal attending	• Eye contact • Leaning forward • Minimal encouragement through head nodding
Verbal attending	• Oral cues, such as "yes," "I understand," "Interesting," etc.
Asking questions	• Open questions: how? what? could? would? • Closed questions: is? are? do? did? Why questions: open and closed
Focusing	• Notice the focus. Is it the speaker, topic, other person, or the listener?
Reflecting	• Reinforce and support the speaker • Clarify meaning of communication • Reflect factual or feeling content
Summarizing	• Recapitulate for easier remembering, better understanding • Show relationship of main points • Go to beginning of discussion ("remembering where we left off") • Summarize in mid-discussion • Drawing together main points at end

any other communication skills. Practicing the following exercises may help sharpen listening skills:

1. After a conversation with someone, a lecture, or any event in which you were primarily a listener, try summarizing what the speaker said immediately, either on paper or in your mind.

2. In note-taking situations, look at the speakers and really listen to them; then record the main ideas, instead of trying to write down every word they say as they say it.

3. Practice paraphrasing others as they speak, but do not interrupt them.

4. Listen to a news story or something primarily factual and then try to summarize what you have heard.

If you are not sure whether you are a good listener, you should take an inventory of your listening habits, by making a list on your own, asking someone you trust to give you feedback, or taking a listening assessment. A little self-awareness will help you realize if improvement is needed and how much.

Motivating and Mentoring

Motivating and developing others tests a leader's emotional intelligence. Leaders need to be particularly sensitive to the feelings of others and able to establish ways to motivate and guide them that work with our personality and with theirs. Employee development and management succession are two of our primary responsibilities as leaders, and we must consciously want to foster the development of those around us and below us.[22] In addition to our own responsibilities for developing others, we are the model for the others in their roles as supervisors, mentors, and coaches.

Motivating, mentoring (the longer-term coaching relationships), and coaching (the shorter-term, usually more specifically focused relationships) all require a willingness to guide and help develop others and the ability to communicate effectively, all abilities associated with being an effective supervisor and leader.

Motivating

Our success as leaders is often measured by our ability to motivate and develop others. "In organizations, leaders or managers are judged by the accomplishments of their team, group, subordinates, or projects. In order to succeed, they must motivate others."[23] The question of what motivates people has been debated for years, with most discussions going back to Maslow's Hierarchy in 1954. Maslow tells us that needs govern people's actions from the lowest level of survival to those less physical and more emotional or psychological, such as the need for esteem and self-actualization.

Going back even further than Maslow to early organizational studies, the famous Hawthorne Studies conducted at Western Electric in 1927 found that personal attention to the workers did more to increase productivity than an improved physical environment, such as better lighting. Frederick Herzberg's research in the 1950s and 60s found that "people are motivated . . . by interesting work, challenge, and increasing responsibility."[24]

A much more recent study found that the following are what a good manager does to motivate subordinates today:

- Provides direct help, adequate resources, and time.
- Reacts to success and failures with a learning orientation versus a purely evaluative one.
- Sets clear goals and clarifies where the work is heading and why it matters.
- Recognizes "real work progress" and praises subordinates for it.
- Works collaboratively as a peer.
- Makes things more fun and relaxing.
- Provides emotional support.[25]

Clearly, motivation is individual, but it is also clear that individuals share similar needs. Skilled leaders will recognize those needs and intentionally address them, both for the betterment of the individuals and for the performance of the organization. Human capital is too important not to invest in it, and it is up to the leaders in organizations to fulfill that obligation. Two actions tied to the motivation responsibility are mentoring and coaching.

Mentoring

All of the leadership communication skills discussed in this text so far—strategy, audience analysis, effective speaking and writing, and emotional intelligence—are required to be effective as a mentor. We should have a comprehensive strategy for providing mentoring throughout our organization and for us personally to mentor the individuals working directly with us. We need to understand those we mentor in the way we would any audience and use all of the effective writing and speaking practices with them. Finally, emotional intelligence takes on even greater importance once we assume the role of mentor. We need to understand ourselves and others, recognize the importance of nonverbal skills in communicating meaning, and be a skilled listener.

To build a successful mentoring program and establish successful mentoring relationships, we need to establish roles and responsibilities for the mentor and the protégé. The Small Business Administration Web site provides a useful outline of the responsibilities for both:

Responsibilities of a Mentor

1. Provide guidance based on past business experiences.
2. Create a positive counseling relationship and climate of open communication.
3. Help your protégé identify problems and solutions.
4. Lead your protégé through problem-solving processes.
5. Offer constructive criticism in a supportive way.
6. Share stories, including mistakes.
7. Assign "homework" if applicable.
8. Refer your protégé to other business associates.
9. Be honest about business expertise.
10. Solicit feedback from your protégé.
11. Come to each meeting prepared to discuss issues.

Responsibilities of the Protégé

1. Shape the overall agenda for the relationship—know what you want!
2. Establish realistic and attainable expectations.
3. Be open in communicating with your mentor.
4. Establish priority issues for action or support.
5. Don't expect your mentor to be an expert in every facet of business.
6. Solicit feedback from your mentor.
7. Come prepared to each meeting to discuss issues.

Source: www.sba.gov/smallbusinessplanner/manage/lead/SERV_MENTORING.html.

Together, the mentor and the protégé must establish an approach for working with each other and, if appropriate, set up a development plan with agreed-upon objectives. They will also need to communicate regularly, but the protégé should be mindful of the mentor's time commitments and be realistic in his or her expectations. Mentors, on the other hand, owe it to protégés not to commit to more than they can deliver and to establish boundaries for the protégés.

On the other side, when looking for a mentor, look for someone accessible and willing. A good mentoring relationship requires a commitment from both sides and is a responsibility both need to respect and honor.

Delivering Feedback

One function that provides ample opportunity for us to use our emotional intelligence to develop others is by providing feedback. Providing constructive feedback is one of the leadership communication skills needed to guide as well as motivate others. The ability to provide feedback, be a coach to others, is essential for transformational leaders:

"The leader emphasizes self-development and offers positive feedback to improve a worker's performance. The transformational leader wants followers to become leaders themselves."[26] It is through feedback that people develop, particularly if the leader providing the feedback recognizes its potential value and uses it as a way to bring about the receivers' growth and development and to help the individuals achieve their own leadership potential.

Feedback should include both praise and criticism. For feedback to be useful to the receivers, the feedback provider must be as specific as possible and use words that will motivate the receivers. For instance, to say, "Your presentation was not very effective" does not tell them much. They certainly would not walk away with anything specific that they could change. Instead, we might want to say, "Your presentation would have been easier for your audience to follow if you had stated your main message very clearly at the beginning, listing your main supporting topics, and then going through each of them in order."

The goal in feedback should be to connect with the receivers in such a way that they are receptive to what we have to say and leave with the specific information they need to perform differently in the future. Planning a feedback session requires the same effort in strategy development and audience analysis that we would apply for any communication situation. The following steps should work effectively when providing feedback in most professional settings.

1. **Be well prepared for the feedback session.** Develop a strategy and analyze your audience. Then, have all of your facts and unbiased appraisal information at hand. Be aware of any cultural differences that may have influenced the person's performance or the way he or she may respond to your feedback. Also, think about all of the other communication strategy components: strategic objectives, medium, timing, and messages.

2. **Create a receptive environment.** Depending on your primary objectives and the type of feedback you are providing, you may want to meet the receivers in their office or a neutral location. If your office seems most logical and you do not see any reasons for the receivers to be uncomfortable there, then at least come from behind your desk to welcome them into your office.

3. **Assume a comfortable demeanor.** Establish eye contact, but not in a challenging way. Smile and exchange some small talk, if appropriate. Use the pronoun "I" instead of "you." For instance, instead of saying, "You are not carrying your load on the team," say, "I have noticed some distancing on your part from the team. Is there anything I should know? Or can I help you in some way?"

4. **Start by setting the context for the meeting.** If it is a yearly performance review, say so. If the person's performance has been

below standard or behavior has been disruptive, perhaps in a team situation, then start off briefly explaining the situation, focusing on the facts only.

5. **Move quickly into your main objectives, which should not be so numerous they overwhelm** (usually three or four at most). Have them organized, so that you can move through them, pausing between each main point to allow the receiver to respond or ask questions.

Throughout, you should focus on behavior rather than the personality of the receiver, and you should be objective and specific. If the receiver is doing well, what can you say to reinforce success? If he or she is making mistakes, what specifically needs to be done differently? If your main focus is on a problem or an issue, first try to bring out any positives in performance or actions, but do not make things up just to make the person feel better. If you can do so honestly, you should begin by focusing on what the receiver is doing well and mention any successes. Direct every criticism at an aspect of performance, behavior, or attitude that is correctable.

6. **Ensure throughout that the receiver understands your points.** Do not take understanding for granted. Ask for questions or whether the receiver needs any clarification.

7. **Finally, close with the next steps,** being very specific about the actions you expect the receiver to undertake as a result of this feedback session and the timing for completing them.

You may find it easier to remember the steps if you put them into the GROW model, used by Max Landsberg in his book *The Tao of Coaching* (Exhibit 7.7).

Any good feedback session depends on listening and doing more asking than telling. We should always go into a session well prepared with specific facts and fair assessments. The goal should be to help the employee, to serve as a coach and mentor. If we display that attitude, the receiver will be much more receptive to our feedback.

From the other perspective, when others give us feedback, listening is important. We do not want to be defensive. Instead, we should listen attentively and show interest in what the person is saying. If we feel he or she is being vague, ask for examples, but do not appear to be challenging the person. There is a big difference between "I do not know what in the world you are talking about; do you have any examples of this?" and "I am not sure I understand; could you give me an example?"

This section's discussion has focused primarily on mentoring and coaching inside an organization, but often leaders mentor individuals outside as well. These mentoring relationships may be more informal, but much of these suggestions apply to these arrangements as well. Mentoring is an important relationship for the mentor and the mentee and is a tremendous opportunity for both sides to teach and to learn.

EXHIBIT 7.7
**Using the
GROW Model
to Structure a
Feedback Session**

Source: Landsberg, M.
(1997). *The Tao of Coach-
ing*. Santa Monica, CA:
Knowledge Exchange 1997.
Used with permission of
Profile Books.

- Agree on topic for discussion
- Agree on specific objective
  of session
- Set long-term aim if
  appropriate

- Invite self-assessment
- Offer specific examples
  of feedback
- Avoid or check assumptions
- Discard irrelevant history

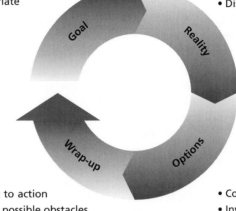

- Commit to action
- Identify possible obstacles
- Make steps specific
  and define timing
- Agree on support

- Cover the full range of options
- Invite suggestions from the
  coachee
- Offer suggestions carefully
- Ensure choices are made

Networking

Just as mentoring is a valuable opportunity for both professionals in the relationship, networking offers another way to connect with others and "give back" in our professional and personal life. Networking calls on our emotional intelligence and interpersonal skills to extend ourselves and connect to communities of practice inside and outside of our organizations. Today, it is a necessary part of doing business in all professions. It is not enough just to be good at what we do; we need to belong to professional organizations and attend events to get to know our colleagues, expand our knowledge base, and be recognized, as well as to advance. All professionals work long hours and find breaking away a challenge, but making the time to network offers learning opportunities and helps us build the relationships that may be essential to advance in many career areas.

Introverts or shy individuals may be somewhat apprehensive about attending networking events. While networking may come more naturally to some than to others, it can be learned by all, and everyone can become good at it. The benefits can be tremendous for us professionally and personally and far outweigh any perceived risks.

As with any important communication activity, before we head out to participate in a professional event, we need to be prepared. This preparation involves four simple steps:

1. Consider the benefits of the event.
2. Prepare an appropriate self-introduction.
3. Be ready to open a conversation and keep it moving.
4. Have a plan for following up after the event.

First, to consider the benefits of the event, we can ask is we are going with the purpose of learning something new. Perhaps we want to meet someone we know will be in attendance at the event. For example, we may want to find someone who is an expert in an area of interest to us.

Next, we need to learn a bit about the organization and the usual participants in an event and to determine what is expected in terms of dress, location, and schedule. All of us feel more confident when we are well prepared; therefore, we should practice our own brief "self-introduction." We should walk into any professional or social networking event ready to deliver our one-minute introduction, our elevator speech on ourselves. It should be a crisp, concise overview of who we are and what we do. It might include our position in an organization with some information about the organization, if unknown to listeners.

Next, we need to be prepared to open a conversation and be an interesting conversational partner. This might sound daunting, but remember that if two people are in a room together, they most likely have something in common. If we determine what that commonality is, we can form an opening question or comment about it. For example, most people can easily relate to the experience of attending a wedding with many people they do not know. After saying "hello," we might ask, "Are you friends with the bride or the groom?" At a professional conference, we might follow up on our self-introduction with a few questions, such as "Were you at the conference last year?" or "Which sessions did you find most helpful to your work?"

After opening a conversation, we can then move to additional topics. To be effective at networking, we need to be good listeners and master the ability to make small talk, which for some personalities is a challenge. However, some advance preparation can be of help, such as reading the news and keeping up with local and professional activities. For example, looking at the blogs or discussion forums for professional conferences can help us identify current topics. We do need to make sure, however, that we can converse about more than just professional topics.

If we know others at the event, we can offer to introduce our new conversational partner to some other attendees. If the timing and situation seem right, we can ask for a business card. After the event, we should write the date of the event and some brief comments about the person we met on the back of the card and enter this information into our contact management system soon before we forget the details.

Finally, what we do after the event can be just as important as the event itself in building our network. We need to stay in touch with our contacts. For example, knowing that they are interested in certain areas, we might see an article or a Web site we think might be of interest to them, which we can send to them. Professional networking, like mentoring, is a two-way street.

New media have changed the face of professional networking, with numerous Web sites available, such as Facebook and LinkedIn, to name just two of the over 100 sites. Even if mainly for the shy or introverted, these new social media can provide avenues to connect professionally to others of similar professional interests. After we have met new contacts at an event, we can invite them to join us online and our network will continue to grow. Many of these sites offer question boards or opportunities for further discussions. In fact, these sites have made it very easy to stay connected with just a few mouse clicks.

One word of caution: We also need to realize that Web sites are public places open to all. We need to be aware of the appropriate security settings and use caution in posting personal information or anything that we would not want professional contacts to see. We all have heard horror stories of individuals losing job opportunities because of inappropriate materials posted on their Facebook page or tagged on the pages of others.

The bottom line is that getting outside ourselves and connecting in sincere and meaningful ways with others inside our professional arena is important, and networking is one method to do so. It can expand our sphere of influence and increase our leadership visibility and potential impact.

Theodore Roosevelt, the 26th president of the United States, said, "The most important single ingredient in the formula of success is knowing how to get along with people." Essentially, that is the thrust of emotional intelligence. People who relate well to others do better in the workplace and as leaders of organizations. They are able to motivate and inspire others to perform up to their potential, a skill every leader should possess, and one particularly important for transformational leaders.

Transformational leaders connect with others openly and honestly. They have emotional intelligence and display their interpersonal skills. They are sensitive to the verbal and nonverbal communication that surrounds them. They are good listeners. They are receptive to being mentored and to mentoring others. Doing so effectively is one approach they use to bring about change. They are sincerely interested in others and care about them, and they show it, whether connecting to others in person individually or in groups or through the numerous electronic channels available today.

**Application 7.1
Improving
Listening Habits**

For this exercise, you will work with two other people. You will each assume one of three roles: speaker, listener, and observer. You will rotate the roles, so that each person has an opportunity to participate in each one. The speaker should spend about two minutes telling the listener about an event or accomplishment that made him or her feel proud or happy while the third person observes. The listener should not interrupt at all in this one-way conversation. After the speaker is finished, the listener should tell the speaker what he or she heard—not only the facts but also some generalizations about the person made on the basis of the facts. The observer should then tell both what he or she heard and observed.

For example, if Galen tells Karim about a time he trained daily for three months to ride his bicycle in a charity marathon, Karim might tell him in return not only the facts he heard about Galen's training but also some assumptions about Galen: perhaps that he is motivated, is dedicated to meeting his goals, and cares about the nonprofit organization for which he was raising funds.

Now, switch roles and repeat the exercise.

Source: Exercise created by Beth O'Sullivan and Deborah J. Barrett. Used with permission.

**Application 7.2
Providing
Feedback**

The Case: Coaching Employees

You are the manager of a small group of people responsible for an introductory training program for new employees at your company. Your group consists of the following people:

- Rosanna, senior-level trainer with 12 years of experience, 10 at your company.
- Susan, senior-level trainer with 7 years of experience, 4 at your company.
- Hari, senior-level trainer with 15 years of experience, 2 at your company.
- Yang, administrative assistant, 7 years with your company.

Your group decides on the specific content of the training material, based on the needs of the trainees, and then creates the materials (including lectures, handouts, and exercises), conducts the training sessions, and provides the feedback. Although the content for the training is fairly consistent from year to year, it does require some adjustments to match the number of attendees, the needs indicated in the assessments of the trainees before each session, and their course evaluations at the end of each session. The exercises, in particular, change frequently. Also, the instruction for each session depends on the previous session. The trainees receive feedback shortly after each session and must complete a lesson successfully before moving on to the next one. Thus, your group has two critical deadlines: one for preparing the materials and one for providing timely feedback.

Susan and Hari are both excellent trainers. In fact, their evaluations have been some of the highest of any trainers you have had working for you in the past, except for Rosanna, who has consistently received the highest rankings since you hired her 10 years ago. All of the trainers are very dedicated to the company and to their jobs. Lately, however, you have received negative comments about trainers' tardiness in returning feedback, particularly directed at Susan. Susan and Hari are called "Perceivers" in the Myers-Briggs Type Indicator terminology, which means they are easygoing, flexible, spontaneous, and open, all very positive qualities for trainers, since it improves their ability to interact with the trainees and to be creative. However, it also means they are not very good at judging time, often wait until the last minute to get things done, and sometimes miss deadlines altogether.

Susan and Hari's frequent tardiness has caused extra work for Rosanna, who is always punctual and ends up having to complete some of Susan's and Hari's feedback forms and step in when they do not make their deadlines in creating materials. It also creates problems for Yang, since she has had to stay late and come in early several times to duplicate materials.

To ensure that all feedback is delivered on time and that all materials are prepared ahead of time, you decide to try what you think of as "micromanaging," even though you do not like doing it. You meet with the group to establish (1) group deadlines for returning feedback and (2) specific responsibilities and deadlines for each lesson (divided up evenly among all of you). You want to make sure each of you has time to review the materials and make any adjustments before they go to the trainees, so you have specified that all materials be completed and sent to each of you at least a week before they need to be sent out for copying and distribution.

So far (you are just three months into the yearlong training program), Susan and Hari have frequently given handouts to Yang at the last minute and in some cases within as little as 10 minutes before a training session, resulting in mistakes in the handouts and late starts for the sessions. They rarely make the one-week-ahead-of-time deadline to distribute their materials to the rest of the group, and they wait until the absolutely last minute to return their comments on the materials sent to them for review. Also, both have been late returning feedback to the attendees, and Hari has completely forgotten to prepare the materials for one of the training sessions, leaving you and Rosanna scrambling at the last minute to get them together. For the sake of your own stress level but, more important, to ensure that the training program continues to receive positive reviews from senior management, you know you must talk to Susan and to Hari.

The Assignment

In breakout groups, answer the following questions:

- What are some of the issues you should resolve before talking to Susan and Hari?
- Should you meet only with both of them individually, with each member of the group individually, or with everyone at the same time?
- How should you conduct the session (consider using the GROW model)?
- How can you ensure that the outcome will be what is best for you and for them?

After answering these questions, individuals may be asked to volunteer to demonstrate a feedback session based on the case.

**Application 7.3
The Elevator
Speech
Introduction to
You**

As discussed in this chapter, we should always have an elevator speech—a very short (30-second) introduction to who we are and what we do—that we can deliver when we meet others. For this exercise, you are being asked to create and practice your introductory elevator speech.

1. Working with a partner, pretend that you are attending an event—a professional conference or some other networking event. In that context, prepare a 30-second crisp, concise self-introduction for someone who does not know you at all.
2. Deliver your introduction to one another.
3. Generate a few opening questions or remarks that could open a conversation.
4. Now, give each other feedback and do it again

Notes

1. The term "emotional intelligence" has been used by organizational psychologists for years, but it first became well known in business after the publication of Daniel Goleman's book by the same name.
2. "Several writers (e.g., Bennis,1989; Megerian & Sosik,1996) have argued that one aspect of EQ, self-awareness, is integral to transformational leadership effectiveness."
3. Gary, L. (2002). Becoming a Resonant Leader, *Harvard Management Update* 7, No. 7, pp. 4–6.
4. Weisinger, H. (1998). *Emotional Intelligence at Work*. San Francisco: Jossey-Bass.
5. Bar-On, R., and Parker, J. D. A. (Eds.). (2000). *Handbook of Emotional Intelligence*. San Francisco: Jossey-Bass.
6. "Obama: A Leadership Report Card," *BusinessWeek*, April 20, 2009.
7. Goleman, D., Boyatzis, R., and McKee, A. (2002). *Primal Leadership: Realizing the Power of Emotional Intelligence*. Boston: Harvard Business School Press.
8. Goleman, Boyatzis, and McKee (2002).
9. Goleman, Boyatzis, and McKee (2002).
10. Goleman, Boyatzis, and McKee (2002).
11. Goleman, Boyatzis, and Mckee (2002).
12. Weisinger (1998).
13. Hoffman, E. (2002). *Psychological Testing at Work*. New York: McGraw-Hill. For a discussion of the reliability of MBTI in studying manager personalities, see Gardner, W. L., and Martinko, M. J. (1996). Using the Myers-Briggs Type Indicator to Study Managers: A Literature Review and Research Agenda, *Journal of Management* 22, No.1, pp. 45–83.
14. Morand, D. A. (Fall 2001). The Emotional Intelligence of Managers: Assessing the Construct Validity of a Nonverbal Measure of "People Skills." *Journal of Business and Psychology* 16, pp. 21–33; Gardner and Martinko (1996).
15. Goleman, Boyatzis, and McKee (2002).
16. (2001). Primal Leadership: The Hidden Driver of Great Performance. *Harvard Business Review*. 79, No. 11, pp. 42–51.

17. Albert Mehrabian found that 55 percent of our message is communicated through our body language and 38 percent through our voice, which means 93 percent of communication is nonverbal.

18. Goleman, D. (1991). Nonverbal Cues Are Easy to Misinterpret, *New York Times*, p. C-1. Also see Morgan, N. (August 2002). The Truth behind the Smile and Other Myths. *Harvard Management Communication Letter.*

19. Morand (2001).

20. Hall, E. T. (1959). *The Silent Language.* Westport, CT: Greenwood Press.

21. Nichols, R. G., and Stevens, L. (1957). *Are You Listening?* New York: McGraw-Hill.

22. Roche, G. R. (1979). Much Ado about Mentors. *Harvard Business Review,* January–February.

23. Harris, T. E., and Nelson, M.D. (2008). *Applied Organizational Communication: Theory and Practice in a Global Environment,* 3rd ed. New York: Lawrence Erlbaum Associates.

24. Herzberg, F. (2003). One More Time: How Do We Motivate Employees. Best of *Harvard Business Review* reprint of 1968 article, 81, No. 1, pp. 30–42.

25. Amabile, T. M., and Kramer, S. J. (2007). Inner Work Life: Understanding the Subtext of Business Performance, *Harvard Business Review.* 85, No. 5, pp. 72–83.

26. Tucker, B. A., and Russell, R. F. (2004). The Influence of the Transformational Leader, *Journal of Leadership and Organizational Studies* 10, No. 4, p. 103

Chapter 8

Cross-Cultural Literacy and Communication

Our globalized, multicultural world requires leaders with a keen understanding of national cultures. By learning from other countries, culturally literate leaders build cultural bridges, enabling them to leverage culture as a tool for competitive advantage.

Robert Rosen (2000). *Global Literacies: Lesson on Business Leadership and National Cultures*. New York: Simon & Schuster

The growing importance of world business creates a strong demand for leaders who are sophisticated in international management and skilled at working with people from other countries. . . . Leaders are . . . faced with the difficult challenge of convincingly presenting their vision to a multicultural and highly diverse workforce and implementing it in an uncertain environment. This requires the ability to decide, communicate, and interact in a culturally sensitive and appropriate manner.

Deanne N. Den Hartog (2004). Leading in a Global Context: Vision in Complexity, *Blackwell Handbook of Global Management*

Chapter Objectives

In this chapter, you will learn to do the following:

- Define culture.
- Recognize major cultural differences.
- Connect and communicate across cultures.

Leaders need an understanding of and appreciation for cultural diversity, called cross-cultural literacy here. It means being literate or knowledgeable about the fundamental differences across cultures. Realizing the value of cultural differences is a key component of emotional intelligence and absolutely essential for leading in today's global environment. Technology has enabled cross-global communication and made working across time zones, geographies, and nationalities a given for most professionals today. In addition, organizations seek diversity in order to compete, and leaders need to be better educated about culture to lead effectively and to take full advantage of the value diversity provides.

We would hope the days of the "Ugly American" depicted in a book of that name published in 1958 are gone, although numerous Web sites suggest that is not the case, and examples abound of companies and U.S. visitors to other countries committing cultural gaffes and lacking sensitivity to cultural differences.

For example, one global computer company, which planned to expand its business by partnering with companies in India, brought the future partners to a meeting at its headquarters, where cowhides were hanging in the elevators. How must the future partners have felt riding in an elevator surrounded by the skins of an animal that they hold sacred, with the slaughter of cows illegal in all but two states in India? Does that mean the company should change its decor for this one meeting? Perhaps not, but it should have a greater awareness of the cultural differences of countries with which it plans to do business on any regular basis.

While bad examples are always easy to find, since they are more visible to the public, examples are becoming more numerous of companies taking cross-cultural literacy seriously and establishing comprehensive cultural diversity training. For example, Royal Dutch Shell, a global group of energy and petrochemical companies headquartered in the Netherlands, has a diversity vision statement and conducts frequent diversity training sessions across all employee groups. Shell uses the "Iceberg of Differences" (Exhibit 8.1) to demonstrate how complex culture is and to illustrate how many cultural differences lie below the surface.[1]

EXHIBIT 8.1
The Iceberg of
Differences

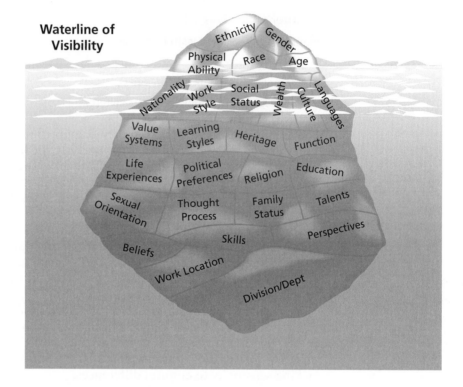

Gender, race, age, physical ability, nationality, religion, and language are the tip of the iceberg, and of course, an understanding of these differences improves a leader's ability to interact with internal and external audiences. An appreciation for all of the differences below the surface will increase a leader's emotional intelligence and greatly improve his or her interpersonal skills and ability to communicate effectively with today's typically diverse workforce.

Countries, areas of a country, companies, and even functions within a company can have different cultures, as can online and face-to-face social networks. Men and women exhibit cultural differences, as do generations. Often, these differences are thought of in a company context as diversity. Fortunately, most companies have come to realize the value of diversity and seek it; many are diverse naturally because they are truly global and contain different nationalities throughout the company.

This chapter will first define culture, then help you understand and manage cultural differences, and conclude with how best to connect and communicate across cultures.

Defining Culture

The term "culture" has numerous definitions, some rather narrow and others much broader. For instance, some think of culture as associated with levels of society or with nationality or geography. For anthropologists, culture is much broader: It is "the way of life of a people, or the sum of their learned behavior patterns, attitudes, and material things."[2] It is the way people make sense of and give meaning to their world. It is the frame of reference and the behavior patterns of groups of people. It includes social characteristics as well as physical characteristics, gender, age, profession, organizational function, and company structure and style. Culture is not personality. Culture is learned and shared equally by those of the same group, whereas personality is highly individual and influenced by our genes and our environment.

A definition that is useful when talking about communicating across cultures is that "culture is a fuzzy set of attitudes, beliefs, behavioral conventions, and basic assumptions and values that are shared by a group of people, and that influence each member's behavior and his/her interpretations of the 'meaning' of other people's behavior."[3] The key words here are "interpretations" and "meaning." Culture is the lens through which we see others, understand them and their words, and interpret the meaning of those words and respond.

The Layers of Culture

Geert Hofstede, a leading researcher on understanding cultural differences, provides a very useful way to look at the layers of the cultures to which we belong (Exhibit 8.2).

Looking closer at the Hofstede's layers of culture helps us realize how complex culture can be. Most of us realize that someone from Japan would differ from someone from Mexico or someone from Germany would differ from someone from Australia in language and behavior, but fewer realize that someone from northern Germany would behave differently than someone from southern Germany and someone from the Northeast coast of the United States would differ from someone from the Midwest. Still fewer recognize that those who use FriendFeed differ in meaningful ways from the Twitter crowd, as do those who prefer MySpace over Facebook.

What we see are finer differences but differences worth realizing when communicating. For example, in business dealings with someone from New York, we would speak in English, but we would find the pace quick and the communication style usually very direct, whereas in a conversation with someone from Dallas, we would also speak English,

EXHIBIT 8.2
The Layers of Culture

Source: Hofstede, G. (1997). *Cultures and Organizations: Software of the Mind.* New York: McGraw-Hill. Used with permission of the author.

1. A **national level** according to one's country (or countries for people who migrated during their lifetime)
2. A **regional/and or ethnic and/or religious and/or linguistic** affiliation level, as most nations are composed of culturally different regions and/or ethnic and/or religious and/or language groups
3. A **gender level,** according to whether a person was born as a girl or as a boy
4. A **generation level,** which separates grandparents from parents from children
5. A **social class level,** associated with educational opportunities and with a person's occupation or profession
6. For those who are employed, an **organizational or corporate level** according to the way employees have been socialized by their work organizations

but the pace would usually be a little shower and the communication style would be more indirect.

Then, if we layer gender on top of these differences, we would probably see more differences in behavior and communication, and even more if we added a generational difference. The behavior and communication style of a 25-year-old woman from New York would differ quite a bit from that of a 40-year-old man from Dallas.

In fact, much has been made of the huge generational differences in the newest group of individuals joining the workforce, the millennials. Exhibit 8.3 shows some of the generalized differences we would probably find across generations.

EXHIBIT 8.3
A Brief Look at Generational Differences

Source: Alsop, R. (2008). *The Trophy Kids Grow Up: How the Millennial Generation Is Shaking Up the Workplace.* San Francisco: Jossey-Bass.

Label	Date of births	Generalized Traits
Traditionalists	1925–1945	Patriotic, dependable, conformisst, respect authority, rigid, socially and financially conservative, solid work ethic
Baby Boomers	1946–1964	Workaholics, idealistic, loyal, competitive, materialistic. seek personal fulfillment, value titles and the corner office
Gen Xers	1965–1979	Self-reliant, adaptable, cynical, distrust authority, resourceful, entrepreneurial, tech savvy
Millennials (also called Gen Y)	1980–2001	Entitled, optimistic, civic minded, close parental involvement, value work–life balance, impatient, multitasking, team-oriented

Anyone looking at Exhibit 8.3 and the description of his or her generation might say, "Wait; I am not like that." What this layering discussion shows us is the complexity of any discussion of culture, but it also highlights the danger of overgeneralizing, or stereotyping. Generalizing is potentially useful but also can be dangerous in cross-cultural communication. People from one country will resemble each other in many ways, but they will also differ.

For example, in the United States are 9,408,802 square miles of geography, a melting pot of cultures representing tremendous diversity, and people brought up to be individualistic. We are also looking at people who have been born and raised in one area and never left it, and others who were born in another country, moved to the United States as a teenager, and are fluent in English and their birth language. We may also be looking at people with little education and travel experiences and those well educated and well traveled.

If we add to this mix different professional interests—such as lawyers, doctors, accountants, philosophers—we cannot help but question the value of any attempt to describe cultural differences, but there is value.

To be sure, academic learning about culture can provide only a basic level of cross-cultural literacy:

> Productive cross-cultural relationships require each individual to embark on a personal learning journey that initially can be even more frustrating than it is rewarding. Academic learning is useful, of course, but it is the direct knowledge accumulated in the day-to-day act of conducting business across cultures that is ultimately most meaningful. This is the kind of learning that allows people to understand not simply the surface signs of cultural differences . . . but, far more importantly, the invisible meanings beneath such differences.[4]

Few would argue that, to understand a culture fully, we must live it—breathing the air, speaking the language, existing as one with the people. However, using standard, reliable frameworks to learn about cultural differences, as well as being exposed to some guiding principles, will aid us in establishing a foundation on which to build a better understanding and appreciation of culture and its impact on the way we interact and communicate.

The next section provides those frameworks and principles and should help you approach diverse audiences with greater confidence and an appreciation for the differences. Understanding another culture requires setting aside a tendency to judge others and being open and flexible. In short, it demands that we draw on the best of our emotional intelligence.

Recognizing Major Cultural Differences

The many books on international communication and on traveling in other countries, such as Roger Axtell's numerous and useful "Do's and Taboos" of international business, provide guidelines on basic verbal and nonverbal communication in most countries. They cover such topics as gestures to avoid, dining customs, gift giving, and even exchange of business cards.

Axtell's books cover many social customs, answering important questions such as the following:

- What are some customs related to lunch and dinner invitations?
- How are gifts viewed? Are they expected in business settings or when visiting someone's home in another culture? If they are expected, what is acceptable?
- What are appropriate greetings?
- What is appropriate to discuss when? For example, are business topics acceptable in informal social gatherings? On the other hand, would it be polite to discuss families at business lunches?
- What gestures should be avoided? See Chapter 7 for more on gestures.

When visiting another culture, we should always review such do's and don'ts, but this section does not provide that kind of information because it is so specific to the country being visited. Instead, it provides frameworks and questions to help you recognize major cultural differences, so that you will better understand the diverse audiences to whom and with whom you will be communicating on a deeper, more universal level.

The frameworks and questions serve as tools to guide you to the areas of differences, and the examples provided illustrate some of those differences. The objective of this discussion is to move you closer to an acceptance level, where you are mindful and respectful of the many differences you will encounter in leading organizations.[5]

A number of frameworks help individuals define and organize the most important cultural differences. It is difficult to cover all of the most universal categories in which to place all the possible cultural differences, but cultural frameworks can be highly useful to give insight into cultural differences and to help us approach culture systematically and nonjudgmentally.

One useful cultural framework in a business or professional context was developed by Mary O'Hara-Devereaux and Robert Johansen for their book *Globalwork*. They argue that, "while the learning process is endless, simple frameworks can help you develop a sense of competence. Understanding the various levels of diversity—physical, social, professional, functional, even spiritual—provides a good beginning.

EXHIBIT 8.4
A Framework for Cultural Variables

Source: O'Hara-Devereaux, M., and Johansen, R. (1994). Globalwork. Jossey-Bass Publishers. Used by permission of John Wiley and Sons, Inc.

The Five Cultural Variables in Holographic Relationship

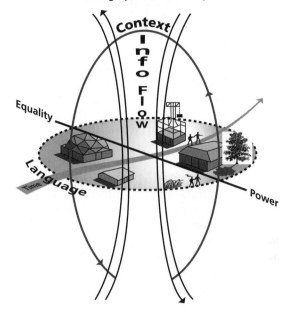

Learning to view each of these levels through the lens of language, context, time, power/equality, and information flow adds invaluable insights."[6] One advantage of their framework is that it shows the interdependence of the variables, each crossing and interrelating with the other (Exhibit 8.4).

These five variables are important to and applicable across all cultures. If we add collectivism versus individualism and spirituality and tradition, we have a very complete list of the differences we will see across cultures:

1. Context
2. Information flow
3. Time
4. Language
5. Power and equality
6. Collectivism versus individualism
7. Spirituality and tradition

These are the variables anthropologists use most often when making distinctions about culture.[7] Understanding each of them will provide you with a platform on which to begin your audience analysis and determine your strategy for communicating and interacting effectively with people from other cultures.

Context

The first topic in almost any discussion of culture will be "context," a theory first explored at length by Edward T. Hall in his groundbreaking work on culture. Context was used in chapter 2 to denote what is going on around us that might affect the choices we make as part of a communication strategy. In cultural studies, context emphasizes what is going on outside **and** what is going on inside individuals that influences the way they interact with others and understand the words and behavior of others. In short, context is anything that surrounds and accompanies communication and gives meaning to it.[8]

Cultures and professions can be arrayed on a spectrum ranging from low-context to high-context. Exhibit 8.5 shows the placement of cultures on the high/low-context spectrum.

High-context cultures rely more extensively on interpersonal relationships to understand meaning and place less importance on verbal messages and more on nonverbal, such as tone, gestures, and facial expressions. They emphasize trust, intuition, and the importance of getting to know people. These cultures tend to be community-oriented, valuing group harmony and consensus over individual accomplishments. Saving face is important to them. Their communication style tends to be indirect.

As a result of the need to get to know people before doing business with them, in high-context cultures, reaching agreements can take much longer than in a low-context culture, which tends to be more impatient and bottom-line driven. Japan and functions such as human resources and corporate communication are high-context cultures. In addition, many social networks tend to be high-context; for example,

EXHIBIT 8.5
Cultures as Usually Placed on the High/Low-Context Spectrum

Source: Cultures column from Copeland, L. & Griggs, L. (1986). Going International: How to Make Friends and Deal Effectively in the Global Marketplace. New York: Random House. Used with permission. Profession/function column, with additions in brackets, from O'Hara-Devereaux, M. & Johansen, R. (1994). The information is used by permission of John Wiley & Sons, Inc.

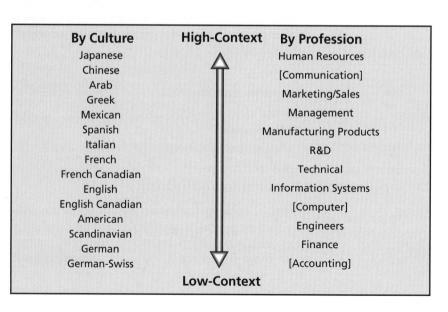

By Culture	High-Context	By Profession
Japanese		Human Resources
Chinese		[Communication]
Arab		Marketing/Sales
Greek		
Mexican		Management
Spanish		Manufacturing Products
Italian		R&D
French		
French Canadian		Technical
English		Information Systems
English Canadian		[Computer]
American		Engineers
Scandinavian		Finance
German		[Accounting]
German-Swiss	Low-Context	

LinkedIn has a place for members to post questions and get a wide variety of answers, and members can vote on the best answer. Many such collaborative decision-making tools have arisen in a variety of social networking spaces.

In contrast, **low-context** cultures depend on explicit verbal messages and rely less on interpersonal relationships for meaning in communication. They tend to value facts and figures, are very direct and to the point when communicating, and expect contracts and legal agreements in business dealings. In fact, the attitude toward agreements and contracts is one major difference between high and low context. In the low-context cultures, contracts are seen as firm and inflexible. Once two sides have shaken hands, and particularly after they have signed the contract, the agreement cannot be modified without major problems and legal intanglements. The United States and accounting and finance functions exemplify low-context cultures.

Low-context cultures tend to use a more direct form of communication, whereas high-context cultures will be more indirect. Exhibit 8.6 demonstrates the range of cultures in terms of direct and indirect communication styles. Cultures using a more direct style will usually emphasize independence and individuality. They will be forthright, appearing confident and authoritative. Their directness may be interpreted by some as being too aggressive when they state their opinions without qualification. In fact, those used to a more indirect style, may see the direct communicator as rude.

Indirect communication, on the other hand, will be used in cultures valuing harmony and community togetherness. They will avoid confrontations and often state their opinion so indirectly that those from direct cultures will not understand them. For example, they will not say "no" directly; instead they may say, "perhaps" or "maybe," which leaves the direct communicator thinking the door is open, when in the mind of the indirect speaker, it may be clearly closed.

Exhibit 8.7 illustrates some of the common differences between low-context and high-context cultures that we might see in a professional setting. As discussed earlier in this text, all communication exists in a context. Recognizing that the importance of context will differ from culture to culture is essential. For some cultures, context is

EXHIBIT 8.6
Direct versus Indirect Communication Styles

Source: Storti, C. (1999). *Figuring Foreigners Out.* Intercultural Press.

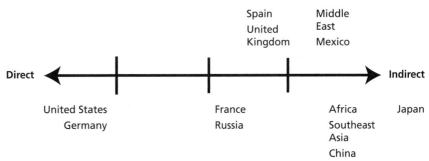

**EXHIBIT 8.7
Differences in
Low- and High-
Context
Professional
Environments**

Source: Table created with
information adapted from
O'Hara-Devereaux, M., and
Johansen, R. (1994). Glob-
alwork the groupings and
some examples supplement
O'Hara-Devereaux and Jo-
hansen and draw on Hall &
Hall (1989) and Samovar &
Porter. The information is
used by permission of
Wiley and Sons, Inc.

Areas	High Context	Low Context
Space	• Executive offices shared and open to all • May have several people in their office at one time, even with formal appointments • Stand close to each other in business conversations and may be offended if someone moves away	• Executive offices separated and access controlled • Expect to meet with one person alone and not have others lingering about during an appointment with someone • Set boundaries and will be uncomfortable if someone moves too close
Information	• Do not expect or want detailed information and feel irritated when pressed for it • Information shared with everyone • Comfortable in a sea of information	• Heavy reliance on detailed background information in written or verbal form • Information highly centralized and distribution controlled by a few people • Overload if information flows in a fast, disorganized manner
Relationships	• Relationships more important than objective data • Overlap between business and social relationships	• Objective (information based) rather than subjective (relationships based) • Business and social relationships compartmentalized
Status	• Authority and status more important than technical skills • Invitations to functions based on person's status rather than competence	• Competence given equal/more weight than position and status • Business meeting invitation based on competence
Meetings	• Meetings often announced on short notice; key people always accept	• Meetings with fixed agendas and plenty of advance notice
Decision Making	• Each new factor and item cautiously evaluated to be sure of implications	• Reluctance to act without a great deal of current information

more important than the words one individual might communicate to another. For others, getting to the point with words is all that matters.

Again, it would be easy to overgeneralize about context differences. It may be typical for a person from the United States or for an accountant to rely less on context and more on the words that are exchanged, looking for actual facts and figures and not for the meaning between the words, the way the words are spoken, or the body language that might accompany the message. However, this stereotypical expectation will not be valid for everyone from the United States or for every accountant.

Information Flow

The importance of context in a culture, high or low, influences how individuals approach exchanges of information and determines how messages flow between people and levels in organizations. It also controls who initiates communication and with whom, what kinds of messages are sent, what channels are preferred, and how formal or informal the exchange of information will be.

For instance, businesspeople in the Untied States are known for their directness and "bottom-line" mentality. They want the "so what?" right up front and do not want to read through a lengthy prologue to get to it. Information flow refers to "how" and "how fast" information is exchanged.

The following are some questions we should ask to understand better the cultural expectations of information flow:

1. How fast does a message travel from one part of the organization to another, from one person to another?
2. Can and does the information travel directly, or must it go through levels or channels?
3. How much context is needed to ensure that the information is understood?
4. How should information be linked and sequenced—or looped—to produce the intended results?
5. What are the most effective means of packaging information to produce the right responses?
6. Does the culture prefer words, graphics, or some combination?
7. How should the information be organized: directly or indirectly?
8. Does the culture prefer written communication to oral?
9. Is the culture comfortable with informality in presentations or meetings?

With the rise of social media, corporations in many areas of the world are feeling the pressure to make their organizations more transparent and to provide more information freely to the public at large. More and more, people expect to be able to connect with organizations through a variety of technologies, and they expect the organizations to respond in kind. This is having a powerful impact on information flow in many companies, and the trend will likely continue.

Time

Henry David Thoreau, a North American writer influenced by Eastern philosophical ideas and North American Indian culture, said, "Time is but a stream I go a-fishing in." This view of time is referred to in discussions of cultural frameworks as **polychronic,** that is, believing that time is a state of being consisting of many events occurring at once. Polychronic time is open-ended and flexible, and people are more important than promptness and schedules. The opposite cultural view of time is called **monochronic.**

People in monochronic cultures believe that time is linear, is divisible, and consists of one event at a time. Time is a commodity and is meant to be measured and managed, conserved or wasted, spent wisely or foolishly. Events are scheduled sequentially, one at a time, and this schedule takes precedence over relationships and people. High-context cultures tend to be polychronic and low-context monochronic. For instance, North Americans see time as a scarce resource, and the expression "time is money" conveys the kind of value placed on time in U.S. business.

In addition to the polychronic/monochronic difference, cultures also differ in how they view the past, present, and future. Some see now as all there is and think it presumptuous to try to control or predict the future. Others value the past more. The typical North American is strongly oriented toward the future and devalues what is happening now as irrelevant. The following questions will help in uncovering differences in time orientation:

1. Does the culture emphasize promptness, or are people relaxed about starting times and even offended by those who arrive "right on time"?
2. Are they involved in several activities at a time, or do they do one thing at a time?
3. Do they take time commitments and deadlines seriously? How are appointments and schedules viewed?
4. How important is the way things were done in the past?
5. Are they more focused on the task or on people?
6. Do they expect privacy and respect private property?
7. What are their usual working hours?
8. When do they typically eat lunch and dinner?

Again, social media and technology are changing people's concepts of time as a commodity. In some work cultures, for example, employees with BlackBerries or other smart phones may be expected to be available at all times and to respond to messages and e-mails even long after standard working hours. Responding in near-real time may be valued, particularly in monochronic cultures.

Language

Language has been described as the "central influence on culture and one of the most highly charged symbols of a culture or a nation. . . . A language does not merely record and transmit perceptions and thoughts; it actually helps to shape both."[9] According to Edward T. Hall, "Culture is language; language is culture."[10] We cannot separate language from culture.

Although language usually presents the most obvious differences when people from different cultures come together, it is not just a matter of someone speaking Spanish and someone else speaking Mandarin. All cultural levels have language differences: industries, professions, functions, and even genders. As Deborah Tannen's research has found, men and women use language so differently at times that it is a wonder they ever connect. Language includes words, syntax, and vocabulary, as well as the various dialects and the jargon of disciplines.

Unfortunately, no easy way exists to solve the problems created by language differences. This is one place where the old adage "A little learning is a dangerous thing" bears out: "Without more than passing familiarity with the language of a culture, it is virtually impossible to scan the environment for business cues, negotiate, or evaluate performance."[11] Learning just a little bit of a language and trying to use it in a professional context could cause problems, although most cultures would appreciate our interest and our attempt. In international business negotiations, we should always consider hiring our own interpreter, even if we feel fairly comfortable with the language, to avoid any misunderstandings or a contractual agreement we did not intend.

Power

Cultures differ tremendously in how they view power and equality. Some believe in strict hierarchies with clear distinctions between levels and formalized respect for people at the higher levels of an organization. Others see everyone as equal, and although a title may command some element of respect, it is not as rigidly observed as in a hierarchical culture. Some cultures respect age; others do not. Some think education demands respect, while others see it as simply another item for a résumé. In other words, titles and position matter more for some cultures than they do for other cultures.

Hofstede discusses the differences in power perception and practice in cultures as "power distance," which he defines as "the extent to which the less powerful members of institutions and organizations within a country expect and accept that power is distributed unequally."[12] He describes a major study measuring power distance from country to country in which the researchers found that some cultures view the possession of power by relatively few people and the resultant inequality as the norm. Such cultures have high power distance values. Other cultures see power as spread fairly evenly across all members and believe all people are equal, resulting in low distance values.

The survey results indicated "high power distance values for Latin countries (both Latin European, like France and Spain, and Latin

EXHIBIT 8.8
Some Differences between High/Low Power Distance Workplaces

Source: Adapted from Hofstede, G. (1997). *Cultures and Organizations: Software of the Mind.* New York: McGraw-Hill. Used with permission of the author.

Low Power Distance	High Power Distance
• Inequalities among people minimized	• Inequalities expected and desired
• Interdependence between less and more powerful people	• Less powerful people dependent on the more powerful people
• More educated hold less authoritarian values than less educated	• Both more and less educated show almost equally authoritarian values
• Hierarchy means inequality of roles, established for convenience	• Hierarchy reflects the existential inequality between higher and lower levels
• Decentralization is popular	• Centralization is popular
• Narrow salary range between top and bottom of organization	• Wide salary range between top and bottom of organization
• Subordinates expect to be consulted	• Subordinates expect to be told what to do
• Ideal boss is a resourceful democrat	• Ideal boss is a benevolent autocrat
• Privileges and status symbols are frowned upon	• Privileges and status symbols for managers are expected and popular

American) and for Asian and African countries" and "lower power distance values" for the "U.S.A., Great Britain and its former Dominions, and for the remaining non-Latin part of Europe."[13]

This difference in how power and equality are viewed leads to tremendous differences in how individuals approach reporting relationships within organizations, how they function on teams, and how they interact with one another on a daily basis. Exhibit 8.8 offers examples of some of the differences found in low power distance and high power distance workplaces.

The differences in how cultures view power affect leadership in particular. "Different cultural groups may have different ideas regarding what leaders typically look like and how they should or should not behave. In some cultures a leader is thought of as typically an autonomous, strong, and decisive person; whereas in other cultures other images of ideal leaders may prevail."[14]

What might be considered leadership in one culture may be seen as tyranny in another. Leaders who move outside of the culture they know must be particularly mindful of how the culture they have entered views power.

In addition, changes in technology and the emphasis on communicating using social media place more pressure on organizations to be open with information and with power. Organizations are having to change power constructs or at least rethink them. Low power cultures will be more receptive to social media and accept their use, whereas high power cultures may try to hang on to traditional behavior and restrict information sharing and communication.

The following questions will help in determining and appreciating some of the differences in cultural perspectives on power and equality:

1. What is the attitude toward titles and positions?
2. Do individuals openly challenge authority?
3. Is the organization multilayered or flat?
4. How are decisions made (by one or many)?
5. Are subordinates consulted or told what to do?
6. What is the attitude toward individualism?
7. How is status displayed?
8. What is the attitude toward women in business?
9. What is the attitude toward age?
10. How open is the organization to social media? Is it an expected way to work or is it discouraged?

A couple of cultural variables that cut across context, information flow, time, language, and power are also important in understanding culture These are questions of individualism versus collectivism and spirituality and tradition.

Collectivism versus Individualism

The individualism versus collectivism cultural difference is included in another popular framework for studying culture, that of Hofstede. Hofstede breaks the cultural differences into power, uncertainty avoidance, individual/collective, masculine/feminine, and long-term/short-term orientation. Cultural emphasis on context, on how information is shared, and how power is viewed are influenced by how individualistc or collectivistic a culture is. Hofstedes explains the terms as follows:

> Individualism pertains to societies in which the ties between indviduals are loose: everyone is expected to look after himself or herself and his or her immediate family. Collectivism as its opposite pertains to societies in which people from birth onwards are integrated into strong, cohesive ingroups, which throughout people's lifetime continue to proect them in exchange for unquestioning loyalty.[14]

The major question to ask is, Does the culture emphasize the individual ("I") or the community ("we")? If a person's culture focuses on the individual, he or she will understand and feel concern about his or her individual needs, expectations, and welfare. On the other hand, persons concerned with the community will be looking for how what happens affects their group and family. The individually focused cultures will look for messages relevant to them specifically, whereas the more collective cultures will want to know what will happen to the group or community

One way to consider whether the culture emphasizes the individual or the community is to examine the social media in which it gets involved. If blogs are common and social networking is less popular, the culture likely indentifies more with the individual. Likewise, if more people are involved in a collaborative online culture, such as Second Life, the focus may be more on the community.

Spirituality and Tradition

Spirituality and tradition include religion and traditional values as defined by Inglehart in his Values Map. Inglehart found that traditional versus secular/rational values and survival/self-expression values dominate all other cultural variables, explaining "more than 70 percent of the cross-national variance."[16]

> The Traditional/Secular-rational values dimension reflects the contrast between societies in which religion is very important and those in which it is not. A wide range of other orientations are closely linked with this dimension. Societies near the traditional pole emphasize the importance of parent-child ties and deference to authority, along with absolute standards and traditional family values.[17]

The religion/tradition value is an important variable in determining behavior and how individuals will communicate and interpret messages. Many of the customs and ways of interacting with others depend on belief systems, and often very traditional cultures will adhere strictly to rituals that honor their beliefs. For example, in Islamic cultures, the call to prayer (Adhan) is honored five times a day with a speaker heard across the communities reciting the lyrical Arabic text of the Adhan. In the Middle East, Friday is a non-work day, since it is a holy day, whereas Sunday is still a non-work day in many traditional Christian countries.

Questions to understand how best to communicate with groups expressing spiritual or other traditional values are as follows:

1. Does this cultural group believe in a higher being or some other source of guidance or power outside themselves?
2. Are they more traditional in their beliefs and values or more secular?
3. What are the predominant religious influences?
4. What are the daily religious practices, expectations, and holidays and how will these influence how they interact on a daily basis?

How persons answer these questions will reflect their value system and will influence how they will respond to whatever messages we are communicating to them. It will influence where they will look for direction and how they will respond emotionally to authority messages in particular.

Again, one of the dangers of any discussion of cultural differences and classifications is stereotyping. The distinctions made in this discussion of all of the variables describe characteristics that are typical of a group but will not necessarily be found in each member of the group. The goal is to make each of us more sensitive to the filters that are deeply embedded in our psyches that affect how we interpret the meaning intended by others in their communication with us so that we are open and flexible and thus better able to connect and to communicate across the different cultures we encounter every day.

Connecting and Communicating across Cultures

By understanding and appreciating cultural diversity, leaders can better know how to connect and communicate with all of the different audiences that form the professional environment and most of the professional world today. If we are leading others, no matter the national or regional origin, race, gender, age, or whatever other cultural difference we will encounter, we want to be able to deliver our messages appropriately and effectively.

First, it may be helpful to dispel a few of the myths about communicating and working in other cultures.

Common Myths About Culture

1. **"We're Really All the Same."** As the discussion of cultural variables demonstrates, we are not all the same, and it can be dangerous to assume that we are. We need to acknowledge and value the differences and avoid "ethnocentrism," the tendency to believe that our own race or ethnic group is somehow better or more important than any other and that all others need to be like the culture to which we feel we belong.
2. **"I Just Need to Be Myself in Order to Really Connect."** While we never want to violate our own sense of identity and will even find it difficult if not impossible to do so, we do need to make an effort to dress and communicate verbally and nonverbally as is appropriate to the day-to-day customs. At times, we may even need to go outside our own "comfort zone" in order to communicate and connect on more than a surface level.
3. **"I Have to Adopt the Practices of the Other Culture in Order to Succeed."** We should "adapt to" instead of trying to "adopt" the practices of another culture. Adopting can result in our being misunderstood and perhaps even considered disrespectful, as if we were mocking the culture. Respect and honor are keys here. We should base any decision to adopt practices of other cultures on an in-depth understanding and a "thorough engagement with the culture."
4. **"It's Really All about Personality."** While personality profiles, such as those discussed previously, are useful in helping us understand behavioral differences, drawing a direct correlation between a personality type and a culture can result in stereotypes that limit our understanding of cultural differences. Also, "while the same range of personality types may exist within any given population, a culture's value orientations provide an overall framework for favoring one particular trait over another." Assuming that personality is the source of unfamiliar behaviors across cultures may cause a misreading of a cultural difference.

Source: Myths and directly quoted passages from Walker, D., Walker, T., and Schmitz, J. (2003). *Doing Business Internationally: A Guide to Cross-Cultural Success.* New York: McGraw-Hill. Used with permission of The McGraw-Hill Companies.

Basically, to connect and communicate, we should adopt the following approaches to any cross-cultural encounter, whether visiting another country, interacting in a new social medium, or meeting someone in our own backyard:

1. **Be open and respectful.** All cultures are valuable and important, and no one is better or right or wrong in the way they think or act; they are just different. We need to be open and value these differences. We also need to respect them, finding out what respect "looks like" to them.

2. **Know the social customs.** Use any of the numerous guides to the social customs to avoid the obvious and potentially dangerous gaffes caused by ignorance. Whether shaking hands, exchanging business cards, or dining, when attempting to connect and communicate with individuals from a culture other than our own, we must know the expectations and behave appropriately.

3. **Learn as much about the culture, history, people, and even languages as reasonable.** When we move outside our own culture into another, we realize the value of learning as much as possible about the culture. If we plan to do business with another country for any length of time, we will ideally want to learn the language, while still realizing that, if we are not fluent, we should use an interpreter before entering into business discussions or decisions.

4. **Obtain pointers and feedback from members of the culture.** Having colleagues and friends in different cultural communities is invaluable, and we should call on them to help us and coach us.

5. **Be patient**, be **flexible, and value the time needed to develop relationships.** Remember, cultures differ in their view of time, and when traveling for business meetings, for example, we need to allow enough time and avoid being rushed. We also need to realize relationship building is important in high-context cultures, and we need to build in adequate time for it to occur.

6. **Keep a sense of humor.** We have to be able to laugh at ourselves and know others will appreciate our ability to do so as well.

7. **Keep language simple and avoid jargon.** All languages are full of idioms and slang, so whenever working across language differences, we need to keep our language as free of jargon and colloquialisms as possible. For example, in English, we frequently use sports and war metaphors. Many of these will not translate well.

Even though we can only obtain a very basic level of cross-cultural literacy from reading about the differences across cultures, having some understanding of the major cultural variables provides a foundation on which to build the greater knowledge we will need if we are communicating cross culturally. At a minimum, the cultural frameworks, examples of some of the differences, and questions to help us probe differences should provide useful tools for our analysis of our audiences and for the development of our communication strategy.

This chapter provides a beginning and should have increased the recognition of the importance and value of understanding and appreciating cultural differences. Cross-Cultural literacy is essential in today's world and required for leadership communication and transformational leaders in particular. This chapter has provided an introduction and basic foundation for leadership communication across cultures.

Further Reading

This chapter has referred to a number of excellent books on culture that would be worth reading in their entirety and would definitely help in further expanding an understanding of cultural differences:

Beamer, L., and Varner, I. (2001). *Intercultural Communication in the Global Workplace.* Boston: McGraw-Hill Irwin.

Bennett, M. J. (1993). Towards Ethnorelativism: A Developmental Model of Intercultural ensitivity. In M. Paige (Ed.), *Education for the Intercultural Experience.* Yarmouth, ME: Intercultural Press.

Hall, E. T. (1990). *Understanding Cultural Differences.* Yarmouth, ME: Intercultural Press.

Hall, E. T. (1989). *Beyond Culture.* New York: Anchor Books.

Hall, E. T. (1980). *The Silent Language.* Westport, CT: Greenwood Press.

Hofstede, G. (1997). *Cultures and Organizations: Software of the Mind.* New York: McGraw-Hill.

Inglehart, R. (1997). *Modernization and Postmodernization: Changing Values and Political Styles in Advanced Industrial Society.* Princeton, NJ: Princeton University Press. Also see www.worldvaluessurvey.org.

Inglehart, R., & Welzel, C. (2005). *Modernization, Culture, Change, and Democracy: The Human Development Sequence.* New York: Cambridge University Press.

Lewis, R. (2000). *When Cultures Collide: Managing Successfully across Cultures.* London: Nicholas Brealey.

O'Hara-Devereaux, M., and Johansen, R. (1994). *Globalwork: Bridging Distance, Culture, and Time.* San Francisco: Jossey-Bass.

Rosen, R. (2000). *Global Literacies: Lessons on Business Leadership and National Cultures.* New York: Simon & Schuster.

Tannen, D. (1990). *You Just Don't Understand.* New York: Ballantine.

Walker, D., Walker, T., and Schmitz, J. (2003). *Doing Business Internationally: A Guide to Cross-Cultural Success.* New York: McGraw-Hill.

**Application 8.1
Proactively
Managing
Diversity**

Case: OmniBank's Diversity Efforts

You have recently been named the new president of OmniBank, a medium-size but rapidly growing suburban bank that meets the needs of individuals and small businesses. During the interview process, you observed that, beyond the front office teller level, the more senior workforce at the bank is very homogeneous—mostly male and predominantly Caucasian. You have reviewed several marketing studies that profile your customer base and you realize that you not only have many customers of different ethnicities but also have a large number of international customers. In addition, you have a large number of "starter" accounts for students in high school who will soon move on to college—and may take their business with them if the bank does not meet their remote banking needs.

As the new president, you decide it is important to launch a comprehensive effort to improve both the diversity of the employees at the bank and the diversity with which it interacts with its constituents. You value diversity and believe that broadening your employee base and social networks as the bank grows will benefit everyone involved. Besides, it makes good business sense.

Your Assignment

You decide to form a committee to jump-start your efforts in improving hiring and networking diversity at the bank. In a group, list the steps you would take to create this committee and establish its charter. Pay special attention to how you would ensure that it accomplishes the goal of greater diversity, both at the bank and in community outreach.

**Application 8.2
Creating
International
Correspondence**

The Case: PTI and Congoil

You are the vice president of operations for Production Tankers, Inc. (PTI), a U.S.-based oil services contractor that provides converted tankers to produce oil from offshore fields. PTI's converted tanker *Ocean Reliable* (*OR*) has been producing oil for Congoil P&P, a small but politically important division of a large West African national oil company, for the past seven years at a field called Naabila. Two years remain on the present contract. PTI hopes to renew the contract with Congoil for use of the vessel at another field when the present contract expires. You know in all honesty that other opportunities for the vessel are very limited. PTI's CEO has made the contract renewal a high priority for you and your group. Congoil pays PTI a fee of $43,000 per day for lease and operation of the *OR*, a rate that has allowed PTI to fully recover its initial investment in the vessel. Oil production has been running at around 7,000 barrels per day, giving Congoil a revenue stream on the order of $140,000 per day at current prices.

Congoil owns Naabila field, is in charge of production operations, and bears all production costs. The large U.S. oil company Amproco serves as commercial and technical advisor to Congoil as part of the agreement granting it the rights to explore and produce other promising areas on the country's continental shelf. Amproco receives no payment for its advisory role and does not pay any share of the costs of operating Naabila field. Amproco is believed to have some influence with Congoil, although the nature of the relationship between the two companies remains rather obscure to outsiders.

Two years ago, as oil production at Naabila began to decline, Congoil asked PTI to install a small natural gas compression system aboard the *OR*, so that it could implement gas lift operations, a technique used to help sustain production from aging fields. The need for gas lift had been anticipated, and PTI's contract with Congoil stipulated that, if a gas lift compression system were ever installed, Congoil would reimburse PTI within 45 days for all documented costs. These costs came to $2.5 million and, under the terms of the contract, were invoiced to Congoil.

Gas lift operations began 18 months ago aboard the *OR*, but despite repeated requests from your operations manager and PTI's in-country business development manager, Congoil has not yet reimbursed PTI the $2.5 million. The difficulty seems to arise from Congoil's belief that some provisions of the contract are unfair and should be overlooked or set aside. Congoil's general manager, Syanga M'bweni Rugeiro, has maintained that installation of the gas lift compressor represents a capital improvement to the *OR*, and thus PTI should bear the cost. He and other Congoil officials have also objected to the fact that Congoil is contractually bound to pay PTI the $43,000 day-rate even if the vessel is not producing oil. They recall with considerable resentment an incident almost four years ago when needed repairs in conjunction with an extension of the original three-year contract required PTI to remove the *OR* from Naabila and take it to port for a 57-day period—during which they continued to pay the day-rate.

As vice president of operations, you have profit and loss responsibility for the *OR* and PTI's other production tankers. PTI's executives have made it clear to you that collecting the $2.5 million, preferably with annual interest of 8 percent, will have a material impact on the company's earnings for the current fiscal year, estimated by analysts to be in the range of $18.5 million on revenues of $390 million. Given the culture of PTI, you understand that securing payment from Congoil would be viewed very favorably and earn you additional status with your peers and superiors.

You decide to write to Syanga Rugeiro requesting immediate payment of the $2.5 million. You have known Syanga for over seven years, and while you did not negotiate the original contract for the *OR*, you did negotiate the follow-on contract at the end of the first three years, when PTI agreed to reduce the original day-rate in exchange for the security afforded by a six-year extension. You feel that you know Syanga about as well as most Westerners get to know African officials, and you feel your relationship with him is sound. You know that he received his geology degree from the local university and later spent a year studying management at a British university. He speaks good English, and your business relations have been cordial. You have talked with him about his family and once even met his oldest son when Syanga brought him along on a business trip to Houston. He asked your assistance in getting the boy accepted into the engineering program at your undergraduate university, something you were happy to do.

Despite all these interactions with him, however, you have never felt that you understood Syanga very well. His Western education and business manner seem like a thin veneer over a much more substantial base of traditional African values and preferences. Your experience and some modest reading on the subject have indicated to you that the local West African culture is collectivist, high-context, high power distance, polychronic, and risk and uncertainty avoiding. Decision making requires consultation among all affected parties, but nothing happens until the highest-ranking official involved signals his approval. You realize you have drawn most of these assumptions from your reading, but you feel you have also seen some of it in Syanga's actions. You feel you need to appeal directly to him to pay the $2.5 million owed to PTI.

You decide also to write to Amproco's assistant country manager, Carl Mouton, asking for his help in getting Congoil to pay PTI the $2.5 million. You have met Carl on several occasions and have a number of common friends in the industry. Also, you have discussed the difficulties contractors can encounter doing business in West Africa. You believe that Carl might be able to influence Syanga to approve your request for payment.

The Assignment

In your role as PTI's vice president of operations, select the appropriate written media for this situation and for the cultures involved (consider text message, e-mail, or snail mail memo or letter) and write two correspondences responding to the situation described in the case:

1. To Syanga Rugeiro, requesting payment of the $2.5 million owed PTI and
2. To Carl Mouton, asking for his assistance in persuading Syanga to pay.

In addition, write a short (one page maximum) explanation of your communication strategy and how your knowledge of intercultural communication issues influenced the decisions you made in organizing the information, expressing your ideas, and developing an appropriate style and tone. In your explanation, comment also on the choice of written media as appropriate for your communication. If given the option, would you choose a medium other than written to communicate these messages? Explain your response.

Syanga Rugeiro's address is 26-30 Avenida Presidente dos Santos, Dist. Norte 4, Kinuanda, Congola.

Source: This case and assignment were prepared by Charles R. McCabe. Copyright Charles R. McCabe, 2002. Used with permission.

Application 8.3 Preparing an International Briefing

For this assignment, you will work in groups to research, prepare, and deliver a 15-minute presentation with 5 minutes for questions and answers. The presentation will show how the culture of an individual nation or world region affects the local business environment and practices. As a starting point for your research and preparation, you should use the information in this chapter on cultural variables and determine the characteristics of your selected country against each variable. For example, is the country high- or low-context? How do they feel about power and equality? Your research should result in an international communication audit for the nation or region you select. In addition, you might want to look at the Web site of a global company that sells its products in many countries—Procter & Gamble, for example (http://www.pg.com/en_US/index.shtml).

Your group should develop its presentation with a specific business-related audience and purpose in mind; for instance, you might want to approach the presentation as a briefing for employees assigned to a newly acquired foreign subsidiary or a negotiating team about to embark on negotiations for an international merger. You should make your presentation appropriate in every respect to this specific audience. You may take a creative approach.

To promote breadth of learning and avoid repetition, each group is encouraged to select a different nation or region.

Application 8.4 Designing International Communication Programs

For this assignment, you are to work in groups to select a country in which a currently established company is not marketing its products. For example, you might look at Dunkin' Donuts and decide to market it in Germany. Each group is to research, prepare, and deliver a presentation of 20 to 25 minutes, with 5 minutes for questions and answers, or 30 minutes total.

The presentation will describe your marketing plan for the introduction of your company's product or service into a country other than your own. Your primary objective is to show that you understand enough about the country and its culture to argue that the country will be a successful target market for the product or service that you have selected. The presentation will address the business opportunity (the market), your product or service, the competitive landscape, your positioning, and your communication strategy (paying special attention to cultural differences).

The overall purpose of the presentation is to showcase to your CEO and senior executive team your team's approach to promoting and marketing your selected product or service. They will want to see your rationale and your preliminary plan for introducing and marketing the product or service.

Your group must decide on (1) the company, (2) the product or service of that company, and (3) the country where the product/service will be introduced. You must be able to make a case for the introduction of your product or service; in other words, there must be a market for the product or service. In addition, you must include your approach to the social media sphere and justify why that approach will work.

Notes

1. This depiction of the Iceberg of Differences is used in Shell's in-house training. They have given us permission to use it here.
2. Hall, E. T. (1959). *The Silent Language*. Westport, CT; Greenwood Press.
3. Spencer-Oatey, H. (2000). *Culturally Speaking: Managing Rapport through Talk across Cultures*. London: Continuum.
4. O'Hara-Devereaux, M., and Johansen, R. (1994). *Globalwork: Bridging Distance, Culture, and Time*. San Francisco: Jossey-Bass.
5. The "acceptance" level of intercultural knowledge, as described by Milton Bennett (cited below), is the fourth stage of the Developmental Model for Intercultural Sensitivity. The stages are as follows: denial, defense, minimization, acceptance, adaptation, and integration.
6. O'Hara-Devareaux X, M., and Johansen, R. (1994).
7. For more on any of the variables, see any of the books by Edward T. Hall, a prolific researcher and writer on culture and the one to whom most recent writers on the subject refer. O'Hara-Devereaux and Johansen rely on

Hall for some of their examples. In addition, you will want to look at Hofstede's *Culture and Organizations* and Inglehart and Welzel's *Modernization, Culture, Change, and Democracy*, as well as their Value Map. If you desire a more complex but also useful, framework, you should look at the one provided by Walker, Walker, and Schmitz in their book *Doing Business Internationally*.

8. O'Hara-Devereaux and Johansen have pulled much of Edward T. Hall's distinctions on space under context, so this discussion will follow that combination as well.

9. Condon, J. C. (1975). *An Introduction to Intercultural Communication*, New York: Macmillan.

10. Hall (1959).

11. O'Hara-Devereaux and Johansen (1994).

12. Hofstede, G. (1997). *Culture and Organizations: Software of the Mind.* New York: McGraw-Hill, p. 28.

13. Hofstede (1997), p. 26.

14. Den Hartog (2004).

15. Hofstede (1997).

16. www.worldvaluessurvey.org/.

17. www.worldvaluessurvey.org/.

Chapter 9

Meetings: Leadership and Productivity

There's nothing better than an in-person meeting. Nothing yet has replicated that, as far as I know. For quick interaction, e-mail and phone are great. But for really getting into something, a physical meeting is much better.

Jeff Bezos, Amazon.com's founder and CEO, *The Wall Street Journal*, February 4, 2000

Chapter Objectives

In this chapter, you will learn to do the following:

- Decide when a meeting is the best forum.
- Complete essential meeting planning.
- Conduct a productive meeting.
- Manage meeting problems and conflict.
- Ensure that meetings lead to action.

A *Harvard Business Review* article several years ago reported that "11 million meetings . . . take place every day in the United States."[1] Today, that figure would probably be even higher with so many companies moving to team-based workplaces. A survey conducted by UCLA and the University of Minnesota found that "executives on average spend 40%–50% of their working hours in meetings."[2] Another survey cited in the same article indicated that "surveyed professionals agree that as much as 50% of that meeting time is unproductive and that up to 25% of meeting time is spent discussing irrelevant issues."[3]

Given the dominance of meetings in business and other professional settings and how often people complain about them, leaders need to be

279

able to plan and conduct effective, productive meetings. Doing so requires leadership communication skills and is important in setting the precedent for the rest of the organization. As one specialist in meeting management says, "Meetings matter because that's where an organization's culture perpetuates itself. . . . Meetings are how an organization says, 'you are a member.' So if every day we go to boring meetings full of boring people, then we can't help but think that it is a boring company. Bad meetings are a source of negative messages about our company and ourselves."[4]

To create a positive atmosphere around meetings in our organizations, we need to avoid the seven deadly sins of meetings.

The Seven Deadly Sins of Meetings

1. People don't take meetings seriously.
2. Meetings are too long.
3. People wander off the topic.
4. Nothing happens once the meeting ends.
5. People don't tell the truth.
6. Meetings are always missing important information, so they postpone critical decisions.
7. Meetings never get better.

Source: The seven sins of deadly meetings. By Eric Matson and William R. Daniels. Reprinted from *Fast Company,* 1997, p. 27. Used with permission.

This chapter will help leaders and other meeting planners avoid these seven deadly sins and plan and conduct productive meetings by determining when a meeting is the best forum for achieving the required result; establishing objectives, outcomes, and agenda; performing essential planning; clarifying roles and establishing ground rules; using common problem-solving techniques; managing meeting problems; and ensuring that follow-up occurs.

Meetings can be small or large, internal or external, frequent or infrequent. This chapter focuses primarily on small-group meetings intended to accomplish tasks or move actions forward inside an organization since these are the most prevalent types of professional meetings.

Deciding When a Meeting Is the Best Forum

Communication purpose and strategy should come first in planning meetings, as in all communication situations. Meeting leaders or planners need to define a clear purpose and analyze the audience to determine whether a meeting is the best forum for what they want to accomplish. One of the frustrations with meetings is that they often seem unnecessary. Groups of all sorts can fall into a habit of meeting daily or weekly or monthly just because they have always done it that way. Beyond tradition or habit, they have no other reasons for meeting.

Even without what appears to be a specific business purpose, meeting periodically can be beneficial. For example, meetings can increase team, department, or company camaraderie. In company meetings, people see others they may not ordinarily see and feel connected to a larger group. Meetings with no specific business objective might have motivation, recreation, or networking as their purpose—all potentially important in certain organizational contexts. The frustration caused when attendees feel as if a meeting accomplishes nothing could perhaps be minimized by making it clear that the purpose for meeting is motivation, recreation, or networking. On the other hand, perhaps instead of a "meeting," what the group or company really needs is a social gathering or party.

Consider Purpose

No set rules apply to answer the question "When is a meeting the best forum?" Referring to the four typical purposes for communication in professional settings—that is, to inform, persuade, instruct, or engage—will help most of us decide. For instance, if our primary purpose is to inform, we should ask if a meeting is required to convey the information or would the Intranet, a blog or forum post, or an e-mail accomplish this goal more efficiently and effectively? If we decide our overall purpose is to instruct, is a meeting better for transferring the skills than an online instructional program?

Consider Audience

Leaders will also want to consider the audience. How do most of their colleagues and employees like to receive information? Does the organization have an online culture where people prefer to stay in their offices and communicate through text messages or e-mails, even to the person next door? Is the culture, on the other hand, one where people move up and down the halls and gather in the coffee room? Are most introverts, those who may prefer to work alone and may need meetings to pull them out of their offices, or extraverts, those who need other people to feel energized but can become distracted from tasks if meetings occur too frequently?

With the purpose and audience settled, we can determine whether a meeting is the best forum for this communication, using the following questions to direct us in our decision:

- What is the purpose? What do I hope to accomplish?
- Will a meeting accomplish that purpose more efficiently? More effectively?
- Can I describe exactly the outcome I am seeking from the meeting?
- Is our group more productive when we meet?

Completing the Essential Planning

To ensure that meetings are productive, we must conduct the necessary planning by answering the following questions:

- What are the purpose and expected outcome?
- What should be included on the agenda?
- Who should attend?
- What is the best setting?
- What is the best timing?
- What information will we need for the meeting?

Clarifying Purpose and Expected Outcome

Meetings often have multiple objectives, but effective meetings, like good presentations and e-mails, usually have one main overall purpose. Our main purpose might be to inform, but we could also intend to persuade, engage, or even instruct in the same meeting. The purpose of an informational meeting could be as significant as introducing a new vision or as mundane as providing a progress report intended to expedite a project. The purpose could be beyond the basic informing, persuading, or instructing. We could have as our purpose to solve a problem or make a decision. For example, a problem-solving meeting could have as its goal to determine alternatives for launching a new product in a new location; or for a decision-making meeting, the goal could be to walk out of the meeting having decided how the launch of a new product will occur.

The care leaders give to defining their purpose and objectives will determine the success of the meeting. We should write out our purpose and objectives very specifically, then, to start the meeting, tell the audience our intentions. We want everyone to know exactly why we are meeting and what we intend to accomplish.

In addition to the objectives, establishing tangible end products helps ensure that the meeting is productive. For example, a meeting to discover and discuss the issues associated with introducing a new product for the first time in South America might have the objectives and end products presented in Exhibit 9.1.

If we have trouble defining an end product, our objective may not be clear enough or tangible enough to accomplish in a meeting. If attendees do not emerge from the meeting with end products, they may feel frustrated with not accomplishing anything. Although it takes some time and thought to list our objectives and end products, doing so will ensure that we avoid a meeting in which people feel they have wasted their time. It will move us toward conducting a productive meeting.

EXHIBIT 9.1
Meeting Purpose and Expected Outcomes

Objective	End Product
• Review past efforts at launching products in South America	• Brief description of each with highlights of what worked and what didn't
• Identify any problems or obstacles to product introduction	• List of potential problems or road-blocks in current proposed launch
• Determine possible approaches to overcoming problems	• Matching list of problem-resolving approaches for each roadblock

Determining Topics for the Agenda

The agenda should follow directly from the objectives and end products and should contain the information shown in Exhibit 9.2.

In determining the agenda topics and the meeting tasks, leaders need to estimate the time it will take to cover each topic and accomplish each objective as realistically as possible; then, they should add at least five minutes to each topic to allow for transitions. They should try to anticipate where possible delays might occur, and allow time to cover each topic and complete each task as planned.

EXHIBIT 9.2
Sample Agenda

Date:	March 5, 2010	Location:	3rd floor conference room
Meeting called by: Beth Shapiro		**Attendees:** See distribution list	
Facilitator: Alice Chang		**Please read:** Memo from Beth on expectations, deadlines, etc.	
Note taker: Bill Smith		**Please bring:** Memo, So. Am. Strategy Plan	

Objectives

• Review past efforts at launching products in South America
• Identify problems or obstacles to product introduction
• Determine possible approaches to overcoming problems
• Assign tasks and establish deadlines

Agenda

Time	Topic	Responsibility
8:30–8:40	• Introductions and review of agenda	Beth Shapiro
8:40–9:00	• Review of past launches in So. America (presentation)	Mario Cisneros
9:00–9:45	• Potential problems and solutions (brainstorming)	Alice Chang
9:45–10:00	• Assignment of action items	Beth Shapiro

Additional Information: This meeting will be the first of two. For this one, the goal is to surface all ideas, so each person should come prepared to contribute. At the end of the brainstorming session, we will decide as a group which solutions to pursue and the facilitator will assign tasks to the appropriate team members.

Selecting Attendees

Selecting the right attendees is important to the success of a meeting. The attendees we invite should be the ones who can contribute to achieving our objectives. The selected attendees will usually include the following:

- Decision maker(s).
- The budget holder (if different).
- Those who must take action on the decisions.
- Those with expert knowledge affecting decisions.
- Representation from those affected by the decision.

Sometimes it is obvious who should attend. For example, for a project team meeting, we would invite all team members. However, sometimes attendance is less clear-cut, and we must make decisions on the attendees. We can determine who should attend by asking the following questions:

- Who can supply information or input to the discussion or decision making?
- Who needs to accept the decisions, so that implementation occurs?
- Who is necessary for us to reach a decision?
- Who needs to understand the information or actions to implement them?
- Who needs to feel part of the decision making?

Considering the Setting

Leaders will want to consider the best setting for the kind of meeting they plan to lead. The setting considerations should include location, equipment, and layout of the room. If they have flexibility on the location, they should consider moving important meetings away from the office to minimize interruptions. For on-site meetings, they should establish ground rules that attempt to protect the meeting time as if it were off-site.

Type of Meeting

We will want to plan ahead, so that the mechanics of meeting management do not interfere with the smooth progress of our agenda. For example, if we are planning an interactive meeting with discussion and an exchange of information, we will need flip charts or whiteboards and a room set up to allow people to see one another and to move around easily. If we are planning an information-sharing meeting with stand-up presentations and attendees sitting and listening, then we need to arrange for computer projections and ensure a setup that allows everyone to see the speaker and screen.

Seating Arrangements

Seating arrangements can be a critical part of room layout for some meetings. In a round-table meeting intended to provide an update on a team's progress, the team leaders might want to seat the team together on one side of the table with the audience on the other. However, if they anticipate some hostility or disagreement from the audience, they might intersperse team members with non-team members to suggest the entire group is part of the team or equal participants in the meeting.

When arranging seating, we may also need to think about cultural differences. In some cultures, the head of the organization always sits at the head of the table with others seated according to rank, and the head person may expect all attendees to remain standing until he or she has taken a seat.

Virtual Meetings

If planning a virtual meeting, we will need to ensure that someone has arranged for the phone conference or VOIP connection, as well as the virtual meeting connection through a videoconferencing or Web conferencing service. These arrangements need to be done far enough in advance to ensure that connections are in place and all participants are informed of the arrangements and what they are expected to do to participate actively in the meeting.

Determining When to Meet

Setting a time for the meeting can be important. To accomplish our goals, we want people when they are at their best. Few leaders would call a team meeting on a Sunday morning after the Saturday night company Christmas party; however, many do hold weekly staff meetings first thing Monday morning, when people's minds may be lingering on weekend activities.

Leaders should think about people's schedules and commitments as much as possible. If they are leading regular meetings, they may want to check with the attendees to get a sense of what works best for them. They should, of course, aim for the meeting time and day that will bring together the most productive group of people within the context of the company and the culture.

Meetings should be no longer than it takes to get through the agenda efficiently and productively. Most meeting planners say that 60 to 90 minutes is about as long as a group will remain attentive, and the number is even lower for virtual sessions. Therefore, if the meeting objectives will necessitate more time, we need to be sure to build in breaks and look for ways to vary the activities. Lengthy meetings will tax anyone's attention and patience; however, if the purpose is significant, everyone is participating, and the meeting is progressing, most people are willing to endure the confinement for several hours.

If we have access to a collaborative workspace, such as Jive Clearspace or Microsoft SharePoint, we may want to consider avoiding lengthy meetings altogether and encourage collaboration using these workspaces. See Chapter 10 for more information on virtual collaboration among teams.

Establishing Needed Meeting Information

Leaders should anticipate and provide any information the group may need before or during the meeting to accomplish the meeting purpose. Too often, attendees end up running down the hall to gather information after a meeting has started, which wastes time and suggests poor planning. If the meeting leaders have clearly defined the purpose and end products, they can review each one and determine what materials will be needed to facilitate the discussion and accomplish each objective. They will probably want to send the agenda out a few days ahead of the meeting, so that others responsible for materials will come prepared. In addition, they will need to bring copies of the agenda with them, since people often forget to bring them.

Finally, if the meeting is a virtual forum, it is particularly important to plan ahead to ensure that all attendees are looking at the same information. If, for instance, they are meeting to discuss the latest numbers, they need to make sure the latest balance sheet has been sent and that any particular columns being discussed are highlighted.

Conducting a Productive Meeting

If leaders have not done so beforehand, they should announce at the start of the meeting the decision-making approach that they plan to use, clarify leader and attendee roles and responsibilities, and establish meeting ground rules. In addition, the meeting will be more productive if the attendees know and use common problem-solving tools.

Deciding on the Decision-Making Approach

The agenda will establish the order of the discussion, but how does the group plan to make decisions? If attendees know the decision-making approach ahead of time, it will make the meeting run more efficiently. Company culture will often determine the decision-making approach as well as the format of the discussion.

For instance, if the organization is very hierarchical and decisions come from the top, meeting attendees will expect to wait for the leader to make the decision. On the other hand, if the culture is open and employees are encouraged to challenge each other and even the leaders, the attendees will expect to speak out and be involved in a process that builds to a vote or a consensus decision, which the leader then accepts.

Usually, the leaders will set the tone and establish the decision-making approach for the organization, carrying it over into the meetings. Their approach may be so pervasive and well understood that no one needs to brings up the subject in a meeting; however, they may want to use different approaches for different types of meetings or problems, in which case they will need to make their approach clear for each meeting.

Clarifying Leader and Attendee Roles and Responsibilities

The leaders should define the meeting roles and responsibilities before or after the meeting starts. Early definition of roles will help avoid confusion. They might want to include the responsibilities in the agenda, as in Exhibit 9.2. The roles recommended for most meetings are as follows:

- Leader
- Facilitator
- Note taker
- Timekeeper

In a small, uncomplicated meeting, one person might play multiple roles, such as leader and facilitator or facilitator and timekeeper; however, it is usually better to separate the leader and facilitator roles, in particular. The leader can then focus on the content of the meeting while the facilitator looks after the process.

In assigning roles, leaders need to be sensitive to diversity issues and people's strengths and weaknesses. They do not want to stereotype attendees into gender roles—for instance, always assigning the note taker role to a female. They also do not want to ask someone to facilitate a brainstorming session if that person tends to criticize every idea anyone else suggests. None of the roles should be minimized. All are important in helping a meeting progress smoothly toward its objectives.

Establishing Meeting Ground Rules

Ground rules should be established for every meeting, no matter how small or uncomplicated. *Robert's Rules of Order* served well in the past to provide strict rules for conducting a meeting. It still serves as the basis for ground rules in formal meetings, particularly for community and civic organizations. Although the *Rules* may be considered too formal for contemporary professional settings, leaders still need to establish either standing ground rules for all of their meetings or specific ground rules for each meeting. Quite often, organizations need both. An organization's standing ground rules may be based in its traditions or culture.

For instance, the organization may have an intensive problem-solving culture in which all people are obligated to contribute in meetings, or it may have an avoidance culture that conditions people to shy away from any open conflict in meetings and avoid openly criticizing or questioning one another. Both could influence how the meeting is managed as well as the outcome.

Even the times that meetings start could reflect the culture, but an organization's leaders should never take for granted that everyone knows the traditions. For instance, every experienced person in a company would know that meetings always begin 10 to 15 minutes late, but those new to the company may see this as tardiness and be frustrated and even offended.

In most organizations, the group will need to determine the ground rules at the beginning of each meeting. The facilitator should write them out so that everyone can see them. They should be actionable. They can be simple or elaborate. They should be specific to the company culture and the type of meeting.

The importance of ground rules cannot be overemphasized; however, they serve little purpose if all attendees do not see them as an agreement, a contract that binds all present. If not enforced, the rules will appear to the attendees as an empty exercise with no value. If, however, ground rules are developed and enforced, the meeting will definitely be more productive.

For virtual meetings, a company will probably need to establish some special ground rules particular to the medium, such as the following.

Example Ground Rules for Virtual Meetings

- Introduce yourself when you join the meeting.
- State your name prior to your comments throughout the call.
- Avoid any side conversations, since not all participants can hear them.
- Keep the speakerphone close to the person who is talking to avoid background noise.
- Avoid tapping pens or shuffling papers, since these sounds may be exaggerated on the other end, or use the mute button when you are not speaking.

Using Common Problem-Solving Approaches

An organization may already have preferred approaches to problem solving, which everyone knows and uses in meetings. If not, leaders may want to introduce some, since most types of meetings will be much more efficient if attendees use common approaches to analysis and problem solving, such as the 10 listed here.

The value in using common analytical tools or problem-solving approaches is twofold: efficiency and creativity. The gain in efficiency is particularly evident when a group or a team is confronted with a complex or a politically sensitive problem. Having a common approach will allow all attendees to work on the problem in a similar way, which will save time and usually result in a better solution. Many of the approaches discussed here are designed specifically to open up the thinking of a group and thus increase creativity.

Shared knowledge of some approaches to analysis or problem solving allows the leader to say, "Let's use brainstorming or the Six Thinking Hats to approach this problem." All attendees will then be able to jump right into the task.

Common analytical tools that work well in many different types of problem-solving meetings are as follows:

1. Brainstorming.
2. Ranking or rating.
3. Sorting by category (logical grouping).
4. Edward de Bono's *Six Thinking Hats*.
5. Opposition analysis.
6. Decision trees.
7. From/to analysis.
8. Force-field analysis.
9. The matrix.
10. Frameworks.

1. Brainstorming

The goal of brainstorming is to generate an exhaustive list of ideas quickly. The characteristics of a brainstorming session are as follows:

- Each person is expected to contribute an idea.
- Ideas are not to be evaluated or judged in any way.
- Ideas must be recorded just as they are and be visible to all.
- Quantity, not quality, is important.
- The facilitator's role is to keep the meeting moving and make sure all ideas are captured.
- The group stops when the ideas stop coming or when time runs out.

At the end of the brainstorming session, the group will emerge with a rather random, unorganized set of ideas. The next step will be to sort and organize, perhaps using one of the next two problem-solving approaches—ranking or sorting.

2. Ranking or Rating

Ranking or rating is performed with an existing set of ideas, perhaps generated from a brainstorming session. As the name implies, ranking involves selecting preferred ideas according to some clearly defined criteria. For instance, if we are looking for ideas about where to market a new product, we might generate 20 possibilities, then go back and select the top five based on our company's ability to implement them.

Next, we might want to use a matrix similar to the one discussed here to evaluate the ideas according to value and difficulty, thus narrowing the list of five to the best one or two of the lot according to where they fall on the matrix. Again, the key to any useful ranking exercise is having group-determined criteria that will produce agreement on the best choices from the list.

3. Sorting by Category (Logical Grouping)

Sorting by category (logical grouping) requires a beginning list, although we might add items as they occur in the discussion as well. We also must have the categories of groups, which we should test to ensure that they are logical. We can test the logic of our groups by asking the MECE questions:

1. Are the groups mutually exclusive?
2. Are they collectively exhaustive?

If the groups overlap at all, we will need to reconsider them and come up with better categories. Once we have the categories, we can usually place the items in them fairly easily; coming up with the categories will often be more challenging than the actual sorting. The Pyramid Principle, introduced in Chapter 2, demonstrates how to group ideas by categories in a major line of an argument (Exhibit 2.10).

4. Edward de Bono's Six Thinking Hats

Edward de Bono designed his Six Thinking Hats approach to problem solving with the goal of encouraging open and complete thinking about a problem by separating ego (thinking our own point of view is best to solve a problem) from performance (the actual solving of the problem).

The Six Thinking Hats approach creates what de Bono calls "parallel thinking," which is thinking that involves looking at the problem in the same way. The example de Bono gives to illustrate parallel thinking is to imagine several people looking at a house from the same point of view—that is, all standing on the same side of the house. They would then more likely see the house in the same or very similar ways versus the differences that would occur if some people were looking at one side of the house and others another side. De Bono uses six distinctly colored hats to represent figuratively the six different ways of approaching a problem (Exhibit 9.3).

To use the approach in a meeting, the attendees would decide figuratively to wear the same hat for the discussion. For instance, they may decide they want to get all the facts out on the table, and thus assume the point of view of someone wearing the white hat; or they may feel

EXHIBIT 9.3
Characteristics of de Bono's Six Thinking Hats

Source: From Six Thinking Hats by Edward de Bono. Copyright 1999 by The McQuaig Group, Inc. Reprinted with permission of The McQuaig Group.

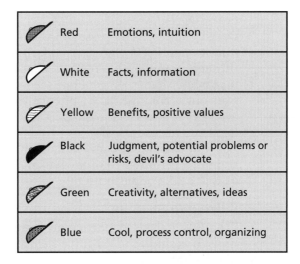

	Red	Emotions, intuition
	White	Facts, information
	Yellow	Benefits, positive values
	Black	Judgment, potential problems or risks, devil's advocate
	Green	Creativity, alternatives, ideas
	Blue	Cool, process control, organizing

they all need to think about the risks associated with an idea and all assume the point of view of someone wearing the black hat. Ideally, the group would spend time wearing all six hats to ensure that they are looking at the problem from every point of view.

Using the hats encourages people to move outside of their usual way of looking at a problem to see it from a fresh perspective. It also keeps the meeting focused on the problem and less on the participants' egos or desire to present their point of view. The result is that, instead of a debate, the meeting attendees achieve parallel thinking, which de Bono says leads to more constructive problem solving.

5. *Opposition Analysis*

Opposition analysis requires the group to look at both sides of an issue. Some common techniques are to list the pros with matching cons, list advantages with matching disadvantages, and apply a test of meaning by using an is/is not approach. For instance, if a company is struggling with the wording of its vision statement, company leaders might assume that not everyone defines the key words in the same way. They might then take each key word and decide if it means this, not this.

For example, if the vision contains the word "world-class," that term can have different meanings to the group members involved in the discussion. If the company wants to establish a common meaning, the facilitator could ask each member what "world-class" means and what it does not mean. Working through every key word in a vision using opposition analysis can be tedious, but it will elicit amazing differences in opinions, lead to greater clarity for all involved, and ensure that the selected words provide the intended meaning.

6. Decision Trees

Decision trees, as discussed in Chapter 2, help break down a problem into its parts. They are particularly useful in finding a way forward through complex, many-faceted problems or issues. Decision trees take many shapes. To generate ideas in writing, for instance, we might state our recommendation or conclusion and then break out the major arguments and facts to support the conclusion. In analyzing a problem, we can use the decision tree to analyze areas of uncertainty or risk. For example, we might map out the decision to build a new coffee shop in a certain area of town using a decision tree to assess the risks as well as the opportunity.

7. From/to Analysis

From/to analysis is particularly useful in diagnosing change situations. It is similar to the force-field analysis discussed next, but it does not include the driving forces or restraining forces. The "from" describes the current situation, and the "to" matches changes that are needed to transform each of the "from's." The from/to analysis is particularly useful in communicating specific changes in activities or focus and works best if used with a framework designed for organizational diagnostics, such as the 7S framework. For instance, we might take the items from the 7S framework that are most important to change in an organization and develop a from/to for each one, as in Exhibit 9.4.

EXHIBIT 9.4
From/to Analysis Using the 7S Framework

Change situation: An IT group in a large medical facility needs to start providing broader MIS support for all of its internal clients.

Selected 7S Categories	From	To
Strategy	Reactive, break-fix approach	Proactive, full-service consulting approach
Skills	Understanding of hardware and software	Understanding of consulting process and how to build client relationships
	Ability to diagnose and fix technical problems	Ability to anticipate and design processes and systems
Style	Reserved and behind the scenes	More outgoing and outspoken
	Seen as followers	Seen as leaders
Structure	Hierarchical, clear reporting relationship and information sharing up and down only	Flatter, open, challenging, communicating up, down, and across

8. Force-Field Analysis

Kurt Lewin, a leading social psychologist, developed force-field analysis as a problem-solving tool to explore the problems and determine approaches to facilitate change in an organization. To use this analytical approach, we would take the following steps:

1. Carefully describe the current problem.
2. Describe the end state we desire.
3. Describe the driving forces included in the situation and pushing it in the direction it is currently heading.
4. Describe the restraining forces that are working against the driving forces and thus inhibiting the desired changes.

For instance, if we applied the force-field analysis to a problem of high turnover in our company, our analysis might be as illustrated in Exhibit 9.5.

By isolating the driving forces, we gain a better understanding of the problem, and then, by finding the restraining forces, we begin to see the reasons for the problem and perhaps ways to solve it. For instance, in the first bullet in Exhibit 9.5, internal competition is keeping the teams from functioning as teams and the current compensation or reward system is causing the competition. To expect people to function as a team yet reward them as individuals is unrealistic. Therefore, to address the problem, the company would need to change its compensation system.

EXHIBIT 9.5
Example of a Force-Field Analysis

Current Situation
- Johnson, Inc.'s employee turnover rate is the highest in the industry
- Our reputation is that we "churn and burn"

Desired Future State
- Johnson, Inc.'s turnover rate one of lowest in industry
- Reputation for job satisfaction and enrichment

Driving Forces
- Competition within the teams
- Regional sales force confused over responsibilities
- Mentoring nonexistent
- Training inadequate

Restraining Forces
- Individual compensation structure rewards individual not team sales
- Regional structure allows overlap of some products
- Senior sales representatives in field; no time for new recruits
- Short time frame to make quotas

EXHIBIT 9.6
Example of a Matrix Problem-Solving Approach

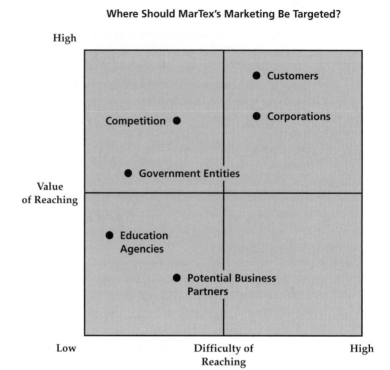

Where Should MarTex's Marketing Be Targeted?

High

● Customers

Competition ●   ● Corporations

● Government Entities

Value of Reaching

● Education Agencies

● Potential Business Partners

Low   Difficulty of Reaching   High

9. The Matrix

A matrix allows a group to evaluate or diagnose problems and the difficulties of making changes and can help a group decide on an approach. A decision-making matrix usually consists of four boxes with each axis assigned an evaluative label. Exhibit 9.6 demonstrates a matrix that a group might create to determine where to place its marketing efforts.

If leaders decide that a matrix will help the group in making a decision, they should first create the matrix by labeling the axes with the characteristics that are the most important in helping to reach a decision. In this case, the decision hinges on two key questions:

1. What is the value of reaching certain groups?
2. What is the difficulty?

Then, the group can weigh the value against the difficulty and decide which is more important at this time. In the example, the matrix has helped the group identify the key question: Should a marketing plan target customers first, even though that will be more difficult, or should it go after an easier but lower-value target?

10. Frameworks

As most of us know well, a framework exists for just about everything an individual might want to analyze. In business, from McKinsey's 7S framework for organizational diagnostics to the Four "P's" of marketing, acronyms abound to diagnose or analyze problems. Frameworks may be original or already in use. Often, the ones already in use work well initially but require modification to fit the specific situation and issues of a particular organization. If a group uses a framework, they will want to be careful not to force it. If they do, they risk invalidating the analysis.

Frameworks are useful and can be an excellent method for organizing analysis and problem solving. They serve as shorthand for discussion and can help simplify a complex idea and make it manageable. In addition, frameworks allow us to capture the elements of a complex problem visually. Further, they not only allow and encourage the logical organization of analysis but also act as an effective communication device to illustrate the topics or questions being addressed.

Managing Meeting Problems and Conflict

Leaders will be able to stop or at least minimize most of the usual meeting problems by careful planning and by developing and enforcing ground rules; however, some issues may arise despite the best planning and meeting processes. All meeting leaders and facilitators must be prepared to handle problems in ways that will not interfere with the meeting objectives or those of the broader organization.

The primary responsibilities of a meeting leader are to plan the meeting, provide the content, anticipate problems, and ensure process facilitation. Fulfilling the last responsibility may call for the use of a skilled facilitator. A facilitator's primary responsibility is to ensure that process problems do not interfere with the success of the meeting. Facilitators help keep the meeting focused on the objectives and ensure redirection if it gets off track. Skilled facilitators should be prepared to (1) handle some of the most common meeting problems, (2) manage meeting conflict, and (3) deal with issues arising from cultural differences.

Handling Specific Meeting Problems

Exhibit 9.7 contains some of the most common meeting problems and methods to manage them. Careful planning and purposeful facilitation will solve most of these process problems; however, problems sometimes arise during meetings that are tied more directly to the personalities of the leader and the attendees than to corporate culture or the issues under discussion.

EXHIBIT 9.7
Common Meeting Problems and Approaches to Managing Them

Problem	Management Approach
1. **Confused Objectives and Expectations**	Create an agenda that includes objectives as well as end products Send agenda out ahead of time and review it at the beginning of the meeting
2. **Unclear Roles and Responsibilities**	Communicate roles and responsibilities with agenda or establish at the beginning of the meeting
3. **Confusion between Process and Content**	Separate the leader and the facilitator role Call time-outs for process checks as soon as confusion is expressed
4. **Drifting Off Topic**	Stop and review meeting objectives. If digression continues, suggest • Discussion continue after meeting • Topic be placed on agenda for next meeting • Topic be tabled, stored for future (write topic down for all to see and make sure it is discussed at end of meeting if time allows or at an agreed future date)
5. **Data Confusion or Overload**	Control handouts to ensure all have same version Create simplified data packs specific to meeting Exclude any data not directly relevant to objectives
6. **Repetition and Wheel Spinning**	Control the discussion by reminding attendees of objectives
7. **Time Violations**	Start on time. Allowing delays at the beginning of meetings cuts efficiency and sends the message that the leader is flexible on time Have a timekeeper If time limits are repeatedly violated, reevaluate agenda topics and time limits and build in cushion time

Two common problems in particular that can interfere with creativity are negative thinking and resistance to the ideas of others or changes of any kind.

Negativity
While a devil's advocate can often stir up useful analysis, negativity—criticizing ideas without good reasons—is deadly in a brainstorming session, where it can destroy morale and shut down creative thinking completely. The leader or facilitator must address negativity immediately.

The best way to stop negativity is to establish a ground rule outlawing it. If no ground rules exist, then the facilitator will have to play a very direct role in confronting the person who is being negative. He or she may not even be aware of the negativity. If, however, the person persists, the leader of the group may need to call the person aside after the meeting, provide feedback on how counterproductive the negative comments are, and see if there is something below the surface that is causing the negative responses. Exhibit 9.8 illustrates a few common negative comments. Imagine trying to have a constructive, creative discussion with such negative comments intruding into the meeting.

It is the facilitator's responsibility to ensure that negative sentiments do not shut down constructive and productive discussion, particularly in brainstorming when looking for creative ideas. In fact, one test of skilled facilitators is how well they can overcome resistance.

Resistance to Ideas

Resistance to the ideas of others is similar to negativism, but not as blatant. Instead of blurting out an obviously negative comment, the person may offer an opposing idea or present roadblocks. For some purposes, the leader might want to encourage the contrary ideas and even encourage someone to play devil's advocate to inspire better ideas as the group argues the pros and cons. If, however, the comments are disrupting rather than helping the discussion progress, the facilitator will need to step in and stop them. Exhibit 9.9 illustrates four techniques to diffuse the situation so that the meeting can continue more productively.

Managing Meeting Conflict

When the common meeting problems turn into direct conflict, perhaps because of personalities or factions within the group, facilitators need to be more aggressive in their tactics. They must be prepared to manage the conflicts and the people involved before they interrupt meeting progress and in some cases even intrude into the overall working environment. Many approaches have been developed for managing conflict.

EXHIBIT 9.8
Common Negatives That Can Shut Down a Discussion

That won't work here.	That's impossible.
We're not ready for that.	That's not feasible.
It can't be done.	That's too expensive.
That failed last time we tried it.	That's not practical.
I don't like it.	That is against company policy.
It is not in the budget.	Not that again.
We'll never sell that idea to _____.	Another one of those management fads.

EXHIBIT 9.9
Techniques to Manage Resistance

Technique	What You Might Say
Verify	"What I understand you to be saying is . . ."
Clarify	"I am not sure I understand your idea completely. Can you explain it in another way?"
Align	"Let's look at the problem from your point of view . . ."
Probe	"Tell me more about your concerns . . ."

One popular technique often used by negotiators calls on the individuals involved in the conflict to apply different levels of assertiveness and cooperation. They can approach the problem by competing, compromising, collaborating, avoiding, or accommodating. The matrix illustrates the trade-offs that occur when selecting any one of these modes of conflict management (Exhibit 9.10).[5]

Collaborating

Any of the five modes can be used to allow the meeting to progress. However, collaborating is usually the best choice to manage meeting conflict because it calls on both sides to work together toward a common goal. Both sides can assert their points of view while still cooperating at a high level. Neither side feels as if it is losing anything; thus, both sides feel as though they have won, which results in a much more positive atmosphere for the meeting.

Compromising

Although compromising allows the meeting to continue, it is usually not a choice to use frequently or for longer-term conflict. On the surface, a compromise seems to be a win for both sides, but the ability of both sides to assert their opinions is only moderate and the level of

EXHIBIT 9.10
Conflict-Handling Modes

Source: From Deborah Borisoff and David Victor, *Conflict Management: A Communication Skills Approach.* Published by Allyn and Bacon, Boston, MA. Copyright 1997 by Pearson Education. Adapted by permission of the publisher.

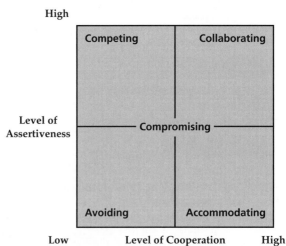

cooperation is moderate as well. Therefore, neither side is likely to feel satisfied by the resolution; they will just accept it. If, however, a compromise is the only way to reach a resolution and will appease most of the group, it is better than the remaining three modes.

Competing

Competing, avoiding, and accommodating may be appropriate in certain situations, but any one of these modes will usually only work as a short-term fix. In the competing mode one party wins, but the other loses. Thus, it frustrates the loser and even affects the others in the meeting, since they may side with the loser or at least feel sympathy for his or her position.

Avoiding

Avoiding is not an optimal approach for the long term because the problem is just buried and both sides feel frustrated. Neither side asserts the problems openly, and neither cooperates to achieve a solution. Avoiding the problem may work for a short time since it will allow the meeting to continue; however, in a longer meeting, or in an organizational context, avoiding problems will usually result in an explosion or sabotage somewhere down the line.

Accommodating

Finally, in most organizational contexts, accommodating is not a good approach as a long-term solution because the level of assertiveness is so low that the conflicting parties may feel as if their opinions are not of value. This approach will allow a meeting to progress, since the level of cooperation is high, which means that the atmosphere of the meeting will not be negatively affected in the short term. Also, in some cultural contexts, cooperation and avoiding conflict may be preferred. Anyone who has to be accommodating too often, however, will become resentful and may eventually withdraw from the group.

Facilitators will find that they need to use all of these modes at one time or another to keep the meeting moving toward their goal; however, all but collaboration—and, if managed right, compromise—are short-term, quick fixes. If used over the long term, they can lead to dissension within an organization or with teams or any group holding a series of meetings.

Other Immediate Approaches

If none of these modes seem the best for the situation, the facilitator may want to try one of the following methods of conflict management to calm the situation, so that the meeting can continue:

1. Turn the question to the group.
2. Use the is/is not approach or a pro/con format.

3. Try listing points of agreement and disagreement.

4. Attempt to get at underlying assumptions.

5. Shift the discussion to the facts (put on the white hat).

Quite often, the white hat approach works well, since it takes the emotions out of the moment, forcing the group to be more objective and to look only at the facts.

Dealing with Cultural and Personality Differences

Chapter 8 contains a complete discussion of the importance of realizing cultural differences, but since meeting conflict may arise from cultural differences, leaders will want to be aware of some of the specific issues related to meetings. Recognizing some of these potential issues will help in managing many of them. Exhibit 9.11 presents selected variables used in Chapter 8 and describes how differing culturally based expectations might disrupt a meeting.

These few examples illustrate only some of the obvious differences leaders might encounter when facilitating a meeting in the global workplace. No one can know enough about every culture to prevent the occurrence of all the offending or marginalizing situations, but we can be aware of the differences and lead or facilitate the meeting in such a way that we help participants feel as comfortable as possible.

EXHIBIT 9.11
Cultural Variables and Meeting Behavior

Cultural Variable	Some Examples of Differences in Meeting Expectations
Context	Individuals from a high-context society or functional area may expect meetings to include time for some casual conversation and relationship building.
Information Flow	People who expect information to come from one direction (top down, for example) may not feel comfortable contributing in a problem-solving or brainstorming session, for instance.
Time	Polychronic people may find agendas and a timekeeper artificial and uncomfortable. The time-is-money, schedule-driven mentality in the United States, for instance, would make them uncomfortable.
Language	People with a different cultural experience than that in the United States might find the bantering and joking exchange of United States attendees offensive, to the extent that they feel left out and isolated because of it.
Power	Societies in which position is equated with power may expect one leader, the person of highest position in the organizational hierarchy, to control a meeting and may be uncomfortable and even confused by the separation of the leader from the facilitator, for instance, or by a leader who takes a backseat for any reason.

Of course, individuals acclimated to the culture of the organization and the country in which the meetings are occurring will have adjusted and will conform, but new employees may not be used to the differences in customs and procedures. Again, if we analyze our audience (prospective meeting attendees) and plan adequately for the meeting, we will mitigate or eliminate entirely most of the potential disruptions.

In addition to the differences arising from national, regional, and functional cultures, we may also encounter differences caused by personality. For example, in the MBTI, the Judging/Perceiving and Introvert/Extravert dichotomies will often be the most visible sources of problems in meetings.

Since Judging personalities are most comfortable with structure and schedules, they will like an agenda and will be uncomfortable if the meeting leader does not provide and follow one. They also may take it personally if people are late for meetings, as many Perceivers are inclined to be.

With Introverts, leaders will need to ensure that they are given an opportunity, and in some cases even encouraged, to contribute, since Extraverts tend to dominate the discussion.

Again, it is dangerous to generalize about personalities and how people will behave in a given situation, but being aware of some of the differences will help us to lead and facilitate our meetings more effectively.

Ensuring That Meetings Lead to Action

Number four in the seven deadly sins of meetings is that nothing happens once the meeting ends. Unfortunately, inaction following a meeting is very common. A good meeting planner, however, can overcome this inertia by performing four steps:

1. **Assign specific tasks to specific people.** Giving tasks to a group is dangerous. The vagueness encourages moral equivocation, and inertia triumphs. When assigned a specific task, an individual is much more likely to deliver than a group is. Accountability is increased when individuals are required to deliver.

2. **Review all actions and responsibilities at the end of the meeting.** Too often, meetings just stop. Never let this happen. Allow time for a review of actions and ensure that the responsibilities are clear to all attending. Any next steps should be spelled out explicitly.

3. **Provide a meeting summary with assigned deliverables included.** If the meeting includes a note taker, that person should write up the minutes of the meeting, confirm all action items and responsibilities, and send the minutes out to all attendees. The minutes do not need to include every word uttered at the meeting, as they would in a traditional civic meeting run by *Robert's Rules*, for instance, but they

should contain the main topics discussed and list every next step task, the person responsible, and the timing if appropriate.

4. **Follow up on action items in a reasonable time.** The leader should contact the responsible people shortly after the meeting to make sure they are clear about what they need to do and to see if they need help. This contact will serve as a gentle reminder and will be enough in most situations to ensure delivery. However, if someone habitually has trouble with deadlines, then the leader should contact that person again as the deadline approaches.

Although these steps may seem like micromanaging, if the meeting contained serious objectives, as it should have, then we are entitled to expect some action to come out of it. Otherwise, we risk sending a message that employees should not take meetings seriously, which will cause them to feel that meetings are busywork, the first deadly sin listed at the beginning of the chapter.

Having employees feel that meetings are a waste of time brings us back to where this chapter started, asking, "Is a meeting necessary?" If we decided that we needed a meeting to accomplish our purpose, we must ensure that it moves tasks forward and makes actions happen. The follow-up to all meetings is not micromanagement; it is simply good leadership.

Application 9.1: Evaluating Experiences in Meetings	Think back to a recent small-group meeting that you attended. Jot down some key information about the meeting:

1. Who called the meeting?
2. What was it about?
3. Was there an agenda?
4. Was the purpose of the meeting accomplished?
5. After the meeting, were minutes distributed that outlined tasks and deadlines?
6. During the meeting, what role did you play all or most of the time (leader, scribe, facilitator, etc.)?
7. What could have been done to make the meeting more effective?

Now work with a partner to compare notes on the meetings you attended to identify similarities and differences in meeting organization and outcomes.

Source: Case and exercise developed by Beth O'Sullivan, Rice University.

Application 9.2 Planning a Meeting	**Case: Wisconsin Frozen Delights**
	You have recently been named the new vice president for operations of Wisconsin Frozen Delights, a regional ice cream manufacturing firm located just outside a large metropolitan area in Wisconsin. The following people report to you:

- Assistant vice president of operations.
- Administrative assistant to the vice president.
- Director of operations.
- Manager of manufacturing.
- Manager of purchasing.
- Manager of shipping.
- Manager of human resources.
- Regulatory compliance officer.

During your first tour of the facilities, you observed a number of safety hazards in the manufacturing areas and you noticed that the factory and adjacent office areas do not have easy access for anyone with disabilities. You are concerned that the building is not in compliance with regulations under the Americans with Disabilities Act and that there are possible Occupational, Safety, and Health Administration (OSHA) violations.

The president has given you full authority to uncover safety concerns, determine areas in which employees have concerns about safety or disabled access, and fix the problems to make the company a safe and healthy place to work. You decide to call a meeting to set the tone for your new administration and to discuss the safety concerns.

The Assignment

Complete the following steps:

1. Decide whom to invite to the meeting.
2. Develop your objectives and end products.
3. Establish the agenda for the meeting.
4. Write an e-mail or a meeting request inviting your selected attendees to the meeting.

In addition, assume that your company has a collaborative workspace solution that allows you to set up a project workspace for the team you are creating. In this space, you can upload documents, create discussion lists, and create project time lines and tasks. Write a brief overview of what you would set up in the project workspace before this meeting and why.

Source: Case and exercise developed by Deborah J. Barrett and Beth O'Sullivan, Rice University. Updated by Sandra Elliott, 2009.

**Application 9.3
Conducting a
Problem-Solving
Meeting**

This exercise, using the OmniBank case from Chapter 8, is designed to provide an opportunity to practice some of the planning techniques and facilitation approaches discussed in this chapter.

Case: OmniBank's Diversity Efforts

You have recently been named the new president of OmniBank, a medium-sized but rapidly growing suburban bank that meets the needs of individuals and small businesses. During the interview process, you observed that, beyond the front office teller level, the more senior workforce at the bank is very homogeneous—mostly male and predominantly Caucasian. You have reviewed several marketing studies that profile your customer base and you realize that not only do you have many customers of different ethnicities but you also have a large number of international customers.

As the new president, you decide it is important to launch a comprehensive effort to improve the diversity at the bank. You value diversity and believe that broadening your employee base as the bank grows will benefit everyone involved, and besides, it makes good business sense.

Your Assignment

You have decided to call a meeting to explore how to alter recruiting efforts for new staff, so that your bank can become more diverse. You want the meeting to be a brainstorming idea-generation meeting with active problem solving that leads to practical solutions.

In groups of four or five, conduct a meeting using the agenda provided in the following table:

Topic/Content	Approach/Process	Responsibility	Timing
Objectives, end products, agenda, roles, decision-making approach	Develop and agree	President, facilitator, note taker, all	
Recruiting ideas	Brainstorming	All	
Selecting and agreeing on best ideas	Grouping—rank order or voting, then agreeing	Facilitator, all	
Next steps	Action plan	Facilitator, all	
Process review	+/Δ	Facilitator, all	

Before starting the meeting, determine how much time you need to allow for each topic. Following the meeting, conduct a +/Δ plus/delta), which is an approach to evaluating your meeting success by looking at the pluses (what worked) and the needed changes (what did not work so well).

Notes

1. Jay, A. (1976). How to Run a Meeting. *Harvard Business Review,* March–April.
2. This survey was originally cited as follows: Introduction to Great Meetings, 3m.com/meetingnetwork/leadingroom/meetingguide_make.html, which is no longer active. However, this statistic is quoted on several other Web sites.
3. Introduction to Great Meetings.
4. Matson, E. (1997). Quoting William R. Daniels, American Consulting & Training, in The Seven Sins of Deadly Meetings, *Fast Company's Handbook of the Business Revolution*, p. 27.
5. Borisoff, D., and Victor, D. (1999). *Conflict Management: A Communication Skills Approach*. Boston, MA: Allyn and Bacon discusses the use of the conflict-handling modes developed by K. W. Thomas and R. Kilmann.

10

High-Performing Team Leadership

Teams are *not* the solution to everyone's current and future organizational needs. . . . Nonetheless, teams usually do outperform other groups and individuals. . . . And executives who really believe that behaviorally based characteristics like quality, innovation, cost effectiveness, and customer service will help build sustainable competitive advantage will give top priority to the development of team performance.

Jon Katzenbach and Doug Smith (1993). *The Wisdom of Teams Boston: Harvard Business School Press.*

Chapter Objectives

In this chapter, you will learn to do the following:

- Build an effective team.
- Establish the necessary team work processes.
- Manage the people side of teams.
- Handle team issues and conflict.
- Help virtual teams succeed.

Since teams are now so prevalent in all organizations, leaders need to know how to build and how to manage them to achieve high performance. Most people have experienced successful as well as unsuccessful teams. Unfortunately, unsuccessful team experiences may outnumber successful ones, a perception that has inspired an abundance of information on how to achieve successful teams. A Google search for the word "teams" yields 178 million hits on every imaginable kind of team from kayak racing to continuous improvement.

Narrowing the search to include "business" with "teams" still yields almost 222,000. A quick scan of the hits reveals that many are organizations, universities, and individuals offering training in how to develop a successful team. Obviously, many are seeking "the way" to build and maintain a high-performing team.

While no one way is likely to guarantee good results for all organizations, most of the skills leaders need to build and manage a high-performing team tie directly to their leadership communication ability. This chapter will guide you through the communication challenges involved in leading a team. You will learn how to build an effective team, establish necessary work processes, manage the people side of teams, and handle team conflict. In addition, you will receive some guidance on leading virtual teams, which are prevalent in today's professional world.

Building an Effective Team

Building an effective team raises both organizational and individual leadership issues. In deciding to use teams across our organization, we will want to look closely at the culture and compensation structure to see if they both support teamwork. In the past decade, many companies have launched the use of teams without establishing the organizational infrastructure for teams to succeed. If we are thinking of forming a team for specific tasks, we first need to determine that a team is the most effective and efficient approach to perform the task, solve the problem, generate the new ideas, or generally move our organization forward in some way.

Deciding to Form Teams

Deciding to form a team is a process very similar to deciding to call a meeting. Both meetings and teams can alienate participants if they are not clearly the best approach. Before moving ahead to establish a team-based organization or to form teams individually, we should be able to answer yes to the following questions:

1. Is a team the best approach to achieve the organizational objectives or a specific goal or targeted result?
2. Does the organization provide the necessary training in diversity, team dynamics, problem solving, and process management to ensure that team members know how to manage team issues and processes?
3. Are the employees accustomed to creating and following team charters and ground rules, and do they know how to resolve team conflicts?

4. Does the current company technology effectively support team communication and collaboration? And do employees know how to use that technology (particularly critical for virtual teams)?

5. Are team performance measures built into the company compensation and performance systems?

Ideally, the answer to each of these questions would be yes; realistically, that may not be the case. Being able to answer yes to all of the questions will ensure a more productive environment for teams if our company intends to take full advantage of a team-based structure using teams throughout the organization. However, answering no to all but the first question does not mean that a team is doomed to fail. High-performing individuals working together in a team with a clear objective and the commitment to achieve it can be an effective team despite the environment. Having a supportive environment will simply make our role in leading and managing teams easier.

Forming the Team

Once we have decided that a team is the best answer, we will need to look closely at how we will form that team. Companies often decide who should be on teams based on functional responsibilities, for instance. If we have the freedom to select the members, however, Katzenbach and Smith's team basics framework is useful in establishing the characteristics of a "real" team (Exhibit 10.1). In their team basics framework, the apex topics—performance results, personal growth, and collective work products—represent the outcome of the work of the team.

The other items in Exhibit 10.1 are the characteristics of what Katzenbach and Smith consider a "real" team:

- Complementary skills (problem solving, technical/functional, interpersonal).
- Accountability (mutual, individual, and small number of people).
- Commitment (specific goals, common approach, meaningful purpose).

Team members should have skills that complement rather than duplicate each other, although teams may develop some of the required skills after the team forms. All members need to recognize and accept mutual as well as individual accountability for the team's work products. The size of the team matters and affects accountability, since a team that is too large will end up dividing into subteams and the work can become so diffused that accountability gets lost. Finally, the team must have specific goals, a purpose that is important to the organization, and a common approach to the work.

Having all of the team basics is more important to achieving high performance than team-building exercises intended to mold a group of individuals into a cohesive, committed, mutually responsible unit:

EXHIBIT 10.1
Katzenbach and Smith's Team Basics

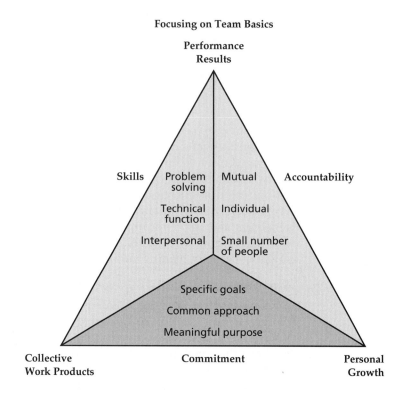

Focusing on Team Basics

Performance Results

Skills — Problem solving / Mutual — Accountability

Technical function / Individual

Interpersonal / Small number of people

Specific goals

Common approach

Meaningful purpose

Collective Work Products — Commitment — Personal Growth

"By focusing on performance and team basics—as opposed to trying 'to become a team'—most small groups can deliver the performance results that require and produce team behavior."[1]

One of the first responsibilities of a team leader is bringing together the right people or, if we do not get to select the members, deciding how to work with the members we have to achieve the performance we seek. As the team leader, we will be the one to communicate to the members individually and collectively the reasons for their selection to the team, the team purpose and objectives, and our expectations of them as a team. The next section covers how best to communicate our expectations of the team as we work with them to establish the purpose, roles and responsibilities, ground rules, and communication protocol.

Establishing the Necessary Team Work Processes

Once the selected team members know they are on our team, we will want to schedule a launch, or kick-off, meeting. Teams tend to begin their work more effectively if leaders take the time to hold an official launch. Having a launch allows the team to address many of the team work process steps discussed here. Although most teams will probably want to jump right into the work without spending the necessary time on process issues, leading them through development of the purpose, goals, and approach (the commitment side of the team basics framework) will help the team work more efficiently and effectively.

The primary causes of conflict in a team are **poorly defined goals** and purposes and **lack of clarity** about the approach to the work and problem solving. Chapter 9 on meetings discussed the importance of using common problem-solving tools in meetings and provided some useful examples that work well with teams. This section addresses the issues of goals, purpose, and approach in a team launch by showing how to create a team charter, action plan, and work plan.

Creating the Team Charter

One of the first steps for a team will be to create a team charter or contract. A charter usually consists of the following:

1. Project purpose and goals.
2. Team member roles and responsibilities.
3. Ground rules.
4. Communication protocol.

Project Purpose and Goals

The leader or the organization may have already established the team's specific purpose, but to make sure the team members understand and have internalized this purpose as a team, team leaders should ask them to write down exactly what they see as their purpose for being a team. Is it a broad, organizational purpose, or is it narrow and specific to one problem or one person? Simply expressing the purpose out loud is not enough. It must be written so that every member of the team can see it and agree to it.

The goals must support and clearly link to the purpose. They should be specific and measurable performance goals. For instance, the purpose of the team might be to establish a marketing strategy and promotional plan for MarTex, Inc. Then, the goals might be (1) to establish a profile of MarTex's current image, reputation, and market perception; (2) to determine MarTex's value proposition, key messages, and target audiences; and (3) to develop a marketing communication plan and materials to reach target audiences.

Team Member Roles and Responsibilities

The team should define all roles and responsibilities for each team member at the first meeting. The basic process roles to consider are similar to the roles in meetings: leader, facilitator, timekeeper, and note taker. The team should consider whether the roles will rotate or if the same person will perform the role throughout the project. In addition, the team needs to assign someone to be the meeting minder (coordinator) and/or work plan manager. This person is responsible for calling meetings or sending out reminders and making meeting arrangements. Depending on the size of the team and the project, the same person could also maintain the work plan, updating and making changes as needed and communicating them to the team.

Team Ground Rules

Teams need ground rules that all the members participate in creating and agree to follow. The rules should be determined at the first team meeting and become a permanent part of the team charter. The rules will probably resemble those the team would establish for meetings, but they will also be longer-term, governing the team's interactions between meetings as well. At a minimum, the team's ground rules should include topics such as those listed in Exhibit 10.2. Some examples are included as well.

Ground rules should fit the culture of the organization and the personality of the team. Some teams like very strict rules with penalties, while others prefer a more relaxed approach. The leader and the team will want to determine what approach is best for this team. Also, the team should build in periodic process checks to review the ground rules and be prepared to adjust them if it appears they are not working.

Communication Protocol

At the first meeting, the team members should decide how they plan to communicate with each other on a regular basis. Will they use IM, e-mail, or voice mail, for instance, or all, with each designated for a specific type of message? Is there a time of day or night that is off-limits for calling a team member, or do some team members respond better and faster to e-mail than phone mail? The team should consider the following questions in developing a team communication protocol:

1. What events or situations will trigger communication with each other?
2. When will we contact a member of the team versus the entire team? Do we copy the entire team on all e-mails? Are there some team members who prefer no calls at home or do not want to receive calls at a certain time?
3. Who will be the spokesperson for most team internal communication? For external communication (that is, with other groups within the company or even outside the company)?
4. What information needs to be communicated to the team? Should we provide regular updates on progress or limit communication to issues, requests, or announcements?

EXHIBIT 10.2
Ground Rule Topics and Examples for Teams

Team Topics	Example Ground Rules
Leadership	One leader for the overall project, but lead persons assigned on the work plan will assume leadership for meetings on their topics.
Communication	The team will follow the communication protocol for all team communication.
Participation	We expect all members to participate equally and actively in all team activities and work.
Work Products	All members will contribute their share of the work, delivering end products complete and on time. The team will follow work plan action items and time line.
Conflict Management and Resolution	We encourage healthy debate about content within the meetings; however, the facilitator will directly address conflict that disrupts the team. Anyone who feels a conflict exists that is not being addressed has the responsibility to bring it to the facilitator or team for resolution.
Preparation	All members must be aware of agenda items for the day and have their portions of the work completed before the meeting starts.
Attendance	We require attendance at all team meetings. If an unexpected conflict arises, the member is responsible for sending in his or her work for the day and for notifying the team. A team member who misses more than three meetings risks being removed from the team.
Timing	We expect all team members to be on time for meetings. If teammates see they will be late, they must notify the team coordinator. Too many late appearances could result in being removed from the team.
Decision Making	The team will determine any decisions by consensus unless the team reaches an impasse, at which time the facilitator or leader can table the item for a future meeting, if appropriate, or call for a vote.
Laptops and Cell Phones	We will try to refrain from using our laptops and cell phones during team meetings. The exception is to retrieve information needed by the team during the meeting.

5. How should we communicate everyday messages, work plan items, end products, questions, emergencies, and the like? Which medium does the team prefer to use for everyday communication? Do some team members strongly prefer one medium over another?

6. To whom do we communicate problems, questions, concerns, and so on?

7. Is there a shared workspace where communication with the team can be centralized? If so, what should be placed in this workspace, when, and by whom?

Exhibit 10.3 provides an example of a typical team charter for an internal team performing a marketing study.

Using Action and Work Plans

For a team project of any complexity or length, an action plan of overall phases is useful and a specific work plan of all action items and end products with responsibilities and time lines is essential. Although any plan has to be updated frequently as the project unfolds, creating one at the beginning of the project is necessary for all team members to know exactly what needs to be done, by whom, and by when. It helps avoid duplication of effort, ensures that all needed activities are included, and allocates adequate time for the planned actions.

EXHIBIT 10.3   Example of a Team Charter

Team Charter for the MarTex Tiger Team (August 25, 2009)		
Purpose:	**Goals:**	
To establish a marketing strategy and promotional plan for MarTex, Inc.	1. Establish a profile of MarTex's current image, reputation, and market perception. 2. Determine MarTex's value proposition, key messages, and target audiences. 3. Develop a marketing communications plan and materials to reach target audiences.	
Team Member Roles and Responsibilities In addition to contributing to problem solving, analysis, research, and document content, members will have the following specific roles and responsibilities:		
Amanda Shay	Team leader	Kick the team off and provide leadership overall. Create drafts of documents.
Miguel Serrato	Meeting facilitator, coordinator, timekeeper	Create agendas, manage the meetings, communicate meeting times and locations.
Tuyen Tran	Work plan master, costing expert	Create work plan, keep it up to date with changes, distribute to team.
Mary Prescott	Benchmarking/data gathering expert	Lead competitive image analysis.
Jane Sudduth	Branding/ communication expert	Lead brand identity and message analysis.
Jodi Pliszka	Design specialist	Create sample promotional materials.

(continued)

EXHIBIT 10.3 (continued)

Team Charter for the MarTex Tiger Team	
Ground Rules: 1. Meetings will start on time (penalties will be enforced for lateness). 2. Members must attend all meetings and be fully prepared to participate. 3. We will stick to our agenda. Any important topics not on the agenda will be placed in the "parking lot"* for future discussion. 4. No sidebars are allowed. 5. No negatives are permitted at any time. 6. Work plan responsibilities must be fulfilled and on time. 7. Consensus approach will be used for decision making, although the leader has right to call for a vote if necessary. 8. Any conflict will be handled immediately, first by the facilitator and then by the whole team if necessary.	**Communication Protocol:** ***Who*** • Miguel will contact members for all meeting items. • Amanda will inform the team of any content issues or other issues from the company perspective. She is to be the only team contact with senior management. ***What and to whom*** • All team-related information (meetings, work plan, questions, etc.) will be sent to all team members. • Correspondence on subteam work will go to members involved only. ***How*** • We will meet daily for the first week. Then, we will meet as needed. Any team member may call a meeting if needed, but he or she must coordinate through Miguel. • We will communicate primarily through e-mail unless urgent; then, we will use phone mail. • Documents will be sent through e-mail and will always contain the initials of the last person working on them and the date and time. • Home phone calls are limited to extremely important team business, such as a last-minute emergency that will cause missing a meeting.

*"Parking lot" is the team's name for items that are important but not for discussion at that meeting or time.

Action plans allow the team members to see the big picture of the project easily and help them organize the individual tasks into blocks of work that make it easier to manage the responsibilities and deliverables. The first step in creating the action plan is to establish the major phases of the project. A project of any complexity or length can usually be mapped into three to five phases. Any more than five phases makes the plan difficult to manage. The phases should correspond to the goals of the project. After the team has determined the phases, they can then list the major activities within each one and the overall timing for the phase. Exhibits 10.4 and 10.5 illustrate that the general action plan activities become the headings for the more specific action items in the work plan with specific responsibilites and deadlines.

EXHIBIT 10.4
Example of a
Team Action Plan

MarTex Tiger Team Action Plan

Phases	Current image, brand identity	Value proposition, key messages	Marketing plan and materials
Actions	• Determine approach to perception analysis • Assess current marketing and promotional efforts	• Conduct surveys and interviews • Identify gaps in perception and materials • Identify audiences • Determine value proposition and messages	• Develop marketing plan • Create preliminary marketing materials • Pilot test plan and materials
Timing	Sept 1–Sept 15	Sept 15–Sept 30	Sept 30–Oct 27

EXHIBIT 10.5   Example of a Team Work Plan

Phase 1 Goal: Establish a Profile of Mar Tex's Current Image, Reputation, and Market Perception

Action Items	Responsibility	End Products	Deadline
Determine approach to perception analysis			
• Create framework and approach	Miguel & Amanda	Framework	9/2
• Establish benchmarking criteria	Mary & Jane	Benchmarking criteria	9/5
• Determine how best to obtain client and marketplace perceptions	Miguel & Amanda	Perception plan	9/8
• Create data instruments (survey interview guides)	Mary & Tuyen	Survey and interview guide and schedule	9/9
• Test survey and interview guides	Mary & Tuyen	Revised version	9/12
• Determine who among competitors to include	Miguel	List of target competitors	9/12
• Determine who among clients to include	Amanda	List of target clients	9/12
Assess current marketing and promotional efforts			
• Research competitors' current promotional efforts	Tuyen & Jodi	Portfolio of material	9/14
• Analyze their marketing approaches	Tuyen & Jodi	Summary of approaches	9/14
• Obtain and evaluate their marketing materials compared to ours	Tuyen & Jodi	Comparative matrix	9/16

The action plan phases should set up the main areas of work for the work plan. In fact, the team might want to repeat the goals at the top of the plan as a reminder for the team.

Delivering the Results

A team's performance will depend on the team's being able to deliver the results of its work. That usually means delivering a presentation, a report, or both. These tasks are often one of the major communication challenges that teams face.

Creating Team Documents and Presentations

Creating a document or presentation as a team requires preplanning and a clearly defined approach. Teams often struggle with dividing up the labor and run into difficulties managing the versions of the documents and presentations. Teams usually use one of two ways to divide the tasks:

1. Single-scribe aproach—one person on the team does all the writing, with the others providing the content to the scribe.
2. Multiple-writer approach—the team divides the writing among the team members according to the sections for which they have provided most of the content.

1. Single-Scribe Approach

The single-scribe approach ensures consistency in style and format. However, one person ends up with tremendous control over the communication's content and style, as well as a heavy work burden at the end of the project. With this approach, the fate of the team's project essentially rests in the hands of one member's ability to communicate the team's ideas effectively.

In addition, despite the amount of work involved, scribes may feel that other members of the team minimize their contribution to the team effort. Thus, to ensure that the single-scribe method works well, the members must share in the ownership of the document by reading and contributing to the drafts. They should also make sure the scribe's contribution is recognized, and that he or she is included in all team meetings.

When using the single-scribe approach, the team needs to build the compilation step into the work plan and be very specific about what each team member is expected to give to the scribe. Teams frequently multitask, with different team members working on different tasks; therefore, the team may want to assign one person to oversee the document production deadlines, ensuring that the schedule is on target.

Despite the best intentions and scheduling, often the final compilation of the document or presentation occurs at the last minute. If team members submit material that is at radically different stages of completion, then the scribe has a huge challenge that could end up harming the quality of the final product. For instance, if one team member brings an outline, another brings a list of bullets, another goes off task and writes on someone else's material, and then another does what is expected and writes out the entire section in detail, the scribe is forced to manage the uneven contribution and fill in the blanks, perhaps without being in full command of the content for each section. In addition, the compilation time expands fourfold. Agreeing specifically to what each team member will give to the scribe will help with efficiency and quality.

2. Multiple-Writer Approach

The multiple-writer, or collaborative, approach divides the writing among team members. This approach has advantages and disadvantages as well. One of the major advantages can be efficiency. When various team members write individual sections of a document or populate the content of a section of a presentation, the work will usually go much faster than the single-scribe approach. The team members know the content well and can ensure that it is complete and correct. Also, they avoid the delays caused when a team member has to rewrite his or her section because the scribe, who is often not close to the content, has misrepresented the meaning in some way. Collaborative writing makes the team labor more efficient and makes it seem more equitable. In the end, the entire team feels greater ownership of the finished product.

However, the approach has some problems. One danger is that the team may be confused about the precise scope of individual assignments, resulting in duplication of effort or neglected tasks. The team may have trouble dividing the sections equitably, and the resulting sections may be uneven and inconsistent. Also, the style and tone will probably differ from section to section. If the differences are extreme, the document can easily come across as fragmented and even incoherent, and a presentation can seem like a compilation of separate presentations rather than the coherent presentation of a team working as one.

To ensure that the writing is performed completely and evenly, the team can divide the document into its different sections and assign responsibilities for them using the pyramid or storyboard. A good pyramid shows the major topics with no overlap. A storyboard can serve a similar function for a team working on a presentation. However, the team members will still need to come together to ensure that the agenda presents a coherent story of their work.

If the team has used the pyramid or a similar structural approach to guide them, the major organizational topics at the first level of their pyramid become the major section headings, or in a longer document, the chapter titles or in a presentation the agenda items. Using the pyramid from Chapter 2 as an example, the team's outline would be as follows:

Launching a New Bank Card in China

I. Market Potential
   A. Political Climate
   B. Competitive Analysis
II. Profitability
   A. Cost Analysis
   B. Potential Revenue
III. Implementation Plan
   A. Staffing Requirements
   B. Marketing Plan Actions

From the outline, the team could assign sections to the team members.

To avoid formatting issues or time-consuming mechanical changes in the compiling phase, the team needs to specify all details of format ahead of time. For example, the team should decide on margins, spacing, body and heading fonts, and the positioning of headings and subheadings in a document and select the background, layout, color scheme, and style and size of fonts for presentations. If they have selected a document or slide template early in the project, each writer would simply be able to type in his or her content and not worry about consistency in formatting.

Finally, to ensure that the document or presentation is consistent and coherent, the team must take time at the beginning to agree on style and format, but also allow time at the end to have one person do the final proofreading after the entire team reviews the document. Although this person does the final proofing, the entire team shares the responsibility for the quality of the end product; therefore, every member of the team should read the final document, with one person giving it the final proofing and quality check before it is delivered.

Controlling Versions

Whether working alone or with a group, we need a method for controlling the versions of our documents. Version control is essential when creating a team document, since multiple team members will touch the document at various times during the writing process.

To keep the versions straight, the team should decide together when drafts are due, who is to receive them, and in what order they are to circulate through the team. In addition, they should establish a tracking method for the versions. One approach is to insert the date and time in the footer and use it as the file name while the document is in drafting stages. Once they have finished all editing, they should make sure to delete the footer from the final version. In addition to the time and date, team members should get in the habit of inserting their initials in the footer and in the file name when saving the document. For example, a team might use the footer "9:00 a.m. 17 05 09 AS" and the file name "Brand Study 17 05 09 AS1" to designate the version as the one completed by Andrew Smith at 9:00 a.m. on May 17, 2009.

Agreeing on a method for tracking the versions and establishing a writing and version control plan will save time and help the team produce higher-quality communication. Such procedures will also help teams avoid some of the conflict that can occur when individuals collaborate in the writing of a document.

With the advent of such shared workspaces as Google Documents, it is far easier for a team to collaborate on documents and presentations. However, these shared documents present their own challenges, since changes to the documents are not saved in previous versions, and information that is deleted cannot be reclaimed. Any team working with such shared material should determine how and when to save previous versions to ensure that vital information is not lost during edits.

Work Plan Specifics

The team will want to include all tasks to create and complete their document or presentation in the action steps of their work plan. Teams typically underestimate the time it will take to create and complete a document or presentation as a team. They make this mistake because they do not push far enough into the details of document or presentation creation and completion. On the work plan, for instance, a team may be tempted simply to write "Create report" as their action step, which does not begin to capture the many steps involved. Instead, the work plan should contain steps, such as the following:

Typical Steps in Creating and Completing Documents or Presentations

1. Develop communication strategy.
2. Decide on medium (round-table or stand-up presentation, Web page, online presentation, or formal written document).
3. Determine format and layout. If creating a presentation, this would include selecting the PowerPoint template.
4. Develop outline, storyboard, or ghost pack.
5. Divide up slides or sections.
6. Create first draft.
7. Pull sections together into one document.
8. Test for coherence and reorganize if necessary.
9. Rewrite sections and complete any editing.
10. Read entire document or presentation as a team.
11. Perform final proofreading.
12. If a presentation, practice, allowing time for revisions if needed; if a document, print and bind copy, if required, or publish online.

Listing all the steps will help the team better estimate the time needed for the creation and completion of the document or presentation. The team should plan for this work just as they do for the research and analysis. Otherwise, they risk not allowing enough time, and the resulting rush may prevent them from delivering the high-quality end product that is characteristic of a high-performing team.

Learning from the Team Experience

Teams should learn from the experiences of being on the team, reflecting on the team work processes and looking at what worked and what did not work so well. Teams working together over an extended period of time may want to build in periodic process checks. Doing so allows them to determine which processes are working well and which may need to be changed. They should revisit their roles and responsibilities, ground rules, and communication protocol. The sample form to assess team process performance in the applications at the end of this chapter provides structure for such a team process discussion.

In addition to periodic reviews during the work, the team will probably want to schedule time as a team to debrief on the experience at the end of the project. Each team member can then learn from the experience, and the team leader will be able to capture the lessons learned from the team's experience for the benefit of future teams in the organization. If the team is using a shared workspace, leaders may be able to take advantage of polls or surveys to get a general feel for the overall success of the team.

The team leader will also want to provide feedback on the performance of individual members and ask for feedback on his or her performance as a team leader (see sample evaluation form in the applications at the end of this chapter). The feedback may cover people issues as well as work process activities, although many of the people issues will be avoided if the team leader ensures that the team attends to the work process activities.

The following list of steps for avoiding team trouble summarizes the process steps discussed in this section.

Keeping Teams Out of Trouble

---

1. Have an official team launch, including an introduction to the team and the creation of a team charter.
2. Obtain any needed training in team management, such as facilitation skills, meeting management, problem solving, and conflict resolution.
3. Develop and post team ground rules and expectations for team behavior.
4. Educate team members about what to expect in team development, such as the traditional stages of forming, storming, norming, and performing.
5. Anticipate the roadblocks to team performance early and deal with them.
6. Provide regular opportunities for feedback among team members and make sure it is done properly.
7. Provide feedback to the team leader on what is working and what isn't.
8. Build in team process checks to monitor the effectiveness of the team.

Source: Adapted from Bens, I. (1999). Keeping Your Teams Out of Trouble. *Journal of Quality and Participation* 22, No. 4, pp. 45–47.

Managing the People Side of Teams

Teams bring together the best talent available to solve a problem; however, sometimes these talented people clash. The previous section covers the more mechanical side of managing team processes, but the success or failure of a team often depends on the softer issues associated with the people and how well they work together. Just as emotional intelligence is important for individuals, it is also important for groups.

One way to improve the team's emotional intelligence or ability to work together smoothly is for the team to take time to know something about each other's current situation, work experiences, expectations, personality, and cultural differences. This knowledge may not result in team bonding or friendships, which are more the by-product of teams than the goal, but since these softer issues influence how the person behaves as a team member, the knowledge can help the team avoid conflict and help the leader anticipate any problems or performance roadblocks.

Shared workspaces, such as Microsoft SharePoint, provide an excellent opportunity for this kind of sharing, offering such tools as profiles, work groups, personal and group blogs, and virtual team rooms the team members can use to find out more about those with whom they are working.

Although team members will get to know each other through day-to-day interactions while working together, the team members can shorten the learning curve by discussing the following information at the first team meeting:

1. Position and responsibilities.
2. Team experiences.
3. Expectations.
4. Personality.
5. Cultural differences.

Position and Responsibilities

What are the person's responsibilities outside the team? If in an organizational setting, what is the position (not just title) of the individual within the organization? What does the person do for the organization? What are his or her day-to-day responsibilities and workload? As was discussed in Chapter 8, high- and low-context preferences affect various functional groups within organizations as well as cultures, and these differences will influence the person's expectations of team dynamics.

Also, unless the individual is relieved of all other responsibilities to work on the team, responsibilities outside the team will influence the time and commitment available for the team, which could leave other team members resentful, particularly if they are unaware of the extent of the individual's outside commitments. While work outside the team is never an excuse for an individual not to carry his or her share of the team work, the team benefits by knowing about the outside demands both for the sake of understanding and for helping the team assign team responsibilities. This knowledge is particularly useful, for instance, when managing someone who tends to overcommit.

Team Experiences

How often have the members worked on a team and on how many teams? If they are new to the team experience, they will need more education in team dynamics, work approaches, and expectations. What kinds of experiences have they had—positive and negative? The team could perhaps learn from discussing both what worked well and what did not work so well on other teams. A decidedly negative team experience could affect a member's attitude toward teams in general; getting that out in the open can help mitigate negative attitudes.

Expectations

What do the members expect from the team and team experience? Do their goals align with the team goals? Are their goals focused more on the project or the process? Are they on the team only to advance their careers? For example, a team member who sees working on the team primarily as a way to garner management attention may pursue individual goals rather than working for team goals. He or she may dominate presentations to management or violate team communication protocol by communicating with management without the team present. The rest of the team will then become frustrated and even angry with this attention-seeking team member.

Another example, frequently encountered in academic settings, occurs when a team is divided between members who want to learn and get the most out of a project or team experience and those who simply want to receive the reward, in this case a good grade. When a team divided like this makes work assignments, instead of giving those who do not know a subject the opportunity to learn it, they assign the substantive work expediently to the person most familiar with the subject to improve their odds of getting the better grade. The people who are there to learn then become frustrated because they feel their learning experiences are limited.

When team members have different expectations and goals, they may work at cross-purposes. This again underscores the importance of establishing goals at the beginning and making sure each member accepts them.

Personality

Chapter 7 discussed the MBTI as a way to help understand individual personalities and how they affect the way people work. Team performance can benefit if the members understand how each other's personalities may affect work behavior and group interactions. For instance, if a Perceiver is frequently late (and while a type characteristic is not an excuse), the other team members will at least know not to take it personally.

Knowing the characteristics of different personality types on the teams can contribute to the ability to lead and manage the team members. It will help the team leaders understand others and how they take in information and approach problem solving. For example, if leaders know that a member is an Introvert and he or she withdraws from the conversation, they will realize that the person is probably not angry or upset, but simply thinking, and the leaders may want to do more to encourage him or her to contribute.

Cultural Differences

Team members' understanding of cultural differences can affect a team's ability to function. Some examples of particular team issues that may arise from diversity are aligned with some of the cultural variables presented in Chapter 8 and discussed in Exhibit 10.6.

Discussing these topics will serve as the first steps toward building the team's emotional intelligence. In research on the importance of developing group emotional intelligence, Druskat and Wolff found that, "to be most effective, the team needs to create emotionally intelligent norms—the attitudes and behaviors that eventually become habits—that support behaviors for building trust, group identity, and group efficacy. The outcome is complete engagement in tasks."[2] Openly discussing some or all of the five topics presented in this section—position and responsibilities, team experiences, expectations, personality, and cultural differences—will shorten the time the team needs to develop trust and a group identity.

It seems obvious that the more team members know about each other the better; however, too often, teams fail to take enough time upfront to understand each other as people. Discussing these topics at the team launch and working to develop the team's combined emotional intelligence will help the team avoid some of the conflicts that typically arise.

EXHIBIT 10.6 **Cultural Variables and Examples of Potential Team Issues**

Cultural Variable	Some Examples of Differences in Team Expectations
Context	• Individuals from a high-context society or functional area may expect teams to socialize some to allow time to build relationships. These individuals could be offended if the social time included discussion of work issues. • Some high-context people may be so dependent on nonverbal cues that they find working electronically limiting. A high-context person may feel that e-mails or shared work spaces fail to capture the meaning of the message and need more direct interaction with others on the team.
Information Flow	• Professionals from different cultures may expect information to flow in a certain way. Some, for instance, may not understand when the team's communication protocol has established only one person as the main contact with senior management; they may see that as face time for them with people of power and resent the team setting limits on their interactions. Others may not be comfortable with including all team members on e-mails when they want to communicate with the team leader. • Some cultures see information as something that is freely shared, and others as a source of power they need to protect. Failure to share information openly on a team can result in hard feelings and a lack of trust, which can completely undermine the team's working relationship and the quality of their work.
Time	• A polychronic person may find action plans and work plans too linear and may not appreciate the importance of attempting to manage time so intensely. • Some people may be very relaxed about meeting times and even deadlines for deliverables, which can cause conflict and place teams in a bind. • Team members may not share the same single-task focus, causing the single-task person to fear that the multitasking individual is not committed to the task or is not well organized.
Language	• Persons from a different cultural experience than that in the United States, for instance, might find joking exchanges offensive; they may see it as a way to keep them from bonding with the team. • Some may have problems with the amount of jargon that tends to emerge in a team environment as well.
Power	• Persons from cultures in which power and position are equated may not recognize the team leader as a person of power if the leader is of the same rank in the company and may resent that person's attempts to lead the team in any meaningful way, for instance, in resolving conflict or determining the best solution when the team is divided. • Some may have trouble seeing team members as equal partners in the project.

Handling Team Issues and Conflict

Despite all of the best planning and time spent on process, teams will likely experience conflict. Some of it will be useful and some not, but the odds are that it will occur. As Katzenbach writes, an effective team is "about hard work, conflict, integration, and collective results."[3] Working on a team is not easy, but the benefits can be very rewarding for the team members, and the results can be much better for the organization. Obtaining the best results can depend on the team's ability to manage conflict. Just as individuals and teams must be able to disagree in meetings, teams need to know how to manage conflict in their overall team activities.

Types of Team Conflict

Internal team conflict will usually be one of four types:

1. Analytical (team's constructive disagreement over a project issue or problem).
2. Task (goal, work process, deliverables).
3. Interpersonal (personality, diversity, communication styles).
4. Roles (leadership, responsibilities, power struggles).

Analytical

Analytical conflict emerges when team members disagree about substantive project issues, approaches to problem solving, or proposed answers to major questions. This type of conflict is usually constructive for the team, since it leads to better answers and greater creativity. It should be encouraged and recognized for the value it brings.

Deriving value from analytical conflict, however, requires that the team separate personality from issues, which is not always easy. The individuals involved must not take disagreements personally. They must see someone's questioning not as a personal attack but as a way to explore and understand all sides of an issue. Putting on the "black hats" (from de Bono's Six Thinking Hats, discussed in Chapter 9) can help team members think critically while removing any associations with personal issues.

Further, a team that wants to be as creative as possible and explore issues rigorously should have a ground rule encouraging members to disagree. For this ground rule to succeed, team members must view analytical conflict as constructive. If it takes on a destructive tone, there is usually a problem below the surface that the team needs to confront.

Task

The second form of team conflict concerns tasks or, quite frequently, a team member's not attending to a task. For example, a team member may not deliver the work product completed or may miss a deadline for an action item. All team members could be at fault if they have not been clear and specific about the expectations for the work product (thus, the value of the end product column in the work plan). However, the individual team member may be at fault if his or her commitment level is not high enough to ensure that the task is done well and delivered on time. Having a ground rule that sets this expectation establishes the esponsibility for every team member to deliver work products complete and on time. If they do not, this kind of conflict can seriously hurt a team's performance.

Interpersonal

Interpersonal conflict can be very disruptive to a team as well. Differences in personality types or cultural backgrounds often cause this kind of conflict. Conflict can also emerge from differences in core values and even ethics. Personality conflict can arise over differences in attitudes. For instance, if one team member has a playful, jocular attitude toward life, and another takes everything very seriously, the joker could offend the more serious teammate.

Personality conflict can also arise over goals and expectations. For example, one team member may see the work the team is doing as a valuable learning experience and enjoy the team problem solving and give-and-take; another may see the team's work as a means to an external end, perhaps a way to gain a promotion or recognition, and thus focus only on the end product, demanding team perfection. Unfortunately, ground rules may not be enough to resolve these kinds of conflicts; the team will thus need to apply some of the approaches to handling team conflict discussed later in this chapter.

Roles

Teams can usually minimize conflict over roles by taking time at the beginning to establish the roles and responsibilities of each member. Role conflicts can still occur if the team gets off course, or individuals start intruding into one another's task area. Conflicts can also occur if individuals have different expectations of the leader's role. One member may see the leader as primarily a facilitator who keeps things moving along smoothly, while another may see the leader as the one to take charge and tell others what to do. Again, clarity about roles and clear ground rules defining team interaction should help manage these kinds of problems.

Whatever the source of the conflict, if it is disruptive, the team needs to address it or risk failing to accomplish planned objectives— and certainly jeopardize obtaining results of the highest quality. The conflict will become distracting and prevent the team from being productive and turning out quality work. The methods and techniques presented in the next section will help teams manage team conflict.

Approaches to Handling Team Conflict

Most teams will use one of the following three approaches to managing conflict:

1. One on one: Individuals involved work it out between themselves.
2. Facilitation: Individuals involved work with a facilitator (mediator).
3. Team: Individuals involved discuss it with the entire team.

One on One

Quite often, a team will decide that the first step in the team's conflict resolution procedure will be to have the two individuals work out the issues alone. However, this one-on-one approach may not be the best approach. The approach should be based on the type of conflict and the personalities of the individuals. For example, if the conflict is a personality conflict and both individuals are Introverts, leaving them alone to solve the problem will probably not yield much progress. Even with an Introvert and an Extravert, the one-on-one approach may not work in a personality conflict. On the other hand, if the problem relates to a task and one member thinks another is not carrying his or her load, the two might be able to discuss it and come to some understanding.

If the individuals decide to resolve the issue themselves, they should follow common ground rules for conflict resolution. They may want to use the following guidelines to manage the discussion:

1. Each person should start in a white hat mode, stating the facts as he or she sees them.
2. Both should listen carefully to the other and not interrupt. Setting a time limit for each person may help manage the exchange of information and avoid the more aggressive person dominating too much.
3. Then, both should explain how they see the issue in relation to the team and how it may disrupt team functioning.
4. Next, the individuals should suggest approaches or ideas to resolve the issues.
5. Finally, they should agree on an approach, write it out, and sign it.

Exhibit 10.7, developed by Deborah Borisoff and David A. Victor, presents a more detailed way of approaching one-on-one conflict management discussions.

Teams could use these steps in most conflict resolution situations, but they will find that they will work particularly well for one-on-one conflict, since they help the individual be more objective. A memory device to help remember the steps is to think of them as the *Five "A's"* and make them action steps as demonstrated below Exhibit 10.7.

EXHIBIT 10.7
Steps to Integrative Conflict Management

Source: From Deborah Borisoff and David Victor, *Conflict Management: A Communication Skills Approach.* Published by Allyn and Bacon, Boston, MA. Copyright 1997 by Pearson Education. Adapted by permission of the publisher.

Steps	Description
Assessment	• Allow yourself time to calm down and to evaluate the situation • Gather appropriate information or documentation • Assess your compromise points • Assess what the other party wants • Make a preliminary determination of the appropriate conflict-handling behavior for the situation, relationship, environment
Acknowledgment	• Listen to the other party's concerns • Try to understand his or her viewpoint
Attitude	• Avoid stereotyping and making predeterminations • Try to remain objective • Remain as flexible and open as possible
Action	• Observe how the other party communicates verbally and nonverbally • Watch your use of language and nonverbal communication • Stick to the issues; don't go off on tangents • Don't make promises you can't keep • Don't present issues in a win-lose context • Don't sidestep the issues • Be sincere and trustworthy • Try to remain open-minded and flexible • Use the appropriate conflict-handling behavior and be able to revise your behavior according to how the transaction progresses • Listen, repeat, clarify information
Analysis	• Make sure all parties' concerns are articulated and considered • Summarize and clarify decisions • Review procedure for implementing any changes

Chevron Chart of Five "A's"

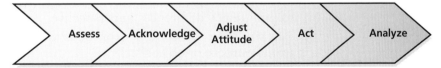

Assess > Acknowledge > Adjust Attitude > Act > Analyze

Facilitation

Having a third person work with the clashing individuals apart from the team is often the best option. If the team decides to use this approach, the facilitator should be skilled in managing conflict. Research indicates that a facilitator can encourage constructive debate and achieve resolution by taking the following steps:

Steps to Facilitate Team Conflict

---

1. Identify and examine the differences to gain understanding of all perspectives.
2. Establish a rule that all involved must listen politely and not interrupt.
3. Have the individuals in conflict paraphrase each other's concerns.
4. Openly address the concerns and translate what they are saying if necessary.
5. If translation is necessary, confirm your understanding of their message.
6. Invite constructive feedback as soon as issues are in the open.
7. Be assertive as a facilitator, intervening when misinterpretation or personal attacks interfere.
8. Bring the discussion to closure, stating what has been agreed and what the next steps will be.

Source: Adapted from Bens, I. (2000). "Facilitating Conflict." *Facilitating with Ease!* San Francisco, CA: Jossey-Bass. Used with permission.

Team

When a team decides all members should meet to solve the problem, they should have a very specific approach in mind and should select one person to facilitate the discussion. They should also take care not to appear to be "ganging up" on one person. If the problem involves one person not performing his or her share of the work, the team might want to select one member to meet with the slacker first, and only then meet with the slacker as a team.

For the team meeting, the team should appoint a spokesperson to present the team's views, rather than having everyone confront the individual. They should even use caution in how they sit around the table to avoid all sitting on one side, with the offending party on the other, as if in an inquisition.

If the problem is broader and involves several team members or the team as a whole, the team should manage the discussion by following these steps:

1. List the concerns, using facts not feelings (white hat again), trying to capture any differences in perspective.
2. Describe how the conflict is at odds with or interferes with the team's purpose or objectives.
3. Reach agreement on what the main issue is as a team, ensuring that all team members have a chance to be heard and all related issues are on the table.
4. Keep the discussion focused on the facts of the main issue and avoid any personal attacks or side issues.
5. Determine if the issue(s) can be resolved by a better understanding of or better implementation of the team's ground rules.

6. Then, write out what the team agrees to do and adjust the ground rules to cover the issue if appropriate. Make sure all actions and responsibilities are clear to everyone on the team.
7. Establish a fallback plan, should the conflict continue.

In all team conflict situations, teams should make sure their team avoids the following mistakes to help keep the conflict from escalating.

Conflict Resolution Mistakes That May Cause Conflict to Escalate

1. Avoid forcing team members to choose from among given options or limited alternatives.
2. Avoid becoming too dependent on having others resolve team problems—because dealing with conflict may be difficult or awkward.
3. Avoid the temptation to ignore conflicts altogether.
4. Prevent individual team members from giving in to the group, who later act as though they are victims of group pressure.
5. Prevent team members from talking about team issues outside the team setting.

Source: Adapted from Fisher, K., Rayner, S., and Belgaard, W. (1995). *Tips for Teams: A Ready Reference for Solving Common Team Problems*. New York: McGraw-Hill, Inc. Used by permission of The McGraw-Hill Companies, Inc.

Finally, teams can prevent most, if not all, team conflict by clarifying and agreeing on their project purpose and goals, defining team member roles and responsibilities, establishing and following team and meeting ground rules, developing a communication protocol, and devoting time to improving their group emotional intelligence.

Helping Virtual Teams Succeed

More and more professionals are using virtual teams to connect to and work with others around the globe. In fact, research shows that today "most teamwork is virtual," with it being rare "to find all team members located in one place" in organizations.[4] As one recent book on virtual teams reported, "The boundary-crossing, virtual team is the new way to work."[5] After September 11, 2001, with the increase in the worldwide threat of terrorism and with the more recent downturn in the global economy, many companies have cut back on business travel and started focusing even more on the use of remote technologies and virtual teams.

It is thus important for all leaders to know how to help virtual teams succeed. Although virtual teams are common, many organizations do not know how to ensure that they function as effectively as a co-located team would. Virtual teams require special effort, and it should not be taken for granted that people who are effective in traditional teams will also work well in a virtual team setting. There are marked differences.

Defining Virtual Teams

Virtual teams are teams whose members are geographically dispersed and who rely primarily on technology (telephone, Internet or intranet, video- or Web conferencing, or some combination) for communication and to accomplish their work as a team. The geographical separation can range from global dispersion to simply being in different locations within a single organization. Exhibit 10.8 illustrates one way to think about the difference between traditional and virtual teams: A traditional team might be working around a computer; the virtual team is *in* the computer or other technology.

Identifying Advantages and Challenges of Virtual Teams

Virtual teams provide several advantages for organizations today: lowering travel and facility costs, reducing project schedules, allowing the leveraging of expertise and vertical integration, improving efficiency, and positioning to compete globally.[6] Some have even argued that virtual team structures may lead to greater team creativity "as a result of more openness, flexibility, diversity, and added access to information."[7]

On the other hand, virtual teams also provide challenges, particularly in communication:

1. **Loss of context and nonverbals.** Much of the context of communication, so important in high-context societies, is lost, particularly if teams rely on voice or text technology only. Even members from low-context societies will find virtual communication more of a challenge, since they cannot see nonverbal cues, which represent as much as 80 to 93 percent of the meaning people receive in face-to-face communication.

EXHIBIT 10.8
**Virtual Team vs.
Co-located Team**

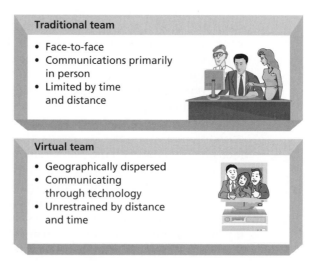

Traditional team
• Face-to-face
• Communications primarily in person
• Limited by time and distance

Virtual team
• Geographically dispersed
• Communicating through technology
• Unrestrained by distance and time

2. **Cultural differences.** Cultural differences can become amplified, and personality conflicts more pronounced. Virtual teams must work harder to build relationships and get to know each other as people.

3. **Sharing information.** Without a shared workspace, it is difficult to share and discuss complex information (diagrams, balance sheets, etc.). Web conferencing is improving but still not perfect, and teams often encounter problems with different document versions and with materials not being formatted for easy and quick focus on the right information.

4. **Trust.** Connection and trust are difficult to build in a virtual environment, and the lack of trust may put a virtual team on a "collision course."[8]

Addressing the Challenges of Virtual Teams

Since training can address some of the challenges of virtual teams, organizations need to be prepared to provide additional resources and training for the people working on virtual teams. They must be trained in how best to use the technology on which their communication will depend. They will need additional diversity training, since "culture is pervasive and even more transparent in virtual working than in face-to-face collaboration."[9]

Using a Shared Workspace

Shared workspaces, such as Jive Software's Social Business Software and Microsoft's SharePoint, provide virtual teams with a shared location in which they can interact. Such tools have become increasingly robust, offering a host of interactive tools. Exhibit 10.9 shows a screenshot of one such shared workspace. Note that a large number of "widgets," from blogs and microblogs to project time lines to discussion boards, can be configured for this workspace.

Many companies use such shared workspaces today, and they are becoming more prevalent, since they make it easier for a large, geographically diverse team to interact more personally with one another and, therefore, foster better communication. In addition, such workspaces make it possible to gather all discussions, notes, brainstorming activities, documents, slides, versions, and the like in one central location that can be accessed by all team members at any time. Of course, however, such tools can only foster such collaboration; clear goals and work processes need to be in place to make these workspaces effective.

Structure and Work Processes

A virtual team needs to have even more structure than a traditional team and must spend even more time on basic good team practices, such as having a clear purpose and objectives, establishing ground

EXHIBIT 10.9 **Example of Shared Workspace: Jive Clearspace Software**

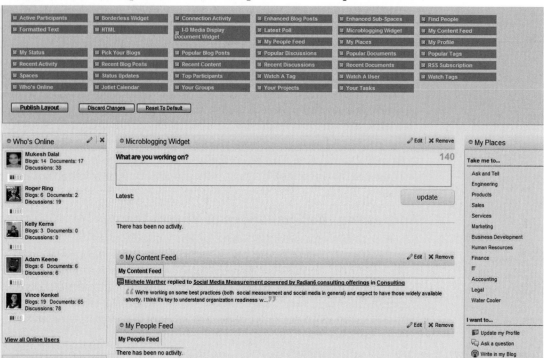

rules, creating work plans, and developing team communication protocols. Virtual team members will need to spend planning time talking through the pros and cons of the meeting options as well as the communication media as part of their team communication protocol (Exhibit 10.10):

What are the advantages yet challenges—

• Of meeting in different places and at different times by using e-mail, voice mail, or Web presentations that can be accessed when each team member has time?

• Of meeting at different times and in the same places using a shared electronic workspace?

• Of meeting at the same time and in different places with Web conferencing?

And how often should they meet face-to-face? They need to determine which option works best for their personalities, their cultural differences, the type of team tasks, and the team timing.

EXHIBIT 10.10
Virtual Team
Meeting Options

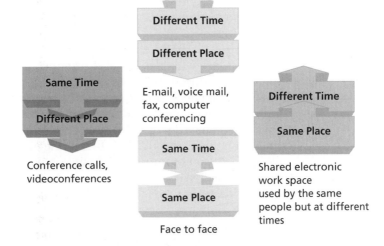

By establishing a shared workspace, team members can start to create a team identity and perhaps begin to develop the connection that is needed to succeed as a team. Such virtual "team rooms" provide a way to meet and a routine for all to share in developing ideas and documents (the "same place/different time" way of working). The team will need to implement procedures for using the space and for informing colleagues about progress.

Trust and Commitment

Studies show that many virtual teams fail because of people problems.[10] As previously mentioned, trust is vital to the success of a virtual team. Unfortunately, trust is not something training can address. It is up to the team members to build it with each other. Jill Nemiro's research on the importance of trust in virtual teams shows that it is difficult to establish and takes time to develop: "Trust developed from a sense of accountability, from seeing that others followed through on what they said they would do. Trust was also based on a belief in the expertise of others, and on positive, ongoing experience with one another."[11]

Just as with a co-located team, virtual team members must be committed to the team and the team's work. They must deliver what they promise, on time, and according to the team's expectations. With a virtual team, a high level of commitment is even more critical than with a traditional team.

In summary, according to an article in *The McKinsey Quarterly*, a virtual team needs the following to be successful:[12]

1. Shared beliefs.
2. A "storehouse of credibility and trust."
3. A shared workspace.

The shared beliefs come from the team members discussing fundamental questions about how they plan to approach the problems, examining areas of potential conflict, and taking time to resolve any differences. To build a storehouse of credibility and trust, all team members need to "pay careful attention to the way others perceive them." In addition, they need to "deliver on their promises, and do so on time; consider other people's schedules; deal straightforwardly with colleagues; and respond promptly to e-mails and voicemails."[12] Creating a shared workspace means that they need to establish a virtual team room through the technology available to them. It should allow them to communicate easily and to share in developing ideas and documents.

A virtual team needs to do all that a co-located team does and more to succeed. They must devote time to the team process and people side of teams. They must communicate frequently and have frequent electronic meetings. Ideally, they should meet in person at least once, if not more. Meeting in person at the launch can speed up the needed trust building. In their in-person meeting, the virtual team should exchange information on position and responsibilities, team experiences, expectations, personality and learning styles, and cultural differences. If an in-person meeting is not feasible, then they will need to devote technology-mediated time to these topics.

Virtual teams are praised, but they are also condemned. On one side, they are hailed: "The new workplace . . . will be a virtual workplace, where productivity, flexibility, and collaboration will reach unprecedented new levels."[13] Others lament the loss of the "human moment" and see decreased performance, confused collaboration, increased anxiety, and diminished creativity when people work virtually.[14]

Virtual teams, however, are here to stay, and their presence will probably increase. They make sense for most organizations today. They can provide benefits for both the organization and the employees. For them to succeed, however, organizations need to be able to answer the five questions with which this chapter started, placing an even greater emphasis on the middle three:

1. Does the organization provide the necessary training in diversity, team dynamics, problem solving, and process management to ensure that team members know how to manage team issues and processes?

2. Are the employees accustomed to creating and following team charters and ground rules, and do they know how to resolve team conflicts?

3. Does the current company technology effectively support team communication and collaboration? And do our people know how to use that technology?

If the answer is yes, then the company has taken some of the basic organizational steps to help virtual teams succeed. That leaves it to the members of the team to do their part. If they follow the instruction provided in this chapter for all teams—combining complementary skills, establishing shared work processes and approaches, devoting some time and attention to the people side of their teams, and constructively managing team conflict—the odds of having a high-performing team are increased tremendously.

To conclude this chapter, it may be helpful to review the activity phases of any team: getting started, doing the work, and delivering the results. The activities within each phase can be thought of as the communication challenges that leaders must meet to support the team. Exhibit 10.11 (for which my colleague John Kimball Kehoe contributed the idea and some of the content) provides a summary of the challenges discussed in this chapter.

This chapter has discussed the best approach to ensuring that all team activities run smoothly so that the team achieves its objectives. It has provided team leaders and team facilitators tools to help them build and manage a team. No doubt, leading a team and working on a team present some challenges, but with the right approach, a team can work through the challenges, achieve high performance, and, in the end as Katzenbach and Smith say, "outperform other groups and individuals."

EXHIBIT 10.11
Summary of Team Work Phases and Challenges

Work Phases	Leadership Communication Challenges
Getting Started	• Selecting team members and communicating to them individually and collectively the reasons for their selection • Establishing the team charter and confirming the understanding/acceptance of it by all team members • Making sure that roles and expectations of team members are clear and accepted • Setting ground rules for the way the team will work • Creating a team communication protocol
Doing the Work	• Guiding or facilitating team meetings • Giving feedback (positive and negative) as work is done • Coordinating the work done by team members; making sure everyone is kept informed • Dealing with and resolving conflicts • Keeping people outside the team informed of what the team is doing when appropriate
Delivering the Results	• Preparing the presentation or report of the team's work • Delivering the presentation or report • Debriefing the experience of the team (what went well and what did not) • Closing out the team, if appropriate

**Application 10.1
Assessing Team
Performance
and Developing
an Improvement
Approach**

Part 1—Team Assessment

Using the following form, assess the team work processes of a team that you have worked with for a while. Your answers are intended to help your team reflect on its performance to date so that it can make any improvements that may be needed. After completing the assessment individually, you should compare your answers with those of other team members and discuss any differences in scores.

Scale:	Needs Improvement		Average		Excellent
	1	2	3	4	5

1 2 3 4 5	How effective is your team in using tools (agendas, team objectives, action plans, or work plans)?
1 2 3 4 5	How productive are your team meetings?
1 2 3 4 5	How orderly and systematic is the team in its overall approach to team projects?
1 2 3 4 5	How conducive is the team atmosphere to effective communication?
1 2 3 4 5	How effective are your team processes?

1. Has your team established ground rules?   Yes   No

2. Do all members of the team have an equal opportunity to participate?   Yes   No

3. Have all members of the team shared equally in team responsibilities and workload?   Yes   No

4. Do all members function as team players (as opposed to putting themselves before the team)?   Yes   No

Part 2—Team Performance Improvement Plan

1. Complete the following table as a way of assessing your current use of team process tools. Make each item as specific and actionable as possible.

Team Tools	Actions We Have Taken	Actions We Plan to Take
Team Objectives		
Team Ground Rules		
Meeting Agendas		
Action Plans		
Work Plans		

2. Complete the following table as a way of determining what you want to continue or change about your current team processes.

Team Activities	What Has Worked	What Needs to Be Improved
Meeting Productivity		
Project Management		
Communications		
Division of Labor		
Team Learning		

3. Working with your team, list the overall actions your team plans to take to ensure that your team continues to perform well.

Application 10.2 Assessing Team Members and Providing Feedback

Using a team you have worked with for some time, apply the following scale to evaluate each team member, *including yourself*, according to the attributes listed. Write the number in the space provided, total the column, average the contribution of this member, and place comments on strengths and weaknesses against the attributes. You will need to complete a separate form for each team member and for yourself.

After completing the forms, meet with your team and review the assessments, using the following approach.

Approach to Providing Constructive Team Member Feedback

The goal of this exercise is to provide constructive feedback to your team members to help them be better at working in a team environment.

You want to be honest and specific but, most of all, constructive in everything you say. Note: You may want to review the information on giving and receiving feedback in Chapter 7 before completing this portion of the exercise.

1. Using the evaluation form that you have completed for each individual in your group, select one or two areas of strength and improvement for each person in your group. You should also have a specific example for both.
2. Ask for a volunteer in your group to be the first recipient of the feedback.
3. Then, move from person to person in the group, presenting the strength and then the improvement area for the first recipient. The person receiving the feedback should listen only and not respond unless he or she needs to ask a clarification question. After receiving the feedback, the recipient should simply say, "Thank you."
4. After everyone has delivered the feedback to the first person, move to the next person to that person's left until all people in the group have received feedback.

For this exercise to be open and honest and to ensure that the information leads to the team improving its approach to working together, it is better that the individual team assessment and information provided in the team's discussion remain confidential to the team; therefore, you should not discuss it with anyone outside your team.

Scale:	Needs Improvement		Average		Excellent
	1	2	3	4	5

Evaluator: Date:		Name of Team Member Being Assessed:	
Attribute	**Number**	**Comments:**	
1. Positive attitude toward team's work			
2. Completed equitable amount of work			
3. Participated actively in all meetings			
4. Cooperative (easy to work with)			
5. Team player (worked with team, not alone)			
6. Made meaningful contributions to team discussions, process, and products			
7. Good listener, responsive to ideas of others			
8. Good problem-solving ability			
9. Good at synthesizing team ideas			
10. Dependable (team could count on him or her)			
Total contribution of this team member (total of column divided by 10)			

Application 10.3 Managing Team Conflict

Consider each of the following five scenarios and decide what may be causing the team's problem (task, interpersonal, or roles) and what steps the team could take to resolve the issues. Consider which of the suggested team conflict resolution approaches would work best (one-on-one, facilitation, or team) and work out how you would structure the discussion. You may want to go back to Exhibit 9.10 on conflict-handling modes and consider one of the approaches discussed there.

Work independently for about 10 minutes; then share your ideas with a breakout group, rotating leadership of the discussion after each scenario. You should assume that all the teams in these scenarios are working on a project that will last several months, so they must resolve any issues they have—merely appeasing one or more members would not be a viable long-term solution.

1. Team One has spent several hours discussing alternative process improvement ideas to streamline the expense reporting system. Tonya frequently interrupts others and is disrespectful of their ideas. She says, "I don't know why we have to spend so much time discussing alternatives when the answers are so obvious! Let's make a decision and get out of here"

   What is causing this conflict and what should the team do to change the disruptive behavior of their member?

2. Team Two is working on an ad hoc project to improve company morale. They are meeting over lunch, since their regular schedule is so full. Two members of the five-person team have brought food to the meeting, which is held in the company's small break room. Tom really objects because he dislikes the strong smell of garlic and curry in the small room. He sends a text to Mary (another team member) to complain, writing,

   "SOS—can't stand the smell!"

   To which Mary rolls her eyes, sighs, and writes,

   "4COL. Say something then."

   Their texting is disrupting the meeting and making other attendees uncomfortable.

   What is the source of the conflict and what should the team do?

3. Team Three is approaching the end of a big project on which each person has been working independently. They are meeting to bring together sections of a report, which is due in the morning. The leader is expecting all to arrive with their analysis complete and with a deck of a few slides they can merge into one 20-slide PowerPoint presentation. However, one member comes in with his Excel sheets and computer, one shows up with 50 PowerPoint slides, and two others arrive with four or five completed graphs. As each person presents his or her part of the work, the leader realizes they will never make their deadline.

   Why is the team in this predicament and how can they prevent this type of misunderstanding from occurring in the future?

4. Team Four has a strong team charter and every member participates. On a major project, the team decides to divide up the work and check in with each other every few days. One member, Gary, is not sure he understands his part of the work. He does his best to complete his section, but he has also been having some personal problems that have kept him from focusing on work for a few weeks, so he gives the group his portion of the project the night before the deadline. The rest of the team members review his work and decide it is unacceptable; they spend all night reworking his section prior to delivering their interim report to the company president. As the next phase of the project starts, the team is concerned that Gary's work will continue to be late and of substandard quality.

What may have led the team to this conflict and how should the team approach Gary to resolve it?

5. Team Five meets on a regular basis every Wednesday at 7:30 a.m. before work begins. Bashirah always arrives late, often bringing donuts and coffee for the other members. She doesn't seem concerned about being late, and she does get right down to business, but one of the other members is really becoming upset about this, saying, "I have to get up at 6:00 to be here on time, but I can make it, why can't she?"

How should the team handle this issue?

Source: *Scenarios developed by Beth O'Sullivan and modified by Deborah Barrett, Rice University. Used with permission.*

Application 10.4
Launching a
Virtual Team

The Case: Zarate Tech Goes Virtual

Zarate Tech has a sales group of 120 located in Chicago, Atlanta, Los Angeles, London, and Sydney. The sales group generates and qualifies leads, meets with existing and potential customers, negotiates deals, and offers technology solutions, focusing primarily on customer relationship management (CRM). The sales force conveys requirements to Zarate's offices in Chicago and London, matching staff capacity with the quantities and types of products needed. The sales group also performs customer service functions, including tracking and confirming delivery and quality of products and solutions. Overall, the sales group moves $2.1 billion of products and consulting services each year.

Traditionally, the company's philosophy was that the sales staff must remain small and in close contact; therefore, they meet in person frequently in either London or Chicago. They see their manufacturing facilities as marketing tools to demonstrate the company's commitment to quality, on-time delivery, and products customized to meet specifications. Despite its focus on providing the latest in CRM technology for its customers, the COO, Jan Ciampi, who oversees Zarate's accounting, finance, and information system, feels the company is behind in its use of technology to manage its sales, sales group interactions, and team communication and problem solving. While Zarate has e-mail, an intranet, and a state-of-the-art internal accounting and telecommunications system, the company rarely uses its technology for team interactions and communication. Although all salespeople have laptops to use on the road, they use them primarily for generating reports and handling e-mail.

You have recently been hired as the new vice president of worldwide sales to help modernize the work processes of the sales group. Senior management is particularly interested in your improving how the company communicates across distances, shares and captures company information, and makes use of computer technology for client and team meetings. They feel the sales group spends too much time and money flying to meetings and even commuting to work. They know some direct contact with customers is important as well as internal meetings of the sales team, which usually consist of a sales rep, an account manager, a technical engineer, a logistics coordinator, and an IT technician; however, they wonder if some of these meetings could be handled virtually. They are also considering using a remote sales force structure, with the salespeople working from their homes instead of coming into the office, which they think would allow them to cut office overhead.

Last week at the company's annual budget planning meeting in Chicago, Ciampi announced the formation of a team to investigate how best to move the sales group toward using virtual team technology and how to encourage them to use the Intranet, Web technology, and Web conferencing to connect, manage accounts, and work and meet directly online. You will be heading up the team. Your charge is to determine what it will take to ensure that the sales group accepts the new way of working and knows how to work effectively as a virtual team.

Once you have decided whom to include from your sales group and from the training, development, and communication departments, you need to draft an e-mail or a meeting request announcing the project to the team and scheduling the team launch. One of your immediate challenges is that your team will be scattered across all the offices, with many of them on the road constantly, so you must confront the challenges of working virtually. In fact, you realize that this team could end up serving as a model for how to work effectively as a virtual team, but you also realize that motivating the sales group to change from their current ways of working and providing the training they need to work effectively using virtual technology will be a challenge.

The Assignment

Draft the e-mail or meeting request to your team establishing the project objectives and inviting them to the team launch, which you have decided to hold in person in the Chicago office. Then, establish an agenda for the meeting and your approach to working as a team. Next, outline what you see as the challenges to this project and some of the best practices in working virtually that you think will help your team get off to a good start. Finally, note the type of interactive tools you will want to include in the team's shared workspace and why these tools will be helpful.

Notes

1. Katzenbach, J. R., and Smith, D. K. (1993). *The Wisdom of Teams: Creating the High-Performance Organization.* Boston: Harvard Business School Press.

2. Druskat, V. U., and Wolff, S. B. (2001). Building the Emotional Intelligence of Groups. *Harvard Business Review* 79, No. 3, pp. 80–91.

3. Katzenbach, J. R. (1998). *The Work of Teams.* Boston: Harvard Business School Press.

4. Duarte, D. L., and Snyder, N. T. (2001). *Mastering Virtual Teams.* San Francisco: Jossey-Bass, p. xi.

5. Lipnack, J., and Stamps, J. (2000). *Virtual Teams.* New York: John Wiley, p. 6.

6. Duarte and Snyder (2001), p. 4.

7. Nemiro, J. E. (2001). Connection in Creative Virtual Teams. *Journal of Behavior and Applied Management* 2, No. 2 (Winter–Spring), also available online at www:jbam.org/articlesarticle2_8.htm.

8. George, J. M. (1996). Virtual Best Practice: How to Successfully Introduce Virtual Team-Working. *Teams Magazine* (November), pp. 38–45.

9. Simons, G. Meeting the Intercultural Challenges of Virtual Work. www .diversophy.com/news_info/downloads.htm.
10. Lipnack and Stamps (2000).
11. www.jbam.org/articles/article2_8.htm.
12. Benson-Armer and Hsieh (1997), p. 25.
13. Townsend, A. M., DeMarie, S. M., and Hendrickson, A. R. (1998). Virtual Teams: Technology and the Workplace of the Future. *Academy of Management Executive*, p. 17.
14. Hallawell, E. M. (1998). The Human Moment at Work. *Harvard Business Review*, January–February, pp. 1–8.

Section 3

Corporate Leadership Communication

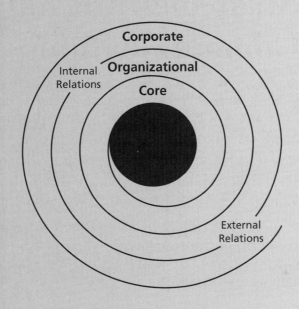

Chapter 11

Leadership Through Strategic Internal Communication

Personal leadership is about communication, openness, and a willingness to speak often and honestly, and with respect for the intelligence of the reader or listener. Leaders don't hide behind corporate double-speak. They don't leave to others the delivery of bad news. They treat every employee as someone who deserves to understand what's going on in the enterprise.

Louis V. Gerstner, Jr., (2002) *Who Says Elephants Can't Dance?* New York: Harper Collins.

Vision, though, is meaningless alone. To be an effective leader, you must communicate consistently, vividly, and so darn frequently that your throat gets sore. You can't, as we've said, communicate too much, especially when you're galvanizing change.

Jack and Suzy Welch, Obama: A Leadership Report Card, *Business Week*, April 20, 2009.

Chapter Objectives

In this chapter, you will learn to do the following:

- Recognize the strategic and cultural role of employee communication.
- Assess internal communication effectiveness.
- Establish effective internal communication.

- Use missions and visions to strengthen internal communication.
- Design and implement effective change communication.

One of the major responsibilities of an organizational leader is communication with employees. Fraser Seitel, former senior vice president of public affairs for Chase Manhattan Bank, argues that it is the most important responsibility: "Employee communications is the most important part of a CEO's many responsibilities. . . . If employees believe in the CEO—trust him [her] and respect him [her]—then they become agents to convince other publics of the goodness of the programs and the company."[1] By communicating effectively with employees, however, CEOs are not simply creating ambassadors of goodwill for their companies; they are providing direction, establishing a positive and productive working environment, and influencing their bottom lines.

Effective internal communication provides organizational direction and employee motivation. Based on its research into 530 companies, Ragan Communications found that "CEOs are not just communicating because they want to be thought of as nice people. They have discovered that effective internal communications will help them achieve their vision for the company and will motivate employees to do their best work."[2]

Organizational direction comes from leaders' having created and effectively communicated a clear and meaningful vision. Developing and communicating a vision is one of the most important communication tasks of leaders.

Individuals are motivated when, through words and actions, the leaders carefully translate their vision and strategic goals into terms that are meaningful to all, particularly inside an organization, where employees contribute daily to seeing the vision become a reality. Motivating employees requires targeting messages to reach them, listening to them, and using emotional intelligence to connect with them. Leaders who appreciate the importance of connecting with all employees through communication and through their actions see results: "An attractive communication climate can contribute significantly to the long-term success of a company. Managers should, therefore, pay serious attention to the internal communication climate by providing each employee the adequate information and the opportunities to speak out, get involved, be listened to, and actively participate."[3]

Direction setting and the creation of a motivated, supportive workforce alone are reasons enough to pursue effective internal communication. Effective employee communication clearly results in higher organizational performance and increased productivity.[4]

In addition, effective internal communication has a measurable financial impact. As one recent study of the ROI (return on investment) of 267 major corporations found, internal communication significantly influences financial performance: "Companies with the highest levels of effective communication experienced a 26 percent total return to shareholders from 1998 to 2002, compared to a −15 percent experienced by firms that communicate least effectively."[5]

From daily information exchanges and interactions with employees to creating and communicating visions, strategic objectives, or other direction-setting messages, to helping employees understand and support major changes—internal communication requires leaders to use all their best leadership communication abilities.

Thus, all of the basic and organizational-level abilities included in leadership communication in this text are applicable to communicating effectively within an organization—in particular, projecting a positive ethos; creating meaningful, purposeful messages; analyzing and understanding audiences; targeting messages to reach different internal audiences; developing communication strategies; and leading through emotional intelligence and cultural literacy.

This chapter focuses on establishing leadership through communicating effectively with an organization's internal audiences. It describes the strategic role employee communication can play by ensuring that employees are well informed and, therefore, positioned to contribute to the success of the organization. It also discusses how to develop and use vision and mission statements to guide the organization and provides an approach to effective change communication, an essential type of communication in today's rapidly changing workplace.

Recognizing the Strategic and Cultural Role of Employee Communication

For employee communication to play a strategic and cultural role in an organization, organizational leaders must realize the importance of keeping all internal audiences well informed and the value of integrating communication into the organization's overall strategy, planning processes, and day-to-day operations. All internal messages should align with and reinforce the organization's goals and objectives, with the mission,vision, and guiding principles helping direct and define the culture and the operational, performance, and financial goals helping establish the expected results.

For example, if a leader's objective is to eliminate the current functional silo approach to decision making and bring the leaders of different groups together to collaborate and make decisions jointly for the good of the organization instead of their individual units, the communication objectives would be (1) to ensure that all functional groups receive the same message that joint decision making is now a priority and (2) to establish forums (meetings if appropriate) for collaboration and joint decision making to occur. The organizational leader's first responsibility will be communicating his or her new vision and objectives for working together clearly; the second will be influencing the group leaders to to act on it.

Essentially, the leader in this situation will be inspiring cultural change, a transformation in the way the group decision makers think about their own operations and behave toward other group leaders. By bringing about such change, the leader will be functioning as a transformational leader: "One primary factor that distinguishes transformational leaders is that they work to change the organization. . . . The culture in transformational organizations inculcates a sense of purpose, long-term commitments, and mutual interests. Such cultures are based on shared interdependence, as well as leaders and followers who can transcend their self-interests for the good of the team and the organization."[6]

Communication helps shape the culture of any organization, and effective internal communication is absolutely essential to bring about any transformation in that culture. Leaders have to make their visions and goals clear, and all communication with internal audiences needs to position all employees to help achieve those goals. To be effective, employee communication should accomplish the following basic objectives:

1. Educate employees in the organization's culture, vision, and strategic goals.
2. Motivate employee support for the organization's goals.
3. Encourage higher performance and discretionary effort to achieve those goals.
4. Limit misunderstandings and rumors that may damage morale and productivity.
5. Align employees behind the organization's performance objectives and position them to help achieve them.

To accomplish these goals, messages need to be clear, consistent, and targeted. Effective employee communication is both the product—the messages that the organization wants to transfer—and the process—the conduit for transferring the messages. Leaders need to pay attention to both, and developing a communication strategy for all internal audiences will help them do so.

Establishing Effective Internal Communication

Creating the internal messages to be sent to employees is a primary leadership responsibility, as is attending to the other main components of any good communication strategy. The Strategic Employee Communication Model in Exhibit 11.1, a model based on the best practices

EXHIBIT 11.1
Strategic
Employee
Communication
Model

Source: This model and the research into the best practices on which it is based appear in Barrett, D. J. (2002). Change communication: Using strategic employee communication to facilitate major change. *Corporate Communication: An International Journal* 7 (4), pp. 219–231. Used with permission of Emerald Press.

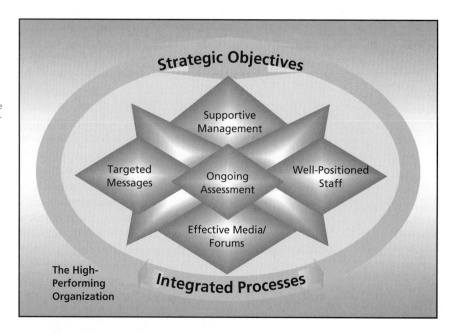

in internal communication found in high-performing organizations, can serve as one analytical technique to measuring and establishing an effective approach to internal communication. It resembles the communication strategy framework introduced in Chapter 2 in its components, but it differs in being specific to developing a strategy for internal communication.

First, the model shows the linking of the company's strategy and strategic messages and suggests the business process integration as a band that ties together all the pieces of an internal communication strategy. Then, it brings in the components of any communication strategy, such as messages and media, and introduces other employee communication components, such as supportive management and well-positioned staff, which best practice research indicates are necessary to have effective employee communication.[7]

To ensure a comprehensive internal communication approach, leaders will find using such an analytical approach helpful. The model serves as a framework for creating an internal communication strategy. In addition, the definitions of each of the components provide benchmarks against which to measure a program to establish possible improvement opportunities.

At its core, the model shows that effective internal communication consists of the following:

1. Supportive management
2. Targeted messages
3. Effective media/forums

4. Well-positioned staff

5. Ongoing assessment

The following definitions describe the best practice approach to each component.

Supportive Management

What does it mean to have supportive management? In short, it means that all employees in leadership positions model the communication behavior they expect of those they supervise. If an organization wants employees to see communication as important, leaders need to demonstrate it. Such demonstrations may mean that managers are directly involved in and assume responsibility for relaying important messages to their direct reports, but they also openly communicate upward and across their peer groups.

Showing management support for communication also means including effective communication on performance reviews and recognizing those who excel in some way. The message that leaders want to send to the organization is that communication is everyone's responsibility and is not to be limited to the activities of the communication staff. Since employees are much more likely to behave as they see their leaders behave than to follow written principles, leaders need to demonstrate support for and belief in the value of communication.

For example, if an organization wants to promote an open, free exchange of ideas, it needs to encourage and establish media and forums for communication to flow up, down, and across all employees. The leaders need to accept good and bad news without penalizing the messenger. In fact, the fear of speaking out can lead to ethical quandaries in some organizations where an employee witnesses something that is questionable but is afraid to take the news to management. In addition, it can lower employee productivity because they have no outlet or recognition for improvement ideas.

Leaders in the organization set the tone for an open or closed culture. Without leadership's positive examples to establish a high priority for open and honest communication, the channels of communication will not flow freely and the rest of the organization will not see communication as important.

Targeted Messages

As has been emphasized throughout this text, effective communication depends on making all messages specific to the audience receiving them. Therefore, leaders need to analyze their many internal audiences and work with other managers to establish groups by function and level and then develop messages each group will understand. While the core messages communicated within the organization must be consistent internally and externally, leaders may need to present messages to specific groups with a slightly different emphasis and maybe even slightly different language. That does not imply that the meaning changes, only the words that are used. The targeted messages need to be relevant and meaningful for each targeted employee group yet consistent with the company's overall strategy and messages, such as those found in the mission, vision, and guiding principles.

For example, in a large company, each business unit or division may need to create a version of important messages for its employees or convert the overall message from the corporate center into digestible and actionable messages the employees can understand and act upon. They may even have their own vision statement specific to their goals in support of the company's vision. This kind of specific message tailoring usually requires the help of individuals closest to the employee groups, so after establishing the overall major messages for the organization, company leaders may want to enlist help in the wording of the messages that follow to each group.

Effective Media and Forums

While most organizations have traditional media and forums for conveying information, they should not take for granted that all employees receive the information through the expected or preferred channels. Organizations may need to communicate internal messages through several different media to reach all employees. Leaders need to look critically at the media, decide when different situations require different media, and survey employees to determine if they are receiving the intended messages through the selected media.

For example, many organizations produce expensive and elaborate employee newsletters and magazines periodically, yet if they were to survey employees on how many read them, they might find that employees do not see much value in them and that they would prefer receiving something less elaborate and more frequent, such as e-mails, IM, corporate blogs, or even recorded voice messages. Gordon Bethune, the former CEO of Continental Airlines, was known for leaving global messages for all employees every Friday in voice mail. These informal, frequent messages were much more effective in reaching the Continental employees than more formal publications or meetings.

With the overuse of e-mail today, some organizations may find that it does not reach their employees with important messages. In that case, they may want to look at using their intranet more effectively. For example, one energy company, El Paso Corporation, has transferred almost all of its internal messages to a well-designed and targeted intranet and has found that it reaches more employees much more effectively than it had through e-mails and hard-copy publications.

If employees prefer direct, face-to-face communication over indirect, print, or electronic media, the organization will need to develop systems and procedures to allow for frequent exchanges among employees at all levels. For example, almost from its very beginning as a company, UPS has held what it calls "three-minute" pre-work meetings every morning at all regional locations to deliver important information for the day and to solicit feedback. This way, they encourage frequent dialogue and make sure they reach all employees with key messages, even those employees not connected to voice mail and e-mail.

Well-Positioned Staff

Organizational leaders serious about ensuring that communication is integrated into the company operations and strategy and effective in reaching all employees with important messages will want to consider the placement of the professional communication staff. Research indicates that the communication staff must be positioned close to the most important business issues and decisions and involved in the strategic and business planning processes for internal communication to be fully effective. They need to have a "seat at the table." For most organizations, that means that the highest-ranking communication person must be at the same level as company presidents and vice presidents. To understand the company's strategy and to participate in the decision making, the senior communication officer must be directly connected to the highest levels of the organization.

If the organization is large enough to have several full-time communication professionals and wants to encourage communication up, down, and across the organization, they should be located at all levels of the organization. Having communication staff close to different functions or within each group or business unit signals the importance of communication and provides local expertise when messages need to be tailored to these different groups. When isolated and seen only as producers of communication products, the communication professionals will not be positioned to help the other leaders deliver and measure the impact of either routine or major change messages.

Ongoing Assessment

For internal communication to be effective, leaders need to demonstrate clearly that they consider good communication to be valuable and important. As is well known, what matters in an organization is what is measured. Therefore, organizations will want to include communication ability and performance in the assessments of the employees. The organization should evaluate communication effectiveness as part of each employee's performance appraisal and give appropriate recognition for excellence.

Employee evaluation forms should include questions on how well employees are communicating to others in their department as well as to people outside their groups. Are they being open and sharing information frequently enough? Do they encourage others to communicate with them? How do they respond to bad news, for instance? Such openness has been found to be one of the major deterrents to unethical practices. It is not as easy to hide questionable activities if all employees feel as though they are being held accountable for communicating everything that is going on within the company openly and honestly.

In addition, the organization should assess companywide communication effectiveness formally and frequently against clearly defined goals. Assessment procedures should include ascertaining whether important messages are reaching all employees and how well these messages are understood. In response to the assessments, leaders should establish ways to ensure that improvement occurs when they uncover breakdowns in communication.

The quickest way to obtain a picture of the "what" and the "how" of internal communication is to survey a stratified sample of the organization. Depending on which channels work best for the organization and the different groups in the company, the organization can send these surveys out electronically through e-mail or set up a company blog, forum, or poll on the company intranet. Web-based survey companies, such as SurveyMonkey, make it very easy to send out surveys electronically and to synthesize the results quickly. Phone surveys work as well, again depending on the culture and the company's preferred way of communicating.

Using the model or a similar analytical framework to develop an internal communication strategy and aiming toward reaching some of the best practices discussed in this section will help an organization achieve improved internal communication. It is up to the leaders of the organization to make communicating with employees a priority and to set the tone for how the organization views employee communication. Failing to approach internal communication strategically and realize its importance will hinder any organization from building a strong and unified culture and limit any leader's ability to accomplish his or her goals.

Assessing Employee Communication Effectiveness

Before attempting to reach internal audiences with important messages, particularly ones intended to transform the organization, leaders may want to determine how the organization's internal communication measures up against the best practices previously described. The scorecard in Exhibit 11.2 is designed to help uncover how an organization stands in relation to the best practices for internal communication. The scorecard uses the components presented in the Strategic Employee Communication Model (Exhibit 11.1) and

EXHIBIT 11.2
Scorecard of
Current Employee
Communication

Source: Barrett, D. J.
(2002). Change communi-
cation: Using strategic
employee communication
to facilitate major change.
Corporate Communication:
An International Journal
7 (4), pp. 219–231. Used
with permission of
Emerald Press.

Where are the company's employee communication practices at present?
Place an "x" on the scale below to indicate your preliminary assessment:

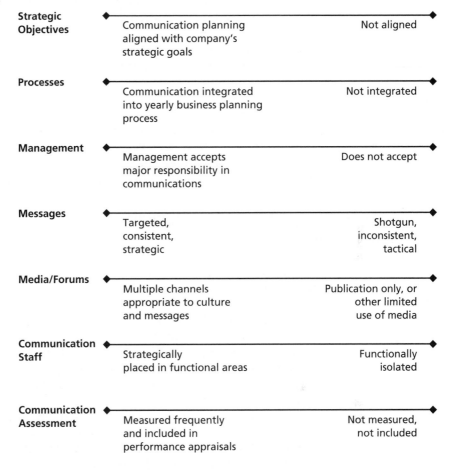

Strategic
Objectives
Communication planning
aligned with company's
strategic goals
Not aligned

Processes
Communication integrated
into yearly business planning
process
Not integrated

Management
Management accepts
major responsibility in
communications
Does not accept

Messages
Targeted,
consistent,
strategic
Shotgun,
inconsistent,
tactical

Media/Forums
Multiple channels
appropriate to culture
and messages
Publication only, or
other limited
use of media

Communication
Staff
Strategically
placed in functional areas
Functionally
isolated

Communication
Assessment
Measured frequently
and included in
performance appraisals
Not measured,
not included

establishes a range of performances. The "x's" will be mostly on the left side for an organization with an effective employee communication program in place. If, however, the "x's" fall more on the right side of the scale, the organization may want to look at improving those components where they fall short.

To obtain a comprehensive appraisal of the current internal communication practices, leaders, particularly ones new to an organization, may want to ask a representative sample of the management team and employees at different levels to complete the scorecard as well. Where an organization falls on the scale beside each component indicates how much time and effort the organization's leaders will need to devote if the organization needs to improve in its current employee communication practices.

For example, if the current media are not reaching employees, leaders will want to find more effective ones immediately. No matter how clear, consistent, and targeted the messages, if they are not reaching the intended audiences, they are useless. If they find that key managers are uninvolved and unsupportive of communication efforts, they may need to coach and encourage them to accept responsibility and accountability for the success or failure of employee communication.

Once leaders have pinpointed areas for improvement, they should take steps to close the gaps and work toward establishing an effective internal communication approach. Otherwise, they will be severely limited in successfully achieving their vision and organizational goals, particularly if those goals include cultural or any other major organizational transformation.

Using Missions and Visions to Strengthen Internal Communication

Missions, visions, values, and guiding principles are major strategic messages that most organizations work hard to ensure their employees understand. Leaders are expected to have a vision and to be able to communicate it clearly and consistently. To quote from the Welches again on U.S. President Obama: "Let's start with vision, the 'thing' without which a person simply cannot lead. And look, whether you like his politics or not, Obama's obviously got it. From the economy to the environment, education to health care, the President has articulated his goals to the nation."[8]

The ability to establish and communicate the mission and the vision effectively strengthens a leader's position in leading in any situation or environment, but in an organization, the clear direction a good vision provides helps ensure that the work everybody is doing is for the right reason and to the right end. Communicating a vision to inspire, motivate, and connect with audiences is a major objective of leadership communication.

Instruction in leadership communication, therefore, must include how best to create and deliver the vision, the mission, and the core directional and transformational messages, so that they are strong and meaningful, not simply feeble slogans good only for adorning T-shirts or coffee cups. This section will help leaders create effective visions by answering the following questions:

1. Why are missions and visions important?
2. What are missions and visions?
3. When are they most effective?
4. How do organizations build them?

Understanding the Importance of Missions and Visions

Leaders should not underestimate the power of a well-crafted, sincere, and meaningful vision. In organizations, visions and missions are needed to guide employees' efforts toward achieving the organization's strategic, operational, and financial goals.

In their book *Built to Last,* James Collins and Jerry Porras argue that visions play an essential role in a company's performance, but to do so, they must be clear, relevant, and directed toward delivering a genuinely useful service or product. They found that the companies they labeled "visionary" achieve the highest profitability: A single dollar invested in general market stocks in 1926 would have grown to $415 by 1990. That same dollar, invested in a "visionary company" with a clear, functioning vision and mission statement, would have reaped $6,356.[9]

Effective mission and vision statements are important to an organization for the following reasons:

1. They inspire individual action, determine behavior, and fuel motivation.
2. They establish a firm foundation of goals, standards, and objectives to guide planners and managers.
3. They satisfy both the organization's need for efficiency and the employees' need for group identity.
4. They provide direction, which is particularly important in times of change, to keep everyone moving toward the same goals.

An organization's success can be facilitated by having a clearly stated, credible, intelligible, actionable, and meaningful vision and mission statement. While organizational leaders usually develop and communicate the mission and the vision, all employees need to understand and accept them.

Defining Missions and Visions

The words "mission" and "vision" are quite often used interchangeably; however, they should not be, and doing so can result in confusion. Since definitions differ slightly from organization to organization, leaders may first want to establish their definitions. The following discussion provides definitions and examples of both words.

Missions

A mission is a statement of the reason an organization exists that is intended primarily for internal use. It should ensure that employees understand the organization's purpose by defining its basic products or services. It should establish a single, noble purpose and an enduring reality.

The following table contains a few mission statements to demonstrate this definition:

Company	Mission
Google	"Google's mission is to organize the world's information and make it universally accessible and useful." www.google.com/corporate/
Microsoft	"At Microsoft, our mission and values are to help people and businesses throughout the world realize their full potential." www.microsoft.com/about/default.mspx
AT&T Labs	"Our mission is to exploit technical innovations for the benefit of AT&T and its customers by implementing next-generation technologies and network advancements in AT&T's services and operations." www.corp.att.com/attlabs/about/mission.html
Sun Microsystems	"Sun's mission is to create technologies and fuel communities that enable sharing and participation." (Corporate Backgrounder at www.sun.com/aboutsun/company/index.jsp)
United Way	"To improve lives by mobilizing the caring power of communities." www.liveunited.org/about/missvis.cfm

Visions

A vision statement establishes the leader's purpose and the organization's aspirations. It describes an inspiring new reality, achievable in a well-understood and reasonable time frame. Organizations often use visions for internal and external audiences, although their greatest purpose is usually to guide internal actions. Motivational visions should reflect the company leaders' willingness to project into the future. "Transformational leaders emphasize new possibilities and promote a compelling vision of the future. A strong sense of purpose guides their vision."[10] A vision usually starts with the words "to become" or "to create."

The following table contains a few vision statements to demonstrate this definition:

Company	Vision
AT&T Labs	"Our vision is to design and create in this decade the new global network, processes, and service platforms that maximize automation, allowing for a reallocation of human resources to more complex and productive work." www.corp.att.com/attlabs/about/mission.html
Amazon	"Our vision is to be earth's most customer centric company; to build a place where people can come to find and discover anything they might want to buy online." http://phx.corporate-ir.net/phoenix.zhtml?c=97664&p=irol-faq# 14296

| Sun Microsystems | "Sun's vision is to see everyone and everything participating on the network. . . . The Network is the Computer." (Corporate Backgrounder at www.sun.com/aboutsun/company/index.jsp) |
| United Way | "We will build a stronger America by mobilizing our communities to improve people's lives." www.liveunited.org/about/missvis.cfm |

One way to differentiate a mission statement from a vision statement is to think of the mission as the "here and now" and to think of the vision as the future. What is most important, however, is that an organization have a clear definition of its reason for being (mission) and of where it wants to go (vision); whether one is called a mission and the other a vision matters less than that both exist and that the organization knows what they are and which is which.

Ensuring That the Mission and Vision Are Effective

To be useful in guiding employees, both the mission and the vision need to be perfectly clear in their meaning and specific to the organization.

To test a mission, the leaders should determine if it has the following characteristics:

- Inspirational and suggestive of excellence.
- Clear, making sense in the marketplace.
- Stable but flexible enough to last with only incremental changes.
- Beacons and controls when all else is up for grabs.
- Aimed at empowering employees first, customers second.[11]

To test the vision, the organizational leaders should ask if it does the following:

- Suggests goals and provides a direction.
- Inspires and prepares for the future but honors the past.
- Applies specifically to the company, providing details that are actionable.

Of course, a vision statement and a mission statement interact, which means that a vision may give rise to a new mission, and a redefined mission may require a changed vision for implementation.

Building an Effective Mission and Vision

In his essay "The Vision Thing," Todd Jick explains three approaches to building a vision:

- CEO/leader developed.
- Leader–senior team visioning.
- Bottom-up visioning.[12]

Depending on the organization's culture, any of the three could work effectively. If, for example, an organization is large and fairly hierarchical company, the CEO/leader approach might work best and even be expected. If, on the other hand, the organization is medium-sized and has a team-based management approach, it might want to use the leader–senior team visioning approach. Finally, if the organization is a nonprofit or a relatively small or flat organization, it might ask a team of employees to develop the vision. For example, a team of 60 employee volunteers developed the Whole Foods Market's "Declaration of Interdependence," which contains their motto, "Whole Foods, Whole People, Whole Planet," and their guiding principles.[13]

For many organizations, some combination of the three approaches seems to work well. This combination approach consists of first having the organization's leaders and senior leadership team create initial vision and mission statements and, then, having employees at different levels participate in refining them.

A mission and vision that emerge at the end of an interactive process, involving a cross section of the organization, will more likely resonate meaning for employees at all levels of the organization. The danger of developing a mission and vision in isolation at the top of the organization is that lower-level employees may not fully understand the leaders' intentions and will not feel any ownership of the statement.

A leader-led, interactive, employee-involved approach to building a mission and vision would include the following steps.

1. Create the Initial Draft

Bring the "right" employees, usually a cross section of organizational leaders, together to create the initial draft of the mission and vision.

To arrive at the mission, the leadership team should work through the following questions:

- What do we do? Why do we exist?
- What are our core products, concepts, or services?
- What are our collateral products and services?
- Why is what we do important?
- What if our organization no longer existed?
- What is our value proposition?

To arrive at the vision, the team should work through the following:

- What does it take for us to succeed in today's marketplace or social, political, or economic environment?
- What will it take in the future?
- What are our current strengths and weaknesses?
- What are our major opportunities and threats?

- How might we increase the value we bring to our stakeholders?
- What do we want to become?
- How do we want competitors and the world to see us?

2. Clarify the Meaning

After the group has answered the preceding questions and completed the first draft, they should look at it critically, word by word. One approach is to take each word and ask what it means. For example, the company vision might read as follows:

> To be the market leader in providing high-performing, cost-effective computer products and services to enable systemwide success for all of our customers.

Then, the exercise to determine the real meaning behind most of the rather abstract words in the vision might look as follows:

Word or Phrase	Means	Does Not Mean
Market Leader	Recognized by peers for innovation	A certain market share percentage
High-Performing	Fast, high-quality, free from defects, low maintenance, compatible with industry standards	The fastest with complete compatibility with all other hardware
Cost-Effective Computer Products and Services	Competitive Central computing, client server, hardware with service and support for all our manufactured products	Lowest cost Peripheral computer equipment such as printers, scanners, external drives, and so forth, with service and support for other companies' products
Systemwide Success	Success for critical enterprise-wide hardware	Success for interfaces and compatibility with all other manufactured products

3. Tell the World in 25 Words or Less What we Are and What we Want to Become

The mission and the vision need to be more than slogans; at the same time, they need to be concise enough that people can remember them. Again, however, they must be meaningful; while some organizations have created visions that capture a lot of meaning in just a few words, it is very difficult to do so.

4. Develop the Strategic Objectives to Make the Vision Specific and Actionable

The strategic objectives should be specific actions designed to help (1) accomplish the vision and (2) bring a sustainable competitive

EXHIBIT 11.3
Relationship of
Mission to Vision
to Strategic
Objectives

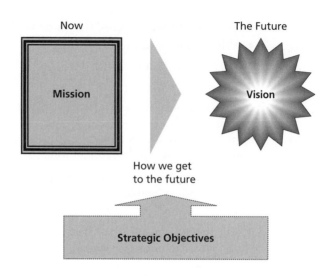

advantage. They are usually measurable targets, divided into quantitative goals (such as financial, market share, or productivity) and qualitative goals (such as personnel development or reputation). Exhibit 11.3 illustrates how the mission, vision, and strategic objectives relate to each other.

Exhibits 11.4 and 11.5 illustrate how the strategic objectives should support the mission and the vision. Strategic objectives help make a vision more meaningful and actionable. Notice in Exhibit 11.4 that the supporting relationship between the strategic objectives and the vision is indicated by the use of the word "by." Exhibit 11.5 provides two examples, one from the United Way and the other from a global chemical company.

EXHIBIT 11.4
Example Vision
with Strategic
Objectives

> **Vision:** To be the market leader in providing high-performing, cost-effective computer products and services to enable systemwide success for all of our customers by
>
> - Creating seamless integration of all system critical components.
> - Providing products of a superior value at prices at or below all major competitors.
> - Supplying management of all products and support for all systems.
> - Establishing partnerships to ensure customers have integrated, highly reliable systemwide solutions.

EXHIBIT 11.5
**Examples of
Mission, Vision,
and Strategic
Objectives**

United Way

Mission
To improve lives by mobilizing the caring power of communities.

Vision:
We will build a stronger America by mobilizing our communities to improve people's lives.

To do this we will:

- Energize and inspire people to make a difference
- Craft human care agendas within and across our communities
- Build coalitions around these agendas
- Increase investments in these agendas by expanding and diversifying our own development efforts and supporting those of others
- Measure, communicate, and learn from the impact of our efforts
- Reflect the diversity of the communities we serve

Major Chemical, Inc.

MISSION
A customer-driven organization, providing industrial chemical products and creative solutions in select markets around the world.

VISION
Major Chemical Inc.'s vision is to become the preferred partner in providing industrial chemical products and creative solutions for our customers by

Strategic Objectives

- Conducting business based on a foundation of environmental responsibility
- Running all operations efficiency but safely
- Generating profitable growth of 15% over the next five years
- Improving the satisfaction of our customers, employees, and shareholders.
- Conducting every aspect of our business guided by our values.
- Developing internal measures of how we are operating and how well we "walk the talk" for our customers and employees

Instead of strategic objectives, often organizations will articulate their values or guiding principles in support of their mission and vision. Usually, these statements of values or principles will not be as measurable as the strategic objective statements; however, they, too, can provide specifics to guide work, as well as behavior. For example, here is Microsoft's statement of values:

> As a company, and as individuals, we value integrity, honesty, openness, personal excellence, constructive self-criticism, continual self-improvement, and mutual respect. We are committed to our customers and

partners and have a passion for technology. We take on big challenges, and pride ourselves on seeing them through. We hold ourselves accountable to our customers, shareholders, partners, and employees by honoring our commitments, providing results, and striving for the highest quality.   http://www.microsoft.com/about/default.mspx

5. Hold Cascading Meetings with Employees to Test the Mission and the Vision

Cascading meetings offer a way to involve as many employees as possible in testing the mission and vision. These meetings or workshops usually start with the upper levels of the organization broken into functions or divisions and then give way to cross-level, functional, or divisional meetings. The first level of these workshops will usually focus on creating and refining the vision and making sure the group involved agrees with the specific language and the meaning of that language to them.

The next round will usually involve a "working draft" of the vision, so that the attendees will feel comfortable suggesting changes. After this round, the leaders may want to regroup and consider which changes to accept and then produce a draft of the vision that incorporates the suggested changes from the other employee groups.

The final round of vision workshops will include a cross section of the next levels, functions, or divisions of the organization. If the organization is large, it will not be practical to involve all employees, so leaders should select a representative group from the levels, functions, or divisions. At this point, the vision should be considered "final" and ready to roll out across the entire organization.

The major reason to approach the development of the vision in face-to-face workshops of this sort is to begin to build support for it. Involving the employees in this way makes them feel part of the process. In addition, should the vision involve a major transformation in the organization's way of working or previous purpose, it can break down some of the barriers to change and allow organizational leaders to obtain important input from the employees in shaping a vision that is actionable and meaningful at all levels.

With most companies, once a few levels or groups of the organization have been involved and a good cross section of employees have had a chance to react to the mission and vision, leaders can feel fairly comfortable that the mission and the vision statements are acceptable and ready for the outside world to see.

Although following the steps outlined in the vision development process here takes time, the process will ensure the creation of a mission and a vision that will guide the actions of the organization. Employees need to know why the company exists and where it plans to go for their work to support the mission and contribute to accomplishing the vision.

Going through some sort of visioning discussion and particularly following a cascading workshop approach can strengthen internal communication by bringing forward agreements and disagreements even among senior management so that the organization can create a shared view of its focus and direction. In fact, in some cases, the process of creating the vision may do more to galvanize the organization by clarifying its direction than the end products of the process—the mission and vision statements.

Designing and Implementing Effective Change Communication

Organizational change is inevitable yet rarely easy. Many organizational change efforts fail to deliver the value the organization seeks. For instance, mergers are one of the most frequent causes of major organizational change, but only a few yield the anticipated or hoped for results. A *Harvard Business Review* article reports that companies spent $3.3 trillion in 1999 on mergers and acquisitions, yet "less than half ever reached their strategic and financial goals."[14] The reason for this failure will usually rest on the softer side of the merger, the side of culture, process, and people.

The greatest difficulty leaders face in bringing about change involves the people. To achieve successful change, leaders must confront the challenges of reaching the employees through effective leadership communication before, during, and after any major, organizationwide change programs. Without effective employee communication and a rigorous approach to the leadership communication, a change program has little chance to succeed.

In her book *The Change Monster*, Jeanie Daniel Duck says, "Communication is always critical but never more so than when you're trying to get others to see and do things differently. . . . If leaders want to change the thinking and actions of others, they must be transparent about their own. If people within the organization don't understand the new thinking or don't agree with it, they will not change their beliefs or make decisions that are aligned with what's desired."[15]

In "Leading Change: Why Transformation Efforts Fail," Kotter lists "undercommunication" as one of the major reasons change efforts do not succeed. As he says, "Transformation is impossible unless hundreds or thousands of people are willing to help, often to the point of making short-term sacrifices. Employees will not make sacrifices, even if they are unhappy with the status quo, unless they believe that useful change is possible. Without credible communication, and a lot of it, the hearts and minds of the troops are never captured."[16]

The organization's leaders bear the primary responsibility for successfully communicating the rationale for the changes, the implementation plans, and the impact on the organization as a whole and on the individual employees. The leaders will need to decide how much communication will be enough and to establish how to manage the change communication effectively.

The following discussion goes through a leadership approach to change communication that begins with determining the scope of the communication program. Next, this section illustrates a best practice approach to structuring a change communication program that includes establishing a change communication leadership team and using interactive change meetings.

Determining the Scope of Change Communication

The magnitude of the proposed organizational changes and the effectiveness of the current internal communication practices will determine the scope of the change communication program. To determine how comprehensive the communication program needs to be, the organization's leaders should first assess how effective the current internal communication practices are and decide if they are strong enough to support major change.

Again, the scorecard presented in Exhibit 11.2 or a similar instrument can serve as a start to the assessment. If the current approach to internal communication falls short in any of the dimensions included in the scorecard, the organization will need to make some improvements in internal communication before launching a change effort.

For example, if the media the organization currently uses are not effectively reaching all employees, how will the organization reach them with major change messages? If the leadership team currently does not see communication as one of its primary responsibilities, how can the organization depend on the team to communicate the change messages effectively?

Internal communication practices need to be working well to facilitate all employees' receiving, understanding, and accepting the change messages.

Next, to establish the level of change being considered and thus, the amount of communication necessary, leaders should ask the following questions:

1. Is the proposed change a major transformation for the organization or does it only consist of incremental adjustments?
2. Does the change involve the entire organization or is it focused on one group or a narrow process?
3. How many people in the organization will be involved and affected?

If the changes are major and essential to the organization's future success or overall performance, the leaders will need to develop a complete

EXHIBIT 11.6
Levels of Change
Communication
Effort

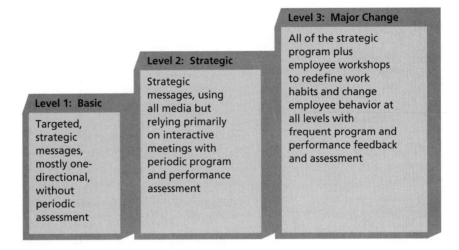

Level 1: Basic

Targeted, strategic messages, mostly one-directional, without periodic assessment

Level 2: Strategic

Strategic messages, using all media but relying primarily on interactive meetings with periodic program and performance assessment

Level 3: Major Change

All of the strategic program plus employee workshops to redefine work habits and change employee behavior at all levels with frequent program and performance feedback and assessment

change communication plan as part of the change program. Exhibit 11.6 demonstrates three possible levels of communication effort, depending on the extent of the change proposed.

For a simple change in policy, for example, the organization could probably succeed by using Level 1: Basic communication. The messages still need to be targeted, but little, if any follow-up assessment would be necessary.

For a more complex change, such as the introduction of new performance measures and reward systems across all groups, leaders might choose the "strategic" level, using several media to ensure that all employees receive the information on the changes and holding meetings to ensure that managers, in particular, understand when and how to use the measures. The leaders would probably follow up with an assessment at some point to make sure all employees understand the proposed changes and their impact on them.

For a major change, such as merging two companies, moving the organization in a new direction, or developing new products or services, leaders would probably want to select Level 3: Major Change and develop a complete change communication program using the following approach.

Structuring a Communication Program for Major Change

Exhibit 11.7 provides an example of a three-phased change communication plan for major change. Each of the three phases specifies actions the leaders would want to take to develop and implement the change communication strategy. Even though an organizationwide change program would not flow linearly or as neatly as depicted in Exhibit 11.7, organizational leaders would still want to create a simple overview map of how they expect the change communication plan to progress.

EXHIBIT 11.7
Three-Phased
Change
Communication
Action Plan

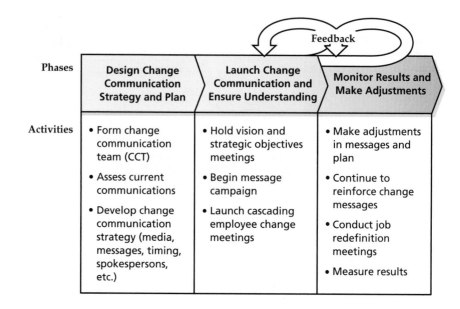

Phases	Design Change Communication Strategy and Plan	Launch Change Communication and Ensure Understanding	Monitor Results and Make Adjustments
Activities	• Form change communication team (CCT) • Assess current communications • Develop change communication strategy (media, messages, timing, spokespersons, etc.)	• Hold vision and strategic objectives meetings • Begin message campaign • Launch cascading employee change meetings	• Make adjustments in messages and plan • Continue to reinforce change messages • Conduct job redefinition meetings • Measure results

Creating such a plan will be useful for thinking through program staging issues and ensuring consideration of all important actions and their timing. In addition, such an action plan can be useful in reassuring the organization. It suggests order and a plan in all of the chaos that usually accompanies major change.

As the discussion in Chapter 10 on team action and work plans pointed out, action plans require frequent updating to remain accurate in guiding activities. They evolve as the project unfolds; therefore, they need periodic feedback loops to capture information coming in that affects the plan once the change program is underway. In addition to this high-level action plan, the leadership team will need a very detailed work plan to specify all actions, responsibilities, and deadlines.

Phase 1: Design Change Communication
Strategy and Plan

The first phase of strategy development is critical to the success of any change communication program. Leaders should use their best leadership skills to guide the organization away from initiating changes immediately without first determining what specific actions are needed and how best to communicate them. Leaders should think carefully about the specific changes the employees will need to understand and make in their day-to-day jobs to accomplish the major organization wide change objectives. The from/to problem-solving tool introduced in Chapter 9 will be useful in analyzing and capturing the specific changes at all levels and of all types (see the example in Exhibit 9.4).

The change leaders will need to develop a communication strategy that includes audiences, media, messages, spokespersons, and timing, at a minimum. Also, they may need to assess the current employee communication situation to determine if they have the media/forums currently in place to ensure that change messages will reach the intended targets. They must know where the communication breakdowns are and how best to reach the organization with the key change messages.

Before assessing the current communication practices or developing the strategy, the change leaders may want to put together a team to help them, since major change requires a lot of leadership's time and attention. A change communication team (CCT) can assist in analyzing the needs and implementing the change communication program. A full-scale change communication program requires resources dedicated to communication.

Depending on the organization and the type of changes, the leaders will probably want the team to consist of a multilevel, cross-functional group of employees and cross-cultural representative of the organization. Having diverse, frontline, operational employees on the team provides definite benefits if the organization is implementing change affecting all employees. It can often mean the difference between the employees' accepting the changes or rejecting them as another management fad of the day. Such a team will often become part of the mechanism to ensure that the changes remain after the "official" team no longer exists.

Although the CCT membership needs to reflect the culture and structure of the organization, team members should have the following basic characteristics:

- Representative of all levels, functions, geographic locations (if relevant).
- Respected and trusted by their peers.
- Open and honest communicators.
- Skilled at interacting with others and facilitating discussions.

Also, team members need to be able to break away from their regular duties to dedicate the time needed. The team members need to be fully dedicated, since they will need to work rapidly to make any needed improvements in employee communication, develop the strategy, and launch into aggressive communication with the entire organization.

Having a team dedicated to communication will make the change program run much more smoothly. In addition to helping develop the strategy, they can serve as change ambassadors who can reach deep into the organization to ensure widespread understanding of the change messages.

EXHIBIT 11.8
Sample Change
Communication
Team Structure

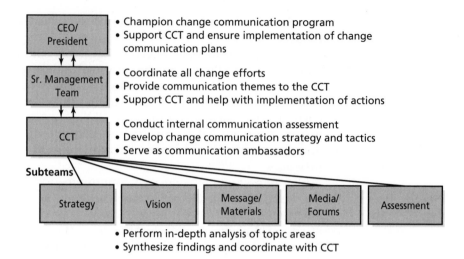

CEO/President
• Champion change communication program
• Support CCT and ensure implementation of change communication plans

Sr. Management Team
• Coordinate all change efforts
• Provide communication themes to the CCT
• Support CCT and help with implementation of actions

CCT
• Conduct internal communication assessment
• Develop change communication strategy and tactics
• Serve as communication ambassadors

Subteams: Strategy | Vision | Message/Materials | Media/Forums | Assessment
• Perform in-depth analysis of topic areas
• Synthesize findings and coordinate with CCT

After change leaders have established the core CCT and the team has completed the preliminary analysis and strategy development, the team may want to break into subteams to focus on different aspects of the change communication strategy. Exhibit 11.8 provides an example of how a CCT might fit into the organization and how the subteams might be organized. In this example, some of the subteams correspond to the components of the strategic employee model, but others are outgrowths of the preliminary assessment and the specific areas determined to be priorities for change communication in this company. The subteams will probably work independently, but to be most effective, they need to interact frequently to avoid duplication of effort and ensure that no issues remain unresolved.

A strong CCT serves as the linchpin of the development and implementation of the change communication strategy and plan. The team can provide information from management to the organization, help translate messages to employees at all levels, and bring credibility to the change communication effort. One additional result of a CCT is that having a cross-functional, multilevel team will help the organization see communication as a responsibility of all employees.

Phase 2: Launch Change Communication and Ensure Employee Understanding

The first step in launching the change communication plan is to start communicating the change messages, getting them out to the organization through the media determined in the CCT's analysis. If an organization already has an acceptable vision, the change leaders may want to measure the organization's understanding of it and reinforce it before launching into delivery of the change messages. Often, however, the vision no longer works for an organization undergoing major changes, and the organization will need to create a new vision with strategic objectives to support it. Since the change communication needs to move fast to stay out in front of the rumor mill, the most efficient approach may be for the organization's leaders to convene and develop a new initial vision that captures the organization's new direction, but to be most effective, they would want to build the development of the vision into the change process and use the leader-driven, employee-involvement approach described previously in this chapter. Allowing employee involvement in the creation of the vision during major change will increase their understanding and acceptance of the new direction and what the changes mean to them.

Once the vision is in place and the communication campaign launched, the change leaders will want to start bringing the organization into the change more directly and specifically. To do so means the organization's leaders and perhaps members of the CCT will need to meet personally with all employees. These should be interactive meetings in which to communicate the case for change and major change messages. The format should allow for and encourage employee questions about and reactions to the proposed changes. The goal in these meetings is to ensure that employees really understand the change messages and know what they mean to them personally, as well as how they are to perform their jobs. All employees need to feel part of the change process, and the more they can contribute to the change discussions, the more they will start to internalize the proposed changes.

Phase 3: Monitor Results and Make Adjustments

As soon as the change messages have reached the entire organization and meetings held with the employees to communicate with them directly, the change leaders should plan to stop and assess the employee understanding. It is a good idea to survey a cross section of the employees and conduct a few carefully planned focus groups.

The survey results will help the change leaders determine if they need to make any changes in the messages or media and if they need to conduct additional meetings. If the changes involve a major change of focus in the organization, then the change leaders may find that they need to conduct some job redefinition sessions that will allow employees to understand better how their specific job activities will need to change within the altered organization.

It helps employees to understand the changes if they can see the key objectives as they are now and as they will be in the new organization once the change program is completed. Again, a from/to analysis is useful in determining the changes and explaining them to employees. For example, a computer company might have the from/to for its strategic objectives as illustrated in Exhibit 11.9.

EXHIBIT 11.9
Example of a From/To Table for Strategic Objectives

Strategic Objectives	From	To
Providing computer products at superior value	Hardware, software, and solutions for all computers Value to us, but high cost to customer	Hardware and solutions for servers and complex enterprise systems only Low cost, high value to customer
Creating integration	Fragmented products and services in isolated pockets	Connected components within the enterprise system

Once the employees can see the changes at a higher level, their immediate supervisors will probably want to meet with them to develop the specific changes in each job function. Again, the from/to works well. The employees would look critically at what their job entails now and what it will involve as a result of the change. For some employees, the change may be small, which will be reassuring to them. For those who have to make major changes in the way they work, these sessions should help make those changes more tangible to them, which again could be reassuring, since any ambiguity around the changes would be removed.

Throughout the change process, the change leaders should involve as many supervisors as possible in the change meetings and job redefinition sessions. Not only does their involvement show their support for the change program, but it also allows them to see employees at work in the organization in ways that differ from day-to-day operations. Often, hidden talent emerges in interactive employee meetings. Organizational leaders may want to elevate some of the high performers to different positions in the organization during or after the change program. Also, the CCT may want to recruit some of the employees who stand out to serve as additional ambassadors and even facilitators for future change meetings.

Just as change leaders want to communicate aggressively at the beginning of the change program to help employees understand the new direction and the meaning of the changes, they will want to communicate successes along the way and ensure that the organization hears how well the change program is progressing. Finally, at the end of the change program, the organization will need to measure the results.

Underlying any successful change communication program are the continual signals along the way that change is happening and that the change is making a positive difference in the way the organization performs. The program will not be judged a success unless it makes a meaningful difference not only for the employees but also for the organization overall. Communication is the key to ensuring that the organization sees and understands the differences being brought about by the changes. Without a well-planned and well-executed change communication strategy, no change program can succeed.

In conclusion, from the day-to-day exchanges to the major efforts associated with organizational change, internal communication is important to the success of any organization. The strategy for internal communication consists of the basic components of any effective communication strategy, such as audience analysis, targeted messages, and appropriate media, but it is also much more than processes and products. Leaders need all their leadership communication abilities to inspire, motivate, and guide employees to support their visions and their goals for the organization.

Through internal communication, organizational leadership emerges and succeeds in creating and transforming organizational culture. Internal communication holds an organization together. Good internal communication enables the smooth operation of the organization when interwoven seamlessly into all other processes of the organization. It is up to the leaders to make internal communication a priority. Leadership inside an organization depends on it.

Application 11.1 **Merging Benefits**	**The Case: Huge Co. Revisited**

Huge Co. (you may want to review the facts in the Huge Co. case in Chapter 4) has now developed the new benefits program for the software managers based on the consulting company's report, which incorporated an assessment of best practices in the industry and consultation with benefits managers at both companies. The new program has the following features:

- Life insurance options will be unchanged for employees from both pre-merger companies. Huge Co. will pay for a base level of insurance (two times salary) and the employee can elect to pay for additional coverage.

- A flexible spending account is a new key feature, under which employees can set aside pretax dollars for medical spending or dependent care. This will be a new feature for the CC employees.

- A vendor who is new to both companies will provide medical insurance, but the new company offers a broader choice of physicians than either plan previously, and employees will retain several choices about the type of plan they enroll in. Employees who actively participate in exercise classes and other health maintenance activities will receive additional credit toward health care deductibles.

- Dental/orthodontic insurance is optional and, if elected, is paid for by the employee.

- Vision will not be offered, but would be covered under the flexible spending account.

- The company will match 401K contributions up to 12 percent of salary, and stock options will be offered to high-performing software engineers.

The change team (CT) has managed the major integration of the two companies, and they have asked for your input on a task that has a smaller scope but is essential to the continued success of the company: advising the software engineers of both companies about their new plan. As Mariel Salinas, the former benefits manager at Computer Co., your new position will encompass all the benefits for the two merged companies.

You believe the new plan is consistent with the mission and vision of the merged companies and that it really is the "best of both worlds" in merging the plans from the two companies. The new flexible spending account will be attractive to the software engineers. Most of the other key features of the plans remain fairly similar, with only a few key changes.

The Assignment

You, as Mariel, have been asked by the CT to develop a communication program to roll out the new benefits to the approximately 5,500 software engineers across the company, which still has offices in four countries. You are expecting delivery of the booklets with all the key details of the plan within two weeks, but the information is readily available on their Web sites right now. You must consider the steps you will need to take to convey this information, the media you will use, the sequence of events, and the content of the communications about the new plan. Develop the communication program to submit to the CT. Remember that a key reason for the merger was adding the software engineers from Computer Co. to the Huge Co. team; they need to understand the new plan and to feel that they are valued members of the new team.

Application 11.2 Communicating Bad News to Internal Audiences

The Case: The HADWIT International Services Company

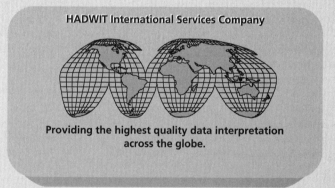

HADWIT International Services Company

Providing the highest quality data interpretation across the globe.

In 1998, you decided to open a small oil field services company based in Houston, Texas. Two friends from graduate school agreed to join you as investors, and you agreed to manage the business. Your company, Have Data Will Travel International Services Company (HADWIT), provides geological/geophysical consulting and computerized interpretation of the 3-D seismic data collected by surveyors working from boats offshore in the Gulf of Mexico, the North Sea, and the Pacific Rim. HADWIT data are critical to the exploration and production (E&P) companies because they form the basis for decisions on where to invest in oil and gas exploration and development. Many of your clients are major oil companies—such as Shell, Exxon/Mobil, and BP/Amoco—as well as a number of independents operating all over the world.

HADWIT's Initial Success

You began operations with 20 employees and trained them well. You are now up to 200 professionals with very specialized backgrounds in geology or geophysics and E&P data analysis. You wanted to develop a company known for high-quality services, and you wanted a stable, loyal workforce to represent you to the client. Your partners agreed with this philosophy, and you provided above-average salaries, paid vacations, health insurance, and annual bonuses.

As the company expanded, you placed employees overseas in offices in Singapore and Aberdeen, Scotland, to meet clients' on-site needs. Things were going well: Employees were happy, and the investors were satisfied with their return on investment. You credit some of the success to your fairly flat, team-based organization (Exhibit 11.10).

You have been operating on a substantial profit margin. Until recently, you had been billing out your professionals at 2 times their gross salary, but the market will now support only 1.5 times gross salary, which leaves you with no capacity for underutilization of people or resources. You have, however, been very generous in the past with bonuses for completing projects ahead of schedule and just for doing good work. In addition, your benefits package is beyond industry standards, with your picking up 80 percent of the premiums.

Market Changes Creating Need for Cost Cutting

In 2009, however, the oil industry went into a downturn, with oil prices fluxating and a worldwide recession tightening the market for everyone. Even though prices rebounded somewhat in 2008 just before the downturn, your customers' E&P budgets going into 2009 were strictly constrained; the ensuing decline in HADWIT projects led you to cut costs by dismissing four employees who were not performing up to par; cutting back on company perks, such as cars and expense accounts; and reducing travel budgets. You have seen similar

EXHIBIT 11.10
The HADWIT Team

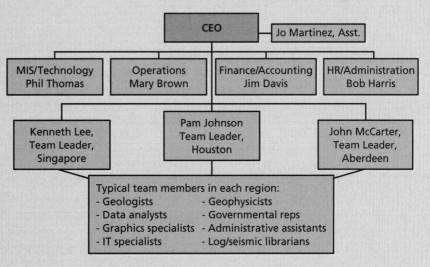

downturns, particularly after September 11, 2001. Now, with the collapse of former corporate giants and a sluggish economy, the demand for your services has fallen more; thus, HADWIT has experienced a serious loss of revenue coupled with increased costs.

So far, the numbers this year are not looking good. In fact, you estimate that profit will be down by around 25 percent this quarter and possibly even 50 percent by the next quarter Your partners are losing patience with the last few months of negative cash flow. Although they understand that HADWIT is a market-driven business and you cannot increase demand for your services, they think that your costs are still too high, and they want you to consider laying off a significant portion of your workforce.

CEO Contemplating Cost-Cutting Measures

To date, you have run a first-class operation and have spared no costs when it comes to providing what your employees need, especially when they are overseas and out of the office, working in your clients' facilities. In fact, compared with your competitors' costs, your research shows that your overhead for each employee averages about 15 percent more per year. In addition, you have just purchased the latest computer hardware and software, which allows you to (1) work more efficiently, (2) provide data services others cannot, and (3) connect virtually across the globe. While you know you can cut some of your overhead, you fear that doing so will result in unhappy employees and dissatisfied customers and will not be enough to turn the company around.

This brings you to the possibility of closing offices and laying off employees. Most of the employees have been with the company for several years and all are doing excellent work. In addition, many of your clients depend on having the pick of your staff on-site anytime they want them; up to now, this "on demand" team formation has never been a problem, since you have had the staff to cover client preferences. Your company is built on the principle that HADWIT should provide clients what they want, when they want it, and where they want it. Thus, you expect that letting staff go will cause some clients to be very uneasy about doing business with your company, particularly since most of your employees have direct relationships with your major clients.

Your clients like having people on the ground in Singapore or Aberdeen. Although they can adjust, it will take away from their flexibility and sense of having a "local" service provider. Even though you may be able to convince the customers that this is a short-term move that will not affect the quality or speed of your services, some of them will not take the news well. You fear that you even run the risk of losing them, which you certainly cannot afford, given the current negative cash flow. You hope that you can convince your clients that, since you have all the equipment you need to service any company anywhere in the world from your offices in Houston, they need not worry. Also, since most of the consultants work on-site, you can still send your people to work with clients in the North Sea, or in any other location, as long as the client picks up per diem (daily) expenses.

Partners Demanding Drastic Measures

You have seen the oil industry recover from cycles like this one before, so you hope that, if you can hold out a while longer, things will turn around; however, you meet with your partners, and they want action now. After some heated discussion, you agree to start reducing your costs by 25 percent immediately, which you know will mean you are going to have to let some portion of your workforce go after all.

Your first step following the meeting with the partners is to look for additional ways to cut costs without downsizing staff. You decide to decrease the company's contribution to health and dental insurance, cancel all bonuses, and eliminate paid vacations. You consider even asking all employees to accept a 10 percent salary cut for next year. Also, you decide that you will have to close your offices in Aberdeen and Singapore, even though you know your clients will not be happy about it. That means you will have to let 10 administrative support staff and some geotechs go, in Aberdeen and in Singapore, and will need to relocate all of the higher-level technical people to Houston, where you will centralize all operations. After your initial analysis, however, you see no way to reach the targeted numbers without a substantial reduction in staff. You are extremely concerned about the effect these cuts will have on your company and your people.

You decide to hold a meeting with the management team, which includes all of your direct reports (team leaders in each location, who will be protective of their staff in each country and want to keep their locations open). In the meeting, you want to work through all possible ways to reduce costs and look at which staff you can cut. You also realize that, given the seriousness of the messages you will be sending internally and externally, you need to devote some of your own time to consider your most important audiences and the messages to send to them.

The Assignment

First, develop a communication strategy for all your internal audiences. Second, write a memo to the management team, delivering the news about the need to cut costs and downsize the workforce and inviting them to the meeting. This memo is an opportunity for you to lay out any issues to be considered and any concerns that you have about the situation, as well as tell them what you expect them to do in general and in preparation for the meeting. Think carefully about this audience. While you will want to provide the truth about what is to happen, you also need to try to allay their concerns as much as possible. These are the leaders in your organization and some of your best people, and you certainly do not want to lose any of them at this crucial time in the company's history. Thus, you need to consider the tone you use and the information these managers will want to have and need to hear. Third, develop an agenda for the meeting establishing objectives, end products, and content.

Source: Case and assignment developed by Deborah J. Barrett and Beth O'Sullivan. Copyright 1999. Revised 2009. Used with permission.

Application 11.3
Developing a
Change
Communication
Strategy

The Case: Rescuing Fly High

The management of Fly High knew they needed to turn the company around immediately. They were constantly rated low in customer satisfaction polls, they were the worst in handling baggage (more lost and more damaged than any of their major competitors), the complaints from passengers had grown by 25 percent, and the employee morale was at its lowest level ever. Fly High was losing money and on the verge of having to lay off hundreds of its 50,000 employees.

The board was placing the company's future in the hands of a new CEO and the management team she was bringing with her. The board had essentially cleaned house, but, then, it was not the first time new management had been brought in to try to turn things around. Fly High had gone through constant change in leadership at the top as well as frequent downsizing and reorganizations, but they had not been able to turn the company around.

The company needed to make drastic changes and fast, and it needed to make them across the entire company, from baggage handlers to pilots. From the reservation desk to the hangars to the corporate offices and the rest of the employees scattered across the globe, no one talked to or worked with anyone else. In fact, the different locations seemed knowingly or unknowingly to work against each other and against the goals of the total company. Some of the middle- and lower-level management adopted an extreme command and control and silo thinking approach to managing, while others used a team-based, participative, cross-functional culture. Employees had reached a point of complacency and cynicism. They lacked a performance ethic and felt management was not open to their ideas about the company. Cutting across all the levels in the organization was a lack of trust for Fly High management and now a lot of skepticism that this new management team would make a difference.

Fly High needed a major change program across the entire company involving all levels of the organization; however, the internal communication was so poor that they did not know where to begin. Communication across the organization or up or down the organizational chain of command was almost nonexistent. A recent HR survey had revealed specific problems in internal communications: Key messages across the company had changed so often that employees were confused and unclear as to the company's vision, many employees felt afraid to express their ideas or concerns, and management appeared isolated and nonreceptive to the employees at lower levels of the organization. It was clear that the company seriously needed to improve internal communications before any change program could have impact.

The Assignment

As part of this new management team, you are charged with addressing the communication challenges and establishing the change communication program. Outline the steps you would take and develop an action plan for improving communication that will feed directly into the larger change program that Fly High needs to undertake.

Notes

1. *Ragan Survey of CEO Communications.* (2001). A Ragan Research Report, supported by the International Association of Business Communication, p. 6.
2. *Ragan Survey of CEO Communication* (2002), p. 7.
3. Smidts, A. Pruyn, A. T. H., and van Riel, C. B. M. (2001). The Impact of Employee Communication and Perceived External Prestige on Organization Identification. *Academy of Management Journal* 49, p. 1059.
4. Clampitt, P. G., and Downs, C. W. (1993). Employee Perceptions of the Relationship between Communication and Productivity: A Field Study. *Journal of Business Communication* 30, pp. 5–28; Downs, C. W., Clampitt, P. G., and Pfeiffer, A. L. (1988). Communication and Organization Outcomes.

In G. M. Goldhaber and G. A. Barnett (Eds.), *Handbook of Organizational Communication.* Norwood, NJ: Ablex, pp. 171–212; Frank, A., and Browness, J. (1989). *Organizational Communication and Behavior: Communicating to Improve Performance.* Orlando, FL: Holt, Rinehart & Winston; Jablin, F. M. (1979). Superior-subordinate Communication: The State of the Art. *Psychological Bulletin* 86, pp. 1201–22.

5. *Connecting Organization Communication to Financial Performance: 2003/2004 Communication ROI Study.* (2004). Watson Wyatt Worldwide.

6. Tucker, B. A., and Russell, R. F. (2004). The Influence of the Transformational Leader. *Journal of Leadership and Organizational Studies* 10, pp. 103–11.

7. The components of this model emerged from the best practices in employee communication found in interviews conducted with and research conducted on several Fortune 500 companies. While no company exemplified all the best practice components exactly as presented in the definitions, they each serve as the ideal components of effective employee communication. The model was created by Deborah J. Barrett based on this research. The model and some of the research have been presented by Deborah J. Barrett at Association for Business Communication and International Association for Business Communication conferences. They are published in her article "Change Communication: Using Strategic Employee Communication to Facilitate Major Change. *Corporate Communication: An International Journal* 7, pp. 219–31, which appeared in 2002.

8. Welch, J., and Welch, S. (April 20, 2009). Obama: A Leadership Report Card, *Business Week*, p. 96.

9. Collins, J., and Porras, J. I. (1994). *Built to Last.* New York: Harper.

10. Tucker and Russell (2004).

11. Peters, T. J. (1988). *Thriving on Chaos: Handbook for a Management Revolution.* New York: Alfred A. Knopf, pp. 399–408. Peters uses these characteristics in a discussion of effective visions, but many of them apply more to missions as defined in this chapter.

12. Jick, T. D. (1989). The Vision Thing. Harvard Business School Case, pp. 1–7.

13. www.wholefoodsmarket.com.

14. Ashkenas, R. N., and Francis, S. C. (2000). Integration Managers: Special Leaders for Special Times. *Harvard Business Review,* November–December, pp. 108–16.

15. Duck, J. D. (2001). *The Change Monster: The Human Forces That Fuel or Foil Corporate Transformation and Change.* New York: Crown.

16. Kotter, J. P. (1995). Leading Change: Why Transformation Efforts Fail. *Harvard Business Review on Change.* Boston: Harvard Business School Press. For information on communicating change across cultures, see Barrett, D. J. (2005/2006). Successful Cross-Cultural Communication during Major Change. *International Journal of Knowledge, Culture, and Change Management* 5, No. 8. www.management-journal.com.

Chapter 12

Leadership Through Effective External Relations

A CEO is ultimately responsible for the growth of a company as evidenced by its financial performance, its capacity for self-renewal, and its character. The only way you can measure character is by reputation.

Roberto Goizueta, CEO, Coca-Cola, quoted in *Fortune,* March 6, 1995

To become well regarded, companies must deserve it. They must develop coherent images and a consistency of posture internally and externally. Identity and self-presentation beget reputation.

Charles J. Fombrun, (1996) *Reputation: Realizing Value from the Corporate Image.* Boston: Harvard Business School Press.

Chapter Objectives

In this chapter, you will learn to do the following:

- Develop an external relations strategy.
- Build and maintain a positive corporate image.
- Work with the news media.
- Handle crisis communications.

A positive public image or reputation affects a company's ability to achieve all other measures of success. The companies with the best corporate reputations outperform all others. The top five companies in the Harris Interactive annual Reputation Quotient survey for 2008 list of the best in corporate reputation—Johnson & Johnson, Google, Sony, Coca-Cola, and Kraft Foods—combine good reputations with strong financial performance.[1]

Hill & Knowlton, one of the leading public relations firms, found in its 2006 study that "90 percent of analysts agree that if a company fails to look after reputational aspects of its performance, it will ultimately suffer financially, too."[2] The Harris Interactive survey included the following categories: "Emotional Appeal, Products & Services, Social Responsibility, Vision & Leadership, Workplace Environment, and Financial Performance," and the companies with the best reputations excelled in all of these areas.

Aon's Global Risk Management Survey 2007, based on responses from 320 organizations in 29 countries, found that "damage to reputation" is the number one risk among the top 10 risks listed by respondents to the survey.[3] Negative public sentiment hurts internal and external reputations, resulting in lost morale among employees and potentially, in tremendous financial loss to a company. Just look at the damage to Domino's Pizza caused by a prank by two Domino employees. They filmed themselves putting food up their noses and placing nasal mucus on food they were supposedly preparing for delivery. They then posted their video on YouTube. In a short time, through the power of social media, "the video had been viewed more than a million times on YouTube. References to it were in five of the 12 results on the first page of Google search for 'Dominos,' and discussions about Domino's had spread throughout Twitter."[4]

Despite the two apologizing for the prank and saying they never delivered any contaminated food, Domino's reputation was damaged and their sales plummeted. According to one online survey, "The perception of its quality among consumers went from positive to negative" overnight.[5] Reputation is so important that Warren Buffet is quoted as saying, "If you lose dollars for the firm, I will be understanding. If you lose reputation for the firm, I will be ruthless." Obtaining a positive reputation is challenging for any organization, but regaining one that is lost can be next to impossible.

Managing the public's perception of an organization is one of the primary jobs of leadership, and in particular, the top leader's personal image affects the company image. Hill & Knowlton's *Corporate Reputation Watch* reports that 84 percent of the CEOs responding to the survey believe that the CEO's reputation "extremely influences" the corporate reputation, and 77 percent report that CEOs are primarily responsible for managing their company's corporate reputation.[6]

Just as the leaders determine the personality of the organization on the inside, they also shape the outside image. An organization has an ethos, just as an individual does. The goal of organizational leaders is to ensure that the company's ethos is positive—that all external audiences consider the company honorable, trustworthy, and ethical. Managing external relations effectively is essential to achieving that goal and essential to leadership communication in any organization.

Any communication activity that touches an organization's outside constituencies—such as advertising, sales promotions, direct marketing, or public relations—falls into the category of external relations. All of these are important and influence how the public perceives the organization. Also, these activities must all be coordinated as part of an overall external relations campaign so that all messages are consistent and delivered effectively.

However, the focus of this chapter is primarily on the activities usually considered public relations, including press and media management, philanthropic activities, community involvement, investor relations, and external publications (for example, annual reports and company magazines). Organizations must manage all aspects of external relations very carefully. They all affect the organization's public ethos. In most organizations, the leadership communication ability of the leaders has the greatest impact on that external ethos through their involvement in public relations.

This chapter provides guidelines to help manage external relations in day-to-day encounters and in crisis situations so that the organization projects a positive image. You will learn how to apply the communication strategy model introduced in Chapter 2 to external relations, how to shape a positive image, how to deal with the media, and finally, how to manage crisis communications.

Developing an External Relations Strategy

Effective external relations require a sound communication strategy. As leaders have done with other communication situations, they can use the communication strategy framework, Exhibit 12.1, to guide them in addressing the entire range of external audiences. With the framework in mind, they should take the following steps to create a strategy for external audiences:

1. Clarify the purpose and strategic objectives.
2. Identify major audiences or stakeholders.
3. Create, refine, and test major messages.
4. Select, limit, and coach the spokesperson(s).
5. Establish the most effective media or forums.
6. Determine the best timing.
7. Monitor the results.

EXHIBIT 12.1
Communication
Strategy
Framework

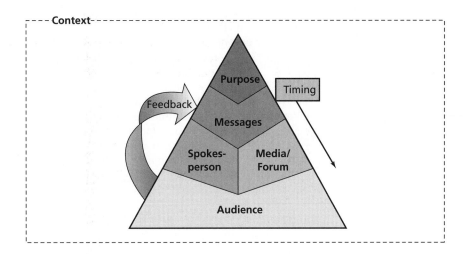

Clarifying Purpose and Strategic Objectives

A company must have a strategy for all of its external relations activities: managing the press and media, coordinating philanthropic activities and community involvement, establishing relationships with financial analysts or investor groups, and creating and managing all publications and electronic interactions with all stakeholders. A central and consistent purpose radiating from the very top of the organization should govern all external communication activities. As discussed in Chapter 7, the CEO and his or her direct reports determine the personality of a company, and as discussed in this chapter, that personality influences the corporate reputation, the ethos of the company. Given these lines of influence, it is clearly the responsibility of the CEO and his or her staff to establish a strategy for external relations.

Ideally, a company's internal ethos and external image will be consistent, with a few central themes permeating all day-to-day activities as well as any crisis situations that may arise. The major corporate themes usually embody the vision, mission, and strategic objectives, as discussed in Chapter 11. The logos, slogans, letterhead, business cards, Web site, blogs, and any promotional materials, often called collaterals, reinforce these themes. Although the logos and slogans are too abbreviated to capture all of the company's themes, they should reflect the major ones and certainly suggest the personality of the organization. Leaders will want to approach the development of all promotional materials strategically and analytically to ensure support for as well as consistency with the organization's strategic purpose and objectives.

For example, a few years ago, the Houston Grand Opera (HGO), one of the premier opera companies in the world, decided to change its logo

EXHIBIT 12.2
Mission Statement
for the Houston
Grand Opera

Source: www.houston
grandopera.org

> The mission of **Houston Grand Opera** is to bring larger and more diverse audiences together for exciting opera in a financially responsible way.
>
> **Supporting Principles** of Houston Grand Opera will
>
> - Be defined by the **excellence** of its work.
> - Provide a **memorable** experience.
> - Be artistically and administratively **imaginative, balanced,** and **responsible**.
> - Make an **impact** locally, regionally, nationally, and internationally.
> - Communicate a **welcoming** atmosphere, be accessible to all, and create an atmosphere of inclusiveness.
> - Hold **discovery** as a valuable goal in itself.

and image. It started by putting together a team to study the company's current reputation and future strategy. The HGO team determined that the messages it wanted to send to the public were that HGO is "fun, for everyone, and innovative." The team surveyed subscribers and nonsubscribers to obtain the public's perception of the opera company. After a few months of synthesizing the results and discussing them internally, HGO emerged with a new mission for the company (Exhibit 12.2).

After developing and testing the mission, HGO launched another team to establish its new logo and look. At first, they met some resistance to changing the logo, since HGO had used that logo for years, and the traditional operagoers loved the look and feel of it (Exhibit 12.3). It had dignity and suggested something solid and long-standing. However, HGO's general director at the time and several of the community leaders who supported the opera felt that the logo needed to be changed to reflect more directly HGO's innovative leadership in the opera world. After several months of surveys and focus groups, the team recommended a new logo (Exhibit 12.3).

The new logo suggested a company that was both traditional and innovative and captured the message of HGO's being expansive yet

EXHIBIT 12.3
Example of Logo
Change to
Emphasize New
Message

Source: Logos used with
permission of David Gock-
ley, director of the Houston
Grand Opera at the time of
the change.

Previous Logo	New Logo

inclusive. Through the new logo and the promotional activity that accompanied it, HGO was able to reinforce its messages to its public: HGO is innovative, is fun, and is for everyone. Soon afterward, the connection of the mission and the logo to the strategy of the company became obvious to the public when HGO unveiled a season with a perfect balance of traditional and innovative operas.

An organization's messages to the public are intertwined with everything that touches that public; to avoid confusion and unwanted associations, the messages communicated in all external materials should be clear and consistent. With this foundation in place, the company can then create specific messages for specific events as needed, from announcing new products to handling crisis communications. All organizations must have central, overarching messages or themes that they intend to deliver to the mass of individuals called their "stakeholders."

Identifying Major External Stakeholders

An organization's external stakeholders consist of any persons, groups, or entities outside the organization that may be affected by the its activities or interested in or influenced by its messages and image. The stakeholders are all audiences for the organization's messages. Depending on the company and industry, a list of stakeholders include the following:

1. Media
2. Community
3. Customers
4. Investors
5. Analysts
6. Board
7. Partners
8. Distributors
9. Suppliers or vendors
10. Trade associations
11. Unions
12. Interest groups
13. Retirees
14. Competitors
15. Government agencies
16. Public at large

The list should include anyone even remotely touched by the organization's products or services.

Once the organization has identified its stakeholders, it needs to establish priorities for reaching each one with its general message as well as specific messages tailored to individual groups. Again, the messages must be consistent, although they may differ slightly in their wording to ensure that the audiences understand them. While companies need to be careful not to exclude any audience or minimize its importance, priorities are necessary to an organized approach. Organizations need to determine how important as well as how difficult it is to reach each stakeholder.

Asking the following questions will help in prioritizing the external stakeholders:

EXHIBIT 12.4
Example Matrix
Analyzing
Stakeholders

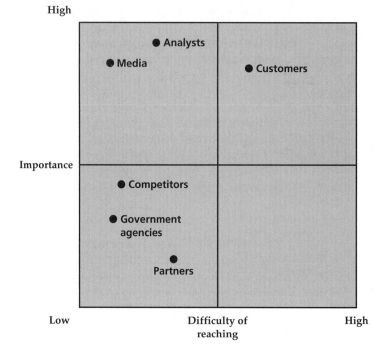

1. Who shapes or influences business or community opinions?
2. Who are the high-profile leaders in the community?
3. Who is well respected? Who is feared?
4. Who has high levels of responsibility within the community?
5. Whom do others regard as important or powerful in the area?
6. Who is actively involved in the community?
7. Who is in a demographic group affected by the organization?
8. Who has a financial or an emotional stake in the organization?
9. Who has the most to gain or lose because of what happens to the organization?
10. Who has a clear role in regulations or policies affecting the organization?
11. Who can undermine the organization's external relations campaign?

Exhibit 12.4 illustrates how an organization might use a matrix to determine the importance as well as the ease of reaching the different stakeholder groups.

Creating the Major Messages

What characterizes effective messages for external audiences? The 2008 Harris Reputation Quotient found that the following measures have the greatest impact on corporate reputations: "Sincerity, correctness and accuracy of information, and consistency."[7] To be most effective in building a positive reputation, leaders should ensure that all messages communicated to their external audiences conform to the following criteria:

- Honest
- Clear
- Consistent
- Meaningful

In addition, leaders need to realize that messages aimed at external audiences are far more vulnerable to interference, interruptions, and barriers than messages to internal audiences. Many external audiences will be only weakly motivated to attend to the messages, and they will often be ignorant of much of the knowledge organizations can assume for their internal audiences. For example, while we may be able to assume that an internal audience will know the jargon of our industry, we cannot assume that outsiders will. Thus, using industry jargon can become a barrier to communication. In addition, we would hope for the best intentions from internal audiences; however, for external audiences, assuming the best can be dangerous.

Leaders should be able to prevent the interruptions and overcome the barriers to reach their external audiences successfully if they ensure that all of their external messages conform to the listed criteria.

Honest

Not all audiences can see through false or deceptive messages, but an organization can do more harm to its reputation by getting caught lying than by telling an unpleasant truth. Honesty should be one of the underlying values and guiding principles of an organization's communication activities for external audiences as it is with internal audiences.

Clear

Assuming that our messages are clear is often not enough when dealing with external audiences. Just as we must scrutinize important internal messages, we should also test messages for external audiences to ensure that they will understand the messages as intended. Companies often use focus groups for this purpose.

Consistent

Consistency is essential in the messages an organization delivers to its public. Internal and external messages must be consistent. Also, messages delivered to different audiences through different networks must be consistent. Consistency does not mean messages cannot be tailored to the different stakeholders. The wording must be targeted to the specific audience, and it may differ slightly or the emphasis may shift to accommodate the varying needs and interests of different stakeholders, but the core message must remain the same.

Meaningful

Finally, the messages must be meaningful. Too often, companies water down their external messages so much that they no longer communicate any substance. This weakening of the message is particularly a problem in a crisis, but it occurs at other times as well. In some cases, the organization may not have taken the necessary time to determine what it wants to communicate. In other cases, organizations are intentionally equivocating or making the message ambiguous to avoid sending a negative message, to sidestep possible legal problems, or to obfuscate the facts.

A press release sent by the U.S. Food and Drug Administration (FDA), printed in its entirety in Exhibit 12.5, makes ambiguous statements

EXHIBIT 12.5
Example of
Ambiguity in a
Press Release

FDA Statement

FOR IMMEDIATE RELEASE
Statement
October 13, 2003

Media Inquiries: 301-827-6242
Consumer Inquiries:
888-INFO-FDA

FDA Statement on Foodborne Illness Risk Assessment

The U.S. Food and Drug Administration (FDA) today issued the following statement:

The headline of a story on the risk of illness from food, "Food Attack Likely, FDA Says" that ran under "Washington in Brief" in the October 11th Washington Post mischaracterizes the FDA report.

FDA prepared this qualitative risk assessment to accompany two new final rules, published October 10th, to improve food safety and security. It discusses both unintentional and intentional contamination of the food supply, because the goals of food safety and security are closely linked.

In drafting the risk assessment FDA relied heavily on the regular occurrence of foodborne illness outbreaks from accidental contamination in reaching the "high likelihood" prediction. The FDA report did not say there is a high likelihood of a terrorist attack in the next year. It did say there is a high likelihood of a significant foodborne illness outbreak in the next year (as there is every year) and that one possibility is that the outbreak would come from a terrorist attack. The actual "likelihood" of a significant terrorist attack on the food supply in the next year is difficult to quantify precisely.

Finally, the report is not "declassified" as the article asserts. FDA compiled the report, which was never classified, from the open literature.

while discussing problems caused by ambiguity in previous releases of information to the public. What the FDA's 12-page report contains is as follows:

> The agency has considered, for the purposes of risk characterization, the known exposure to food that has been inadvertently contaminated and the past incidents of deliberate contamination, as well as the evidence that terrorists have targeted our food supply. In light of this information and the uncertainties attendant to characterizing the risk of an act of food terrorism, FDA has concluded that there is a high likelihood, over the course of a year, that a significant number of people will be affected by an act of food terrorism or by an incident of unintentional food contamination that results in serious foodborne illness.[8]

What appeared in the newspaper is illustrated in Exhibit 12.6. When an organization sends unclear messages, it risks misinterpretation by the media and by the public. If, in addition, the organization has obscured the information, intentionally or unintentionally, by embedding the "sound bites" (concise messages designed to capture the

EXHIBIT 12.6
The Press's Coverage of the FDA Story

Food Attack Likely, FDA Says

WASHINGTON IN BRIEF
Saturday, October 11, 2003;
Page A13
Washington Post

There is a "high likelihood" within the coming year of a deliberate attack or accidental outbreak in the U.S. food supply that sickens a large number of people, the Food and Drug Administration said yesterday.

Although no specific threats were identified, the FDA said it came to the conclusion because of recent food-borne outbreaks and recent reports that al Qaeda was plotting to poison the food supply.

"FDA has concluded that there is a high likelihood, over the course of a year, that a significant number of people will be affected by an act of food terrorism or by an incident of unintentional food contami-nation that results in serious food-borne illness," the agency said in a declassified report.

The food supply was especially vulnerable because of the broad range of biological and chemical agents that can be used, the FDA said.

The agency said salmonella, E. coli 0157:H7 and ricin pose a significant threat because of their easy dissemination in food. Anthrax and botulism were considered the most deadly.

"so what?" in broadcast journalism) in long releases or complex reports, as in the example here, the organization risks distorted messages being conveyed to the public.

Messages that an organization sends to the broadcast media for transmission to the public need to be very brief so that they conform to the length of the typical sound bite. The essential information—the who, what, when, where, why, and how—must be covered in 10 to 20 seconds. Certainly, such conciseness can result in loss of substantive meaning; therefore, to counter media dilution, organizations should create the sound bites themselves. In addition to the sound bite version, however, organizations should have at their fingertips the details behind the "so what?" message.

Messages need to be concise and simple, but they also need to contain enough real information to be meaningful to any audience. The habit of using business jargon may interfere with clear communication, as discussed in Chapter 3. Other messaging faults can lead to more serious consequences. Business pronouncements that contain doublespeak (the use of ambiguous and often meaningless language) or fluff not only will frustrate the public and leave the organization open to misquoting and misunderstanding but cause the stakeholders to feel as though they are being deceived, which can destroy a company's ethos. For example, look at the following company announcement of pending layoffs:

> "As a result of our recently completed cost rationalization study, Proteus, Inc., will be performing some staff reduction activities in order to rightsize the organization and eliminate redundancies in the human resources area. We expect these workforce adjustments to start right away with some repositioning of staff and with termination services provided for all those employees who may be displaced."

No doubt the company is going to be firing employees, but by choosing to attempt to obscure the bad news, the company risks creating a strongly negative impression with their stakeholders.

In summary, when developing external messages, an organization's leaders need to spend the time to ensure that all messages are honest, clear, consistent, and meaningful. The time spent in the beginning will be fully justified if it avoids confusion or negative communication to any stakeholder. In the end, it is the organization's reputation that will suffer, and trying to correct misconceptions or a negative image is much more difficult than spending the time upfront to communicate with all stakeholders effectively.

Selecting and Coaching the Spokesperson(s)

Selecting the right spokesperson to deliver external messages can be almost as critical as the messages themselves. Three major rules apply to selecting spokespersons:

1. They must be at the right level for the problem.
2. They must project a positive ethos.
3. They should have received media training.

The rank of the spokesperson sends a message in itself. For instance, if the person is too high-ranking for the message being delivered, it could suggest that the issue being discussed is more important than it is. If the person is too low-ranking, it could signal that the organization does not view the issue as important enough to warrant the CEO's time.

An example from a fairly recent crisis communication situation concerns the Ford and Firestone/Bridgestone controversy, involving rollover accidents in Ford Explorers. Some people were very critical of Firestone/Bridgestone's choosing a vice president, instead of the CEO, to address the public, as Ford did. Although Firestone/Bridgestone may have had very good reasons for its decision, the public felt that the company did not view the accidents and resulting deaths as important enough to justify the CEO's time.

Next, the spokesperson must project a positive ethos. His or her credibility must be above reproach; otherwise, no message he or she delivers will be received as intended. Ethos relates both to how the person appears to the public and to how close he or she is to the situation. For example, in a crisis situation involving a pipeline explosion, an engineer on-site would have more firsthand knowledge and could answer the media's questions more specifically on the causes and mechanical problems; medical personnel would have better answers about the injuries; and depending on how serious the explosion is, the highest-level executive may be needed to suggest the company's concern for the injured. Deciding on the spokesperson is not easy and can require almost as much deliberation as is required for creating the messages.

Thinking back to the sources of ethos discussed in Chapter 1, it is best to select the spokesperson based on the following three of French and Raven's sources of power:

1. Legitimate—position or title.
2. Referent—charisma.
3. Expert—knowledge.

Even if the spokespersons possess all the sources of ethos, however, they should still receive media training before facing the press, opening a Twitter account, or creating a blog or social network presence. Many organizations provide formal training for any employees who might have to face the media or the public at any time. That training will usually include the who, what, when, and where of dealing with the media and the public as well as coaching on projecting a positive image (see "Working with the News Media" later in this chapter).

Establishing the Most Effective Medium or Forum

Deciding on the most effective medium or forum to ensure reaching the identified stakeholders is yet another critical component of external relations. An organization will often use several different media to reach external audiences, depending on the importance and magnitude of the communication event. For example, when the SEC was investigating Putnam Investments, Putnam used every available medium to reach its stakeholders. They sent letters to investors and e-mails to internal audiences; they crafted a carefully written press release for the news media and conducted a press conference with them; they posted releases, letters, and a video clip of two senior-level executives explaining the investigation on their Web site; and they published a "tombstone" (advertising statement). The table in Exhibit 12.7 provides an alphabetical list and describes each of the most frequently used external media and the limitations on using each one effectively.

Today, it is not enough to simply send messages out and wait for a reponse. The sending and the responding need to be immediate. The damage done by the Domino's Pizza's prank is a perfect example of what can happen if an organization is slow to become aware of negative press or slow to respond: "Domino's Pizza has become the latest company to learn how quickly a brand can be tainted in a Web 2.0 world—and how important it is to monitor social media. . . . If there's a lesson here, experts say, it's that companies must have an active presence on the Web—to monitor their brands continuously, perhaps enlisting loyal customers to help deal immediately with any damage."[9] Many of the traditional media used in the past are limited in their reach and response rate; thus, organizations must invest in current technology and leverage the power and speed of all the available social media.

Determining the Best Timing

As Domino's Pizza learned, timing is critical. With today's technology, being slow to respond makes the situation much worse. Domino's supposedly learned of the prank from a blogger. Then, the company responded with a Twitter account, and the president conveyed "his outrage" on YouTube. Domino's messages came 48 hours after the employee's video was posted and had already reached millions, too late

EXHIBIT 12.7   Characteristics and Limitations of External Media and Forums

Media/Forums	Characteristics	Limitations
Analyst's briefings	• Usually a presentation in person or as a phone or video conference. • Include a short, prepared statement on financial performance with backup financial information and time for Q&A.	• Require time to prepare materials and answers to anticipated questions and reliable financial analysis. • Spokesperson must be well prepared and credible.
Blogs	• Usually informal, even casual, so they foster connection. • Allows for public feedback and discussion	• Reach a limited audience. • Public feedback is unpredictable.
Editorials (in online or hard-copy news outlets)	• Allow company to voice an opinion on newsworthy topics. • Often, reliability of medium source adds credibility.	• Reach is limited to those who read newspapers. • May be seen as biased.
Fact sheets, or backgrounders	• Compilation of relevant information for the press or for analysts. • Usually contain information similar to a press release but presented in bullet form with highlights emphasized.	• Must be very carefully crafted to ensure that the major messages are captured and enough supporting information is supplied to appear substantive. • Too short to provide much more than the sound bites.
Hotlines	• Easily established numbers for stakeholders to call with specific questions or comments.	• Require coaching of respondents to ensure consistency of responses. • Need constant oversight.
Microblogs (Twitter, FriendFeed)	• Provide near real-time release of information. • Foster subscriptions • Allow information to be passed on easily.	• Very short (140 characters), so they can lead to misunderstanding. • Immediacy can lead to carelessness.
Podcasts or online videos	• Informative, focused, and short. • Inexpensive to produce. • Quick to release. • Foster subscriptions or sharing. • Can build positive brand reputation.	• Difficult to quantify impact. • Can damage image or brand.
Press conferences	• Meetings to which media are invited. • Company spokespersons present prepared statements and usually take questions. • May or may not be broadcast.	• Most influential media may not come. • Require careful planning and practice for the participants, not only in delivering the statements but also in anticipating the questions.

Press or media kits	• Usually contain the following:
	  – Press release.
	  – Fact sheet of company history.
	  – Relevant biographies and pictures.
	  – Contact information.
	  – Video clips.
		• Limited in space or press tolerance, so information must be very carefully organized for selective reading.

(continued)

EXHIBIT 12.7 (continued)

Media/forums	Characteristics	Limitations
Press releases	• Short, usually no more than a one-page definitive statement intended to be quoted by the media. • Start with the most important information and end with the least (releases are cut from the bottom); also contain contact information. • Intended for wide media distribution quickly.	• If sent as a blast fax and not followed up with personal contact, press releases have a hit-or-miss effect; therefore, they may not reach the intended audience and may attract no media interest or coverage.
RSS feeds	• Provide feeds of information that can be updated rapidly. • Encourage subscriptions.	• Only reach audience of subscribers.
Social networks (LinkedIn, Facebook)	• Places where organizations can create groups and share information with "fans." • Provide means of interacting with and reaching dedicated audience. • Can build brand reputation.	• Only reach those who opt in. • If not maintained, can damage brand reputation.
Town hall meetings	• Local gatherings of selected stakeholders. • Usually include prepared statements but allow for informal but controlled interaction between company representatives and stakeholders.	• Need to be facilitated skillfully or can turn into gripe sessions if the message being communicated is bad news.
Tombstones, or advertising statements	• Notices published in newspapers intended to reach the public with a specific message from the company.	• Expensive. • May be dismissed by the public as simply advertising.
Web sites	• May be specially designed Web sites for particular events or additions to the company's current Web site. • Convenient method for reaching a broad audience. • Allow for rapid dissemination of information that can be very persuasively crafted.	• Creation should be by a Web site design expert. • To be effective, they should meet the necessary criteria of an effective site: easy to navigate and informative, with contact information.

for their messages to do much more than fuel the story.[10] In this case, a rapid response was critical.

When organizations have the time to develop a communication strategy for communicating external messages, such as in announcements of new products or services or other news that can impact their external stakeholders, they need to consider the context, asking what is going on around their communication event that will influence how their audience receives their message. For example, announcing a major layoff at the same time as promoting and advertising an expensive sponsorship of a major sporting event will cause many employees to be even more resentful than they might have been if the announcement had been better timed. Google's announcement of its new e-mail product on April 1 was certainly questionable timing, since it left many thinking it was an April Fool's joke.

Also, the organization needs to consider the sequencing of the messages around a communication event. For instance, if a company is involved in a merger, it will need to consider the timing of every announcement down to the minute for both internal and all external stakeholders. Ideally, they will want their internal audiences to receive the announcement first, which can be challenging, since often the best timing for a merger announcement is not the best time to reach employees—early enough on Monday to influence the stock price. Depending on the company's public profile, how and when the public hears or sees the announcement will affect how they respond to it, just as when the announcement hits the market will impact investors' responses around the globe. Legal and regulatory requirements could also affect the timing of any announcements related to a merger.

What the Domino story teaches is that organizations must monitor all channels and know what stories about them are circulating through all the social media channels and be ready to respond in real time. Just as a crisis communication plan needs to be in place **before** the crisis, a plan for managing negative stories does as well. Any delay only makes the situation worse. However, when an organization can control the timing, they should look at it strategically and consider the context and their audiences.

Monitoring the Results

Organizations need to monitor their reputations constantly, but they also need to measure specifically the impact of day-to-day and major messages on their major constituencies. Larger, well-known companies will find their reputations monitored for them in yearly surveys, such as *Fortune*'s "Most Admired List," Harris Interactive's "Reputation Quotient," or The Customer Respect Group's online reports.

Two of the most common traditional methods used to obtain feedback from external stakeholders are focus groups and surveys (phone, Web, or mail). Holding effective focus groups and conducting useful surveys, however, require very careful planning and a clear and specific purpose. In-house employees must be proficient at survey methods and analysis to obtain reliable results. If they are not, a company should hire a market research firm or one of the many PR, external relations, or HR consulting firms that offer these services, since the

Corporate Leadership Communication

established firms have efficient and effective approaches to conducting focus groups and surveys and to analyzing the results.

One method gaining in popularity is online community forums. An example explored in *Groundswell* is a forum established by members of the National Comprehensive Cancer Network, including M.D. Anderson in Houston and Memorial Sloan-Kettering in New York. They hired Communispace, "one of the most rapidly growing vendors in the groundswell" to help them set up, monitor, and synthesize the results from the forum. Communispace "recruits three hundred to five hundred people in the client's target market . . . that looks like any other online social network, with profiles, discussion forums, online chat, and uploaded photos."[11] No one sees the forum site except the members, the moderators, and the organization.

For their efforts, the members receive gift certificates and agree to spend an hour a week on the site; however, patients in the cancer community group reported they participate more for the information they obtain from others with similar problems.[12] The benefits are that the organization can ask the groups whatever questions they want and can ask and adjust them easily to the answers they receive. The results are real-time and actionable.

Organizations must establish a procedure for frequently monitoring the Web conversations about them through blogs, Twitter, online news sources, and, depending on their product or service, even consumer activist sites. Entering the organization's name into a common search engine will indicate the conversation about the company on the Web. They may also want to subscribe to an online clipping service, which will collect any media hits, whether broadcast, newsprint, or Web.

However companies decide to measure the results of their public relations activities and their reputations, they need to make sure they target all constituencies. They must have a strategy for routine as well as periodic comprehensive assessments of their public perception. The key is being proactive, anticipating responses, and planning ahead for what, when, and how monitoring will occur.

Building and Maintaining a Positive Corporate Image

Reputation affects the bottom line, and even the strongest companies will have difficulty surviving damage to their reputations. Leaders of organizations must give high priority to establishing and maintaining a positive corporate image and, today more than ever, that means keeping the public, customers, and all other external stakeholders happy. According to Li and Bernoff, in their book *Groundswell,*: "Your brand is whatever your customers say it is. And in the groundswell where they communicate with each other, they decide."[13]

EXHIBIT 12.8
Companies That
Are Considered
Good at External
Relations

Source: Corporate
Reputation Watch (October
1997). *The State of
Corporate Communications,*
written by Hill & Knowlton
and based on research
conducted by Yankelovich
Partners. Used with permission of Hill & Knowlton.

Type	Company
Media Relations	1. Microsoft
	2. Coca-Cola
	IBM
	GE
	Disney
Corporate Public Relations	1. Coca-Cola
	2. Microsoft
	3. GE
Corporate Identity	1. Coca-Cola
	2. IBM
	3. Nike
Government Relations	1. Boeing
	2. GE
	3. Phillip Morris
	4. AT&T
Investor Relations	1. Microsoft
	Intel
	2. GE
	Coca-Cola

All companies can learn something about effective management of external relations by looking at others that are considered good at it. In *The State of Corporate Communications,* written by Hill & Knowlton and based on research conducted by Yankelovich Partners, the corporate communication chiefs identified the companies listed in Exhibit 12.8 as good at managing the different types of external relations.

Many of the same companies are also included at the top of the Harris Interactive Reputation Quotient of 2008 for effectively managing their corporate communication: "Microsoft ranks in the top 5 positive rating for 6 of the 8 measures [sincere, consistent, distinctive, transparent, providing correct and accurate information, having common look and feel, easily recognizable, and proving consistent messages] used to describe perceptions of corporate communications of companies. Coca-Cola, Johnson & Johnson, and Apple rank in the top 5 for 5 of the 8 measures."[14]

Of course, an organization's presence and use of the Internet also has an effect on its reputation. For example, a Customer Respect Group's *2004 Online Customer Respect Study of the Top 100 U.S. Companies* looked at how well companies manage their Internet customer relations. They established what matters to Internet customers and found the following criteria at the top: simplicity, privacy, responsiveness, transparency, and attitude. Interestingly, responsiveness is very low for some of the world's most respected companies, despite the risk

EXHIBIT 12.9
Most and Least
Respectful Web
Sites—Companies
and Scores

Source: 2005 Online
Customer Respect Study
of the Country's Largest
100 Companies. www
.customerrespect.com.
Results reported in *USA
Today,* June 29, 2005.

Most Respectful (top 10)	Least Respectful (bottom 10)
Hewlett-Packard	Wellpoint Health Networks
Medco Health Solutions	Johnson Controls
Sprint	Marathon Oil
Intel	Plains All American Pipeline
American Express	Northrup Grumman
UPS	Boeing
Bank of America	Weyerhauser
Microsoft	Honeywell
Dell	Morgan Stanley
Wachovia	Berkshire Hathaway

of losing customers, yet Customer Respect Group found that 70 percent of the consumers surveyed move their business to a competitor if they do not receive a timely response. Exhibit 12.9 shows the most respectful and least respectful Web sites out of the 100 largest U.S. companies in the 2005 survey.

CustomerRespect.com found that 37 percent of the companies surveyed did not respond at all to customer inquiries, while 41 percent responded in 48 hours, 12 percent in 72 hours, and 10 percent in more than 72 hours. Importantly, Customer Respect Group found a correlation between the companies with a low "Customer Respect Index" and a publicized lack of respect for shareholders and employees.[15] They argue that "respect for the customer, respect for investors, respect for employees, are all borne out of self-respect and moral fiber." In other words, the lack of respect a company shows for its customers may suggest a lack of respect for its investors and its employees and a fundamentally flawed ethical core. Whether the logic follows exactly may be questionable, but the study shows that customer respect does affect image and potential profitability.

Everything an organization does influences public opinion and reputation; therefore, every organization should look carefully at building and maintaining a positive reputation. In *Reputation: Realizing Value from the Corporate Image,* Charles Fombrun identifies six ways companies can build and maintain a positive corporate image:

1. Design campaigns to promote the company as a whole.
2. Carry out ambitious programs to champion product quality and customer service.
3. Maintain systems to screen employee activities for reputation side effects.
4. Demonstrate sensitivity to the environment.
5. Hire internal communication staff and retain public relations firms.
6. Demonstrate "corporate citizenship."[16]

This list reveals the importance of being proactive and comprehensive in fostering a corporate reputation. The organization needs to be perceived as one unit with one unified message, no matter how many individual groups or business units exist or how globally diverse it is. It needs to place a high priority on customer service and ensure that all employees realize their importance as representatives of the company.

Shaping a positive corporate image involves every employee and the total commitment of senior management. It also involves taking advantage of the resources available to help, from internal communication professionals to public relations firms. In fact, for a large, global company in particular, the assistance of a strong public relations firm is invaluable. These firms have the contacts in local communities and the news media and the expertise to reach these as well as online outlets, and they can often do more to build a reputation than a public advertising campaign.

Building and maintaining a positive corporate image requires having an external relations strategy that is vigilant, vigorous, and comprehensive. It involves developing a strategy for managing the press and media, making meaningful and sincere philanthropic contributions, being actively involved in the community, obeying all the legal and regulatory requirements of investor relations, and ensuring that all external communication vehicles carry honest, clear, consistent, and meaningful messages to all stakeholders. One mistake in any of these areas can cause repercussions from which a company may never recover.

Working with the News Media

The mistakes or missteps that tarnish a company's reputation may be uncovered by any number of possible means, including by disgrutled employees in chatrooms or on corporate blogs, and spread through the Web as quickly as they are started, but often the greatest amount of coverage and how negative the spin of the story depend on the news media. To increase chances for favorable treatment, it is important for organizations to establish a positive relationship with the media and for the organization's leaders to know how to work effectively with them. Hill & Knowlton's 2002 Corporate Reputation Watch survey reported that CEOs see media criticism as "the greatest threat to corporate reputation." Any leader of an organization should know why the media are important, when to talk to them, and how to manage encounters with them.

Understanding the Media's Role and Importance

Print, broadcast, and Internet media are the primary channels for much that is communicated in our society. While some coverage is given to business in almost all traditional media, certain newspapers and TV news networks and programs provide more coverage of corporations than others. A study by Media Tenor found that *The Wall Street Journal, The Washington Post,* and *USA Today* publish most extensively on corporate management, with *The Wall Street Journal,* not surprisingly, providing three times the coverage of the other two.[17] Unfortunately, as the Media Tenor study also found, the media are much more likely to pick up a negative story than a positive one. As is well known, the bigger the story, the more media attention it attracts, and since the media are businesses, they seek the news that will sell—and they sell it across multiple networks, from Web pages and RSS feed to Facebook and Twitter updates.

Since all major newspapers and most TV networks provide coverage of major corporations and are definitely interested in sensational news from smaller organizations, every organization needs to recognize the importance of the media and take the time to interact with media representatives and learn a little about their needs and interests.

In addition, companies need to understand the value of positive public relations and realize that establishing a relationship with the media, either directly or through a public relations firm, can open the door to a tremendous amount of "free" publicity. Of course, "free" is relative, since companies have to pay for public relations resources and services; however, if handled effectively, a good public relations campaign will usually reach more people more economically than an advertising campaign. A public relations campaign can also achieve more positive results, since most people are more skeptical of advertising than they are of what they think of as "news."

Deciding When to Talk to the Media

Interactions with the media can allow an organization to reach a large and globally dispersed audience, present their point of view proactively, and establish a positive public ethos. However, a company must be cautious and think through the answers to these key questions before deciding to talk to the media:

1. What will the company gain by talking to the media, and what might it lose?
2. Why would the media be interested in our company or our story?
3. Could our story fall within the context of a negative story about another company or topic?
4. Who is the reporter? Is he or she reputable and known for covering "real" news or for doing features or lighter reporting?
5. Do we have all the facts that a reporter might seek on the story?
6. Will we be able to come across as knowledgeable and credible?
7. Will the coverage result in additional positive interest in our company?
8. What are the ways an interview could turn negative?

Preparing for and Delivering a Media Interview

Any leader or high-level manager should receive training and, ideally, specific coaching in preparation for an encounter with the media. The training should include the following at a minimum: preparation for the interview, performance during the interview, and steps to take afterward.

1. Preparation

Preparation is key to an effective interview. No one should go into an interview without it. Interviewees must not only have the content well under control but also know how to dress and how to appear credible to the reporter. They should develop their strategy with a public relations expert. That strategy should include the description and understanding of the context, target audiences, strategic objectives, and major messages. They should work with the content and know it well enough that they need only minimal notes. Ideally, in a live interview, they should be able to speak without notes. It is important to know something about the reporter's background and mode of operation in interviews and to establish ground rules with him or her before the interview starts. Finally, the interviewee should practice in a setting similar to the one in which the interview will be conducted.

2. Performance During the Interview

If being interviewed over the phone, interviewees want to be very well prepared and have their notes handy, although they should not sound as though they are reading. They should keep all of their answers simple, thinking in terms of sound bites. If they respond with long sentences or complicated prose, the writer will do the cutting to get the sound bite, taking control of the message out of the interviewees' hands and greatly increasing the odds of their being misquoted. If given clear and concise responses, the reporter will be more likely to quote the words exactly, which will make it more likely that what is said is what is published or broadcast. Also, interviewees should be very careful to stay focused on their core message and not let the reporter take them away from it.

If the meeting with the media is a press conference, the interviewees will have a prepared statement to deliver, but after that, they must be ready to answer any questions that may arise. They should have full command of information and subjects closely related to the main messages of their statement. They may bring notes to the interview, but again, they need to make sure they use sound bites that they know well. If they have to read responses, they will not look confident, so any notes should be very brief and include only facts and figures. Interviewees need to dress appropriately and look pulled together. Most of all, they want to be themselves and maintain their composure no matter what questions are thrown at them.

Exhibit 12.10 provides 10 rules for dealing with the media that apply for any media encounter, but particularly when meeting with them in person.

EXHIBIT 12.10
TEN Rules of
Effective
Communication
with the Media

Source: Adapted from
Burger, C. How to meet the
press. From *Harvard
Business Review*, July-
August 1975. Copyright ©
1975 by Harvard Business
School Publishing
Corporation. All rights
reserved.

1. Talk from the viewpoint of the public's interest, not the company's.
2. Speak in personal terms whenever possible.
3. If you do not want some statement quoted, do not make it. There is no such thing as "off the record."
4. State the most important fact at the beginning.
5. Do not argue with the reporter or lose your cool.
6. If a question contains offensive language or simply words you do not like, do not repeat them, even to deny them.
7. If the reporter asks a direct question, he [or she] is entitled to an equally direct answer.
8. If you do not know the answer to a question, simply say, "I don't know, but I'll find out for you."
9. Tell the truth, even if it hurts.
10. Do not exaggerate the facts.

As a final note for any encounter with the media, we need to remember that nothing is "off the record"; we should never be misled into believing that it is. We must aways be very careful what we say and do in the presence of the media, and always tell the truth.

3. *Steps to Take after the Interview*

After the interview, reporters may or may not let the interviewees see how they are going to report the statements. Most often, however, reporters will not. If the story has a longer lead time and is more a public interest piece than hard news, they may allow interviewees to see it. Interviewees should certainly review it if possible. If the reporter does not offer, then the interviewee should ask. If the story is breaking with a short lead time, interviewees will have to trust that the reporter will quote them exactly, emphasizing again the importance of being very careful about what is said and of providing only sound bites. Whether the interviewees have a chance to review the story as written or not, they should still follow up by thanking the reporter and, if appropriate, complimenting him or her on how well he or she conducted the interview or on the importance of the topic. Building strong relationships with the media is important and will serve all organizational leaders particularly well should they ever face a crisis communication situation.

Handling Crisis Communications

At one time or another, most organizations will face a crisis. A situation requiring crisis communications involves "a specific, unexpected and non-routine event or series of events that create high levels of uncertainty and threaten or are perceived to threaten an organization's high priority goals."[18] If the company has established and maintained a positive relationship with the media and their stakeholders, the job of managing the crisis will be somewhat easier.[19] In fact, "an important part of crisis planning . . . entails identifying stakeholders prior to a crisis and cultivating positive relationships with these groups. . . . The organization's leadership plays a fundamental role in establishing value positions with key stakeholders before a crisis as well as after the event."[20]

Although establishing positive relationships with external audiences prior to a crisis will help in all but the most extreme situations, no amount of goodwill can guarantee the positive coverage that is necessary to avoid permanent damage to a company's reputation. History is full of examples of companies handling a crisis well and not so well. Johnson & Johnson's effective handling of the Tylenol tampering incident is legendary, while Exxon's bungling of the *Valdez* oil spill is infamous.

More recently, the world witnessed how companies and a city responded to one of the worst crises of modern times, the destruction of the World Trade Center buildings in New York City. No one was untouched by the disaster, and examples of effective and ineffective communication efforts during the crisis abound, from the companies located in or near the World Trade Center to organizations scattered across the world, which had to decide how to reach their employees with the news and how to answer their questions about performing their daily duties.

The following guidelines will help companies respond appropriately in most crisis situations:

1. **Develop a general crisis communication plan and communicate it.** No organizations should take for granted that they have no risk of encountering a crisis. Nothing will replace preparation and a knowledgeable, informed workforce to implement it.

2. **Once the crisis occurs, respond quickly.** Implement the plan immediately. The first few hours are critical. While the organization needs time to gather the facts, it must do so quickly so that it is the first to the media and the public with the information they need and want. It is a very good idea to have staff members ready to blog, Tweet, and post information as it comes available, directing both the media and the public to a central location (such as its Web site) for information.

3. **Make sure the organization has the right people ready to respond and that they all respond with the same message.** Corporate crises of any significance require the organization's top leaders to respond, which usually means the CEO. In fact, one of the criticisms of Exxon's handling of the *Valdez* disaster was that the CEO sent two lower-level executives to Alaska. Other executives should also be trained to respond appropriately to the media in a crisis situation and should be prepared to accept the responsibility for implementing the

communication plan. The people preparation includes at least minimal training for all employees who might come in contact with the media, even if that training consists simply of telling them where to refer questions. The designated spokespersons should be accessible and visible and should deliver a consistent message.

4. **Understand the audience; try to see the crisis from their perspective.** What do they want and need to know? What will be their major concerns? Leaders want to focus on the facts but ensure that they touch the feelings of the people on both sides of the crisis. All messages should be honest and compassionate.

5. **Realize and leverage the value of the Web.** Use of the Web during a crisis is essential. Reporters as well as the public and even employees go to the Web for information during a crisis; therefore, in any crisis communication plan, every organization must use the Web as a virtual crisis communication center for internal and external audiences.

6. **Revisit the crisis communication plan frequently.** Since situations and people in companies change constantly, the organization must build in periodic reviews and revisions of the plan. Any major changes to the plan need to be communicated to the employees responsible for its implementation. One way to make the plan easier to update is to keep it on the company's intranet.

7. **Build in a way to monitor the coverage.** Monitor blogs, microblogs, and social networks, and use electronic clipping services to collect media hits. Again, the Web can be a tremendous resource for measuring the public's response to the messages.

8. **Perform a post-crisis evaluation.** After a crisis, management should look critically at what worked and did not work and collect the lessons learned for the future. In addition, the organization needs to develop a strategy for moving forward and quickly communicate it once the crisis is under control.

Just as managing the crisis and most of the communication that surrounds it falls to the organization's leaders, often the CEO, establishing the direction out of the crisis is the CEO's responsibility as well. In his book *Who Says Elephants Can't Dance?* Lou Gerstner, CEO of IBM from 1993 to 2002, writes, "So there must be a crisis, and it is the job of the CEO to define and communicate that crisis, its magnitude, its severity, and its impact. Just as important, the CEO must also be able to communicate how to end the crisis—the new strategy, the new company model, the new culture."[21]

All organizations, no matter the size, must have a crisis communication plan. Nothing will replace being prepared. When a crisis happens, it is too late to develop a communication strategy and select target audiences, create appropriate message content, determine what media to use or how best to use social media, and choose spokespersons. Everyone must be ready to move quickly or the organization risks its reputation, and a lost reputation damages the organization, often irreparably.

To conclude, managing external relations effectively is essential for organizational leaders; however, external relations do not exist in isolation. Organizations must link all communication activities to ensure that what the outside world sees and hears reflects what the inside world lives. As one CEO said when interviewed in a survey of 2,000 top private- and public-sector organizations conducted by Aon Consulting, "The fundamental truth, which you only discover when you have gone through the fires of hell, is that your reputation will always mirror the absolute reality of who you are. . . . Anyone who thinks that they can change their reputation without changing the company is mistaken."[22] Today, more than ever before, the public expects companies to demonstrate social responsibility and to behave ethically in all they do internally and externally.[23]

All leaders of organizations must realize that their companies' reputations depend on their internal ethos and the perceptions of their many external stakeholders. They cannot ignore the importance of establishing and maintaining a positive reputation or the need to manage external relations to keep it.

Application 12.1 Communication with Customers after a Crisis	**The Case: Spree Cruise Lines Revisited**

(Begin by reviewing the facts in the Spree Cruise Lines case from Chapter 2.)

Within several days after the cruise returned to New Orleans, Tara was able to learn more about what happened on the ship. Approximately 350 passengers made their own arrangements to fly home and disembarked from the ship in Cozumel, but the remainder stayed on board. The cruise line offered them a shipboard voucher of $100 per person, but there were still some extremely unhappy customers, and they shared their dissatisfaction openly on their blogs, Facebook profiles, and Twitter and FriendFeed accounts.

Marcie Smith, the senior vice president of sales and marketing, has asked Tara to draft a letter for her signature to be sent to all customers who were aboard that cruise, whether they disembarked or stayed aboard. Since research shows that many cruisers are repeat customers, upper management approved an offer of a 50 percent discount on another three- to five-day cruise, so that these passengers might give Spree Cruise Lines a second chance. The cruise line set up a special booking phone number to accommodate the return guests, 1-800-724-4000; the offer stipulated that new reservations must be made within the coming year to qualify for the discount.

The Assignment

Draft the letter to go out to all the customers who were on the cruise, offering them the discount and explaining the terms of the offer. Then, make at least one additional recommendation to Marcie Smith about how to mitigate the damage and improve the company's image in the social networking sphere.

**Application 12.2
Writing a Press
Release**

The Case: Spree Cruise Lines Revisited, Again

Teams of mechanics greeted the *Sensation* upon its arrival back in NewOrleans. They were able to repair the ship sufficiently so that the propulsion system would hold up for the next few cruises, which were already fully booked. As the vessel departed for its next trip, teams of city engineers carried out tests to determine whether the vibrations reported from the last trip were indeed linked to the vessel's departure from port. They concluded that the vibrations *were* caused by the vessel: They had nothing to do with the malfunctioning propulsion system that hampered the last cruise, but the vibrations did seem to relate to the frequency set up when the engines were run at a particular power level. The vessel's captain could easily be directed to reduce power during departures and entries into port.

Even though the vibration and frequency problems could easily be solved, Spree's vice president of operations decided to accelerate the timetable for the dry dock, which had initially been planned to occur in several months. The vessel would go into dry dock for a multimillion-dollar makeover, including a new purser's lobby, a new restaurant decor, upgraded passenger rooms, and a complete engine system refurbishment. The dry dock would require about two months, during which time one of Spree's other ships, the *Plentitude*, would serve the New Orleans market.

The Assignment

Draft a media plan, including the appropriate social media, that announces the dry dock plans for the *Sensation*. Include any other information you feel should be addressed and be prepared to discuss your reasoning for including specific pieces of information in one medium and not another. For example, what might you say on the corporate Web site or in a blog or Twitter account versus in a press release sent out broadly to the media and the public? As you know from the chapter, any messages to external audiences must be clear, so be very careful with the language you use. Also, remember that all announcements to external audiences, in particular, serve two primary purposes: (1) They inform the public and (2) they create an image.

For the press release, you should follow these guidelines:

1. Answer the journalist's questions of who, what, where, when, and why.
2. Place your most important information in the first sentence or two.
3. Since news editors cut press releases from the bottom up, you need to make sure all of the most important information comes as early in the release as possible, leaving the "nice-to-knows" to the end.
4. Place contact information (name and phone number) at the top.
5. Try to limit the release to one page, but if it runs over, type "more" in the center at the bottom of the first page.

6. Leave adequate margins and double-space.
7. Use concise sentences (think in terms of sound bites) and proofread carefully.
8. Use "-30-" to indicate the end of the release.

Releases through other social media will include much of the same information, but you will not be able to provide as much detail in some of them.

**Application 12.3
Developing an
External
Communication
Strategy**

The Case: HADWIT, Revisited

Review the HADWIT case in Chapter 11, paying particular attention to the information on HADWIT's relationship with its clients.

The Assignment

Develop a complete communication strategy, including all the external audiences you need to consider. After developing the strategy, create a notice to clients for your Web page and prepare written correspondence directly to each one personally. Use e-mail or a letter, whichever seems appropriate to you; explain the changes you will be making at the company.

Notes

1. The Best Corporate Reputations. (1999). *The Wall Street Journal*; Annual Reputation Quotient Survey results for 2005. www.harrisinteractive.com.
2. (2001). *Corporate Reputation Watch*. :Hill & Knowlton.
3. *Aon's Global Risk Management Survey: Some Multinationals Not Ready for Risk.* http://aon.mediaroom.com/index.php?s=43&item=554 (accessed May 2, 2009).
4. Video Prank at Domino's Taints Brand. (April 15, 2009). *New York Times*. www.nytimes.com/2009/04/16/business/media/16dominos.html?_r=4.
5. Video Prank at Domino's Taints Brand (April 15, 2009).
6. *Corporate Reputation Watch* (2001).
7. *The 10th Annual RQ: Reputations of the 60 Most Visible Companies. A Survey of the U.S. General Public* (20,483 Interviewed) Harris Interactive. December 31, 2008 – February 2, 2009. http://www.harrisinteractive.com/services/pubs/HI_BSC_REPORT_AnnualRQ2008_Summary Report.pdf.
8. Risk Assessment for Food Terrorism and Other Safety Concerns. (October 7, 2003). www.cfsan.fda.gov/~dms/rabtact.html#i.
9. Levisohn, B., and & Gibson, E. (May 4, 2009). An Unwelcome Delivery. *BusinessWeek*.
10. Levisohn and Gibson (May 4, 2009).
11. Li, C., and Bernoff, J. (2008). *Groundswell: Winning in a World Transformed by Social Technologies*. Boston: Harvard Business School Press.
12. Li and Bernoff (2008).
13. Li and Bernoff (2008).
14. Harris Interactive (2008).
15. *Online Customer Respect: Study of Fortune 100 Companies* (2002), p. 7.
16. Fombrun, C. J. (1996). *Reputation: Realizing Value from the Corporate Image*. Boston: Harvard Business School Press.

17. Media Tenor International, March 2003.

18. Seeger, M. W., Sellnow, T. L., and Ulmer, R. R. (1998). Communication, Organization, and Crisis. In M. E. Roloff (Ed.), *Communication Yearbook*, Vol. 21, pp. 231–275. Thousand Oaks, CA: Sage.

19. Ulmer, R. R. (2001). Effective Crisis Management through Established Stakeholder Relationships. *Management Communication Quarterly* 14, No. 4, pp. 590–615.

20. Ulmer (2001), p. 594.

21. Gerstner (2002). New York: HarperCollins.

22. Steve Marshall (2003), CEO of Railtrack, quoted in *Corporate Reputation: Not Worth Risking*, p. 3.

23. Kitchen, P. J., & Laurence, A. (2003). Corporate reputation: An eight country analysis. *Corporate Reputation Review* 6 (2), pp. 103–117.

Appendix

Self-Assessment of Leadership Communication Capabilities*

Read through the list of skills and for each one check off your present capability in the chart below.

1. Excel = mastered this skill and am excellent in it.
2. Competent = competent in this skill but could polish it some.
3. Need to Develop = need to develop further

Area and Capability	1 Excel	2 Competent	3 Need to Develop
Part I – Assessment of Core Capabilities			
Audience Analysis and Strategy			
1. Analyzing the context for communication			
2. Analyzing audiences			
3. Tailoring messages to different audiences			
4. Selecting the most effective medium (channel)			
5. Developing a complete communication strategy			
Written Communication			
1. Deciding on communication purpose			
2. Clarifying purpose			
3. Generating support for each purpose			
4. Organizing written communication			

* The format and some of the capabilities listed were inspired by an assessment in the book *Client-Centered Consulting* by Peter Cockman, Bill Evans, and Peter Reynolds. Used with permission of McGraw-Hill.

Area and Capability	1 Excel	2 Competent	3 Need to Develop
Written Communication (continued)			
5. Using formatting effectively			
6. Using language correctly			
7. Writing clearly			
8. Writing concisely			
9. Writing confidently			
10. Using an appropriate tone			
11. Writing correspondence (e-mails, memos, text messages)			
12. Writing formal reports			
13. Writing executive summaries			
14. Proofreading own work			
Oral Communication			
1. Delivering an impromptu presentation			
2. Delivering an extemporaneous presentation			
3. Organizing a presentation			
4. Creating PowerPoint slides			
5. Talking in small groups			
6. Talking in large groups			
7. Answering questions			
8. Asking questions			
9. Drawing others out			
10. Summarizing and clarifying others' ideas			
11. Keeping to the topic			
12. Summarizing a discussion			
13. Dealing publicly with more senior people			
Visual Communication Capabilities			
1. Recognizing when to use graphics			
2. Selecting and designing effective data charts			
3. Creating meaningful and effective text layouts			
4. Employing fundamental graphics content and design principles			
5. Ensuring that "so what?" is captured			
6. Creating presentation visuals and slides			

Area and Capability	1 Excel	2 Competent	3 Need to Develop
Part II – Organizational Capabilities			
Ethos/Image			
1. Understanding how I am seen by others			
2. Knowing how my personal style differs from others			
3. Asking others to comment on my style			
4. Assessing my own strengths and weaknesses			
5. Setting goals for personal change			
6. Willing to work on improving personal effectiveness			
7. Influencing the behavior of others			
8. Inspiring trust in others			
9. Projecting confidence			
10. Making ethical decisions			
11. Creating an ethical environment			
Emotional Intelligence 1: Dealing with Own Feelings			
1. Being aware of own feelings			
2. Identifying feelings			
3. Asserting own ideas and rights			
4. Stating own needs			
5. Expressing feelings to others			
Emotional Intelligence 2: Dealing with Others			
1. Listening			
2. Recognizing nonverbals			
3. Being sensitive to others' feelings			
4. Asking people how they feel			
5. Acknowledging people's feelings			
6. Helping others express their feelings			
7. Dealing with anger			
8. Dealing with hostility and suspicion			
9. Being comfortable with conflict			
10. Withstanding silences			
11. Mentoring others			
12. Coaching others			
13. Networking			

Area and Capability	1 Excel	2 Competent	3 Need to Develop
Emotional Intelligence 3: Observation and Feedback			
1. Being aware of high and low participators			
2. Noting if people are excluded			
3. Recognizing who talks to whom			
4. Being aware of who takes on leadership roles			
5. Giving feedback on behavior in the group			
6. Giving praise and appreciation			
7. Providing constructive feedback to individuals or groups			
8. Helping team members give each other feedback			
9. Soliciting feedback from others			
10. Receiving feedback without being defensive			
Cross-Cultural Literacy and Communication			
1. Realizing the value of cross-cultural literacy			
2. Defining and appreciating cultural differences			
3. Understanding differences in values and preferences			
4. Recognizing general communication preferences (direct or indirect, explicit or implicit, high or low context)			
5. Understanding differences in attitudes toward authority, time, risk, and change			
6. Knowing customs common to cultures encountering			
7. Communicating in social situations			
Team Communication and Dynamics			
1. Sensing tension in the group			
2. Being sensitive to how people in the group are feeling			
3. Being aware of how open or closed the group is			
4. Identifying those issues which are avoided			
5. Identifying and clarifying goals and objectives			
6. Clearly defining the problem under discussion			
7. Examining all facets of the problem			
8. Exploring people aspects of the problem			
9. Surfacing vested interests and feelings about the problem			
10. Encouraging others to generate ideas			
11. Using creativity to develop new ideas			

Area and Capability	1 Excel	2 Competent	3 Need to Develop
12. Evaluating options			
13. Helping groups make decisions			
14. Helping groups explore their commitment to group decisions and/or agreements			
15. Encouraging groups to develop action plans			
16. Helping the team confront difficult issues			
17. Drawing attention to unhelpful behavior			
18. Helping the team deal with conflict or other tension			
19. Supporting individuals against group pressure			
20. Helping team members acknowledge each other's strengths			
21. Facilitating team review and critique			
Part III – Corporate Communication Capabilities			
1. Developing an internal communication strategy			
2. Developing a vision			
3. Communicating a vision			
4. Targeting messages to different levels in an organization			
5. Creating a change communication program			
6. Implementing a change communication program			
7. Developing an external communication strategy			
8. Managing corporate image			
9. Analyzing external stakeholders			
10. Developing targeted messages for all external stakeholders			
11. Communicating with the news media			
12. Dealing with a communication crisis situation			
Total marks in each column			

Worksheet to Develop Personal Leadership Communication Development Plan

1. Using the information gained from completing the *Self-Assessment of Overall Leadership Communication Capabilities,* assign a score for your improvement need in each Capability area (use the scale provided next to the table) based on the number of checks under Excel, Competent, and Need to Develop.

Score	Capability Area
	Communication strategy
	Written communication
	Oral communication
	Visual communication
	Ethos/image
	Dealing with own feelings
	Dealing with others
	Observation and feedback
	Cultural literacy
	Team communications and dynamics
	Internal corporate communication
	External corporate communication

1 = substantial need to improve
2 = some need to improve
3 = little need to improve
4 = no need to improve at this time

2. What do you consider your major communication strengths?

3. What do you consider your major communication weaknesses?

4. What leadership communication roles do you currently play in your organization?

Part 2—Determining Your Leadership Communication Goals

Answer the following questions to help you develop your goals and plan.

1. What communication leadership roles would you like to play in the future (at your organization or in your career overall)?

2. What are your short-term and long-term leadership communication improvement goals?

3. What new skill do you want to work on first, second, third, etc.?

4. What barriers do you anticipate having to overcome to reach your improvement goals?

5. How long do you think it will take you to achieve your goals?

6. How will you know you are succeeding?

7. How will you obtain feedback?

Part 3—Developing a Plan to Achieve your Goals

Using the table below, list your primary improvement goals, and then establish actions, deadlines, and measurement for each. The more specific the goal, the more likely you are to achieve it.

Improvement Goal	Action Steps to Achieve Goal	Deadline	Method to Measure Success

Appendix B

The Business of Grammar

Each specialization has a jargon. To know how to talk about style and usage at an advanced level, you need to know the jargon of grammarians. Also, the more you know about the foundation of a language, its grammar, the more confident you will be in using it.

Grammar, just as any subject, needs to be reviewed periodically. What follows is a brief review of traditional English grammar designed to give you the basics of the business of grammar, so that you can be proficient in the business of leadership communication.

Parts of Speech

Following Priscian's Latin grammar in the 6th century AD, the first grammarians broke the English language down into eight parts of speech: *nouns, pronouns, verbs, adverbs, adjectives, prepositions, conjunctions,* and *interjections.* The use of Latin grammar causes problems when we try to apply the different labels of the parts of speech because the classification definitions are not consistent:

1. Three parts of speech are defined by meaning—*noun, verb,* and *interjection.*
2. Four by function—*adjective, adverb, conjunction,* and *pronoun.*
3. One by function and form—*preposition.*

When you start paying attention to how words work in sentences, you quickly realize that you can determine the part of speech by the position of the word in the sentence. For example, if you were asked what parts of speech the nonsense words "rehpog" and "gud" are in the following sentence, you would recognize "rehpog" as a noun and "gud" as a verb because of their positions and the context provided by the other words: The *rehpog gud* a deep tunnel in the woods.

What follows is a brief explanation of the eight parts of speech.

1. **Nouns.** Nouns name persons, places, things, and abstractions. Properties of nouns are more appropriate for Latin, but in case you hear the terms for the properties, the following definitions should help you:

   a. **Number**—singular (one) or plural (many). Plurals are indicated by *-s* or *-es,* which will be pronounced *s, z, ez,* or *iz.*

   b. **Case**—in Latin, there were five cases. Cases did in Latin what word order does in English.

   - Nominative or subjective—subject (*David* gave the report to Mary.)
   - Accusative—direct object (David gave *the report* to Mary.)
   - Dative—indirect object (David gave *Mary* the report.)
   - Genitive—possession -*'s* (*David's* report is complete.)
   - Ablative—preposition (from, with, in, etc.)

2. **Verbs.** Verbs show action or states of being. There are two kinds of verbs:

   a. Active verbs express action.
      (1) **Transitive** active verbs require objects.
          Example: The CEO *gave her* the report.

          V I.O. D.O.
      (2) **Intransitive** active verbs are complete without objects.
          Example: He *ran.*

   b. Linking verbs express a state of being. They may be followed by predicate adjectives or predicate nominatives.
      (1) Predicate adjective
          Example: She is brilliant.
      (2) Predicate nominative
          Example: She is the boss.

   Either active or linking verbs may appear with auxiliary (or helping) verbs, such as *can, could, may, might, must, shall, should, will,* or *would.*
   Five terms apply to verbs:

   a. **Person**—*who* is performing the action or doing something.
First:	person speaking (I, me)
Second:	person spoken to (you)
Third:	person spoken about (he, she, they)

b. **Number**—*how many* are performing the action or doing something.

Singular	Plural
I am	We are
You are	You are
S/he is	They are

c. **Tense**—*when* the action is performed.

Present:	I am; action taking place now
Past:	I was; action that has taken place
Future: I	will be; action that will take place
Perfect:	I was to be; action that took place at one time in the past; indicated in English by a verb phrase: *will go, was going, had gone,* etc.

d. **Mood**—the *attitude of the speaker* or way in which the speaker thinks about the action.

Subjunctive:	conditional, contingent, possible, contrary to fact; if he were (thought mood)
Imperative:	command, request, prayer (will mood)
Indicative:	statements and questions (fact mood)

e. **Voice**—indicated by the *relationship* between the verb and the subject.

Active:	The subject performs the action.
	Example: *He* hit the target.
Passive:	The subject is what is acted upon.
	Example: *The target* was hit by him.

Another way to think about the passive voice is to focus on the *actor* in the sentence instead of the subject. Ask yourself who is performing the action and where he or she is positioned in the sentence. The actor is *before* the verb in the active voice and *after* the verb in the passive voice.

Quite often, the passive voice will be constructed as it is in this sentence without identifying the actor:

Examples: The target was hit. (By whom?)

The report will be written. (By whom?)

Verbals make up a subgroup of verbs. Verbals are formed from verbs, but they function as nouns, adjectives, and adverbs. The three types of verbals are the following:

a. **Gerund**—an *-ing* form of a verb that functions as a noun.

Examples: *Finishing* the report was all that occupied Pierce's mind. Mary hoped the team's *completing* the report ahead of schedule would impress her boss. (Note the possessive before the gerund.)

b. **Participle**—a verb form ending in *-ing* if present tense and *-ed,* *-en,* or *-d* if past that functions as an adjective.

Examples: A *malfunctioning* computer is worse than no computer. A *completed* report is a relief.

c. **Infinitive**—the root form of the verb preceded by *to* that may be used as a noun, an adjective, or an adverb.

Examples: *To finish* the report was all that occupied Pierce's mind. (noun)

He has a report *to finish.* (adjective modifying report)

He has gone *to finish* the report. (adverb modifying *gone*)

3. **Pronouns.** Pronouns take the place of nouns. A pronoun must refer to a specific noun, called its antecedent or referent, in the same or a previous sentence. An English pronoun must agree with its antecedent in person and number. Pronouns have the following gender properties: masculine (he), feminine (she), neutral (it).

We have six types of pronouns in the English language:

a. **Personal** pronouns—refer to a specific person or thing mentioned previously.

First: I, me, my, mine, we, us, our, ours
Second: you, your, yours
Third: he, she, it, him, her, his, hers, its, they, them, their, theirs

b. **Relative** pronouns—can function as connecting words and reference words. As connecting words, they are used to relate subordinate clauses to main clauses. As reference words, they refer to and stand for their antecedents, making the repetition of the antecedent unnecessary.

Simple relative pronouns: who, which, that
Compound relative pronouns: whoever, whomever, whichever, whatever, whatsoever

c. **Demonstrative** pronouns—pointing words used to indicate which one or ones: this, that, these, those.

d. **Reflexive** pronouns—used to indicate that the action is reflected or comes back to the subject: myself, herself, themselves, ourselves, etc.

e. **Indefinite** pronouns—pronouns that do not refer to any particular person or thing. The most common ones are the following:

any, anybody, anyone
everyone, everybody, everything
some, someone, somebody, something
one, none, nobody
other, another, all, many, each, both, either

Be very careful with agreement in number—singular or plural—when using indefinite pronouns. They are the ones that often cause mistakes in pronoun antecedent agreement.

Remember to say *Everybody must file his or her report.* Employ the following verb test: Would you say, *"Everybody is"* or *"Everybody are"*? Since the verb would be *is,* you know that the indefinite pronoun is singular and requires a singular pronoun for reference.

All of the indefinite pronouns in the *any* and *everyone* groups are *singular. Some* and *none* may be singular or plural depending on the meaning in the sentence.

Example: *Some* of the employees *were* upset over the decision.
But—
Some of the confetti *was* left on the floor.

A related pronoun reference, which often causes problems in business communication, is the reference to a collective noun, such as *board, committee, corporation, department,* or *company.* In the United States, collective nouns are usually thought of as singular and take singular verbs and pronouns. For example, in the United States, a company is treated as singular and would be referred to by "it," as in the following example: "Brown & Partners, LLP, is considered successful in its market area." In other countries, such as Great Britain and Australia, a company is treated as plural, which would mean that the previous sentence would read "Brown & Partners, LLP, are considered successful in their market area." As with other differences across countries, you should usually follow the conventions of the country in which the company has its headquarters.

f. **Interrogative** pronouns—used in questions: *who, whose, whom, what, which.* A pronoun must agree in person (1st, 2nd, or 3rd) and number (singular or plural) with its antecedent noun. Remember that *who* stands for people. *Which* stands for things and objects and denotes properties.

Also, with pronouns, watch the cases. Is the pronoun performing the action or receiving it? Use *I, who, he, she* in the subjective case (action performers) and *me, whom, him, her* in the objective cases (action receivers).

Say: Divide the money between him and me.
Not: Divide the money between he and I.

You need to take care to use the correct case, since the incorrect pronoun is used often in casual conversation and, unfortunately, on the radio and television as well. Trust your knowledge of the use of the pronoun: Ask, Is it functioning as an actor or as a receiver? Do not be misled by common misuse. Also, since the use of pronouns is a foundation for our grammar, no amount of misuse will make it correct.

4. **Adjectives.** Adjectives modify (describe or point out) nouns and pronouns by telling color, kind, size, amount, or other qualities.

5. **Adverbs.** Adverbs modify verbs, adjectives, and other adverbs, telling when, where, how, or to what extent.

   Modifiers in English do not have to agree with the nouns or words they modify, but we do use endings to indicate degrees of comparison.

   a. **Positive (no comparison):** good, bad, large, useful

   b. **Comparative (comparison between two):** better, worse, larger, more useful

   c. **Superlative (comparison among three or more):** best, worst, largest, most useful

   Most modifiers add *-er* and *-est* endings, a few use *more* or *most,* and some, such as *good* and *bad,* have special forms. With one-syllable words, you will usually add *-er* and *-est,* but there are some exceptions, so be careful. With many *two-syllable* words and practically all words with *three or more syllables,* you should use *more* and *most.* Some modifiers, such as *unique* and *ubiquitous,* are absolute in their meaning and cannot be used as comparatives or superlatives. The phrases "more unique" and "most unique" are illogical and should not be used.

   Remember to place modifiers close to the word(s) being modified, so that the sentence is clear and not ambiguous. Watch for *dangling modifiers* in particular.

   Example: Balancing the books, the accounts had to be recalculated.

   (*Accounts* cannot perform the task of balancing, thus the dangling modifier.)

6. **Prepositions.** Prepositions show relationships between other words.

   One way to recognize the largest group of prepositions, those indicating position or direction, is to think of anything that you can do to a log: *across, around, at, beside, beyond, in, over, out, through, to,* and *under.*

   Another commonly used group shows relationships of words or phrases to other words in a sentence: *as, of, except, for, besides,* etc.

7. **Conjunctions.** Conjunctions join other words or connect two or more grammatical units.

   The three types of conjunctions in English are as follows:

   a. **Coordinating conjunctions:** and, or, for, but, yet, nor, so

   b. **Subordinating conjunctions:** after, as, although, as if, because, before, even though, if, until, when, since, unless, whenever, where, whereas, while

   c. **Conjunctive adverbs:** however, therefore, nevertheless, thus, then

A reminder about punctuating conjunctions: **Coordinating** conjunctions require a comma before them if they join two independent clauses (see examples that follow).

Example: Zhang finished writing the report last night, and she plans to give the rest of the group copies today.

However, coordinating conjunctions should not have a comma if they separate an independent and dependent clause:

Example: Zhang finished writing the report last night and plans to give the rest of the group copies tomorrow.

Subordinating conjunctions make the sentence following them dependent, so they only need a comma before them if the following clause is nonessential to the meaning of the sentence:

Essential (no comma needed):   Lee left the company because he found another job.

Nonessential (comma needed):   We need to finish the analysis by tomorrow afternoon, because Ms. Johnson needs to take it with her to the board meeting tomorrow.

Conjunctive adverbs require a semicolon before them and a comma after them when they join two independent clauses. They require a comma only if they start a sentence, and they need commas around them if they serve as interrupters.

Examples: The analysts are reporting on the company's performance in the morning; *however,* the word on the street is that the news will not be good.

The analysts are reporting on the company's performance in the morning. *However,* the word on the street is that the news will not be good.

The analysts are reporting on the company's performance in the morning; the word on the street, however, is that the news will not be good.

8. **Interjections.** Interjections express emotions: Ouch! Ah!

Sentence Structure

The parts of speech are combined to form the following larger structures:

1. **Phrases** are groups of two or more words that act as a single element in a sentence but do not have a *subject* (what is talked about) and *predicate* (what is said about the subject).

2. **Clauses** are groups of words with subjects and predicates. Clauses are main (independent) if they can stand alone and still make sense and subordinate (dependent) if they depend on a main clause to make sense:

a. **Independent clause**

Example: The employees were pleased with the extra holiday this year.

b. **Independent clause followed by a dependent clause**

Example: The employees were pleased with the extra holiday until they were told that they would have to make it up next year.

c. **Dependent clause followed by an independent clause**

Example: Because the employees were pleased with the extra holiday, management decided to make it permanent.

If a clause is introduced by a *subordinating conjunction* (after, although, as, as if, because, before, if, since, because, or whereas), it is a *dependent clause*. A dependent clause cannot stand alone, so when you have used a subordinating conjunction, always make sure that your clause is attached to an independent clause.

3. A **sentence** is an independent clause that contains both a subject (could be implied and not stated) and a verb. Sentences are traditionally said to convey a complete thought; that is, they make a meaningful statement.

The three types of sentence structures are as follows:

a. A **simple** sentence consists of one independent clause by itself.

Example: We are going to work now.

b. A **compound** sentence consists of two or more independent clauses, joined by a coordinating conjunction (and, or, but, for, so, yet) or a semicolon.

Examples: We are going to work now, and we would like you to join us. We are going to work now; we would like you to join us.

Remember to use strong punctuation to separate two independent clauses. A comma alone is too weak and would create a comma splice. No punctuation between two independent clauses creates a run-on sentence.

Comma splice: We are going to work now, we would like you to join us.

Run-on: We are going to work now we would like you to join us.

c. A **complex** sentence consists of at least one independent clause and one or more dependent clauses.

Example: *Although* you would like to extend the lunch hour to two hours, we are going to work now and want you to join us.

In a complex sentence, the dependent clause is usually set off by a comma if it begins the sentence, as in the previous example.

If the dependent clause comes after the independent clause, as previously mentioned, the punctuation depends on the conjunction and if the following clause is essential or nonessential.

Examples: We are going to lunch now and want you to join us, *although* you would like to extend the lunch hour to two hours. We are going to lunch now and want you to join us before it is too late. The four kinds of sentences are as follows:

1. **Declarative**—usual straightforward statement that may be active or passive.
   Example: We are going to work now.
2. **Imperative**—begins with *you* (stated or implied) and issues a command or request.
   Example: Go to work now.
3. **Interrogative**—begins with a finite verb or a question word and ends with a question mark.
   Examples: Get to work now?
   Who did you say was going to the meeting?
4. **Exclamatory**—ends with an exclamation mark.
   Example: We are going to work *now!*

A Final Note on the Study of Grammar

English grammar and the rules that govern its use need to be reviewed just as any other subject needs to be from time to time. People tend to forget what they do not use regularly. Also, usage rules do change because the way that we use our language influences the way we expect it to be used, and there are some differences among academic, journalistic, and business writing. Journalism, in particular, has influenced usage because we hear and see the reporters and newscasters daily. A knowledge of grammar helps you recognize the differences between everyday, casual usage and the more traditional, correct usage, and it develops your recognition for what can be changed and what cannot. As you realize now after reviewing traditional grammar, usage may vary, but the basic structure of a language—the grammar—remains constant.

Certainly, you can use the language without understanding its foundation or workings, just as most people use the computer without knowing what makes it run or drive a car without knowing how the engine works; however, by knowing how something works and the terminology for its parts, you have a greater sense of freedom and control. How often have you said or heard someone else say upon reading a sentence with a mistake in it, "I don't know exactly what's wrong, but it just doesn't sound right"? Now, perhaps, you will not only recognize that it is wrong but also know why and what options you have to correct it.

Appendix C

Usage Self-Assessment

Instructions: Each of the following sentences requires adding or changing punctuation (or a word or two) or correcting usage errors. *You should keep your changes to a minimum. Do just what is necessary to correct any errors. Avoid completely rewriting sentences.* Sentences may contain more than one error.

You should allow approximately 30 minutes to complete the assessment and should not go beyond a maximum of 45 minutes.

After completing the assessment, compare your responses to the answer key that follows.

1. Our top executives, several of our account directors and myself met to discuss the need for change across the company.

2. Everyone must complete their monthly report before they can leave for the holidays.

3. Balancing the books, and completing performance appraisals is the worst aspect of the job.

4. My boss thinks its selfish not to share all of my ideas with John, I think its prudent.

5. By having a clear vision and strategic direction, our clients will be better served in the future.

6. In John Smiths new book Watching Giants Fall, the best chapter is "Saving the Corporation".

7. Since Engineering has lead the list in placement opportunities in the past, many students select it as their major.

8. This approach will create shareholder value, and increase the markets confidence in our companies continued success.

9. Mary worked on the report to long, now its past the deadline set by the home office.

10. The team members cannot expect to do good if they never practice their speech, therefore, I do not understand why they think to constantly complain will get them anywhere.

11. ABC Corporation decided to redesign their website so it appeals to a wider customer audience.

12. Having been employed by Johnson, Inc., for 8 years, his dismissal with only one day notice caught Bill completely off guard.

13. Scheduling all full time employees and to actually expect to need part-time people as well is to optimistic in my opinion; we never have received that many orders in the Summer, but their has been more activity this quarter then ever before.

14. Three major newspapers, The New York Times, The London Herald, USA Today, and The Washington Post, carried full-page ads for the new e-commerce cite. It must have cost the company a small fortune which is such a waste since no Web savvy person pays attention to this anymore.

15. The board of directors ran out of time before our department could deliver the quarterly report, therefore, we will have to come back tomorrow at 10:00 am.

16. Ms. Zavier claims to have been VP for Operations at Jones and Porter, Inc., from May, 1994 to June, 1998, but between you and I, she does not seem to know that much about Operations management.

17. The team knew there was a problem when Mary exclaimed, "You going out of town last weekend caused us to miss the deadline"!

Answer Key

Instructions: After completing the usage self-assessment, compare your responses to this answer key. The corrections are in **bold** to make them more visible for you. The number in parentheses at the end of each sentence is the number of corrections *required* in the sentence. Other answers besides those provided here are possible.

1. Our top executives, several of our account directors, and I met to discuss the need for change across the company. (2) **The way to test this one is to say, "We met." You would not say, "Us met"; thus, you need to use a pronoun in the subjective case (in this case, "I").**

2. Everyone must complete ~~their~~ **his or her** monthly report before ~~they~~ **he or she** can leave for the holidays. (2)

   Or: **All employees must complete their monthly report before they can leave for the holidays.**

3. Balancing the books, and completing performance appraisals ~~is~~ **are** the worst aspects of the job. (3)

4. My boss thinks **it's** selfish not to share all of my ideas with John~~,~~**;** I think **it's** prudent. (3)

5. By having a clear vision and strategic direction, ~~our clients will be better served in the future~~ **we will serve our clients better in the future.** (1)

6. In John Smith's new book, *Watching Giants Fall,* the best chapter is "Saving the Corporation ~~.~~**.**" (4)

   U.S. business communication standards call for periods and commas to be placed inside quotation marks. Many other country standards do the opposite. Follow the standards of the corporate headquarters.

7. Since ~~E~~ engineering has ~~lead~~ **led** the list in placement opportunities recently, many students still select it as their major. (2)

8. This approach will create shareholder value~~,~~ and increase the market**'s** confidence in our compan~~ies~~ **y's** continued success. (3)

9. Mary worked on the report **too** long, ; now, **it's** past the deadline set by the home office. (4)

10. The team members cannot expect to do ~~good~~ **well** if they never practice their speech~~,~~; therefore, I do not understand why they think to ~~constantly~~ complain **constantly** [or complaining constantly] will get them anywhere. (3)

11. ABC Corporation decided to redesign ~~their~~ **its** Web site so **that** it appeals to a wider customer audience. (3)

    Selection of "its" or "their" is country specific.

12. Having been employed by Johnson, Inc., for ~~8~~ **eight** years, **Bill was caught completely off guard by** his dismissal with only **one day's** notice ~~caught Bill completely off guard~~. (3)

13. Scheduling all full-time employees and ~~to~~ actually **expecting** to need part-time people as well ~~is~~ **are too** optimistic in my opinion; we never have received that many orders in the ~~S~~ summer, but ~~their~~ **there** has been more activity this quarter ~~then~~ **than** ever before. (6)

14. ~~Three~~ **Four** major newspapers, *The New York Times, The London Herald, USA Today,* and *The Washington Post,* carried full-page ads for the new e-commerce ~~cite~~ **site. The ads** must have cost the company a small fortune, which is such a waste, since no Web-savvy person pays attention to this **form of advertising** anymore. (7)

15. The board of directors [if you capitalized it, count it as one error] ran out of time before our ~~D~~ **d**epartment could deliver the quarterly report~~,~~ ; therefore, we will have to come back tomorrow at 10:00 a.m. (3)

16. Ms. Zavier claims to have been VP [if you wrote it out, that is okay] for Operations at Jones and Porter, Inc., from May 1994 to June~~,~~ 1998, but between you and ~~I~~ **me,** she does not seem to know that much about ~~O~~operations management. (3)

17. The team knew there was a problem when Mary exclaimed, "Your going out of town last weekend caused us to miss the deadline"~~!~~ !"(2)

Scale

      0–10 = In good shape
   11–18 = Need some review
   19–25 = Need more review
   26–52 = Need lots of review

Appendix D

Successful Case Analysis and Discussion

The ability to read and learn from cases is an important skill for any business leader. Cases provide examples of good and bad business decisions along with enough of the story for you to learn from the challenges and approaches in them. They also provide an opportunity to test your business judgment and decision-making ability in the context of real business problems.

As is typical of problems within an organization, a case rarely provides facts and information you would like to have before making a decision. Therefore, you must be able to think critically and uncover the assumptions underlying the case information.

You must also learn to be comfortable with ambiguity in the information as well as in the "answers." In fact, one of the most valuable lessons to learn from case analysis and discussion is that there is no one "right" answer. A good case is open to many interpretations and the case problems to many possible resolutions.

Since case analysis and discussion are standard approaches to learning in the business school classroom, this appendix is intended to help you approach both with some of the traditional techniques needed to succeed in the case classroom and to obtain the most out of the case experience. The discussion here contains hints on how to do the following:

- Perform a successful case analysis.
- Contribute to a case discussion.
- Organize a case analysis report.
- Stay within the ethical boundaries of case discussions.
- Get the most out of the learning experience that case discussions provide.

Performing a Successful Case Analysis

To prepare for a case discussion, you should approach the case analysis as follows:

1. Skim the case quickly.
2. Write out what you see as the central problem(s) in the case.
3. Read the case through more carefully, highlighting key issues and facts to support the central problem.
4. List the possible solutions to the case problem.
5. Select a solution and develop your defense.
6. Outline how you would implement the solution.

When reading the case, you should focus on exploring the problems and pulling out the issues and the facts instead of focusing on specific courses of action. You might find it helpful to think about approaching a case as you would the analysis of a short story. Try looking for the conflicts and sources of tension, outline the plot of the story, and examine the motives of the characters involved.

Contributing to the Case Discussion

In the case classroom, you will want to sit where you are visible, if possible, which usually means sitting in the middle of the room at the case discussion leader's eye level. You want to avoid the far right or left unless you are unprepared and want to lower the risk of the discussion leader's calling on you, although you should not show up to any case discussion unprepared. Doing so wastes your time, your colleagues' time, and the discussion leader's time.

To benefit from the case experience, you must be prepared to contribute positively to the discussion, whether in the classroom or with your team. You should not assume a combative pose, although you can and should challenge ideas. Instead of attacking people, challenge the ideas and look for ways to work toward building on their point of view or ideas. What most discussion leaders want to see is an active exchange among class members, not simply a routine Q&A between the discussion leader and the class.

Most case discussions will begin with the discussion leader's asking for someone to summarize the case. This type of contribution provides a chance for you to speak up early in the discussion, before the rapid exchange that soon erupts once the discussion gets started. If you are new to the case discussion or perhaps hesitant to jump in, you may want to take advantage of this opening opportunity to speak. The following are usually considered legitimate contributions to a case discussion:

1. Summary of the case.
2. Your solution.
3. An alternate solution to one suggested by a classmate.
4. An explanation of any underlying assumptions in the case.
5. Transition to another area of the case.
6. Connections to other cases read for this class.
7. Clarification of relevant financial or quantitative information.
8. Application of an analytical approach.
9. Synthesis of key learnings from the case.
10. A summary of the discussion.
11. Suggested next steps.

Overall, you want to avoid broad generalizations or superficial statements.

Organizing a Case Analysis or Report

If you are not given a suggested organizational structure for writing your case analysis, you will probably want to use one of the following popular structures:

1. Inductive or indirect.
   - Strategic issues and problems.
   - Analysis of problems.
   - Recommendations.

2. Deductive or direct.
   - Recommendation or solution.
   - Support for solution or evidence for recommendation.
   - Brief discussion of alternative solutions.

3. Issues and results (executive).
   - Crucial strategic issues.
   - Assumptions about issues.
   - Recommended strategies.
   - Justification for recommendation.
   - Plan of action.
   - Expected results.

4. Elimination of alternatives.
   - Discussion of at least three alternative solutions.
   - Summary of why only one is the best.
   - Reinforcement of that one.

5. Pros and cons.
   - Introduction of two best solutions.
   - Advantages and disadvantages of each.
   - Conclusion, recommending the preferred alternative.
6. Thesis-antithesis-synthesis.
   - Solution.
   - Counters or objections to that solution.
   - Combination with solution emphasized.

What is most important in writing your analysis is that you organize it logically and make it easy for the reader to find your analysis of the problems and clear explanation of any solutions.

Staying within the Ethical Boundaries of Case Analysis

Staying within the case ethical boundaries means you do not do the following:

1. Pass along case notes or old case reports to students who have not yet taken the course.
2. Discuss the case with someone who has not yet had the case in class.
3. Attempt to find out "what happened in the case" (as if what the company did was the correct answer, or that someone else's "right" answer is right for you).
4. Contact a case company without permission to gather more information about the case situation.
5. Identify the real company in a disguised case.
6. Take advantage of group members by letting them do the bulk of the work instead of reading and analyzing the case yourself.

Getting the Most Out of the Case Experience

As with most learning experiences, you get out of the case method what you put into it. To get the most out of the case experience, you should do the following:

1. Prepare for the discussion by skimming, reading, thinking about the case.
2. Emphasize the student-to-student learning over the teacher-to-student learning.
3. Listen carefully to colleagues and synthesize their ideas and yours to develop your own critical analytical abilities.
4. Develop your own personal system of case analysis.
5. Remember, case analysis is designed to sharpen your analytical skills.

Index